RETAINING BALANCE
THE ETERNAL WAY

RETAINING BALANCE
THE ETERNAL WAY

Dr. M R Venkatesh

KNOWLEDGE WORLD

KW Publishers Pvt Ltd
New Delhi

ISBN 978-93-91490-25-6 Hardback
ISBN 978-93-91490-27-0 Paperback
ISBN 978-93-91490-26-3 ebook

Published in India by Kalpana Shukla

KNOWLEDGE WORLD

KW Publishers Pvt Ltd
4676/21, First Floor, Ansari Road
Daryaganj, New Delhi 110002
Phone: +91 11 43528107
Marketing: kw@kwpub.in
Editorial: production@kwpub.in
Website: www.kwpub.in

Printed and Bound in India

Contents

Dedicated to the
Civilisational God
– Lord Rama

Family – Marriage – Culture

Civilisation – Monogamy –

Polygamy – Economics – Implosion –

Discipline – Excess – Rights –

Duties – Citizens – Society –

Welfare – Markets – Crisis – Taxes –

Finance – Failure – Original Sin –

Feminism – Entropy – Rights –

State – Individualism – Constitution –

Gender Equity – New Economic

Order – Balance – Civilisational

Economics – Ram Rajya

Family as a Balancer Between

Man and Woman

Individuals and Society

Society and State

State and Citizens

Savings and Consumption

Consumption and Production

Production and Environment

Piety and Progress

Progress and Security

Security and Tolerance

Divine Intervention and Individual Initiative

Initiative and Excesses

Markets and Governments

Liberty and Equality

Equality and Equity

Equity and Welfare

Welfare and Taxes

Taxes and Citizens

Citizens and Rights

Rights and Duties

Preview

"*Retaining Balance* is an original contribution to Indian political economic thought. I have purposely hyphenated politics with economics because economics merely looks at human beings as a material person looking solely for fulfilment of his/her material desires. MRV takes an entirely fresh look at this assumption. He establishes that there has been far too much emphasis on the individual and alternatively suggests that family needs to be at the centre of all economic policies. He is a right-wing economist with moorings in Bharatiya culture, that does not believe in absolute unrestricted freedom. His expansive sweep of study takes in all that is good or bad with Western civilisation, economic and political thought. He doesn't mind mincing words when he claims that most modern western philosophies are primarily based on Christian theology. He goes into classical capitalist theories and also into disruptive and miserable communist theories. Simultaneously, he goes on to pick up wisdom from Indian classical knowledge system and its *Itihasa,* its civilisational guiding literature of Ramayan and Mahabharat and then presents the spirit of Ram Rajya in modern perspective. He is frank, unapologetic and objective in his criticism as well as his advocacy of Ram Rajya as the guiding principle in modern terminology.

MRV takes off from where Integral Humanism left off **or I would suggest that he picks up the threads from Integral Humanism and takes the idea forward in his own way.** It is not a book out to grab headlines. It is a serious treatise created with years of research and thoughts as any reader will find out. I am sure, this magnum opus will be a required reading in humanities and for policy makers."

– Dr **Ratan Sharda**

Author and Researcher

"*Retaining Balance* is a book about economics but it is also a book about marriage, specifically monogamy, and the singular impact it has (and has always played until the industrial revolution) in deciding the economic destiny of nations. A progressively lethal impact that the post-industrial world has increasingly had across the globe is the near-complete erasure of our historical and cultural memory. Remarking on this in a tangential fashion, the Swiss intellectual and writer, Alain De Botton observes how, decades ago, people in the West lost contact with the person who actually grew and produced their food. This phenomenon known variously as the atomisation of the society, has grown at an alarming pace in India as well. And it does not bode well. This in turn, has come with the destruction of the family system largely owing to two major ideological factors. While both are opposed to each other, their destructive impact has been the same; they have merely taken opposite paths which have met at the same destination of destruction. Capitalism which has reduced the human to a mere 'resource' and Communism and its contemporary avatars, whose goal is to enslave the individual to the State. Both have economics as their premise, and in their own ways, both have destroyed culture by destroying the monogamous family institution, the bedrock and upholder of culture since time immemorial.

Thus, shorn of the protective embrace and the balmy consolation that culture offers, contemporary economics has been reduced to a jungle law of competing theories which have repeatedly proven disastrous in practice. The more worrying reality is the fact that this patented American brand of economics has been universalised. And those nations which have resisted it have been physically bombed – for example, the poor nations of Africa. One is reminded of Lee Kuan Yew's memorable words in this context: 'Americans believe their ideas are universal – the supremacy of the individual and free, unfettered expression. But they are not – never were.'

Using this and related underlying themes, Sri M.R. Venkatesh explores a wide range of fundamental issues in this book. Without revealing too much, it may be said that he approaches the problem from a civilisational and cultural standpoint and makes a convincing argument that the roots of the present, jumbled and rudderless approach to economics lie in the Christian doctrine. To a student of comparative religions and cultures, and to one deeply moored in the Sanatana ethos, Sri Venkatesh's thesis makes eminent sense.

The book's scholarly approach also presents an impressive gamut of research including but not limited to Scarlet Johansson (yes!), Samuel Huntington, Koenraad Elst, S. Gurumurty, Alan Greenspan and uses relevant material from the Hindu Puranas and epics. In many ways, the book presents the renewed wisdom of the ages applied to contemporary problems, using the "modern" framework of analysis.

Primarily aimed at a specialist audience, the proverbial ordinary reader will also benefit from reading *Retaining Balance.*"

– Sandeep Balakrishnan
Author

"*Retaining Balance* is one of the most interesting books that I have come across in recent times. Departing from usual prescriptions, MRV has taken a new approach to deal with what he calls the 'indiscipline of economics.' In the process, the author has taken a broad sweep on several issues and has sought to examine the interface of economics, theology, culture and civilisation. Retaining Balance is an important work for the contemporary situation. I wish the author well."

– Prof **R. Vaidyanathan**
IIMB (Retd)
Chair Professor of Public Policy at Sastra University

"M R Venkatesh's book Retaining Balance is a work that can be loved or hated but cannot be ignored. He passionately argues for placing families at the centre of all programs and succeeds in getting one to question policies that we take for granted as common sense. There is something in this book that will rankle almost all groups – leftist, rightist, Hindu, Muslim, Christian, Brahmin, Dalit, liberal, conservative, capitalist, socialist – and Venkatesh seems happy to cock a snook at everything that policymakers have considered inalienable. Voltaire famously said, 'I disapprove of what you say, but I will defend to the death your right to say it.' Read this with a bookmark of Voltaire's words nestled within the pages."

– Ashwin Sanghi
Author

"The title of the latest book of Dr M R Venkatesh, Retaining Balance, reveals the theme underlying what is an original and fascinating book. As with those who refuse to follow the herd, some of the views are provocative, and hence may not be met with agreement from a few if not more readers. This is not an argument for avoiding reading *Retaining Balance*, but precisely why the book needs to be perused. In a world where problems are many and solutions to an increasing number seem distant, opening wide the doors and windows of the mind to the flow of ideas from different directions is essential, rather than shutting them off to live in the silos. Such ghettoes of the mind, where those who think on the same lines as we ourselves do believe represent truth, a truth found nowhere else, is based on illusion. *Sanatan Dharma* mandates a universality of outlook, and this foundation of Indian thought is why Retaining Balance needs to be read."

– Professor **Madhav Nalapat**
Manipal Academy of Higher Education

"*RETAINING BALANCE: THE ETERNAL WAY*, is perhaps one of the most insightful books you will ever read. It marries economics; human behaviour and most importantly, human frailty in a manner that is both rare and in short supply. M R Venkatesh has captured the essence of the many pillars that support human existence and human society putting in context the myths and realities and juxtaposing them against our historical and cultural legacy. I would call this work deeply philosophical as also rooted in reality."

– **Suhel Seth**
Noted Brand Guru

"After three decades of policies based on the advice of the West, realisation is coming all over the globe, especially in the countries of the third world, that something really has gone wrong. Majority of the countries have not been any gainer, if we see in terms of the well-being of the masses. Rather rich have got richer, and masses are still reeling under extreme poverty and hunger, with an extremely slow improvement in the goals of sustainable development. Even socialistic policies, as suggested by likes of A K Sen have proved to a utter failure, as production system guided by profit, continues to create jobless growth and excessive exploitation of nature without any reprieve from poverty and hunger.

Though, I come from the discipline of economics, I believe that mainstream economists have failed to address the problems faced by the humanity, due to faulty compartmentalised approach. Need of the hour is to go back to our routes and adopt an integrated approach, and give rise to a decentralised production system, aimed at creating jobs and raising incomes for the lowliest strata, which can only sustain growth in the long run, with wellbeing of all.

May MRV's book *Retaining Balance* opens the closed minds, imprisoned by failed fundamentalist economic thinking. May the discipline of economics grow with fresh thinking, bringing humans back in the centre of our approach to development.

– **Ashwani Mahajan**
Author and Columnist
Professor of Economics, University of Delhi
National Co-Convenor Swadeshi Jagaran Manch

"Economics is a complex field. There are as many theories as there are eminent economists. However, it is not often that we think of family, culture and civilisations as important influences on the economies of the world. Over centuries the field of economics appeared to have insulated itself from a slew of external influences, certainly those of family and culture. Or has it? *Retaining Balance* by M. R. Venkatesh delves into this fascinating topic. The book combines inputs from history, psychology, sociology and yes economics too to get us thinking on a new path. Very interesting read."

– Dr. **Sumanth C Raman**, MD.DCH
Medical Consultant and Television personality

"Hindu Dharma had never frowned upon acquiring wealth and fulfilling your desires in a rightful honest way, unlike Abrahamic religions. On the contrary it has always emphasised on the *Purusharthas* at different stages of life. This balance stressed upon in our scriptures between the material and spiritual world has been brought out beautifully in this book in contemporary idiom. Congratulations to the author."

– **V S Chandralekha** IAS (Retd)

"On first read *Retaining Balance* came across as provocative, almost in-your-face. But when you dig into it you realise it is not trying to incite, but to provide insight. One of those rare books that transitions across genres (economics, theology, anthropology, and more) smoothly and seamlessly. I personally ask myself the question often, 'When was the last time you learnt something for the first time?'. *Retaining Balance* fills that barrel of firsts for me. Having devoured it over a weekend, I've been fascinated by its ability to not only inform (most books do that), but to spark a series of thoughts and realisations. A powerful book that forces you to question your assumptions!"

– **Anuraag Saxena**

Market-entry, Public Policy & Growth Strategist

"Every civilisation is a complex amalgam of individuals, families, culture, history and sense of purpose. Economics as evolved in the West seeks to reduce human behaviour to rational choices largely ignoring the impact of culture, family and behaviour. Because of the economic domination of the West, their cultural mores including their Christian upbringing, dominates their thoughts. Older civilisations like India, China, Japan and others often find western economic theory contradictory as their cultural behaviour is very different. This book seeks to explore economic thought from the cultural and family point of view."

– **T. V. Mohandas Pai**

Chairman, Aarin Capital Partners

"To understand economics is to understanding the nature of balances. The author MR Venkatesh in *Retaining Balance: The Eternal Way* opens your mind to understanding economics by understanding the nature of balances. Understanding the nature of balances comes from understanding nature itself. Economy moves with society; and society moves ahead with different push and pulls driven by economic activities. The book is well-written and interesting in its analysis of retaining balance in the world today which is bordering on chaos and anarchy.

Retaining Balance notes that national economics works on the four fundamental principles of production, consumption, Retaining balance argues that these cycles are an inevitable by-product of individual excesses and points out that the most natural and effective way of addressing this imbalance is through the institution of family. Therefore, it argues that it is imperative that economic policies world over must revert to placing family at the centre of policy frameworks globally."

– Savio Rodrigues
Founder & Editor-in-Chief, *Goa Chronicle*

"Although a book on economics – MRV's deep research and thought has given the book philosophical undertones. The Great Indian Family – appreciated and criticised is the basic unit of a country's development. An exposition on the family juxtaposed with the individual's contribution to the economy – this book is a view through the Bharatiya lens. A unique study which will be sure to influence and change minds.

– Advaita Kala
Best Selling Author & Screenwriter

"The book *Retaining Balance: The Eternal Way* is an extraordinary attempt to provide indigenous ideas and practices rooted in the Bharatiya ethos as an alternative to the euro-centric economic thinking revolving around liberalism or socialism. The book substantiates the concept of 'familial globalisation' articulated by Late Dattopant Thengadi Ji in the early 1990s. While arguing for a 'family' based economic model, M R Venkatesh, in his typical engaging and epic style, has not minced words about the fundamental difference between the Bharatiya systems that sustained for centuries and the Christian values that shaped the Anglo-Saxon economic ideas. I am sure this book, rightly dedicated to the civilisational icon, Maryada Purushottam Shri Rama, will be a pathbreaking intellectual exercise in guiding us towards the path of Rama-Rajya."

– Prafulla Ketkar
Editor, *Organiser* (Weekly)

"The answers to the conflicts between unbridled rights of an atomised individual and his duties is defined differently by different cultures. When ideas are imported from alien cultures and imposed on a civilisation, they are bound to create major disruptions and economic pain. What is essentially an Abrahamic concept of redemption through external support and the binaries that stem from it has driven the economic concepts of the modern western world, be it capitalism or communism, one being the redemption through market forces and the other through the force of the state. What is common between both those concepts is the aspect of irresponsible exploitation of resources. The Bharatiya economic concept lays larger emphasis on duties and responsibilities rather than rights. Even in aspects pertaining to rights, there are rules defined by the *Purusharthas* of *Dharma, Artha, Kama and Moksha*. Resource usage or personal pleasure was subject to guidance from the rules of *Dharma*. Bharatiya economic concepts had built in checks and balances in the form of family followed by Varna or community.

MRV's book *Retaining Balance* brings out the concept of balancing as opposed to unchallenged exploitative behaviours. He has brought out this fundamental difference between the existing rights based atomised level economic models and Bharat's ancient responsibilities-based family and community level economic model. MRV aptly argues that not factoring in civilisational and cultural aspects into economic policies has resulted in a common Indian citizen seeking only rights from his state without pressure of any matching duties on his shoulders while dealing with the affairs of the state. The same individual is quite dutiful in his private and social life even if it is at the cost of his rights. This is a thought-provoking book and is a must read for all intellectuals to help them understand the wisdom of ancient Bharat and its relevance in today's world. Policy makers should read this book to get ideas that will help them reshape the economy that can bring back balance between rights and duties of its citizens.

Among the several competing schools of economic thought – Classical, Marxist, Keynesian or the Chicago school, the preoccupation is often with markets, labour or welfare and redistribution, thereby curiously and safely staying away from the civilisational or cultural prisms to economic analysis. But in a first, in a masterly and innovative approach to the philosophy of economic thought with a uniquely Indian perspective, M. R. Venkatesh brings to his readers these missing cogs in the wheel – family, culture and civilisation to the study of economics. As a keen student of both economics and politics, Venkatesh skilfully integrates the two to literally 'Retain Balance' to economic analysis in a magisterial manner. Significantly, he traces the emanation of several 'modern' or 'rational' concepts in the world today to Christian theological constructs that got imposed on countries across the world, especially colonies such as India. This permeation in turn impacted the drafting of Constitutions, policy frameworks, governance and of course, economic theories and attitudes thereof, as well. Here is where Venkatesh brings in the much-needed balance to the paradigm by integrating fundamentally Indian concepts that value the institution of marriage, monogamy, the rights-versus-duties conundrum and advocates the agency of family to address macroeconomic imbalances. Venkatesh's approach to economic thought is a novel one that is richly nuanced, meticulously researched, felicitously written and elegantly argued to build a robust case for this new prism. Even as I wish M R Venkatesh the greatest of success with this wonderfully crafted new work of his, I also earnestly hope that policy-makers in our corridors of power are keeping the doors and windows of their mind open to such ideas, like the Rig Veda aspired for us: *Aano Bhadraha Kratavo Yanthu Vishwataha* (Let noble thoughts come to us from all directions)."

– Dr. Vikram Sampath
Author & Historian

"The answers to the conflicts between unbridled rights of an atomised individual and his duties is defined differently by different cultures. When ideas are imported from alien cultures and imposed on a civilization, they are bound to create major disruptions and economic pain. What is essentially an Abrahamic concept of redemption through external support and the binaries that stem from it has driven the economic concepts of the modern western world, be it capitalism or communism, one being the redemption through market forces and the other through the force of the state. What is common between both those concepts is the aspect of irresponsible exploitation of resources. The Bharateeya economic concept lays larger emphasis on duties and responsibilities rather than rights. Even in aspects pertaining to rights, there are rules defined by the Purusharthas of Dharma, Artha, Kama and Moksha. Resource usage or personal pleasure was subject to guidance from the rules of Dharma. Bharateeya economic concepts had built in checks and balances in the form of family followed by Varna or community.

MRV's book "Retaining Balance" brings out the concept of balancing as opposed to unchallenged exploitative behaviours. He has brought out this fundamental difference between the existing rights based atomised level economic models and Bharat's ancient responsibilities-based family and community level economic model. MRV aptly argues that not factoring in civilizational and cultural aspects into economic policies has resulted in a common Indian citizen seeking only rights from his state without pressure of any matching duties on his shoulders while dealing with the affairs of the state. The same individual is quite dutiful in his private and social life even if it is at the cost of his rights. This is a thought-provoking book and is a must read for all intellectuals to help them understand the wisdom of ancient Bharat and its relevance in today's world. Policy makers should read this book to get ideas that will help them reshape the economy that can bring back balance between rights and duties of its citizens.

I congratulate MRV on this wonderful work and wish for the success and wider readership of this book."

– CA Giridhar Mamidi, B.Com, FCA, LLB
State Vice-President, Pragna Bharati Telangana

Foreword

As a fervent believer in the India story and as a newsman, I have observed from close quarters, the shift in the arc of the Indian economy from the onset of liberalisation to the push towards Atma Nirbhar Bharat. And in the middle of it all, I have witnessed firsthand, the squeamishness to own the India story with the confidence it deserves. The true potential of the Indian economy cannot be actualised by ignoring its rich culture and glorious civilisation or the beliefs that bind us over several millennia which forms the foundation of all our societal norms.

A macro-economic understanding of the Indian economy cannot come from subtracting civilisational dimensions of critical importance. M. R. Venkatesh has by writing "Retaining Balance" provided a contemporary yet civilisational perspective on current day economics and has seamlessly communicated how '*culture is symbiotically linked to the world of economics.*' In the process he has raised a profound question of what constitutes the discipline of economics. If human beings are central to economics, it is obvious that the rich corpus of what constitutes human evolution too has to be integral to the study of economics. Political economy or economics cannot confine itself to a study to truncate the discipline and treat humans as a bundle of demands of for that matter rights, which the all-powerful state or markets can bestow or bludgeon. The more economics drifted away from its alter-ego – culture and civilisation, it became more recondite and abstruse. It is time that experts revisited the discipline of economics as a product of culture and as an emanation of civilisation. This is what "Retaining Balance" all about.

M. R. Venkatesh's work is solution-oriented – not only does he successfully bring to light as to how the current international order modeled on the west is ridden with serious flaws but goes on to unravel a truly native solution to it. He has succinctly traversed through the need for the '*institution of monogamous marriage*' as the basis for a strong economy and how family is the '*the First Building Block in an Economy.*' He has copiously drawn from the Bhagavad Gita, for example, as he elucidates on the idea of '*placing duty above everything*' – an idea that is alien to Western philosophy. Simultaneously, he has adduced and juxtaposed concepts like entropy in Thermodynamics and Homeostasis in biology to give a scientific explanation for how '*exclusion of the missing middle*' i.e., the middle ground between markets and governments is proving fatal to the management of economies.

The book analyses theories of the west, provides well-researched contrasts of the Orient, and makes a case for balance between governance, markets, social institutions, individual duties and civilisational restraints. M. R. Venkatesh has studied, broken down, condensed, analysed and questioned the ideas of those like Adam Smith, John Maynard Keynes, Francis Fukuyama, William Tucker, Samuel Huntington, Paul Kengor and Yuval Noah Harari. He makes a novel case to not only realise the pitfall in Nehruvian economics but actively break away from it. This makes the book a compelling read for those in power who seek to break out of those decrepit ideas.

Throughout the book, M. R. Venkatesh has raised pressing questions that often get overlooked – how did British colonisation and its corrosive taxation regime impact Indian civilisation? Whether questions posed in any macro-economic modeling are obnoxiously simplified? Whether there is an appropriate weightage provided to families and their decision-making process? And importantly, is the antidote to cyclical economic boom and doom available with us in the form of cultural and civilisational values rooted to individual restraints?

Retaining Balance makes a fascinating case to break free from the conventional rigmarole of Western thinking. Rooted in *Bhartiyata thoughts, idea and civilisation* the book makes a persuasive case for rethinking the economic narrative from a critical lens by relying on '*eternal ideas.*' One such *eternal idea* that he has constantly referenced is the idea of individual duty. He identifies and notes how "*eternal ideas flow from ancient texts like the Ramayana or the Mahabharath where at every twist and turn the virtues of adhering to one's duty is repeatedly emphasized.*" The logical endgame in this argument of Venkatesh is that the Constitution of India needs to factor individual duties along with rights and make such duties justiciable.

M. R. Venkatesh has been unafraid to venture into a more theological perspective. He urges us to move away from the Christian idea of the "*broken self*," and "*a corresponding reliance on an external divinity to provide salvation*" towards a more inclusive and perhaps efficient concept of Rama Rajya. He highlights how '*the life-message of Lord Rama explained through Ramayana only re-emphasises the prerequisite for building the national economy through individual restraint*.'

In a New India, where the nation is charting the course to be a superpower, this book is a timely reminder that the solution may just lie in our cultural and civilisation roots. It advocates a *Bhartiya* perspective to economics, that is not based on isolation, excessive regulation, or Western dominance. At a time when India is making its place felt in the new world order, the current ideas handed down by the west and the Left must be reconsidered and possibly jettisoned in governance, policy-making, and individual choices. 'Retaining Balance – The Eternal Way' is an essential first step for all those looking to understand how our economic system can level-up.

My friend M. R. Venkatesh is both a practicing lawyer and a qualified Chartered Accountant. He thinks critically, is deeply well-read, and remains acutely precise in problems he identifies and solutions he provides. As someone who has known him for years now, interacted with him on-air, and has been friends off-air, agreed with him, and debated against him – one thing I can say with certainty is that his book is a highly relevant and thought-provoking read. It made me, and I am sure it will make any reader, see the Indian economy and the global economy from a whole new lens.

New Delhi
10 August 2021

Arnab Goswami
Editor-in-Chief
Republic Media Network

Preface

"Third and final call for passengers travelling to New Delhi….." the public announcement system blared incessantly at the Chennai airport. Even as I was rushing to the boarding gate to catch my flight that evening, a book on display at the popular airport outlet caught my attention. The title of the book was indeed inviting: "*Great Economists - How Their Ideas Can Help Us Today.*" I instantly flipped to the first page where the author Linda Yueh had dedicated the book "To my family." Logically, I assumed that a person who could write about the greatest of economists and simultaneously dedicate her labour of love to her family would certainly have dealt with how various economists - classical to modern - had approached the subject from the family perspective. I picked up the book for some serious in-flight reading. Within minutes even as the flight soared, my hopes from the book rapidly evaporated. The reason for the same was not far to seek. Despite being a brilliant analysis of the work of twelve great economists, post that first page, the word "family" was conspicuous by its absence! This peculiar approach of disregarding family, civilisation, and culture from any discussion on any formal study of economics had always left me befuddled. For too long this had been bothering my inner self too. Consciously I wondered, whether I should undertake an exposition on the link between family, culture and civilisation on one hand and economics on the other in the form of a book. By the time the flight landed in New Delhi, the idea of *Retaining Balance - The Eternal Way* had germinated in my mind.

At the outset, I need to make an upfront confession to my reader. I was never formally trained in the discipline of economics. Nevertheless, economics as a subject, has always excited me. Each time I delved deeper into the subject, I become more convinced about a fascinating fact surrounding it - that it has never been understood in all its dimensions even by the very experts who proclaim to have mastered it. Without meaning any offence to such experts, it appears to me that the proverbial 'elephant in the room' was being explored by the visually challenged who never got to know the elephant in all its completeness. From economists who looked at the subject from the angle of accumulation and distribution of wealth; to those who propounded welfare theories; to those who added the spice of communism and to those who politicised economics, it appeared to me that economists romanticised the discipline of economics by safely avoiding looking at it from the civilisational prism. In the process, I would make it bold to say that they defied economics. Thus, in my understanding, the subject continues to be examined and taught by ignoring the basic building block in every society viz., family. Therefore, I call family, culture and civilisation, in the study of economics, as the missing middle. In my view, this truncated vision of economists ultimately resulted in fatal flaws in their approach to the discipline of economics. In turn, this caused serious imbalances in their prescriptions. *Retaining Balance* seeks to look into these imbalances and attempts at providing appropriate prescriptions.

Lest it be misunderstood that I am critical of legendary economists, I must hasten to add that at appropriate places in the book, I have eulogised them for their perceptions too. Nevertheless, the incompleteness of the understanding of a complex subject is the issue on hand. Influenced by what I experienced on a daily basis; I began assimilating my views on economics from cultural as well as civilisational standpoints. It is therefore natural that it appears to me that the discipline of economics, bereft of civilisational values, is fast imploding. Economists too of late have been near unanimous in their view that they do not have the necessary answers even to some of the most pressing challenges posed to their respective national economies. *Retaining Balance* attempts to seek answers for such convoluted questions.

Policy framers now realise that for too long, the 'battle for the commanding heights of the economy' has been, at best, binary. In the absence of a viable alternative to the dominance of governments (socialism) or markets (liberalism), the world of economics has invariably alternated between the two grand ideas posited by Keynes and Hayek. The resultant oscillation in the macro-economic policy formulation across the globe in the past 50 years has been more out of sheer compulsion, than any conviction.

In the process, the solution to every economic crisis contained the seeds for the next. It is in this connection in a recent article in the magazine *World Finance*, Charlotte Gifford, a UK-based researcher writes as follows:

> Towards the end of the twentieth century, economists began to see the pitfalls of imposing economic policies without paying heed to culture. The Washington Consensus, for example - a set of neoliberal policies presented to the International Monetary Fund in 1989 - is broadly seen as having failed to achieve its goal of bringing prosperity to Latin America. In the thirty years after the Washington Consensus was implemented, Latin America grew less than 1 percent per year per capita terms, compared to 2.6 percent annual growth between 1960 and 1981.
>
> This shows that, while a certain kind of institutional reform may succeed in one country, it won't necessarily succeed in another, and culture may be the reason why. "One example is Italy," said Thierry Verdier, Professor of Economics at Paris School of Economics, "where you had reforms that worked in the north but not in the south. Why? People have begun to think that it's down to very long-term factors such as the development of cities in the north of Italy and the building up of social capital there that happened over a long period of time. It didn't exist in the south because of other historical developments."
>
> There are many scenarios where economics alone cannot account for the behaviour of a certain group. For example, immigrants and their children often exhibit different behaviour despite being in the same economic environment as other citizens.
>
> "Immigrant children of a certain origin systematically outperform US-born students in the country, even if they attend the same school. These differences hold after taking into account the income and the education of the parent," said Sapienza. "If the explanation for these differences in behaviour were economic conditions or the quality of the institution, we would not observe these differences."
>
> By identifying the cultural beliefs that proliferate in more productive and innovative countries, we could advance our understanding of the conditions needed for economic success.

While dealing with these issues, I also realised that most modern theories, not merely in economics but also in several other disciplines, owe their origins to Christian theology. Consequently, several contemporary ideas emanating from the western world are built around a Christian idea of a 'broken self' that constantly requires external intermediation for its 'salvation.' That explains the importance to governments and markets in modern economics. Thus, what is predominantly a Christian view of the discipline of economics became over time the western thought or understanding of the world, which subsequently became the acceptable global order! And this idea is not merely limited to economics. It permeates the entire constitutional construct in the western countries which has been adopted in substantial measure by India too. *Retaining Balance* addresses this skew in our understanding of ourselves.

In contrast, I put forth the argument that *Bhartiya* civilisation has repeatedly emphasised on the individual, his actions, enterprise and his efforts. However, I must hasten to add that the individual in *Bhartiya* civilisation is not completely atomised without any regulatory or supervisory oversight. This is where the importance of family and society comes to play - both as a functional and as an oversight, body. This makes us culturally different and the global economic order arising out of Christian theology, probably unworkable. *Retaining Balance,* therefore, argues that the macro-economic policies pursued by the Government of India needs to factor in these differentials.

Simultaneously, I have argued that marriage - more particularly monogamous marriage as the first known institution created by mankind - has a far greater influence on the functioning of economies. Monogamy brought with it a specific social order that has helped man to achieve individual peace, social harmony and therefore, extraordinary all-round progress. Importantly, monogamous marriage taught us the importance of civilisational restraints. It is these restraints that make societies stable and economies functional. It is in this connection that I put forth the view that national economics, works on the four fundamental principles of production, consumption, investment and savings. Experiences demonstrate that excesses in one result in cycles of boom or depression in the economy. Modern economics is in a constant quest for an external balancing factor to prevent such excesses and the resultant cycles of boom and doom. In the absence of an auto self-correcting mechanism caused by individual excesses, I am fairly convinced in my view that these cycles of booms and bursts are inevitable. As a policy alternative, I suggest that the most natural and effective way of addressing this macro-economic imbalance is through the institution of family that acts as an oversight body to correct individual excesses. Therefore, I argue that policy framers, world over, must revert to placing family at the centre of economics. This is the core of *Retaining Balance*.

This naturally takes us to the eternal conflict between the rights and duties of every citizen. Ideally, the levels of responsibility cast on every citizen should be no less than his rights. But when the citizens themselves contrive to dilute their own responsibilities - in favour of their individual rights - the consequences are indeed disastrous. The framers of the Indian Constitution who encapsulated the various fundamental rights to its basic structure strangely ignored our civilisational emphasis on duties. Thus, placing rights at the centre of our Constitution we spawned an omnipotent, yet ineffective, state. To counter-balance the emergence of the omnipotent state, we allowed the proliferation of individual rights. And all our economic policies are built on this premise of individual rights. Such a constitutional arrangement may suit the British, or for that matter the Americans even today, but cannot be thrust on a nation which has deep-rooted civilisational values, especially on individual duties. This gives rise to a new fault-line - between an Indian who swears by his constitutional right while dealing with the state and a *Bhartiya*, who adheres to his duties. *Retaining Balance* addresses this bi-polar disorder afflicting each one of us.

Mahatma Gandhi, at various times, vocally propounded the concept of an ideal state. He did not hesitate to call that as Ram Rajya, implying it to be a system of good governance where duties preceded rights, both for the state and the individual. He surely implied an ideal post-independent government where values of justice, equality, idealism, renunciation and sacrifice are practised, both by the state and its citizens. *Ramayana* and *Mahabharat*, the unparalleled epics of our nation are replete with such sagacious advices on good and ideal governance as well as the disciplined, duty-conscious and cultured lifestyles of the people. Commenting on these inherent strengths of our people, the first Governor-General of India Sri C. Rajagopalachari succinctly observed:

> "If there is any honesty in India today, any hospitality, any chastity, any philanthropy, any tenderness to the dumb creatures, any aversion to evil, any love to do good, it is due to whatever remains of the old faith and the old culture."

Sadly, the founding fathers of our Constitution, have inadvertently thrust Christendom's "broken self" (arising from the original sin of Adam and Eve) on our citizenry in the making of our Constitution. In the process, individual rights have preceded duties. This, in turn, has spawned a series of imbalances that needs decisive intervention. We need to cognise this skew in our constitutional construct and address it forthwith. While I realise that these cannot be addressed overnight, I also understand that we need to make a beginning somewhere. *Retaining Balance* precisely does that.

In this book, I have not enunciated any principles. Nor have I postulated any theories. I have simply penned my thoughts and expressed my apprehensions. In the process, I have tried to raise some questions with stoic scepticism. In my attempt to seek answers to those questions I deliberately chose to leave some of the questions to be answered by the readers themselves. However, the most pertinent question that I would like to ask is: Are we made to miss and ignore the ultimate concepts of family, culture and civilisation in our skewed understanding of economics and if so, is it by design? If I stir some minds into serious thinking on these lines, the trouble I have taken would perhaps be worth the while.

This work of mine, which has taken more than 18 months of intense research, studying and assimilating humongous number of materials and writing nearly two lakh words, though energy-sapping physically, has been a great learning expedition for me. Of course, I must admit that a discerning reader may find some occasional flippant tone in the narration, but then I am incapable of camouflaging disturbing facts in pleasant language. Of course, there are exceptions to the rule of the verse of Manu Smriti *"Sathyam Bruyath: Priyam Bruyath."* I must admit that I have relied heavily on the exception.

Chennai
31.05.2021

M R Venkatesh
mrv10000@gmail.com

Acknowledgements

The independence of India, rather than paving the way for a fresh thinking and thereby leading us to a new beginning in arranging our public affairs, led to a recycling of many ideas that flourished during the British Raj. The Constitution, according to several scholars, is one of them. Writing the introductory chapter to the book - *Ayodhya and the Future India* - Shri JK Bajaj, Director of the Centre for Policy Studies, opines: "Having taken over the levers and the trappings of imperial power in India, the new ruling elite quickly convinced itself that the courthouses, the circuit bungalows, and the magisterial residences built by the British, as also the various manuals and codes of departmental and courtly procedure created by them and the earlier Mughal rulers, were essential to the governance of Indian people." It is this introductory chapter that had a profound impact on me, which ultimately compelled me to explore the discipline of economics from a civilisational i.e., *Bhartiya* perspective. I must thank Shri Bajaj, and in particular, the Centre for Policy Studies, for providing me with the inspiration for writing this book.

I am fortunate to have attended several lectures of Shri S Gurumurthy, who has dealt with a range of issues on economics and the impact of culture on economics. Since then, he has had a profound impact on my thinking. My innumerable personal interactions with him that revolved around several issues relating to law, economics, politics, and spirituality, have refined my understanding of economics in general, and *Bhartiya* economics in particular. But for his insightful guidance to several issues from a nationalistic perspective, I would not have been able to appreciate them in all their dimensions. I have no words to express my gratitude to Shri Gurumurthy.

I have been equally fortunate in discussing several of these issues with Dr Subramanian Swamy. After shifting base to New Delhi in 2015, I have been privileged to interact with him on several issues relating to political economy, usually, as a student would with his master. I thank Dr Swamy for his guidance and sagacious advice.

This book would not have been completed but for the painful task undertaken by my good friend Shri PS Prabhakar, chartered accountant in Chennai, of reading the manuscript, even as the book was being written and course corrected instantly. He has been a long-standing friend, guide, and a philosopher to me, who has constantly refined my thinking on such an ambitious idea.

My sincere thanks are to my friend Shri Shankar Bharadhwaj and my cousin Shri M K Suresh for having meticulously gone through the manuscripts and for suggesting appropriate improvements. My thanks are also to my colleagues, advocates Bharat Upreti, Surabhi Singh, G Karthikeyan, Rakesh Karela, and CA Vijay Kumar Gupta for having gone through the manuscript and suggested important changes. But for their decisive interventions, this work would not have seen the light of day.

I must also thank the publishers, KW Publishers Pvt Ltd, New Delhi, especially its Managing Director, Kalpana Shukla, for having done a remarkable job. Their professionalism has indeed been admirable. I also take this opportunity of thanking Vanit Sethi for editing this book.

My sincere thanks to the unknown author of the cover design of Lord Nataraja exemplifying both apocalypse and creation – in a way symbolising the cosmic balance.

I also thank all my family members for having left me unburdened by the pressures of domestic commitments while writing this book. I have no words to express my thanks to my parents, my wife Priya, and our sons Siddharth and Pranav for their support during this project.

While ensuring that all references contained in this book are appropriately acknowledged, I must admit that I could have missed some due to oversight. My sincere apologies to all those whose references I might not have appropriately acknowledged in the book or recognised their contributions to this work.

Chennai **M R Venkatesh**
31.05.2021 mrv10000@gmail.com

1. Strange Alliance, Stranger Bed Fellows

I don't think it's natural to be a monogamous person

– Scarlett Johansson

Monogamy is not a choice; it is a responsibility of a genuine human

– Abhijit Naskar, Wise Mating: A Treatise on Monogamy

The evolution of man is coextensive with the development of institutions. However, the use of the term 'institution' has acquired widespread usage in the political lexicon only in recent years. Institutions define the contemporary man and reflect the current development of mankind. Yet, we do not seek to understand the importance of institutions.

Institutions are the foundation on which the grand edifice of a societal order rests. Institution, as a concept in modern times, is increasingly becoming relevant in several disciplines, including economics, philosophy, sociology, politics, and geography. Our progress is constantly measured by the evolution of these institutions. Dynamic, self-sustaining, and continuously evolving, institutions capture the robustness of our societies. Some believe it is these institutions that historically make or break civilisations, governments, or even nations. This stems from the fact that there is an increasing acknowledgement, at least in the second half of the 20th century, of the crucial role of institutions in most spheres of human activity. Institutions are thus rule-setters, regulators, moderators, oversight bodies, providers of justice, and amongst several others, rule-enforcers. To this extent, institutions both constrain and enable human behaviour. By structuring, constraining, and enabling individual behaviours, institutions have the power to mould the capacities and behaviour of humans in fundamental ways; they have a capacity to change aspirations instead of merely enabling or constraining them. Whatever be it, one must hasten to add that institutions as an idea are nebulous and hence probably hard to define, but definitely not difficult to comprehend. Hence, let us at the outset ideate on the functions of institutions to understand it in all its dimensions.

One of the most important functions of these modern institutions is to constrain, structure, regulate, and enable human activities and make them more codified and predictable. They have strong self-reinforcing and self-perpetuating characteristics. They make rules for us. In the process, they guarantee peace for mankind. Peace ensures progress. These institutions are accountable for our collective freedom and answerable for our individual liberty. Simultaneously, they regulate our behaviour and fuel our aspirations. They punish us for our excesses, while protecting our rights, life, and property. They channel our individual and collective thinking. They are the moral compass for modern society to navigate between what we collectively believe are rights and wrongs. And thus, they permeate virtually every aspect of our lives. While institutions depend upon the character of men who drive them, paradoxically they mould men and their collective behaviour. And when institutions fail men, it is often seen that men at the helm of affairs have failed the institutions. That is understandable, and to a large extent logical. But what we, in these modern times, probably fail to appreciate is how the collapse of any institution has a debilitating impact on society and men.

Whenever we refer to institutions, instantly we refer to formal institutions created by man – socio-economic-political institutions like the parliament, judiciary, army, trade unions, police, central banks, or for that matter social ones, like hospitals, schools or colleges, commercial ones like say a large corporate, or a scientific one like say a space centre or for that matter a research and development organisation. Most of these institutions are formal, backed by the force of law or have in the least, governed by a written charter. The development of each of these institutions signals a quantum leap for man. Nurturing these institutions ensures the continuous progress of modern societies. Reforming and restoring these institutions are necessary as most of these institutions, being governed by men, are invariably fallible. Restoring and sustaining these institutions has thus become synonymous with reforms and progress.

Institutions are invariably interlinked. Governments are mandated to constantly monitor or regulate their functioning. Laws are enacted to protect these institutions and prevent them from becoming dysfunctional. We are continuously on the lookout to make these institutions more efficient. Globally, the efficiency of every government is measured by the ability of these institutions to deliver. Delivery, for all the reasons, stated above, by these institutions is crucial. Functionally, these institutions have their own grammar of working in different countries. Though diverse in their Constitutions, expectations from these institutions worldwide, more or less fall within a narrow compass of ensuring peace and prosperity. In more ways than one, each of these man-made institutions have become essential to the very functioning of modern societies.

However, there is an institution that predates all these institutions named above – the institution of marriage. This institution is probably the first institution set up by man that codified his individual as well as social behaviour. Setting up the institution of marriage had a great consequence for mankind as it signalled the dawn of civilisation. It is only after setting up this institution that probably man could conceptualise or feel the need for other institutions. Marriage, as an institution, regulates, dominates, and controls all other human institutions. In more ways than one, marriage is the mother of all institutions. No institution can probably claim to precede its existence. Yet, despite the fact that the institution of marriage predates virtually all other institutions, it has received scant attention from economists, sociologists, constitutionalists, and probably even social anthropologists. For a variety of reasons, of late the institution of marriage is under tremendous attack. Some fear this may ultimately lead to its collapse. And this could probably have a snowballing effect as several institutions too could come under severe stress. Expectedly, this could have profound implications on the economy, society, and even on the polity. Significantly, there is not much study on the impact of family on economics.

The Trigger

Given this paradigm, a few intriguing questions, which have been haunting me from within for well over a decade, has become the trigger for this book. Is consummation vital to the institution of marriage? By definition, is the institution of marriage monogamous or polygamous, or both? Is monogamy a natural instinct or polygamy? How do these societies, monogamous or otherwise, deal with the institution of marriage? How did societal norms germinate and fashion the development of philosophies across generations that govern the institution of monogamous marriage? How did society define taboos? And why does an individual follow these societal taboos? Do polygamous societies structurally function and differ from a monogamous one? If so, how?

How do men and women view each other in polygamous societies? Is it significantly different from how they view each other in say a monogamous society? Does polygamy result in societal imbalance? What is the theological drive that sustains polygamy and for that matter monogamy? What happens in a society, like say an Islamic one, where some men are allowed to have multiple wives, and therefore, some are left with none to marry? What happens to those men who do not get any women for marriage in a polygamous society? Does polygamy lead to economic instability? If so, why? Are polygamous societies equitable? If they are not, are they in the least, sustainable? Does it make macro-economic sense for a society to be monogamous? Either way, how does each society sustain itself in the long run? How does Mother Nature-when there is a design to ensure a male for a female in the first-place deal with this and correct the imbalance, if any? Crucially, and perhaps finally, how does family and societal norms impact the functioning of national, and by extension, global economy – the fundamental question that we seek answers throughout the length and breadth of this book.

Polygamy keeps society perpetually on the boil

To answer all this, a bit of historical reference to societies that practiced polygamy in the first place is absolutely critical. In the course of history, it is believed, based on anthropological researches, that approximately 85 percent of societies have practised polygamy. Modern history postulates the idea of monogamous marriage as one of recent origin. It believes that the history of man has been one of alpha male; a polygamous one at that. In his book *The Moral Animal: The New Science of Evolutionary Psychology*, Robert Wright notes that a 'huge majority' of the human societies (for which social anthropologists have copious data) have been polygamous. Virtually, all of those have been polygynous: that is, one husband-multiple wives. Polyandry (one wife-many husbands) is vanishingly rare. It is undeniable that in the evolution of mankind, polygamy is the general rule and monogamy the exception, that too in recent times.

Expectedly, some modern liberals argue that it is irrational and bigoted for contemporary society to limit marriage to just two people of the same sex or otherwise. Post-modernity, thy name is polygamy? Of late, some American campaigners have argued that polygamy should be made legal. If the Constitution of the United States of America (US) allows gay marriage, as the US Supreme Court ruled in 2015, then assuredly some argue, it is unconstitutional in the US to disallow plural marriage. "Group marriage is the next horizon of social liberalism," writes Fredrik DeBoer, an academic, in *Politico*, on the basis that long-term polygamous relationships deserve as much legal protection as any others freely entered into. According to him, "The question presents itself: Where does the next advance come? The answer is going to make nearly everyone uncomfortable: Now that we've defined that love, devotion, and family aren't driven by gender alone, why should they be limited to just two individuals? The most natural advance next for marriage lies in legalised polygamy. Yet, many of the same people who pressed for marriage equality for gay couples oppose it."

It is obvious that the nascent idea of monogamy is already under intense ideological and sociological challenge. And in all these developments, India is not far behind. India, at this point in time, does not explicitly recognise same-sex marriages. None of the marital laws expressly recognise same-sex marriages. Recently, a Public Interest Litigation (PIL) was filed in the High Court of Delhi, India, seeking declaration of the marriage rights of the gay community under the Hindu Marriage Act, 1955. The petition points out that the Act merely allows marriages between 'two Hindus' and does not discriminate between heterosexual and homosexual couples. It is argued that it is nowhere mentioned under Section 5 of the Act that a marriage must be solemnised between only a man and a woman. Placing the argument on a much different pedestal, advocates of same-sex marriage point out that the right to choose one's partner, whether of the opposite sex or of the same sex, is guaranteed by Article 21 of the Constitution of India. Interestingly, opposing the petition, the Union Government through its Solicitor-General, stated that "Our legal system, society, and values do not recognise same-sex marriages." Of course, some countries have legalised same-sex marriages. But the question is whether India too should follow this development? The question is obviously no longer limited to gender but the number of persons one could legally marry. Crucially, this calls for a complete understanding of individual rights and the extant constitutional arrangements. We will deal with more of this in greater detail in the ensuing chapters. But first, let us deal with the idea of polygamy.

Theoretically, there are three main forms of polygamous relationships: polygyny (a man takes multiple wives), polyandry (a woman takes more than one husband) and polygynandry (multiple men take multiple wives). Polygyny, by far the most common form of polygamy, is the subject of this book. In this entire work, we discuss polygamy as synonymous with polygyny and do not discuss the other forms of polygamy.

Statistically speaking, it is pertinent to note that more male than female babies are born (approximately 105 boys to 100 girls). But this is balanced over time as boys are more likely to die of natural causes as infants than girls. That ensures the gender balance as in any given society there will be approximately 100 males to every 100 females. Given this fundamental biological fact, polygamy does not ensure enough females for every male. And this absence of females for every male has a profound impact on the society, and as we will see increasingly, polygamy de-shapes the very society that accepts, justifies, and glamourises it. Polygamy is the mother of all imbalance, increasingly iniquitous and violent, having a profound impact on the economics, both at the national and the global level. The reason for this disparity is not far to seek. In a monogamous society, for instance, each man has an even chance of marrying a woman. But in a polygamous society, that chance dwindles and possibly even evaporates. Monogamous society gives every person at least a reasonable chance to mate, and possibly marry, with his or her opposite sex. In contrast, in a polygamous society, a few men take multiple wives. This leaves other men with little or no chance of marrying altogether, and thereby giving a go-by to the most natural of all biological needs – mating, and the most crucial of all social needs – marriage! The immediate question, therefore, is what are the social consequences of polygamy?

In their 2012 article, *The Puzzle of Monogamous Marriage*, appearing in *Philosophical Transactions of the Royal Society*, Joseph Henrich, Robert Boyd, and Peter J Richerson compared how polygamous and monogamous societies functioned and possibly differed from each other. Interestingly, they found that polygamous societies significantly differ from monogamous societies in terms of violent crimes, female educational attainment, domestic violence, parental investment in children, and economic productivity. In many polygamous, non-industrialised societies, anthropological studies suggest that young unmarried men waged war primarily to steal wealth and wives, while raping and pillaging. Empirical studies carried out across continents suggest polygynous societies engage in more warfare, often with the primary goal of capturing women to meet the demand of their men. Polygamy is the origin of all imbalances.

Polygamy and its debilitating impact

More pertinently, criminologists have repeatedly pointed out the fact that single men commit the vast majority of violent crimes. Statistically, women and married men seldom carry out heinous crimes like murder, rape, and assault in comparison to a single man or a group of unmarried men. As there are many single men at any given point in time in polygamous societies, such societies have higher incidences of violent crime. Cultural anthropologists and modern sociologists too have backed these findings. The reason for the same is not far to seek. Being fully aware of a bleak statistical chance of having one long-term mate, unmarried men – especially of lower status and income – see no great future for themselves. Remarkably, such men of low status and income, indulge in risky status-elevating acts to jump the queue, improve their economic status, and thereby increase their chance of getting married. In the alternative, they indulge in serious deviant behaviour, which includes violent sexual crimes against women they so desperately seek.

An analysis of most crimes committed against women in most societies including murder, rape, social disruption, kidnapping of women, sexual slavery, and prostitution can be traced to such unmarried men. What is galling to note is that some young males with a bleak future become victims of the violence they seek to unleash. And this is a self-fulfilling prophecy where young men, by force of circumstances in a polygamous society, are compelled to take significant risks to get married. This unholy competition, in turn, distorts the male-female ratio and skews the same. That finally turns society into a polygamous one. In short, if the social order of ensuring a male for a female altogether disappears, and if a few males in a society by virtue of their economic status or for other reasons monopolise the available females in the society, the results could indeed be troubling, if not disastrous. It is the social order called monogamous marriage that settles the origin of most disputes within a society, ensures peace, progress, and prosperity. Should this social order be disrupted – the results could indeed be socially and economically chaotic. This social arrangement that ensured a man for a woman and vice-versa in the process elevated animals called *homo sapiens* into civilised men. If this is as elementary as it seems on first blush, why did it take several millennia for our forefathers to understand its importance? Is this social order easy to destroy as many suggest and some fear? If so, what are the consequences? We shall attempt to answer these questions as we proceed along.

Valerie M Hudson and Andrea M den Boer, ponder some of these consequences in their 2004 book *Bare Branches: Security Implications of Asia's Surplus Male Population*. Summarising their findings in a *Washington Post* article, they succinctly put across their entire findings: "Scarcity of women leads to a situation in which men with advantages – money, skills, education will marry, but men without such advantages – poor, unskilled, illiterate will not. A permanent sub-class of bare branches (read unmarriageable men) from the lowest socio-economic classes is created." They further note that "bare branches are more likely than other males to turn to vice and violence."

To get ahead, they "may turn to appropriation of resources, using force if necessary." Such men are ripe for recruitment by gangs, and in groups, they "exhibit even more exaggerated risky and violent behaviour." The result is "a significant increase in societal, and possibly inter-societal, violence."

Similarly, Kanazawa S and others in an unpublished document titled *Why men commit crimes (and why they desist)* in 2000 demonstrate that greater the percentage of unmarried men in the national population, greater will be the rates of rape, murder, assault, theft, and fraud. The percentage of unmarried men is a highly significant predictor of all these crime rates. In fact, the percentage of unmarried men is the only predictor that is consistently important across most crimes. In China, for instance, sex ratios (males to females) rose markedly from 1,053 to 1,095 between 1988 and 2004, nearly doubling the number of unmarried or 'surplus' men. This distortion in sex ratio was plausibly created by the implementation of China's one-child policy which forced the Chinese to prefer a son. At the same time, crime rates nearly doubled, 90 percent of which were committed by men. The inescapable conclusions from all such diverse studies reiterate the same point – unmarried low-status men, often in bachelor-bands, engage in higher levels of aggressive, violent, and anti-social activities.

Importance of Gender Balance

India too has her share of bare branches, as some parts of India practise female infanticide by which the sex of foetus is sought to be determined to eliminate the female ones. Expectedly, the sex ratio has been turned on its head with certain states within India reporting less than 900 females to every 1,000 males. Elimination of female foetus also has a psychological impact in such parts of the country, where boys grow up without sisters, cousins, and even female friends in their neighbourhood. This skew in the sex ratio is the fundamental cause for increased violence against females in certain parts of India, especially in some north Indian states. The response to this sociological malaise is typically bureaucratic – legislate criminal laws and make existing ones far stringent. But while criminal laws punish the deviant, the moot question remains unanswered – can it prevent the crime in the first place? Does it deal with the root cause of the malaise – the skew in the sex ratio? The answer to this is pretty obvious – Indians need to get rid of the skew in their sex ratio, one that does not allow a young boy to naturally deal with a person of the same age in the opposite sex without being violent to the opposite sex. And for that to happen, Indians have to go back to the age-old tradition of worshipping the girl child (*Kanya Puja*), married women (*Sumangali Puja*) and married couple (*Dhampathi Puja*). Modern India forgot this societal insurance offered by traditional India, even to a female foetus. The consequences are pretty chilling, as more than five million female foetuses have been estimated to have been aborted in the past decade or so. It is this imbalance between a man and a woman that brings about societal imbalances. And we are already paying a price for this.

Other studies carried out demonstrate that in every polygamous society, as a significant number of unmarried men compete for scarce sexual partners, their testosterone levels tend to rise, which has been correlated with higher crime rates. And this paradigm is not limited to young unmarried men alone. Increased testosterone levels in an elephant in *musth* can be as much as 60 times greater than in the same elephant at other times. Even the most placid of male elephants become highly violent toward humans and other elephants during *musth*. Although the link between testosterone levels (demonstrated to be lower among married men and higher among unmarried men) and higher crime rates is speculative at this point in time, the correlation between large pools of unmarried men and criminal behaviour has been amply documented. Statistically speaking, higher testosterone levels and crime go hand in hand.

Even terrorist groups understand the threat posed by large numbers of unmarried men. One of the most notorious terrorist groups ever, the Black September movement, conducted the seizure of Israeli athletes at the Munich Olympics in 1972. When Arafat's organisation sought to dismantle this group for fear of their violence undermining broader political objectives, military leaders decided to simply marry them off. Through a system of financial incentives and structured 'mixers,' members of Black September married attractive young Palestinian women. When such men were later asked to leave the country with legal passports, not a single one agreed to go, for fear of losing his family because of past terrorist activities. The Northern

Ireland Prison Service is reported to have used similar strategies when they offered early release to former IRA and loyalist terrorists. The larger point remains those unmarried men simply have less to lose. They also have more incentive to seek dominance through less conventional and more dangerous means, in hopes of garnering the resources required to attract sexual partners.

That explains substantially, if not wholly, the Indian wisdom of suggesting marriage of young male family members whenever elders in the family noticed deviant behaviour in youngsters. Certainly, Indians at some point in time must have realised how marriage has an uncanny knack of disciplining a young deviant male. Interestingly, marriage makes most men with deviant behaviour instantly responsible family men. From the point of economics, an unmarried young male who otherwise would find every occasion and excuse to spend till his marriage would suddenly find virtues in savings after his marriage. The institution of family, besides the benign idea of taming the young male and making him responsible, has macro-economic implications – it forces him to save instead of indulging in reckless consumption. This household savings is central to the national savings and goes on to fund investments for the national economy. Per contra, when the institution of marriage is damaged or even destroyed, at once, we notice the concomitant fall in the savings rate of the respective national economies. That forces the government to borrow internally or from the other countries to balance their lack of domestic savings to finance domestic investments. In the process, it considerably strains the finances of the countries who lend in the first place and hampers their development. We will revisit this link between marriage, savings, and spending in greater detail in subsequent chapters.

Polygamy and Impact on Women

But that is one side of the story. The impact of the female half of the population in a polygamous society is equally disastrous. As men accumulate wives, it is obvious, that there is and will always be a significant shortage of wives. With a scarcity of women of their own age, men actively seek younger women. The incessant demand leads to ever lowering of the marriageable age of the females to ensure a steady supply. That eventually means that in a polygamous society, it is most likely that the age of marriage will be lower for females than in a monogamous society. Early marriage, in turn, leads to much higher rates of reproduction, but at a lower age of women when she is not yet ready for motherhood. She is physically unprepared and psychologically underprepared for teenage pregnancy – at times more than one – when she reaches the age of 20. Modern medical studies clearly establish that such teen motherhood is detrimental not only for the mother but also for the new born. This, in turn, produces a society that is malnourished and undernourished. In most cases, sudden marriage and unplanned pregnancy do not allow a woman to complete her education. The difference in age exacerbates gender differences, and, for men, is more likely to give rise to jealous fears that their young wives will be unfaithful. No wonder, marriage at a young age to a much older man is also linked to lethal domestic violence. Inside every polygamous home, the senior wives worry that they will be replaced by younger wives, and the younger wives in turn worry about the dominance exerted by the senior wives. There is another biological reason for the domestic violence in polygamous homes – wives seek to preserve their place with their shared husband. The struggle becomes intense as they seek to secure family assets, businesses, and resources for their own biological children. Sometimes and often tragically, children are victims of such violence and the urge to dominate.

If polygamy is bad for men and worse for women, it is far worse for children. As polygamous wives tend to be younger and less well-educated, their children suffer in not having more mature mothers, as would be more typical of their counterparts in a monogamous society. As a family, especially mothers, are constantly in a state of unnatural, unhealthy competition with their step-mothers, children are constantly prepared for a state of conflict. Half-siblings compete for limited resources. Weaker genetic bonds do not help in mitigating the conflict within the family, especially in the allocation of scarce resources. This, in turn, sows the seeds of discontentment among young males in the family that eventually shapes their deviant behavioural patterns as they grow older. Girls, in turn, are prepared through ocular demonstration as to how their father and brothers treat their mother or stepmother or sister-in-law, as the case may be, and thereby are psychologically trained and mentally prepared to get married to older men, which in turn sows the seeds of their deviant behaviour.

All these suppress women's freedom and rights (sharing husband must be the cruellest of them), increasing gender inequality, and prompting domestic violence – a fact lost on most who assume to take cudgels on behalf of such women in the first place. What is lost in the melee is the fact that a streak of unbridled behaviour of an individual – especially a male -which is passed off as 'fundamental right,' 'theological right,' or 'inalienable right,' depending on the societal norm, has a consequence – a cost to the individual, his family, and to the society as a whole. But do we realise this? The resultant cost of deviant individual behaviour to the society and its impact on the macro-economics of the nation is one of the subjects that will be dealt with, in greater detail in subsequent chapters.

Given all these, is the institution of marriage centred on monogamy associated with the great cultural leap that was undertaken by our forefathers? Is the taming of the alpha male – one who monopolises every available female – the inflexion point in our history? Or is polygamous marriage as much a robust institution as the monogamous one? Was the risk associated with polygamy denounced somewhere down the line by different societies and cultures, which re-worked themselves into monogamous ones? If so, how? Was monogamy the great de-risking factor in our evolution that allowed our cultural and scientific progress? Did monogamy, as a special social app, reduce the emergence of a surplus-risk-undertaking-unmarried-men, and in the process become an important factor in reducing crime rates? Did this arrangement ensure durable peace in societies and thereby lend itself to scientific progress and economic prosperity? If monogamy is the killer app for peace, progress, and prosperity, why is it so fragile and under constant attack? The next obvious question – attack by whom? And if so, what should be done to save, if at all, it requires to be saved? Are governments by their actions and policies unwittingly a part of this attack? Well, we shall seek answers to these convoluted questions as we proceed further. But first, let us look at the downsides of a polygamous society, and how polygamy ensures that a society is always in a constant state of boil.

Suffice to state at this point in time, that the social dynamics in a polygamous society are indeed ugly. For starters, as we pointed out, it creates a numerological imbalance between men and women in a society. In a polygamous world, men cannot take marriage for granted and have to be competitive, and at times even brutal, for getting married. And those who have won in the present are in persistent fear of losing in the near future – and hence seek to physically eliminate any and every potential competitor, often through violent means. This endless cycle where violence begets more violence is a race to the bottom. Sociologists who have studied the devastating consequences of polygamy have commented on its retrograde consequences on women who are condemned to sharing a husband with several co-wives, or whether men are at the greater receiving end in a polygamous society as a larger number of men who never stand a chance of becoming a husband and raise a family or children in such societies (which is in a constant state of boil) are psychologically tormented.

Polygamy is when a man seizes possession of the woman and holds her as a sexual object in the same sense in which he has other goods of the outer world. Tragically, in polygamous societies, woman becomes completely a thing; an object. In the process, in such a society, a woman is stolen, bought, given away, or sold. In short, she instantly becomes a property in a polygamous society. In such polygamous societies, it is perfectly legitimate for a man to have as many wives as he can afford or defend from other predators. As wives are a form of property, it is always better to have more than a few. Resultantly, when polygamy is the norm, violence is universal.

It is perhaps these evolutionary experiences that had taught mankind of the enormous downsides of polygamy. For primers, a polygamous society, by its very definition, is the anti-thesis to a liberal democracy. For too long, we have ducked the issue of understanding the impact of polygamy on society, and by extension on national and global economics. But remaining oblivious to this problem further may cause immense damage to the very idea of civilisation as we have come to understand now. As societies move away from hierarchy and towards equal opportunity i.e., democracy, they have an indispensable pre-condition – leave polygamy behind. Put pithily, societies become liberal, and hence sow the seeds of democracy when they are monogamous, not otherwise. It cannot be the other way around. While one can endlessly argue about the sequence – liberty-democracy-monogamy in any society, it is often seen that it is only this triumvirate that co-exists in most societies. It is all or none!

Culture, Civilisation and Family

Throughout this book, the words culture and civilisation are used as alternatives, though it must be conceded at the outset that there is a fine difference between the two. Civilisation, it is often remarked, is what we were, and culture is what we are. The term 'culture' is believed to be a derivative of the Latin world 'cultus,' which refers to cultivating or refining something; more particularly in constructive terms. The cultural anthropologist E B Taylor defines culture as a "complex whole which includes knowledge, belief, art, morals, law, custom and any other capabilities and habits acquired by man as a member of society." Thus, the behaviour of an individual is shaped by culture and therefore almost all the members of a specific culture share its prominent characteristics. It is also important to note that culture is acquired both by training and inheritance. It includes all that is summarily termed as habits, practised by a person at an individual level and manifest subtly through restraints and abstentions. It is everything an individual achieves as a member of a social group and relates to the other members of the group.

Civilisation too has its root in the Latin word 'Civis' implying someone who lives in town. (By extended logic, one who lives in the village is uncivilised!). Civilisation, in contrast to culture which deals with men at an individual level, deals with developing the state of human society as a whole and includes industry, technology, and government so as to satisfy the collective needs of people by organising them as a whole. Civilisation, therefore, is the bigger set of which culture is a sub-set – it is both a process and a destination. In theory, the former can encompass several units of the latter. That makes civilisation a complex aggregate of the society, and culture is just a spec or a portion of an entire civilisation. In short, a culture ordinarily exists within a civilisation. In this regard, each civilisation can contain not only one, but several cultures – which is both its strength and weakness. Being a microcosm of civilisation, culture can exist by itself whereas civilisation requires a multitude of cultures. Because of its complexity and magnitude, all of the raw aggregates of a civilisation need to be entirely passed on to successive generations, usually through the medium of language, though language is not a necessary pre-condition to preserve civilisation.

Before we proceed further, a word about family too. Let us concede that it is probably very difficult to define the term family. But given the context of what we have set out to address we have held a family to be an aggregate of individuals of opposite sex and their union recognised either by civil laws of the country where they normally reside or by the religion that they follow and their children arising out of their wedlock. But beyond this, one is afraid that it is always a nebulous idea that is incapable of precise definition. For instance, the Census Bureau of the US defines a family as "a group of two people or more (one of whom is the householder) related by birth, marriage, or adoption, and residing together." Several scholars have pointed out that this definition is highly subjective for what is 'residing together' may vary from family to family, person to person. Interestingly, one could not trace even a nebulous definition in the case of the Ministry of Health and Family Welfare, Union Government of India. Yet, billions of rupees are spent on the 'families' by the successive governments. Disturbingly, it is also not clear what is meant by 'welfare.' This is how most governments across continents view families – the basic institution on which the entire civilisation of mankind rests – with a lack of understanding of family, its civilisational importance, and importance in national and possibly global economics. That explains the 'why' of the book.

Alberto Alesina and Paola Giuliano in their working paper with the American National Bureau of Economic Research (NBER) argue based on world value surveys that when family ties are strong, there is more reliance on home production and less participation in market activities. Importantly, they point out that since strong family ties produce social insurance, less is needed from the government. In other words, when family ties are strong – both market and government have a secondary, residual role. Naturally, family, as we will see in Chapter 3, is a common natural adversary of both markets and governments. No wonder, both government and markets seek to weaken it, as a strong family is an antithesis of both reckless markets and overbearing governments. With strong family ties, participation in market activities is no doubt lower, but productivity in the aggregate is higher. Since home production is by and large not included in GDP statistics, the latter could display a downward bias as a measure of total production (home and market) in countries with strong family ties. Even though lower market participation may imply a lower income, the NBER working paper argues persuasively that family ties reduce the variances in income by providing psychological as well as financial insurance. The moot question therefore is, are people happier or not in cultures with strong family ties? We seek to answer this question in this book.

Importantly, the authors of the working paper point out that the North European group has the lowest family ties followed by continental Europe, central and east Europe, and the group including the US, Canada, the UK, Australia, and New Zealand, that is the group of English-speaking Anglo-Saxons OECD countries. The relatively weak family ties of many central and east European former communist countries, they point out, may be the result of communist collectivist ideology and propaganda. It is apparent that whatever be the definition of family, there is a huge range in the manner family is viewed and perceived by people across continents. Crucially, there are differences in the societies that are rooted to family values and those where which are not family-centric. These differentials are not subjected to any great socio-economic studies. The fault lines are distinctly noticeable. Nevertheless, economic theories for countries where family ties are weak are as a matter of routine imposed on the countries where family ties are strong. This is simply because economic theories, unfortunately, have degenerated into a one-size fit all, more so in the past three decades or so. As ideas fail, economists are clueless as to how and why economic theories that worked so well in one country fails to work in another. Probably we do not realise in the case of economic policies what is cheese for the goose may not entirely be cheese for the gander.

Fascinatingly, most countries where family ties are lower, seem to be economically developed, and those where family ties are strong are 'developing.' But is the 'development' in the developed world sustainable over a longer period of time? Are economies that are dependent on the markets infallible? The answer, in the absence of a precise study on this subject, may be at best, tentative. It may be recalled that economies that placed the government at the commanding heights of their respective national economy too have imploded, some beyond recognition. Countries that have proudly proclaimed they have reached the macro-economic nirvana, perfected an all-encompassing economic model, and pontificated the rest of the world to follow them, have gone bust before our own eyes, all within our lifetime. We will look into this issue in Chapter 9 of this book. Whatever be it, the world is well and truly in search of a durable economic model. Will it be one that placed family – not markets or government – at the centre of policy formulations? Well, this is one question that we will seek to answer as we proceed further.

Polygamy and Violence

Now let us revert to the core issue of polygamy. In civilisational parlance, polygamy was taboo for probably the whole of the 20th century, at least in parts of the non-Islamic world – and remained so out of sight, and hence out of mind until recently. But that taboo is crumbling. And crumbling fast. An HBO television series in America called *Big Love*, which benignly portrayed a one-husband, three-wife family set off the latest round of polygamy debate. Likewise, the American Civil Liberties Union's stand for polygamy rights, and the rising voices of pro-polygamy groups such as TruthBearer.org (an evangelical Christian group) and Principle Voices (which *Newsweek* describes as "a Utah-based group run by wives from polygamous marriages") were already making the topic of polygamy hard to side-step.

This, in turn, has compelled some to approach the question of polygamy as an issue of individual choice intertwined with individual rights and further fortified by the constitutional mandates across continents, while turning to a blind eye to the debilitating consequences arising out of such a social approach. This debate on individual rights and constitutional guarantees that follow it – all in the name of social contract theory – is now cast in stone, and a rethink of some of these issues are virtually impossible. This has been elaborately dealt with in subsequent chapters of this book. This substantially clarifies why conservatives have been rather defensive, especially in face of hydraulic pressure exerted by public opinion generated by the mass frenzy on the subject of individual rights and subjects like polygamy that arise with it. This frenzy by libertarians on the one hand and silence of the conservatives on the other has left the ubiquitous common man completely befuddled. The public opposes polygamy – more out of emotional impulse than any serious understanding of the subject – and is unsure why. Worryingly, there is hardly any serious thinking about the impact of polygamy (even as the taboo on the subject is fast evaporating), and its resultant impact on the socio-economic policies of national governments – one that has profound impact on the manner in which the discipline of economics is fashioned. When one man marries two women, some other man marries no woman. When one man marries three women, two other men cannot marry. When one man marries four women, three other men go without wives. Thus, polygamy is a zero-sum game that skews the marriage market so that some men marry at the expense of others. Despite all these, monogamy that gives everyone a shot at marriage is lampooned as conservative, old-fashioned, and an affront to individual rights.

A monogamous marriage results in significant improvements in child welfare, including lower rates of child neglect, abuse, accidental death, homicide, and intra-household conflict. These benefits result from greater levels of parental investment, smaller households, and increased direct 'blood-relatedness' in monogamous family households, says Henrich, who served as an expert witness for British Columbia's Supreme Court case involving the polygamous community of Bountiful in British Columbia. Monogamous marriages have largely preceded democracy and voting rights for women in the nations whenever and wherever it has been institutionalised, opines Henrich. By decreasing competition for younger and younger brides, a monogamous marriage increases the age of first marriage for women, decreases the spousal age-gap, and elevates female influence in household decisions, which decreases total fertility and increases gender equality.

Do we ever realise the net consequence of monogamy or for that matter polygamy? The effect on an individual who is denied a natural probability of taking a person of the opposite sex as his partner is devastating. And that natural deprivation leads to an unnatural sexual preference in the form of becoming gay and ending up marrying up persons of the same sex. Even as libertarians applaud the explicit manifestation of an individual choice, little do they realise the probable cause – polygamy – the denial of rights to practice natural sexual preferences that could probably force some to become gay, which may not be their first or natural choice. So much for the concern for individuals and their rights that the modern-day libertarians seek to espouse. While sexual preferences are indeed a matter of personal choice, the fact remains that a study on the correlation between polygamous societies and the increased incidence of gays in such societies calls for greater research and study. This imbalance of sexes within the marriage market destabilises society, and when society is destabilised, the economics that flows within too is destabilised with chilling consequences. That is a recurring theme of this book.

Nevertheless, Hudson and den Boer suggest that societies become inherently unstable when sex ratios reach something like 120 males to 100 females – in other words, when one-sixth of the men are surplus goods in the marriage market. India, as a whole, would reach that ratio if, for example, 5 percent of men took two wives, 3 percent took three wives, and 2 percent took four wives – numbers that are quite imaginable and possible if polygamy continued to be legal. In particular communities, polygamy could take a far bigger toll much more quickly than most anticipate.

Worse, high-sex-ratio societies are governable only by authoritarian regimes capable of suppressing violence at home and exporting it abroad through colonisation or war. In medieval Portugal for instance, Hudson and den Boer argue that "the regime would send bare branches on foreign adventures of conquest and colonisation." In 19th century China, where as many as 25 percent of men were unable to marry, "these young men became natural recruits for bandit gangs and local militia," which nearly toppled the government. In what is now Taiwan, unattached males fomented regular revolts and became 'entrepreneurs of violence.'

Based on anecdotal references from history and social arrangements across continents, it can be safely demonstrated how polygamy significantly contributes to turning societies violent. Naturally, such violence was either curbed within the borders by far greater violence, or was tactfully exported to distant lands, mostly the latter. That, in turn, had two-fold objectives – first was to unleash violence in other lands by channelling the frustrations of their unmarried men, and second to seek women from distant lands for such men and thereby address the shortage of women in their own land for their men. Thus, the never-ending cycle of violence begins – frustrations of young men who cannot get women in their own society compels them to seek women, mostly by force, from distant lands and other societies which are usually monogamous ones. Worse still, polygamous societies thrust war and violence on unsuspecting lands for the least likely reason – excess of unmarried men at their own end. What is indeed exasperating to note here is that monogamous societies end up paying a price for the indiscipline of polygamous societies. Unless the world is uniformly monogamous, it will indeed be a case where a monogamous society has and will continue to bleed for the machinations and indiscretions of polygamous societies. This inequity – where the disciplined have always to pay a heavy price – is yet another issue that is sought to be addressed in this book.

It is the consistent view of modern sociologists and emerging frontiers of modern societal values that wherever it is widely practised, polygamy destabilises society, not only the very society where polygamy is practiced, but also runs the risk of destabilising societies afar, largely because it is a form of inequality which creates massive distress in the hearts and loins of young men. Every time a rich man takes an extra wife, another poor man must remain single. Young men, in such a scenario, naturally will take desperate measures. It is precisely these reasons that are blamed by Robert Guest in an article titled *The Link Between Polygamy and War,* and illuminates as to why Arab Spring erupted in the first place, why the jihadists of Boko Haram and Islamic State were able to conquer swathes of Nigeria, Iraq, and Syria, and why the polygamous parts of Indonesia and Haiti are so turbulent.

Well, while this work does not aim to establish the precise mathematical correlation between polygamy and violence, the fact remains that several authors, quoted above, do point out to the inherent contradictions in the social structure of a polygamous society – one that is iniquitous and unstable, hence breed violence. Structurally, it would seem polygamous societies are inherently unsuited for democracy. Is that why large parts of the Islamic world are not democratic, and whenever they have their tryst with democracy, it is at best tenuous? While it might be essentially difficult to directly link polygamy to violence, it is apparent that polygamous societies exhibit certain characteristics that are unique and remain distinct from monogamous societies. If it is iniquitous as demonstrated above, what explains the how and why of its longevity? Is it because polygamy is 'natural?' But that is not the only reason for why it has been practised for long. It is now evident that polygamy requires better reasons – theological for instance – to sustain on a long-term basis. Else it would be unfathomable as to why women would agree to be a part of the polygamous society without demur? Likewise, what would explain the unnatural behaviour of young men in such societies who let go of their prospects of getting married for generations after generations? To understand the long-term effects of polygamy and its devastating impact on societies, far and near, it may be profitable at this point to make a brief reference to the manner in which Islamic societies have been influenced by the theological sanction to polygamy by Islam.

But polygamy is not the sole reason for making a reference to Islam. To the uninitiated, Islam offers polygamy as part of a much larger package. Islam, it may be noted, has an imperialistic view, mandates global dominance, necessitates conversion by force or otherwise, legitimises polygamy, and of course, rationalises jihad. All of these are symbiotically linked to one another, and polygamy is an integral part of this package. In contrast, other religions may or may not sanction polygamy. But surely some aspects of Islam, jihad, for instance, is absent in most other religions. And the absence of such a holistic package in other religions does not provide us the scope for deeper research on the convoluted subject of polygamy and its ubiquitous link with violence, as much as an Islamic society does. That, in turn, compels a reference to polygamy within Islamic societies.

Polygamy and Islam

While scholars usually differ – sometimes boisterously – in their interpretation of the Koran, there is near unanimity among scholars about the fact that Islam does permit polygamy. Probably, Islam is one of the major religions of the world that unabashedly accepts polygamy. Under Islamic marital jurisprudence, Muslim men are allowed to practise polygamy, that is, they can have more than one wife at the same time, and as per some scholars, up to a total of four. Polyandry, the practice of a woman having more than one husband, by contrast, is not permitted. More importantly, Prophet Muhammed – the founder of Islam himself – is supposed to have married over 11 women during his lifetime. It may be interesting to note that Prophet Muhammad was monogamous for 25 years. After his first wife Khadija bint Khuwaylid died, he proceeded to marry several times over, and most of them were widows. Francis Edward Peters (Professor Emeritus of History, Religion and Middle Eastern and Islamic Studies at New York University) says it is hard to make generalisations about Muhammad's marriages: many of them were political, some compassionate, and some perhaps affairs of the heart – in short, several reasons that rationalised his marriage. But that is not our concern. Islam makes imperial demands of Muslims – and one such demand is that every follower shall faithfully clone his life in line with that of the Prophet. Mohammed is the perfect Muslim, and all Muslims are to pattern their life after his. He is the perfect father, husband, judge, leader, warrior, businessman, and politician. That explains why Muslim men, in view of the theological sanction obtained in the Koran and practised by Prophet Mohammed himself, see no moral conflict in polygamy. Women, thereby in Islamic societies, are presented with a fait accompli – one by which they have to necessarily follow, or else be labelled as an infidel and face its consequences, mostly brutal.

The verse most commonly referred to with the topic of polygyny in the Koran is Verse 3 of Surah 4. A translation by Yusuf Ali as quoted by several sources in public domain, is faithfully reproduced hereunder:

> If ye fear that ye shall not be able to deal justly with the orphans, Marry women of your choice, Two or three or four; but if ye fear that ye shall not be able to deal justly (with them), then only one, or (a captive) that your right hands possess, that will be more suitable, to prevent you from doing injustice. – *Koran, Surah 4*

At first glance, this can be interpreted in many different ways, depending on one's agenda. However, it is important to understand the verse in context of both the Koran as well as the historical context when it was revealed. These verses were revealed after the Battle of Uhud, in which many Muslim men were killed, leaving widows and orphans. Thus, some Islamic scholars argue that these verses have been revealed "because of Allah's concern for the welfare of women and orphans who were left without husbands and fathers who died fighting for the Prophet and for Islam. It is a verse about compassion towards women and their children; it is not about men or their sexuality."

In the Hadith collection compiled by al-Bukhari, the historical context of Verse 4:3 is further explained when 'Ursa narrates:

> He asked Aisha about the Statement of Allah: If you fear that you shall not be able to deal justly with the orphan girls, then marry (other) women of your choice, two or three or four; but if you fear that you shall not be able to deal justly (with them), then only one, or (the captives) that your right hands possess. That will be nearer to prevent you from doing injustice. (4.3) Aisha said, "O my nephew! This Verse has been revealed in connection with an orphan girl under the guardianship of her guardian who is attracted by her wealth and beauty and intends to marry her with a Mahr less than what other women of her standard deserve. So they (such guardians) have been forbidden to marry them unless they do justice to them and give them their full Mahr, and they are ordered to marry other women instead of them."

The Koranic context can be further explained by Surah 4:2, which states "To orphans restore their property (When they reach their age), nor substitute (your) worthless things for (their) good ones; and devour not their substance (by mixing it up) with your own. For this is indeed a great sin." Therefore, the first part of verse 4:3 is dealing with orphan women who are under the protection of a male guardian, and it is advising the guardian to deal justly with the orphans.

In the second part of Verse 4:3, the Koran states "but if ye fear that ye shall not be able to deal justly (with them), then only one, or (a captive) that your right hands possess, that will be more suitable, to prevent you from doing injustice. If a man cannot deal justly with more than one wife, then he must marry only one." It is clear that this quote was revealed out of compassion towards women, and not as a means to please male sexuality, which is a common modern interpretation of such verses.

Putting the verses regarding polygamy into the broader context by examining the nature of marriage in Islam helps to understand them. The Koran (4:21) – *"And how could ye take it when ye have gone in unto each other, and they have Taken from you a solemn covenant?"* refers to marriage as a *mithaq*, i.e., a solemn covenant or agreement between husband and wife, and enjoin that it be put down in writing (4:21). Marriage is more than just a 'solemn covenant' however, with Surah 30 verse 21 stating *"And among His Signs is this, that He created for you mates from among yourselves, that ye may dwell in tranquillity with them, and He has put love and mercy between your (hearts): verily in that are Signs for those who reflect."* Love and mercy are very much a part of marriage as described in the Koran. Although the Koran may prescribe different roles for males (husbands often seen as the provider), the equality between husband and wife is promoted when it is dictated in Surah 2 verse 187 that *"They (your wives) are as a garment to you, and you are as a garment to them."* It is thus clear that there is more to polygamy in the scriptural basis of the Koran than simply the citation of certain verses.

One can say without the fear of contradiction that these are benign interpretations and available in the public domain of polygamy in the Koran. But to restrict polygamy to mere theological sanctions would be taking a rather narrow view of the subject. Let us not forget that Islam has a political view too. Polygamy is permitted, as it is believed to benefit its ultimate political goal – *Ummah* – the Muslim Nation. Muslims understand that numbers are vital to their political agenda of being a globally dominant religion. This has been a consistent feature of the writings of the finest minds in Islam for a thousand years. Given this paradigm, Islamic reformer Sultan Shaheen's remarks that "For hundreds of years now, major Muslim theologians have been engaged in creating a coherent theology of intolerance and violence in order to expand the Islamic reach." He further amplifies, "Luminaries of Islam have established a theology which primarily says that Islam must conquer the world." Certain Islamic scholars like Sheikh Muhammed Salih Al-Munajjid, for instance, have unabashedly rationalised polygamy for the simple reason that it helps to increase the numbers of the Ummah. They believe that numbers can only be increased through marriage, and the number of offspring gained through polygamous marriages will be greater than that achieved through monogamous marriages. Secondly, polygamy is necessitated, as according to them, there are some men who may have strong physical desires, for whom one wife is not enough. Some Islamic scholars opine: "If the door is closed to such a man and he is told, you are not allowed more than one wife, this will cause great hardship to him, and his desire may find outlets in forbidden ways." Thirdly, in addition to that they add, a woman menstruates each month, and when she gives birth, she bleeds for forty days (this post-partum bleeding is called *nifaas* in Arabic), at which time a man cannot have intercourse with his wife, because intercourse at the time of menstruation or *nifaas* is forbidden. So, for all these reasons, polygamy is 'approved' by Islamic theologians.

Thus, at a theological, level Islam sanctions polygamy, while it also allows conquest and conversion through violent means as a political agenda. In contrast, Indic religions do not positively sanction polygamy. Neither do Indic societies approve of polygamy. Thus, while some of the Hindus, Buddhists, Jains, or Sikhs are likely to be polygamous, it is considered a deviant behaviour, never approved by the respective theology or by their societal practice. But what would be interesting is that never in the history of these religions have armies crossed borders for conquests, much less in search of women for their unmarried men. Did the societal norm of monogamy make the Indic civilisation less violent, tolerant, and peaceful? Is the traditional way of looking at women as an integral part of man in these civilisations much to do with their approach to life? Crucially, did this allow a delicate balance within the society – as the rules of engagement between men and women were well defined? We will seek answers to these questions also in subsequent chapters.

Before we delve into the link between polygamy and violence in Islamic societies, first let us explore the issue of conquest and conversion in Islam. It is pertinent to note that Islam periodically augmented its missionary agenda with military conquest, and the rise of Islam is intimately connected with military and spiritual conquest. Mohammed himself served as a religious, political, and military leader. This experience, many scholars argue, served to distinguish Islam from all other major religions in its imperialistic attitudes, as only Islam has its genesis in armed conflict. Yet, even on this fundamental point, the Koran lends itself to glaring contradictions where it claims that "there is no compulsion in religion" (2:256) on one hand and calls for war, slavery, and death to those who refuse to submit to Islam (9:5) in others. Stephen M Kirby precisely examines these contradictions in his book *Islam's Militant Prophet: Muhammad and Forced Conversion to Islam* in an objective and meticulous fashion. According to him, the command of 'no compulsion in Islam' was a unique command that had doctrinal authority for only a little over two years. It was abrogated both by the Sunnah and the Koran. Its short lifetime was preceded and followed by commands that non-Muslims were to be given the option of converting to Islam, fighting to death, or at times, paying the *Jizya*. Muhammad was indeed the militant Prophet of a militant religion that supported forced conversions to Islam. In the process, increasingly he offered only two choices to all those who did not believe in his doctrine – convert or suffer the consequences, the latter of which often manifested as wholesale brutal bloody massacres. Substantial evidences exist to suggest that the overwhelming majority of those who were the first converts to Islam did so under tremendous duress. Even Islamic scholars have summarised the following three paradigms as an essential feature of its teachings: One, forced conversions, two, imperialism including the conquest of other lands for establishing Islamic rule, and three, slavery and slave trade.

Coerced conversion is especially evident in Muhammad's conquest of Mecca. When Islam's prophet – at the head of a vast army which had already put several tribes to the sword for refusing to convert – was approaching the polytheists of Mecca, the latter were warned: "Embrace Islam and you shall be safe. You have been surrounded on all sides. You are confronted by a hard case that is beyond your power." When the leader of Mecca, Abu

Sufyan who had long mocked Muhammad as a false Prophet approached the Muslim camp to parley, he too was warned: "Embrace Islam before you lose your head." Abu Sufyan then recited the confession of faith and entered Islam. The Meccans soon followed suit.

Koenraad Elst, the noted historian, captures the inherent violence of the Islamic invasion of India in *Negation in India*. According to him, the Islamic conquests, down to the 16th century, were for the Hindus a pure struggle of life and death. Entire cities were burnt down and the populations massacred, with hundreds of thousands killed in every campaign, and similar numbers deported as slaves. Every new invader made, often literally, his hills of Hindus' skulls. Thus, the conquest of Afghanistan in the year 1000 AD was followed by the annihilation of the Hindu population; the region is still called the Hindu Kush, i.e., Hindu slaughter. The Bahmani sultans (1347-1480) in central India made it a rule to kill a lakh captive in a single day, and many more on other occasions. Yet, to this day, strangely Islam is called the religion of peace. Similarly, in *Back of History*, historian William White Howells wrote that "first, invaders conquer a civilisation, then marry it." Islam, it would seem, provided a ready rationale for polygamy and armed conquest.

Rather tellingly, the Muslim historians who recorded these non-Muslim conversions to Islam saw no contradiction between the coercion and the Koran's claim that "there is no compulsion in religion." In short, this claim seems more of an assertion, a statement of fact, than a command for Muslims to uphold. But history is evidence of precisely the opposite. After all, it is true that no Muslim can make a non-Muslim say the words "There is no god but Allah, and Muhammad is the messenger of Allah." But Koran gives a licence to every Muslim to enslave, extort, plunder, torture, and slaughter such non-believers if they refuse. And Islam also ensured through polygamy a readymade army of young men who were compelled to take to violence for their basic biological needs. If these young men failed to indulge in violence, Islam condemned them to lifelong celibacy. Incidentally, Prophet Mohamed has repeatedly frowned on celibacy and thereby compelled these young men to act violently and seek women for themselves, even if it were from distant lands. And that makes the study of Islam compelling.

The Origins of Sleeper Cells

William Tucker, the author of the celebrated book *Marriage and Civilisation: How Monogamy Made Us Human,* asks the key question: "What happens in a society, like Islamic society, where men at the top can accumulate multiple wives and men at the bottom are left with nothing?" While the answers in some parts are indeed on expected lines, what makes Tucker's work epochal is the fact that he is the first scholar to trace the practice of killing oneself under theological compulsions. The answer is best left by quoting from his work.

According to Tucker, the holy war, jihad, was part of Islam from the beginning. After conquering the Middle East and North Africa, Muslim armies pushed into sub-Saharan Africa and the Caucasus in search of slaves. In the West, slavery was about work. When Western merchants shipped slaves to the New World, male slaves outnumbered females two to one. In Islamic countries, female slaves outnumbered male slaves by the same ratio. These 'slaves' were actually extra wives and concubines. Even the steady supply of women slaves from conquered lands did not solve the problem.

Despite the steady supply of women from conquered provinces, there was always a shortage, and the most common reaction of lower-caste Islamic men deprived of women became the desert retreat where dissident sects plotted the overthrow of the regime. Of these, perhaps the most extraordinary was the 'Assassins,' a Shia sect founded in Egypt in the 11th century that became the scourge of rulers all over the Islamic world. The Assassins established themselves in the Castle of Alamut, a mountain resort in northern Persia that is still difficult to reach today. There, they set up an early version of Al Qaeda, training young recruits to plant 'sleeper cells' around the Middle East, and manage to plant themselves into the circles of the prominent officials they wanted to assassinate.

The famous traveller and explorer, Marco Polo, in 1273, described what he saw when he passed through this same area: The Old Man kept in his court such boys of 12 years old as seemed to him destined to become courageous men. When the Old Man sent them into the garden in groups of four, ten or twenty, he gave them hashish to drink. They slept for three days, then they were carried sleeping into the garden where he had them awakened.

When these young men woke up, and found themselves in the garden with all these marvellous things, they truly believed themselves to be in paradise. And these damsels were always with them in songs and great entertainments; they received everything they asked for, so that they would never have left that garden of their own will. And when the Old Man wished to kill someone, he would take him and say: "Go and do this thing. I do this because I want to make you return to paradise." And the assassins go and perform the deed willingly.

So began the familiar Islamic pattern: young men with very little hope of rising in society are offered enlistment in a dissident sect that sanctifies violence, promises revolution, and offers martyrs a prize of 72 virgins up there. This is how polygamous societies end up at war with their neighbours that cause societal inequity and economic imbalance.

Tucker concludes: "A shortage of women means a volatile male population. Seventy-two virgins await in heaven – a reward, it should be noted, that does not have any particular appeal to the female half of the population. In short, Islam excludes women and has very little for young married men." What Tucker implies is the obvious – when a society cannot ensure one woman for every male, it contrives, often violently, to provide not one, not two, but 72 women for such men, of course, in a convoluted way. Has anyone ever wondered why married wealthy Muslim men never blow themselves up in the name of jihad, and often that is left to unmarried men? Why do women not blow themselves up in the name of jihad? Well, that job is left to mostly unmarried men! After all, if such unmarried men blow themselves up, they have been promised an extraordinary reward – not one, not two, but 72 virgins in heaven by the holy Koran, no less.

That, in a way, validates the imperialistic design of Islam, and how it has been sustaining itself over centuries. While all these – life, death, and life-after-death are matters of personal choices and belief, one cannot and should not question them. We do not intend to do so either. But when such dogmas come to intrude life and death in other societies, one cannot but comment on such beliefs, critically examine them, and suggest reforms.

Violence and Imbalanced Societies

Tucker opines that the history of Islam has been one continuous story of rebel groups off in the desert deciding that the religion being practised by the authorities and their harems back in the cities is not the 'true Islam.' They come crashing back upon the palaces, overthrowing the leaders (no Ottoman Sultan ever died of natural causes), and establishing a new regime that is just like the old one, where the powerful are allowed to take multiple wives.

Tucker surely has a powerful argument when he points out that Prophet Muhammad had a wonderful solution to this problem caused by polygamy by allowing conquest by unmarried young Muslims of other neighbouring societies and bringing home their women. If the men die in the process, the reward will be even greater – 72 virgins waiting for you in heaven! 'Jihad' has been a clever and effective incentive of redirecting the hostilities of the 'bachelor herd' that polygamy inevitably produces. In the alternative, should this army of unmarried men be successful in their conquest, they can virtually share the spoils of war and take any number of women from the conquered lands – marry them or treat them as sexual slaves, which too is permitted by Islam. In this connection, Tucker quotes Ibn Khaldun, the famous Islamic philosopher who wrote, "In the Muslim community, the holy war is a religious duty, because of the universalism of the (Muslim) mission and (the obligation to) convert everybody to Islam either by persuasion or by force. The other religious groups did not have a universal mission, and the holy war was not a religious duty for them, save only for purposes of defence. Islam is under obligation to gain power over other nations."

Interestingly, M A Khan, in his well-researched and acclaimed book *Islamic Jihad – A Legacy of Forced Conversion, Imperialism, and Slavery* points out that in Islamic belief, Muslims who live their life as perfectly as that of Prophet Muhammad will enter paradise without ever serving any time in hell. But it is almost impossible for a Muslim to emulate Muhammad's sinless life. Therefore, most Muslims will first serve some period of time, being roasted in the horrifying fire of Islamic hell. Obviously, the length of their residence in hell will be determined by the quantum of sins they commit in this life. They will, thereafter, enter paradise to live there for eternity.

The only other group of Muslims who will directly enter paradise, according to Khan, bypassing the roasting in hellfire, are those who would die as martyrs while fighting in the cause of Allah, while engaging in jihad or holy war (Koran 9:111). Therefore, those hundreds of Muslims, who died while fighting in the wars commanded and or directed by Prophet Muhammad in his lifetime as well as those hundreds of thousands, who died in Islamic holy wars over the subsequent centuries and those dying at present and will die in future, would have/will directly land in the Islamic paradise. Other Muslims, who die a normal death, will have to wait until the Judgement Day after the end of the world for Allah to judge how much time they will have to spend in hell before they can enter paradise.

Let us now indulge in some counter factual analysis. What if Islam practices monogamy instead of polygamy? What if the promise to marry 72 virgins no longer existed in Koran? In such a scenario, will young unmarried men continue to kill themselves? If so, how will Islam get recruits to furthering its imperialistic agenda? If Islam prohibits polygamy, would the world be a less violent place? Critically, not many even within the Islamic community seem to have asked this basic question – how does a religion that does not guarantee, much less facilitate even one wife in this life, takes upon itself to promise 72 in its aftermath? What is the philosophical underpinning of a religion that does not promise much but certain death in the most gruesome manner at the prime of one's life? And for those outside of Islam, the question is how does one deal with a religion which does not care for its own followers?

The problem is that those who question Islam can no longer be 'true Muslims,' Islam is a complete and completed religion. Probably, this also is one reason why not many scientific researches are ever done by any Islamic society. Why run the risk of discovering anything that is un-Islamic and face its ugly consequences? It is reiterated that Islam is a complete and completed religion with virtually no space for any contrarian findings. This universality of Islamic doctrine is said to be contained in the Sharia, which includes topics not limited to theology, but includes on subjects including but not limited to how to pray, conduct funerals, pay taxes, business law, banking law including payment of interest and share of profits, manner of writing wills, performing marriage, sex, divorce, criminal law, political rule, including dealing with *Kafirs* (the non-believers), how, when, and why to carry out jihad and against whom, punishment, family law, food, ethics, art, dress, and finally even to the use of toilets, how to say hello, knock on a door, a structure of government, and on and on. Being a complete religion, nothing can be added to it and being a completed religion, it cannot be reformed.

Let us amplify further. For instance, Muslims believe that Allah, the monotheistic Islamic God – claimed by Muslims to be the very same God as that of the Jews and Christians – had sent several prophets in succession for the benefit of mankind. Adam was the first and Muhammad was the last in this succession of prophets; the final Prophet – Prophet Mohammed – was the best of them all. The final and best Prophet also brought God's perfect, final divine revelation through the Koran and founded God's finalised religion, Islam. The earlier revelations and creeds sent by God, such as the Jewish and Christian scriptures and religions were imperfect and inferior to the final one. The net implications of all that was there in the past were to be rejected, the future was simultaneously made tamper-proof by excluding any other Prophet at a later point in time.

For instance, soon after its independence, Pakistan, despite having a predominantly Islamic population and an Islamic bias in its Constitution targeted the Ahmadiya sect, which takes its name from its founder Mirza Ghulam Ahmad. The Ahmadis are considered heretical by orthodox Muslims, not because they do not believe in Prophet Mohammed or his teachings, but because they do not believe that Mohammed was the final prophet. A sustained anti-Ahmadi campaign by Sunni religious groups starting in the 1950s led the government to designate Ahmadis as non-Muslims through a constitutional amendment in 1974. This is the fate of those who dare to challenge the prevailing Islamic orthodoxy. Thus, there is not much scope for any rethink much less revisiting any of the tenets of Islam, whether fundamental or otherwise.

Unsurprisingly, given the myriad issues involved and the refusal by its believers to see any reason, the Indian Supreme Court refused to comment on the issue of polygamy within Islamic society as late as 2017, even as it declared instant triple talaq as not being an integral part of Islam. Probably, the highest court in India did not dare to tread an area, where angels fear to go for the simple reason that abolishing polygamy has the calculated effect of reforming Islamic society. The Indian Supreme Court exercised the choice to evade which it did eloquently by postponing to address the issue to another day. Frankly, Islamic societies do not have this luxury of ducking the issue of polygamy to another day. It is now or never.

Political Islam

Nonetheless, the answer to these questions raised above may even be shocking to some. Islam is alleged to be highly imbalanced in its ideals. For starters, it has no answer to the imbalance created between every man and woman who are born in Islamic societies. Muslims are compelled by Islam not only to abide by the Koran but follow the sayings, deeds and actions of Prophet Mohammad, collectively called the Sunnah or Hadith. The Surah (biography) along with the Hadith (traditions established by the Prophet) and Koran (the religious text) completes the trilogy within Islam. Through these three, Islam regulates the daily life of the Muslims as few other religions have ever attempted or done to their respective followers. Amongst the rules laid out in these are the rules governing polygamy. Prophet Mohammed sanctioned the practice but tried to limit it by prescribing that a man could take only four wives and had to support all equally. Since Mohammad was the best amongst God's numerous prophets and the embodiment of the highest perfection of human life ever to walk on the earth, the only way for Muslims, indeed for all human beings, to live a perfect human life for achieving paradise is to walk in the footsteps of the Prophet. That is the core of Islam.

But that is not all. What is interesting is that Islam is not only designed for believers, it is also designed as to how such believers of Islam should deal with non-believers which necessarily mandates violence. Therefore, violence becomes inadvertently central to most of its even seemingly benign agenda. It is obvious to any lay reader of Islam that there are only two roads to Paradise – one, is by following the life of Prophet Mohammed including his multiple marriages (which in turn spawns an army of young unmarried men) and the other is participating in the holy war or jihad (which is a direct consequence of polygamy within the Islamic societies). There is, unfortunately, no third way of leading a simple, monogamous and nonviolent life that could lead a Muslim to Paradise. This is the truth about Islam. Thus, Islam can never answer the neat question – why does it promise something in the nether world what it fails to comprehend and deliver in the present world. It does not to this day have a solution for all those men who are victims of its polygamous agenda. These men are potential and actual destroyers of peace, not only within Islamic societies, but also the world over. History is a testimony to their brutal aggression, primarily caused by a lack of domestic harmony.

That begs a question: when did any Islamic society bring about any significant scientific invention for the benefit of mankind? The answer to this question is indeed murky. For its 1,400-year of existence, Islamic societies probably have very little to offer by way of scientific discoveries. And even if they did, not many scientists, are celebrated. Is the lack of domestic peace within Islamic societies stunting scientific researches within these societies? The answer to this question seems to be an emphatic 'yes.' At first blush, all that Islam promises is 72 virgins in heaven as a reward for being violent even when it does not have a solution to provide one, now and here. Worse still, as it mandates all faithful to follow the examples by the Prophet himself, any reform within Islamic society is virtually impossible. In fact, Islam mandates every 'True Muslim' to clone the life of the Prophet Mohammed as far and as much possible.

Until Islamic society introspects and reforms itself, the world will be witness to a steady supply of men who will get inspired by Islam to lay their life for the establishment of Islam at a global level and simultaneously search for their elusive brides in the other world. In the process, millions of innocents will continue to lose their lives. Unsuspecting women in far-off places run the potential risk of being raped, carried away as spoils of war, and turned into sex slaves. Children run the risk of 'Black Swan' events several times over within even their childhood – where the resultant violence could leave them orphaned – all thanks to Islam.

Will Durant, the famous historian who sums up rather succinctly the entire argument of the risk arising from Islamic societies to other non-

Islamic societies: "The Islamic conquest of India is probably the bloodiest story in history. It is a discouraging tale, for its evident moral is that civilisation is a precious good, whose delicate complex of order and freedom, culture and peace, can at any moment be overthrown by barbarians invading from without or multiplying within." This happened in the past, continues in our living times, and contains the seeds for future conflicts. For instance, according to the Global Terrorism Index (GTI), created by the Institute for Economics and Peace, in 2013, nearly 18,000 people around the world died from terrorist attacks. Eighty-two percent of the victims were in just five countries: Iraq, Afghanistan, Pakistan, Nigeria, and Syria – and all of them are either avowedly Islamic countries or countries with a majority of Muslims. Of the attacks for which groups claimed responsibility, 66 percent were executed by ISIS, Boko Haram, the Taliban, or al-Qaeda. In contrast, during the past 14 years, just 5 percent of deaths from terrorist attacks have occurred in the industrialised countries of the Organisation for Economic Cooperation and Development (OECD), which includes the US. Of the 162 countries in the GTI study, Iraq ranks as the nation most affected by terrorism. Forget others, it is obvious that Islam is not in peace with itself. In view of this historical position, the billion-dollar question is whether polygamy lies at the root of Islamic violence? Is the internal arrangement within Islamic societies creating an army of young men who apparently die in the name of their religion, but in fact are in search of a person of opposite sex to marry and raise a family?

Islam is one religion that exhorts global dominance, mandates forcible conversion, recognises polygamy, in the process prepares an army of unmarried men, and allows brutalising other societies in the name of fighting infidels. It is instructive to see how the trilogy of Koran, Surah, and Hadith deals with *Kafirs*, as Islam claims to be a final judge to all religions. More than half of Islamic doctrine concerns itself with the *Kafir*, that is non-believers. The *Kafir* is outside of the religion of Islam, and yet is an integral part of Islamic doctrine. Thus, Islam ends up making rules not only for its believers, but also how these believers should deal with non-believers. This doctrinal relationship is unabashedly political, and it is neither religious nor cultural. Political Islam defines the Islamic doctrine and refers to Islamic theology of dealing with *Kafirs*, while cultural Islam diffuses the subject in any debate. It is a clever ploy that one cannot ignore. If Islam were only a religion, it would be of no concern to those who do not seek to follow it. Islam makes imperial demands on every facet of society – Islamic, cultural, political or otherwise. This differentiation is irrelevant. That makes Political Islam the engine that drives cultural and theological Islam. While we assume that Muslims are concerned only with religious Islam, the fact remains that because of its rules for non-believers, the entire humanity is affected by political Islam. Therefore, Islam has a position or rule for every aspect of life, including for those who do not believe in it. It is a religion, culture, and political system, a complete way of life. It promises heaven to those who believe in it and die in the process with an added incentive of being presented 72 virgins and a polygamous life to those who survive these violent events. In short, it is a complete package of promoting polygamy to sustain its imperialistic design and an expansionist political agenda. Or is it the other way around – promoting violence to sustain polygamy? Whatever be it, if Islam has to give up jihad, especially its violent variant, it has to give up polygamy. Per contra, if Islam gives up polygamy, it will contain violence in the name of Jihad.

That, in a nutshell, is Islam for you – polygamous, and hence violent. And violence unleashed by Islamic societies are a derivative of polygamy. It is time for Islam to introspect and reform itself. But neither can it nor will it. Therefore, the non-Islamic world has to reform Islam in its own supreme self-interest. Else the consequences would be cataclysmic for the rest of the world. If Islam were to deal with its believers and their religious duties only, one had no compulsions, moral or otherwise, in reforming Islam. But the sad fact is that Islam encompasses non-believers too, and lays down rules for the believers in dealing with the non-believers.

Historically, Islam – for reasons stated above – is incapable of reforms from within. And the non-Islamic world, for its own self-preservation, has to necessarily carry out reforms for and on behalf of Islamic societies. For starters, how about banning polygamy within Islamic societies? How about restoring the delicate balance between man and woman the world over, more so, more specifically within Islamic societies? If non-Islamic societies fail to reform Islam and Islamic societies, at least to the limited extent of banning polygamy to help restore the balance between men and women within Islamic societies, the former runs a huge risk of the unknown overtaking us all.

Of course, admittedly this work is not about Islam. Nor is it about its core beliefs. This is about family, its civilisational importance, and its impact on macro-economics. Nevertheless, Islam is an important religion of the world with nearly two billion followers. Sustainable world economic growth and macro-economic stability are rooted in global peace and functional social order. The moot question is whether the practice of polygamy is increasingly becoming an impediment to a monogamous family, stable society, and a sustainable economic model? While the research on this vexatious subject has indeed been far and few, the fact of the matter is that common sense tells us that successful economic model cannot be linked to an inherently unstable society. Unstable societies in turn are products of unstable families. And unstable families, let us not forget, are an extension of an evolving *homo sapiens* – or those who may be called civilisationally challenged. The moot question is whether economic theories specifically crafted for civilisationally challenged (as is the case now with most modern economic theories) be imposed on those who are culturally and civilisationally rooted? And when such economic ideas do not work for obvious reasons, the ubiquitous demand is that people must jettison their family values, their culture, and civilisational values to make the economic theories work. Put differently, modern economics works only when the undisciplined untethered to any family, cultural, or civilisational values are in play. Not otherwise. This begs the question – should economics be a discipline tailored for the civilisationally superior, and the endeavour made to uplift those who are civilisationally challenged? Or should it be otherwise? We will seek answers to this question as we proceed along in the subsequent chapters of this book.

Courts world over get it wrong

In a celebrated judgement, oblivious to all these convoluted issues concerning the institution of marriage, its importance and its impact on the national economy, the sanctity associated especially with monogamous marriage, the Hon'ble Supreme Court of India declared the 150-year-old adultery law as it stood in the statute books as unconstitutional. This judgment, passed in 2018 by a bench of five judges of the Hon'ble Supreme Court of India on a writ filed by a non-resident, Joseph Shine, struck down section 497 of Indian Penal Code (IPC), 1860 along with section 198 of Criminal Procedure Code (CrPC) as unconstitutional, thereby decriminalising the very offence of adultery. Obviously, this judgement is going to have a profound impact in the near and long run. In a country beset with rising divorce rates and increasing cases of marital infidelity, the decriminalisation of adultery will critically endanger the already fragile institution of marriage. Worse still, it is feared by some that this judgement will increase extra-marital affairs and some will use this judgement without any let or fear to break their own marriages. In the process, do our courts realise the disastrous consequences of such individual actions on the institution of marriage, their spouse, society, and of course on young children born out of extra-marital affairs or out of marriages?

Before we proceed further, a reference to Section 497, the law in question, would be in order: Section 497: Adultery – Whoever has sexual intercourse with a person who is and whom he knows or has reason to believe to be the wife of another man, without the consent or connivance of that man, such sexual intercourse not amounting to the offence of rape, is guilty of the offence of adultery, and shall be punished with imprisonment of either description for a term which may extend to five years, or with fine, or with both. In such a case, the wife shall not be punishable as an abettor.

Thus, under Section 497 of the IPC, only the husband of the woman had the right to file a case against the man with whom his wife commits adultery, provided his wife did not take his consent while carrying out the act of adultery. And even in such cases, the wife was not to be punished as an abettor. Interestingly, this law gives the right to prosecute only to the husband of the adulterous wife. On the other hand, the wife of the adulterous man, had no similar right to prosecute her husband or his paramour. What is therefore punished under the then prevailing law was adultery but the proprietary interest of a married man in his wife. Surely, this is iniquitous and hence repulsive. The Hon'ble Supreme Court rightly frowned on this. Further, the heteronormative nature of the law left a gaping legal loophole to be wilfully exploited by married and unfaithful men to the great detriment of their respective wives. To this extent, the law was not gender-neutral and hence ran afoul of the Indian Constitution.

This law written over 150 years ago, probably under the influence of Victorian morality, was no doubt antediluvian, anomalous and incongruous. But on the question of adultery – the core of the subject matter in this writ – can we conclude that the modern-day socio-economic-political values are different from what they were when the provisions were first introduced in the statute book? Or for that matter ever before? Or ever after? Some values like monogamy are eternal and hence need to be respected. Some institutions, like family though fragile, are sacrosanct. The institution of monogamous family has made us cultured and hence over a period of time, made men civilised. This in turn has allowed peace to prevail and peace, in turn, ensured social, economic and scientific progress. Of course, nurturing the values of monogamy and allowing the institution of family to evolve, required a complex trade-off for mankind. This was dextrously done over the millennia by several civilisations through a method of constant trial and error till the sweet spot of monogamous family was finally arrived upon, probably as we pointed out earlier, serendipitously.

Despite its overwhelming importance, judges, world over seem to have a contrarian view of both monogamy as a virtue, and the family as an institution. Worryingly, courts view monogamy as an affront to individual rights, privacy, and personal liberty as guaranteed by their respective Constitution. To them, adultery is a private affair with absolutely no consequences, economic or societal. This, in quintessence, is the challenge to the modern economists who seem to be oblivious to these grave developments in the field of law that is set to have a profound impact in the next few decades on all spheres of life.

Justice Indu Malhotra, one of the five judges who decided the Joseph Shine case, drew reference to contemporary international jurisprudence in her separate but concurring judgement which is worth referring to know how courts across the world look into the issue of adultery, and thereby by extension, the sanctity of the institution of marriage. For instance, Justice Indu Malhotra points out that in the US, 17 out of 50 States continue to treat 'adultery' as a criminal offence under the respective state law. The characterisation of the offence differs from state to state. In the case of Oliverson v. West Valley City, the constitutionality of the Utah adultery statute was challenged. It was contended that the statute offends the right to privacy and violates substantive due process of law under the US Constitution. The Court held that adultery is a transgression against the relationship of marriage which the law endeavours to protect. The State of Utah had an interest in preventing adultery and given the special interest of the state, it was considered rational to classify adultery as a crime. A similar provision exists in the state of New York, wherein adultery is treated as a Class B misdemeanour.

By way of contrast, in the state of North Carolina, it was held in the Judgment of Hobbs v. Smith, that adultery should not be treated as a criminal offence. The Superior Court of North Carolina, relied on the judgment of the US Supreme Court, in Lawrence v. Texas wherein it was recognised that the right to liberty provides substantial protection to consenting adults with respect to decisions regarding their private sexual conduct. The decision of an individual to commit adultery is a personal decision, which is sufficiently similar to other personal choices regarding marriage, family, procreation, contraception, and sexuality, which fall within the area of privacy. Following this reasoning in Lawrence, the Superior Court of the state of North Carolina held that the state law criminalizing adultery violated the substantive due process, and the right to liberty under the fourteenth amendment to the US Constitution, and the provision criminalizing adultery was declared unconstitutional. However, in Canada, the Criminal Code of Canada under Section 172 imposes criminal sanctions for adulterous conduct. This provision was introduced in 1918, and continues to remain on the Criminal Code. The Criminal Code of Canada prohibits endangering the morals of children in a home where one "participates in adultery or sexual immorality or indulges in habitual drunkenness or any other form of vice."

In Malaysia, adultery is punishable as a crime under the Islamic Laws. However, the Law Reform (Marriage and Divorce) Act, 1976 made it a civil wrong, for all non-Muslims. Similar to the position in Canada, this Act makes adultery a ground for granting divorce, as it is a proof of 'Breakdown of Marriage.' Interestingly though, the Act also allows either spouse, to be an aggrieved party and claim damages from the adulterer or adulteress.

In Japan, the provision for adultery was somewhat similar to the present Section 497 of IPC; it punished the woman and the adulterer only on the basis of the complaint filed by the husband. In case the act of adultery was committed with the consent of the husband, there would be no valid demand for prosecution of the offence. This provision has since been deleted. Adultery is now only a ground for divorce in Japan under the Civil Code.

In South Africa, in the case of DE v. RH40, the Constitutional Court of South Africa struck down adultery as a ground for seeking compensation by the aggrieved persons. The Court relied on an earlier judgment of Green v. Fitzgerald wherein it was held that the offence of adultery has fallen in disuse, and has ceased to be regarded as a crime. The Court noted that even though adultery was of frequent occurrence in South Africa, and the reports of divorce cases were daily published in the newspapers in South Africa, the authorities took no notice of the offence.

In Turkey, the decision of the Constitutional Court of Turkey is another instance where the Court struck down the provision of adultery as a criminal offence from the Turkish Penal Code of 1926. The Court noted that the provision was violative of the Right to Equality, as guaranteed by the Turkish Constitution since it treated men and women differently for the same act.

In South Korea, adultery as a criminal offence was struck down by the Constitutional Court of Korea in, what is popularly known as, the Adultery Case of February 26, 2015. The Constitutional Court of Korea held that Article 241, which provided for the offence of adultery, was unconstitutional as it violated Article 10 of the Constitution, which promotes the right to personality, the right to pursue happiness, and the right to self-determination. The right to self-determination connotes the right to sexual self-determination that is the freedom to choose sexual activities and partners. Article 241 was considered to restrict the right to privacy protected under Article 17 of the Constitution since it restricts activities arising out of sexual life belonging to the intimate private domain. Even though the provision had a legitimate objective to preserve marital fidelity between spouses, and monogamy, the court struck it down as the provision failed to achieve the "appropriateness of means and least restrictiveness."

The Court concluded that it was difficult to see how criminalisation of adultery could any longer serve the public interest of protecting the monogamy-based marriage system, maintain a good sexual culture, and the marital fidelity between spouses. A consideration of Article 241 which punishes adultery failed to achieve the appropriateness of means and least restrictiveness. Since the provision excessively restricted a person's sexual autonomy and privacy by criminally punishing the private and intimate domain of sexual life, the said penal provision was said to have lost the balance of state interest and individual autonomy. Thus, in balance, courts in the whole of the US barring seventeen states, Canada, South Korea, Japan and even conservative societies like Turkey and Malaysia have de-criminalised adultery. The core that was determined by these courts as well as in India was whether 'adultery' must be treated as a penal offence subject to criminal sanctions, or marital wrong which at best is a valid ground for divorce.

One view canvassed before the courts was that the family being the fundamental unit in society, if the same was disrupted, would impact stability and progress of the society. The state, therefore, it was argued, has a legitimate public interest in preserving the institution of marriage. It was further argued that though adultery may be an act committed in private by two consenting adults, it is nevertheless not a victim-less crime. It violates the sanctity of marriage and impacts society as it breaks the fundamental unit of the family, causing injury not only to the spouse of those practicing adultery, but also impacts the growth and well-being of the children, the family, and society in general, and therefore must be subject to penal consequences. Throughout history, the state has long retained an area of regulation in the institution of marriage by determining the age when an adult can enter into marriage; it grants legal recognition to marriage; it creates rights in respect of inheritance and succession; it provides for remedies like judicial separation, alimony, restitution of conjugal rights; it regulates surrogacy, adoption, child custody, guardianship, partition, parental responsibility; guardianship and welfare of the child. These are all areas of private interest in which the state retains a legitimate interest, since these are areas which concern society and public well-being as a whole. Adultery has the effect of not only jeopardising the marriage between the two consenting adults, but also affects the growth and moral fibre of children. Hence, it was vehemently argued that the state has a legitimate public interest in making it a criminal offence.

The view of the Hon'ble Supreme Court was that adultery is at best a marital wrong, which could have only civil consequences. In the considered opinion of the Court, a wrong punishable with criminal sanctions, must be a public wrong against society as a whole, and not merely an act committed against an individual victim. Adultery, in its opinion, was not a public wrong. Like most Courts world over, the Hon'ble Supreme Court of India, viewed adultery as a moral issue and refused to intercede thereon. Chief Justice Dipak Misra, and Justice A M Khanwilkar, while allowing the writ and the attendant challenge on the Constitution, concluded that "In case of adultery, the law expects the parties to remain loyal and maintain fidelity throughout and also makes the adulterer the culprit. This expectation by law is a command which gets into the core of privacy. That apart, it is a discriminatory command and also a socio-moral one. Two individuals may part on the said ground but to attach criminality to the same is inapposite." With great respect to the Hon'ble Supreme Court, this judgement is seriously flawed as it does not take into account several other aspects.

Interestingly, the very same Supreme Court which decriminalised adultery is now looking into the issue of whether polygamy, as sanctioned by Islamic theology, is compatible with the Indian Constitution. Let us not delude ourselves – polygamy, even if it is backed by theological or for that matter Constitutional approvals, is nothing but adultery couched with a fig-leaf of theological sanction. One cannot see any difference between the two. Will the Supreme Court resist the great temptation to invoke the nebulous idea of 'constitutional morality' while deciding on the constitutional validity of polygamy? If so, how? Will it find anything amiss in polygamy when it has emphatically opined that adultery is purely a personal affair of an individual and the very same 'constitutional morality' prevents it from holding such acts as criminal? It would be interesting to see how the Hon'ble Supreme Court reconciles polygamy and adultery.

Justice Chandrachud, in his separate but concurring judgement on the issue of decriminalising adultery, opined that Section 497 was unconstitutional and had to be struck down as it sought to "preserve a patriarchal conception of marriage which is at odds with constitutional morality." Concurring with Nivedita Menon, a noted feminist, and quoting from her celebrated book *Seeing like a Feminist*, Justice Chandrachud tells us "Infidelity was born on the day that natural flows of sexual desire were bound into the legal and formal permanence of marriage; in the process of ensuring male control over progeny and property, women were chained within the fetters of fidelity."

That once again raises a fundamental question. Is feminism all about infidelity? Should a feminist be necessarily an infidel? Is it the sole test? Have we reduced feminism and women to this bizarre idea? Civilisation and culture, as we briefly saw, is all about transforming animals into homo sapiens. In the process, society did frown on unrestrained behaviour, notably unbridled sexual desires of every individual. Nevertheless, through the institution of marriage, it allowed everyone to have an equal chance of getting a partner of opposite sex. All these were originally codified by the society through an elaborate process spanning several millennia. Probably the social oversight was insufficient. Laws were introduced subsequently to punish the deviant. While the law on the subject is indeed crass, can we afford the pendulum to swing to the other extreme? Did the formal and legal permanence of marriage lead to infidelity? Or did codification of monogamous marriage lead to social taboos on polygamy, infidelity and adultery? Or did controlling these natural urges lead us to civilisation and its attendant benefits? Is constitutional morality at odds with marital fidelity? Is monogamous family a vice or a virtue? Is it necessarily patriarchal? Is everything that is patriarchal to be condemned? Or is it that we first label something as patriarchal and then condemn it as patriarchal so that we need not explain anything to anyone? What is this new animal called constitutional morality? If constitutional morality has an inexplicable force why not matrimonial morality or for that matter societal morality? Crucially who is to decide on all these? Finally, is fidelity limited only to one partner in a marriage viz., the wife and does it not apply to the husband? Or does it apply to both? If it does not apply to both what is wrong with being infidel? If so, what is wrong with polygamy? And if polygamy is to be accepted what is so unacceptable about its resultant consequences explained in the context of Islam and of course jihad?

We will attempt to answer all these questions in the subsequent chapters of this book. We are conscious of the fact that criminalisation or otherwise of adultery will not stop a person from being unfaithful to his or her spouse, just as stringent punishments to rape will not eradicate rape or for that matter any crime. Criminology is still in an embryonic stage even as criminologists are grappling with this vexatious subject of dealing with adultery as an offence. Nevertheless, reference to the Judgement of the Hon'ble Supreme Court in Joseph Shine case is illustrative of the fact that evolving thought process within the modern liberal world approximates to the belief that the days of monogamous marriage and fidelity in marriage are well and truly over. If conservative Islam believes in polygamy, the modern liberal world does not believe in the institution of marriage at all. That is the challenge before us – strange yet powerful alliance of those who believe in theological underpinnings of polygamy and those who do not believe in the institution of marriage itself. Strange alliance this!

References

1. What Are Institutions? By Geoffrey M. Hodgson – Journal of Economic Issues – Vol. XL No. 1 March 2006.
2. The Moral Animal: Why We Are, the Way We Are: The New Science of Evolutionary Psychology By Robert Wright.
3. It's Time to Legalize polygamy- Why group marriage is the next horizon of social liberalism By Fredrik Deboer, Politico, June 26, 2015.
4. Perils of polygamy By ChiristopherKaczor; Public Discourse – The Whiterspoon Institute.
5. One Man, Many Wives, Big Problems By Jonathan Rauch April 2006 Issue – The Atlantic's Politics & Policy Daily.
6. The puzzle of monogamous marriage By Joseph Henrich, Robert Boyd, Peter J. Richerson-- Published 23rd January 2012.
7. Science Daily -monogamy reduces major social problems of polygamist cultures – Dated January 24 2012.
8. Marriage and Civilization: How Monogamy Made Us Human – William Tucker.

9. www.Wikipedia.com/Islam
10. The link between polygamy and war -By Robert Guest; The Economist -Christmas Issue 2017.
11. The Unanswered Question of Same-Sex Marriages in India – By Paras Sharma – Jurist – October 9, 2020.
12. Did We Evolve to Be Monogamous? By Samuel Veissière.
13. https://en.wikipedia.org/wiki/Muhammad%27s_wives
14. Muhammad and Forced Conversions to Islam By Raymond Ibrahim – FrontPage Magazine, February 1, 2017.
15. Bare Branches – The Security Implications of Asia's Surplus Male Population By Valerie M. Hudson and Andrea M. den Boer (The MIT Press – 2005).
16. https://keydifferences.com/difference-between-culture-and-civilization.html
17. The Power of the Family By Alberto Alesina and Paola Giuliano, http://www.nber.org/papers/w13051
18. http://www.differencebetween.net/miscellaneous/difference-between-culture-and-civilization/
19. Islam's Militant Prophet: Muhammad and Forced Conversion to Islam By Stephen M. Kirbey.
20. ISIS: 'Holy war is an integral part of Islam'- They've got a pretty good argument By CounterJihad March 25, 2016.
21. Islam Question and Answer -By Shaykh Muhammad Saalih al-Munajjid.
22. https://en.wikipedia.org/wiki/Musth
23. Polygamy fuels Violence By Matt Riddley in The Times, 24th December 2014.
24. ISLAMIC JIHAD – A Legacy of Forced Conversion, Imperialism and Slavery By M. A. Khan.
25. Is polygamy the cause of Muslim violence? By William Tucker Feb 18, 2014 in Human Events.
26. Islam and Politics in Pakistan – By Jayshree Bajoria, April 20, 2011, Council on Foreign Relations.
27. Political Islam, a Totalitarian Doctrine, By Bill Warner, April 4 2017.
28. Writ Petition (Criminal) No. 194 OF 2017 in The Supreme Court of India, Joseph Shine, Petitioner Vs Union of India, Respondent.
29. Decriminalisation of Adultery – A Setback To The Institution Of Marriage In India By Abha Singh, Outlook Magazine, 27th September 2018.

2. "Mummy, What is a Daddy?"

> *A nanny state is hostile to liberty. Any attempt to institute or continue it should be opposed, root and branch. Government intervention is never the solution; it is always part of the problem.*
>
> – Laurence M. Vance

> *You are free to choose, but you are not free from the consequence of your choice*
>
> – Unknown

The 'Question' when did *homo sapiens* (the animal) evolve into a man is perhaps the most complex one faced by social, cultural and legal anthropologists. Equally important is when did mating become marriage, especially one of monogamy? While the 'questions' by themselves may be apparently challenging, the fact of the matter is that the answer to these questions may not be so. It can now be well-argued that monogamous marriage, the setting of terms between two persons of opposite genders, is the quintessence of civilisation. Absent the institution of monogamous marriage, we are all animals with our primaeval instincts let loose. Let us not forget that polygamy and by extension, life, without any restriction, is the dominant characteristic of most animals including several mammals, *homo sapiens* included. Culture and by extension civilisation meant that we curbed this basic instinct and moved on from a polygamous society to a monogamous one.

There is indeed sufficient evidence to suggest that monogamous marriage elevates us – the primaeval animals – into civilised men. Put differently, monogamous marriage is the inflexion point in the evolution of man that emphatically distinguishes between the evolution of *homo sapiens* into men and marks the 'progress of mankind' thereafter. Interestingly, this institution of monogamous marriage may well be the first institution set up by man, an institution that has probably survived over time to become one of the most durable one set up by him. No other institution, not even any government, judiciary, or for that matter the army, set up by him has been as robust as the institution of marriage, more so that of monogamous marriage. No other institution did ever impact the progress of mankind as much as the institution of marriage did in our collective history. We have discussed most of these issues in the previous chapter.

The day when a person agreed to take another one from the opposite gender as a life partner, and both promised to remain faithful to each other life-long, and their coming together was guaranteed by the society by granting legitimacy to the children born out of such wedlock, the institution of monogamous marriage was born. In several ways, monogamous marriage was unique – it was at once biological, social, and even legal, not to speak of being sacred in some societies. The evolution of human race and the events that have fashioned our subsequent progress can be traced to this pairing of opposite genders through a set of well-defined societal norms. At the root of this artificial construct was the cold natural calculation – a man for a woman, and a woman for a man – one that ensured all-round social equity. Remarkably, this was guaranteed by society.

What was till then essentially a biological issue was codified through a set of rules, laws, and regulations in various societies, mostly by religion, but sometimes outside of religion too. In the process, the institution of monogamous marriage has come to be defined through a complex structure of marriage, which also set the terms *inter se* between the man and a woman. Attaining this balance remains at the root of achieving peace and progress. Disturbing this delicate balance, as we saw in the previous chapter, can have disastrous consequences. Importantly, this societal norm has, in effect, ensured that mating, the physical, became marriage, the metaphysical. The question, therefore, is what happens when society is unable to guarantee that both the parties would adhere to the societal code? Or when society itself unravels in a substantial measure, resulting in a situation where there is no social code, or for that matter society ceases to exist in the first place to provide that guarantee? We will seek answers to these questions shortly.

Monogamy – the inflexion Point in Civilisation

The perpetual narrative of the history of mankind since the institution of marriage was set up has been marriage, family, and an oversight body, mostly society, to guarantee that the players adhere to a pre-determined norm. The reason for the same is obvious. The institution of family demanded loyalty between partners. That, in more ways than one, ensured marriage by definition to be monogamous, which in turn was guaranteed by societal norms and overseen by players in a society. This substantially explains why monogamy, and not polygamy, is the general rule in every civilisation, despite the latter being in practice for a longer period of time. Monogamous marriage thus ensured cooperation between players both at an individual and collective level. Eventually, as we saw in the previous chapter, monogamy ensured lowering of sexual competition among otherwise fiercely competing players, freeing them significantly for other useful, creative, and productive efforts. It is, therefore, no wonder that monogamous marriage offered greater potential for peace, probably durable peace. It is this potential for durable peace arising from a monogamous marriage that has consistently ensured progress and prosperity for mankind. This stable paradigm of uninterrupted peace allowed scientific developments, democratic institutions, and commercial rules to develop and flourish in societies. Simultaneously, it has been observed that whenever the institution of a monogamous family has been destroyed, the progress of mankind has been greatly stunted.

In the evolution of mankind, as *homo sapiens* got elevated into a civilised man, polygamy was the first pitstop, and monogamy the ultimate destination. It is now increasingly being seen by cultural anthropologists that monogamy and probably monogamy alone that defines, expresses and sustains culture, and by extension, civilisation. The history of human civilisation is predominantly the history of development of the rules of engagement of a monogamous society and sustaining the institution of monogamous marriage. This is for the simple reason that monogamy is based on the laws of nature – for every baby girl, a baby boy is born. This, in turn, sows the seeds of a monogamous society where a man for a woman is the fundamental rule. Whether the idea of monogamy was well thought through in all its dimensions before being made the social norm by our forefathers, or whether they theoretically anticipated the cultural, social, economic, political, and scientific benefit in a monogamous society and then went about practically implementing the idea of monogamy is still unclear. What will remain an eternal puzzle is the trigger that ensured the emergence of monogamy. While the sequence of events leading to the emergence of monogamy is indeed blurred at this distant point in time, our experience with monogamy since its evolution demonstrates that it was indeed a defining moment in our history.

Joseph Henrich argues possibly by chance, whim, or insight, some ancient societies began to impose monogamy, and they consequently began to prosper and spread because of the palpable group benefits of monogamy. According to him, modern monogamy can be traced back to the Greek city-states, where Athens and Sparta instituted early versions of monogamy laws to galvanise internal solidarity and compete more effectively with other city-states. This tradition passed into Rome, where Augustus and other emperors further sought to fortify monogamous marriage, with the notion that this would strengthen Rome. From Rome, monogamy infused into Christianity, where it was mixed with Greek stoicism by the early churches. It is pertinent to note that monogamy is not preached in the gospels. Rather, the Old Testament implicitly endorses polygamy. Over a long period, the Church gradually managed to compel the European aristocracy, who were initially polygamous, to become monogamous.

This system, according to Joseph Henrich spread to the rest of the world during the European expansion after 1500 AD, and continues to spread to this day. Well, that is one version of history, a compelling one at that. As benefits flew from a monogamous society, societal norms on monogamy were probably created, refined, experimented, and subsequently tweaked over a period of time, and from one civilisation to another. Notwithstanding the scholarly work of Henrich, one must hasten to state that its initial contours are indeed indeterminate at this distant point in time. However, this simple societal norm of monogamy as we see it remains at the core of the intricate design of any culture, which in turn defines the sophisticated idea of civilisation.

Threat to Monogamy

But monogamy, despite all its seeming benefits, has always been and will always be under threat. Historically, it has been seen that the seeming success of monogamy is its soft underbelly – especially from societies that are not yet civilised. In Chapter 1, we saw how certain societies were polygamous and had experienced the debilitating impact of polygamy. Consequently, unmarried men are either forced to lay siege on other societies to satisfy their fundamental biological needs or remain unmarried. Without the compassionate touch of a woman in their life, these men, it is observed had the potential to turn violent, probably even into terrorists. Whatever be it and wherever be it, it is also seen that the soft target for a terrorist attack is invariably a monogamous society – one that is peaceful and progressive.

Strangely, it has been our experience that while monogamy ensured equity in the biological needs of every individual in a society, the institution of monogamous marriage remains under a constant threat. Remember, most mammals including men (which includes women too) are prone to be polygamous. Critically, for the institution of a monogamous family to succeed, there needs to be a functional oversight body i.e., society in the instant case. If monogamy is the hardware, societal norms are the software. Absent the regulator society, the institution of family goes into a downward spiral. When societies go into a downward spin, it requires tremendous efforts to get them back on the rails. It is fascinating to note that governments do not have any structural ability or wherewithal to create these norms (or for that matter regulate society) but do have the innate ability to destroy societal norms through their myopic policies or introducing laws. As we will increasingly see shortly, more often than not, government provide incentives that encourage individual deviant behaviour which in turn destroys the fragile institution of monogamous marriage. Paradoxically, while this seems to be lost on most policy-framers within the government, there seems to be increasing realisation of the importance of culture in economics and the limitation of government in managing economics. We will deal with this issue in greater detail in subsequent chapters.

When societal norms get destroyed by war as Arjuna argued with Lord Krishna in Chapter I of *Bhagavad Gita* or by governmental incentive for deviant behaviour, for instance, the results are indeed cataclysmic for society. When social norms disappear, economics too goes for a downward spiral. An imploding society – felled primarily by the absence of social norms that oversees the sustenance of a monogamous marriage – cannot have a successful economy. Such societies are a massive burden on the rest of the world. It is often seen that social norms (including an oversight mechanism), monogamous marriage, and a stable economy are an intricately linked triumvirate. We will continuously argue in this book that the first two are the pre-conditions for sustained growth and the consequent stability of the third – viz, the national economy. We will explore these links in greater detail as it is one of the underlying themes that continues to recur throughout the length and breadth of this book.

Noted author Francis Fukuyama in his celebrated book *Trust: The Social Virtues and the Creation of Prosperity* argues that much of the economic policies are not only ineffective, but in many cases, seen as contributing to the very problem they sought to solve. What was understated by Fukuyama was the manner in which welfare economics has played out in the past five decades or so, and its deleterious impact on the issues it sought to address in the first instance. A generation or more ago, Fukuyama points out, there would have been a broad consensus among social scientists of a largely one-way causal relationship between poverty and family breakdown, flowing from the former to the latter. Today, people are far less certain of the reasons for the breakdown of the family, and definitely clueless in resolving it. It is easy, especially given our experiences of the past five decades or so, to see how government policies actually encourage the breakdown of families, even as they support, subsidise, and encourage single motherhood. What is indeed perturbing, as Fukuyama points out, is how government policies can hardly restore family structure once it is broken. Now that the family structure has been broken, possibly beyond redemption, economists do not have much of an idea of how to fix it.

When societal norms give way, for reasons including war, invasion, or misplaced government incentives, society becomes lax in enforcing the necessary standards of social discipline – a pre-requisite for sustaining the institution of monogamous marriage. Under such ruinous circumstances, society begins to unravel. A war or misdirected governmental incentives have the potential to destroy, not create, societal norms. When that happens, economic revival, or for that matter balanced economic growth, becomes a gargantuan challenge.

Preserving Culture

While Joseph Henrich traces the history of the evolution of institution of monogamous marriage to the ancient Greeks and Roman, the fact remains that the Indian civilisation probably had the occasion to deal with this issue in far greater detail and arguably far earlier than other civilisations. Let us elaborate. The abduction of Mother Sita by the demon king Ravana in the great Indian epic *Ramayana* was a direct assault on this institution of a monogamous family and in upholding the virtues of monogamy. The war in *Ramayana* between Lord Rama and Ravana was, at a superficial level, to protect the honour of Mother Sita and secure her. But at a much profound level, it was to establish a significant societal norm. While Lord Rama spurned the advances of every lady after his marriage to Mother Sita, it was equally his duty to protect Mother Sita and rescue her from her abductor, as she too was steadfast in her devotion to Lord Rama. In doing so, Lord Rama re-established the ultimate social norm and sought to re-emphasize the importance of the institution of a monogamous family. This is the subtle message of *Ramayana*, the classic Indian epic. No wonder Lord Rama is hailed as *Maryada Purushotam* (ideal man) even to this day by every Indian – not only for his valour in rescuing Mother Sita from a distant land in Sri Lanka, but also for reiterating the virtues of a social norm, more specifically monogamy, one that has withstood the ravages of time and has come about to define the Indian civilisation too. We will revisit this subject once again in Chapter 10.

While *Ramayana* symbolises the Indian culture, the Ministry of Culture, Government of India, continuously glosses over this crucial point. For instance, a perusal of the website of the Ministry of Culture, Union of India, reveals the mission statement of the Ministry of Culture. Accordingly, the mission of the department is intended "to preserve, promote, and disseminate all forms of art and culture." But what precisely is culture remains undefined by the government. Fascinatingly, how can governments defend culture when it does not even define it? The theory as to how Indian culture, which has its roots in *Ramayana* and modelled itself on the ideals of Lord Rama and Mother Sita and their life-teachings that has fashioned Indian civilisation for time immemorial, is never expounded by the Union Government. If only this point is fully understood, marketed and passionately articulated by the Indian government to governments abroad as a pre-condition for a successful and robust functioning of respective national economy, India would be seen to offer much in the world of economics than all other theories put together. Crucially, the final question remains beyond the realm of successive Indian governments, or for that matter governments abroad: What is the link between the traditional state and society, society and family, and finally family and an individual?

And pray how does the Union of India propose to 'preserve, promote, and disseminate' culture? Of course, through two-year term officials, one-year budgetary allocations, and monthly review meetings. A frightening thought indeed that a civilisation as old as time, and one which has withstood the ravages of several violent intrusions from abroad – and is yet, according to experts, probably the only one to retain its pristine glory even to this day – is sought to be 'preserved and promoted' in such a cavalier fashion by not even defining what constitutes Indian culture. But there is more to come. In order to achieve its 'mission,' the department of culture seeks to undertake the following activities:

- Maintenance and conservation of heritage, historic sites, and ancient monuments
- Administration of libraries
- Promotion of literary, visual, and performing arts
- Observation of centenaries and anniversaries of important national personalities and events
- Promotion of institutions and organisations of Buddhist and Tibetan Studies
- Promotion of institutional and individual non-official initiatives in the fields of art and culture
- Entering into cultural agreements with foreign countries.

- The functional spectrum of the Department ranges from creating cultural awareness from the grassroot level to the international cultural exchange level.

Amusing to note that the Government of India seeks to 'preserve, promote, and disseminate' by entering into cultural agreements with foreign countries. While all these are important activities, no doubt, it is unfathomable as to how can a government, merely by undertaking these activities in any way 'preserve, promote, and disseminate' Indian culture. The moot question remains – even as the ordinary Indian believes that Indian culture is defined by the acts and deeds of Lord Rama and Mother Sita, the Ministry of Culture does not even make a cursory reference to both Lord Rama and Mother Sita. That is not all. The Ministry of Culture does not seem to realise that culture is symbiotically linked to the world of economics. And as a pioneer of this subject linking culture to economics, India must now take centre stage in explaining the link between culture and economics to the global audience. We will deal with this issue in subsequent Chapters.

Oblivious of this historical responsibility cast on it, the Ministry of Culture, in an absolutely insensitive move in 2007, admitted through an affidavit filed in the Supreme Court of India that while several versions of *Ramayana* "form an important part of ancient Indian literature, these cannot be said to be historical records to incontrovertibly prove the existence of the characters and occurrences of events depicted therein." This naturally sparked a furore in India, and the affidavit had to be subsequently withdrawn. Is it not for the Government of India, more specifically the Ministry of Culture, to collect and collate such evidences? Should it not have produced these evidences before the court instead of demanding them? In effect, the Ministry of Culture in the instant case abdicated its responsibility by filing a terse affidavit on such a searching issue. This explains as to how successive governments by their very definition are completely disconnected from the sublime idea of culture or civilisation, what sustains it, and what is needed to fortify it. This work is not about examining the role of the Indian Government in 'preserving, promoting, and disseminating' Indian culture, but the reference to the same is nevertheless made, merely to highlight the complete disconnect between government and culture, and simultaneously to highlight the fact that the very genetic composition of the governments precludes it from preserving, promoting, and disseminating culture. We will revert to the issue of how governments, by their misplaced priorities and muddled economic policies, end up actually destroying culture and by extension, economics.

Understanding the Indian Culture

What must be captivating to note here is that Indian culture is not a monolith; it has several layers. Within the Indian culture are regional cultures like the Tamil or Bengali cultures. To a person from a distant land, it may be very difficult to comprehend what precisely is Indian culture, or for that matter is Tamil or Bengali culture. Even to an Indian, sometimes it might be a bit too heavy to distinguish between the national and the regional cultures as much, and to find out the unifying force between them. Cutting across the frills associated with this seemingly endless debate, let us unambiguously declare that in the Indian context, the Indian culture is the Tamil culture which is identical to the Bengali, or for that matter any other regional culture. At the core of this kaleidoscope is the societal norm established by Lord Rama – a man for a woman, and a woman for a man.

But the story of *Ramayana* is not the sole reference point in Indian civilisation to the issue of establishing this particular social norm. In fact, the story of Indian civilisation revolves around five chaste women, and each one is revered to this day. These five are: Mother Sita (from the *Ramayana*), Mother Draupadi (from the other great Indian epic *Mahabharat*), Mother Savitri, Mother Damayanthi, and Mother Kannagi. It is pertinent to note at this point in time that each one of them have come to epitomise the ancient Indian civilisation. Absent these feminine characters and their adherence to steadfast chastity with an abiding faith in the institution of monogamous marriage, there would probably be very less of Indian culture and Indian civilisation. More to the point, India as a nation and Indian civilisation would not have withstood the ravages of time and her invaders, but for the fact that she had a moral compass that guided her functioning from generation to generation.

More tellingly, monogamy as an age-old wisdom has ample support and stress in all the major literary works in all key languages of India, including the oldest of languages spoken – Sanskrit and Tamil. The reference to these two ancient languages here is to demonstrate that higher thoughts flowing from greater consciousness are possible only if expressed in such wonderful languages capable of capturing the range of human emotions. And in all these literary works, the life of Lord Rama and message of *Ramayana* was repeatedly mirrored, some subtly and in some, otherwise. More to the point, the idea of monogamy did not evolve overnight. Nor did it possibly begin with *Ramayana*. The idea of monogamy had probably evolved even before the *Ramayana*. Thus, the concept of monogamy, at least as a gold standard for society, was not alien or new to the Indian sub-continent from the days of *Ramayana*. It is quite possible that this idea existed before *Ramayana* and was probably exemplified by the great epic with greater emphasis on the chastity of women, and subsequently men. Thus, monogamy in the Indian context became the cultural norm for society, and possibly a driver for civilisational progress over a period of time. This idea, therefore, remained at the core of the prevailing culture within the Indian sub-continent for several millennia. There are sufficient evidences in the delightful literary traditions of both Sanskrit and Tamil that the entire landscape south of Himalayas and even regions up to present-day Iran, Afghanistan, and spreading to Cambodia and Burma, were more unified and homogenous by the religious and moral thought revolving around the central idea of monogamy.

That a mere nebulous idea survived the ravages of time for this long by itself is indeed fascinating. At some point in time, societies also understood that they had a choice – individual deviancy could not be controlled by society, but could definitely be condemned by it. In the least, such persons and their behaviour would not be celebrated by any society. A person, by his personal choice, could remain deviant and hence break the societal norm. In some societies or in some civilisations, he could have even been subjected to some severe punishment or mild chastisement as determined by that society. In some, individual deviancies have been defended, rationalised, and at times even celebrated. In contrast, while Indian society did not punish the deviants, it never was widely celebrated. Indian society, on most occasions, was irrelevantly neutral towards individual delinquents, probably to the point of ignoring them.

That is remarkably unique when compared to other civilisations. More to the point, it was chaste women and steadfast men that definitely became the examples in the Indian context – one that the society followed and a template for the forthcoming generations to emulate. Nevertheless, this benign approach to delinquents probably ensured that monogamy as a sublime idea survived for this long. This is the power of restraint – the power that makes ideas eternal. We will deal with this in greater detail in Chapter 9. More to the point, the social order from time immemorial in the Indian context was to celebrate the disciplined and simply ignore the delinquent. A tall order if one looks at the complexity of the subject but reinforces the power of restraint. Yet, this is what Indian society aimed to achieve. And over time, the impact of this social order on national economy is immeasurable. Captivatingly, when governments fashion their economic policies that encourage individuals to be deviant, the results could be calamitous for society as much as for economic arrangements within society. We will look into this issue shortly.

The uplifting idea of the institution of marriage, as author Steve Tucker points out, arising out of monogamy turned into ensuring honour of women, not only in India but probably over other civilisations too. It happened when Odysseus decided that he would return to his wife and family than live with a goddess. It was equally underlined by Penelope who fended off every suitor, awaiting the return of Odysseus. Ancient Greeks through their epics were re-emphasising the very same message that lay in the great Indian epic *Ramayana* – a man for a woman, and a woman for a man. In medieval France, Suzanne, a character in the novel titled *Barber of Seville* defined the societal norms of a monogamous marriage when she preferred her Figaro to the Count as did the immortal character Pamela in England in Samuel Richardson's novel *Virtue Rewarded*. But what went wrong, especially in the West, which is seeing a collapse of the family structure, more specifically the monogamous family? If monogamy was indeed the norm in the West, as Tucker argues, why are monogamous families rapidly withering? Is the state and its economic policies responsible for the collapse of the monogamous families? If the state is indeed responsible, then how?

Emergence of a rights-based society

Barring occasional exceptions, once the societal norm of a man for a woman and woman for a man was established, the acceptance of the benefit of the family as an institution more or less continued worldwide probably till the end of the World War II. Even as late as the 1950s, 75 percent of households in the US were occupied by married couples. Eighty percent of children were living with natural parents, and illegitimacy was frowned upon. The phenomenon of a 'single mother' was virtually unknown. Steve Tucker explains how Swedish actress Ingrid Bergman was banned from coming to the US because she had a 'love child' with Italian director Roberto Rossellini, obviously without getting married to him. This may seem ridiculously quaint and prudish by today's moral standards, but people in those not-so-distant times in the US believed that movie stars could possibly set standards for society, and if someone of Bergman's stature could do it, youngsters could imitate as well. The underlying concern was what if youngsters imitated Bergman, societal norms could get destroyed. When societal norms get destroyed, the Americans feared the debilitating impact on the economy. It was a classic case of self-preservation. All these were not formally codified by American society, but a code, albeit informally, did exist. Neither was this fear limited to Bergman alone or for that matter, celebrities of her ilk. Before the 1960s, single mothers, for instance, were not allowed in New York City public housing. Before 1970, the stigma of unwed motherhood, even within the US, was so great that few women were willing to bear children outside marriage. The only circumstance that would cause women to engage in sexual activity was a promise of marriage in the event of pregnancy. Men were willing to make and were forced by the then American society to keep that promise for they knew that in leaving one woman, they would be unlikely to find another who would not make the same demand. Even women who would be willing to bear children out-of-wedlock could demand a promise of marriage in the event of pregnancy. That was the US, the high priest of liberal, modern, and market economics just a few decades ago – conservative, conventional, and conformist. So, what explains the complete turnaround in just a few decades?

The answer to the same is not easy and no single explanation is plausible. We can call it the conspiracy of coincidences – medical, social, and legal. The discovery of contraception, birth pill, and safe abortions meant pregnancy was solely a woman's decision. It was as if women and only women had a choice and she knowingly exercised it. The man was no longer a party to this decision of a woman – of continuing with her pregnancy or terminating the same. Simultaneously, the debate on women's rights, single motherhood, and patriarchal families gained traction in the West, notably the US in the 1960s and 1970s. Illogical as it may sound, the feminist lobby fell into this 'rights' trap. If they sought the participation of men in the decision to take the woman's pregnancy to a logical conclusion, they ran the risk of dynamiting the very idea of feminism. In the alternative, if they agreed to be liberated from men, they liberated men too from the responsibility of pregnancy of the women – a classic case of *Catch-22*. Meanwhile, within the American establishment, the debate shifted dramatically from the cause, consequence, and prevention of single motherhood to how to assist single mothers. Once the state stepped in to assist single mothers and children born out of wedlock – all hell broke loose. All in all, the societal norms that frowned on 'single mothers' suddenly evaporated.

To many, the explosion of 'rights' within the US, the simultaneous proliferation of 'single mothers,' and their collective impact on the national and probably global economics may appear at first blush to be superficial. But it is not. This requires some greater explanation. In 2008, an article titled *Why the US is an economic burden on the world?* I had pointed out to a news report from the US, where 17 schoolgirls reportedly entered into a 'pregnancy pact.' Staff at a secondary school health clinic in the city of Gloucester, Massachusetts, became suspicious after seeing a surge in girls seeking pregnancy tests, most of whom were below the age of 16. But that was just the beginning. The school's principal is reported to have said: "Some girls seemed more upset when they weren't pregnant." The school is reported to have administered 150 pregnancy tests in the previous year alone. In an ironic twist to the tale, press reports suggested that the school itself allowed distribution of condoms and contraception with 'parental consent.' This transformation in attitudes was best captured by the *New York Times* way back in 1993 itself: "In the old days of the 1960s, '50s, and '40s, pregnant teenagers were pariahs, banished from schools, ostracized by their peers or scurried out of town to give birth in secret." Today, they are supported and embraced in their decision to give birth, keep their babies, continue their education, and participate in school activities. All this has raised many questions, and the answers could equally be many. Adults in Gloucester, according to press reports, blamed economic depression, broken families, skewed sense of status, and movies like *Juno* and *Knocked Up* that glamourise teenage pregnancy. Experts, according to reports, feel that celebrities like Jamie Lynn Spears, sister of Britney Spears, sent out the wrong message to teens by getting pregnant at 16. All these are not remote happenings in some corner of the world that can be brushed aside. Rather, in a globalised world, they affect you and me – not only within the confines of civilisational values – but also through the prism of economics.

As 16-year-olds became pregnant, schools set up nurseries for the benefit of child-bearing teenagers. As we would see in Chapter 6, constitutional norms ensured extreme atomisation of the individuals so much so that even parents could not question any deviant behaviour of their own child. Well, the ostensible idea was to substitute the state for the parents. While parents were liberated of their responsibilities, the state could not by any stretch of imagination remotely mimic the role of the parents. This created an imbalance which needs to be recognised and addressed. Nevertheless, social welfare programmes were re-jigged to meet the new demand of unwed mothers. Political parties competed to sound more concerned than the other. Academicians came with newer ideas to deal with the situation by rationalising it. Economists began writing newer theories capturing the socio-economic paradigm. As Governor Mario Cuomo of New York once said: "If we take a 16-year-old-single mother, get her welfare, give her food stamps, get her own apartment, and have her back in school taking classes, what is the problem?" The problem for many with understanding economics, especially when articulated by career politicians, is that they understand and explain economics as a discipline, completely disconnected from the larger question of how culture and civilisational values impact economics. And least of all, they never answer the question of who foots the bill? We will look into this particular issue in Chapter 7.

In short, government programmes were fashioned with a necessary presumption – there will be unwed teenage mothers in the US, and the society or her parents can and, more importantly, should do nothing about it. Expectedly, it is the sole responsibility of the state to ensure that such 16-year-old single mothers are taken care of. Thus, dramatically the state was compelled to step in even as societal norms collapsed. So, what was an unwritten, nebulous, yet powerful link between an individual and his or her family, family and society, and society and government – the bedrock of culture was given a direct go-by. In its stead, a new link between the state and individual was directly established – one that is precise and probably enforceable legally. This potential collapse of culture and societal oversights has a profound impact on the functioning of modern economics, and by extension, the state too.

Missing link in Modern Economics

In fact, most modern theories of welfare state, taxation as well as role of markets are worked out without any great understanding of culture and its subtle yet powerful impact on economics. Fukuyama, for instance, argues that the expansion of the welfare state from the New Deal tended to make federal, state, and local governments responsible for many social welfare functions that were previously under the purview of civil society, mostly families. The rise of the 'welfare state' can, in short, be explained as the steady transfer of the 'dependency' of an individual from his own family to the state; from persons tied together by blood, marriage to a faceless, emotionless yet all pervasive state. (We shall refer to this arrangement whenever we refer to as welfare, in this book.) This shift in responsibility, obviously meant that the macro-economic assumptions – for instance, the manner in which taxes were raised, collected, and distributed by the governments – were completely reset. Questions naturally arise – "Do we fully comprehend the implications of welfare policies laid out by governments?" This is not to mean that the state should not engage in welfare at all. On the contrary, one needs to first understand the impact of mindless welfare in all its dimensions before we proceed to comment on the intervention by the state.

To do so, a brief reference to the manner in which society is arranged becomes absolutely necessary. Francis Fukuyama has elaborately dealt with these issues in his celebrated book, titled *Trust*. According to him, the US had undergone a 'rights revolution' in the second half of the 20th century. According to him, rights-based individualism is deeply embedded in American political theory and constitutional law. This revolution, he believes, has its roots in Christian Protestantism, which provided a moral basis for the promotion of individualist behaviour, while simultaneously weakening other tendencies towards group life. This is evidenced by the disintegration of even the nuclear family and community, with a concomitant rise in social isolation within the US. It may be amazing to note that these thoughts and ideas are not merely the products of the late 20th century. In fact, such thoughts permeate the entire length and breadth of the US Constitution as it pervades in the political thinking of eminent Western political thinkers, notably Thomas Hobbes and Thomas Jefferson. The fundamental assumption that has driven such political thought has been that man is born not with duties, but with rights and rights alone. Whatever duties he takes on, he acquires as a result of his free will, neither necessitated by law nor to be expected by society.

Fukuyama argues that Americans have developed a 'culture of rights; that is quite distinctive among other modern liberal democracies. Constitutional scholar Mary Ann Glendon has pointed out that although most other modern democracies have adopted the American-style 'Bill of Rights,' there remains a unique character to the American 'language of rights.' For Americans, rights have an absolute character that is not balanced or moderated by constitutional language outlining duties to the community or responsibilities to the people. In contrast, the constitutional or basic laws of most European countries contain, in addition to the enumerated right, language to the effect that "everyone has duties to the community." American law does not support any kind of duty to rescue or otherwise enjoin citizens to do good to strangers in need. A good Samaritan in the US is much more likely to be sued for administering the wrong kind of help than rewarded for his troubles. As Glendon points out, the American language of rights gives political discourse in the US an absolute and uncompromising character. It is this uncompromising character that unites the Left and the Right in the US, which is in turn based on the belief that the end of any government is to protect the sphere of autonomy in which every individual can enjoy their natural rights, free of pressures, constraints, or obligations to those around them. Having boxed themselves to an extreme position, the Americans are now becoming increasingly aware that they have to pay a very heavy price for the same. And they are doing so.

This primacy of individual rights is substantiated by the words contained in the American Declaration of Independence: 'Man is endowed with certain inalienable rights.' Subsequent thinkers have even suggested that not even the family is necessary for human sustenance. Based on such extreme ideas, constitutional experts in the US argue that parents and children may have mutual obligations of love and respect, but parental authority should end when the children are capable of reasoning things out on their own. The culmination of all these political and social thoughts, evolution of constitutional law and of course, societal values result in 16-year-olds getting pregnant in the US without any let or fear from parents, or for that matter, society. But what is the incentive for these 16-year-olds in the US to get pregnant at such an early stage of their life? Why is it that American parents are unable to prevent such deviant behaviour? Are the successive US administrations – whether headed by a Democrat or Republican – not guilty of encouraging such conduct? Does not the US Government, in the garb of encouraging individual rights, end up encouraging deviant individual behaviour? Is it not a fact that these rights and the potential deviant behaviour come with a cost to the US Government? The billion-dollar question that naturally follows is 'Who foots the bill?'

While the answers to all these questions are not easy, the answer to the last question is obvious – it is the disciplined, hard-working, tax-paying American who finally bears the cost of such deviant individual behaviour. As we will increasingly see in this work, in a globalised world it is not only the disciplined American tax payer who foots the bill, in a globalised world it is the disciplined people worldwide who also end up footing the bill on all those who are not disciplined. In a world of undisciplined, it seems that it is foolish to stay disciplined. Strangely, not many economists seem to understand this particular fact that the cost of individual indiscipline is, more often than not, picked up by the disciplined. While the economists can indeed choose to ignore this, the fact is that the disciplined foot the bill of the undisciplined cannot and should not forgotten by the former, if not the latter.

Enter a Nanny State

But if the answer to the last question – that the disciplined foot the bill of the undisciplined – is so obvious, why is it that the US, or for that matter most countries, perusing such bizarre economic policies? Why does it not put an end to such outlandish welfare measures? Why does it continue to incentivise the undisciplined? Why does it tax the disciplined? The answers to these are complex. Contrary to the popular belief that the US is deeply rooted to the market economy, the fact remains that the US is a nanny state and hence wedded to mindless and probably reckless welfarism. Is this a direct consequence of allowing unfettered proliferation of individual rights? While there are no clear-cut answers to this question, the fact remains that a state can destroy societal norms (as it has done in the past four decades or so in the US), it cannot recreate them through a fiat. This is the havoc that the US has wrecked on itself. Having encouraged the idea of 'single mothers' and footed their bill for too long, the US cannot create a societal norm that would once again ensure monogamy and respect for the institution of marriage. Having placed individual at the centre of its economic policies, it has inadvertently destroyed a virtuous societal norm that prevailed till the 50s within the next three decades or so. Dan Quale, the then US Vice-President in the 80s attacked the Democrats on the issue of family values by arguing that the cultural Left was glorifying single parenthood through TV characters like Murphy Brown. But it was too feeble, too little, and too late. Interestingly, economists too in the US over the past generation have consistently held the view that family was an obstacle to development. Though authors like Francis Fukuyama suggest – and as the Dan Quale debate indicate – that this view has softened considerably and even in the US there seems to be a re-think on this issue. According to him, in retrospect, it is clear that modernisation theorists writing in the 1950s or 1960s were wrong to assume that the breakdown of family structure would end with the nuclear family, whose stability and cohesion they took for granted. As it turned out, nuclear families began to break down into single-parent families at an alarming rate with much greater consequences than the breakdown of the extended family in earlier generations. The end result of heightened state intervention is that individuals in the US are left standing all alone in a dependent relationship with the government with little or no relationship with their own blood relatives. It would seem that experiment at the atomisation of the US society has gone completely awry.

By the time this realisation had drawn, too much water had flown through the Potomac. It was clear that by the mid-1970s, the US had irrevocably become a welfare state, at least in so far as it related to single mothers. In the process, let us not forget that this tectonic shift to welfare in the US destroyed the institution of monogamous marriage. Or was it the other way round – did the implosion of families lead to the welfare state? While the causation may still be a matter of debate, the fact remains that the correlation of the destruction of family values in the US and the simultaneous rise of such welfare programmes as mentioned above since the 1950s is near perfect. The only beneficiary of all this is obviously the Democratic Party (backed by Left-liberals of course) which gains immensely since women who look to the state for deliverance, vote overwhelmingly in their favour. Some surveys suggest African-American women vote 95 percent for the Democratic Party, and thus have become a decisive block, read vote bank, in elections in the US.

This narrative of the Left-liberals in fashioning the economic policies and favouring deviant individual behaviour even in the US demonstrates the fault lines in the debate on economic policies of the government. Anyone who speaks against these deeply flawed approaches to economics is instantly labelled, stereotyped, and lampooned. Worryingly, world over, this has become the mainstream narrative. If this is the case in the US, what to speak of developing countries like India where the Left-liberal lobby control every institution, direct the course of every narrative, and seek to have a veto on every policy formulation? That, in a way, explains the rationale for this book – the impact of family and its implosion on economics and how it shapes, de-shapes and re-shapes economic policies of governments across continents.

It is through this formal intellectual intimidation that traditional family values have come under extraordinary assault even in the US, not to speak of other parts of the world. As a direct consequence, the institution of family is under direct threat – a fact not many are ready to acknowledge. And those who acknowledge, feel very little can be done, on the extant state of affairs. What is worrying some, is that as the institution of marriage collapses, the state is forced to step in to take the responsibilities of the family. This is colourfully termed as the nationalisation of families. This destruction of the family (and the resultant nationalisation of the filial responsibilities) has extraordinary consequences, giving rise to the modern welfare state – where the state is compelled to deal with situations where it has no expertise, comprehension, or emotional bandwidth. It is equally quixotic for some to argue for privatising the affairs of the state even as the state continues to devour much of the responsibilities of the families. As the state steps in, what must worry economists is that the resources are transferred from the most productive segment within the economy – read disciplined family – to the most unproductive segment within the economy – read the state. This transfer of wealth from the most productive and disciplined sector in the economy in the name of taxes and levies to the most undisciplined and unaccountable sector of the economy, passed off as welfare to citizens who demonstrated deviant behaviour, is at the root of the modern social-politico-economic conundrum. The moot point, therefore is, what is the role of the state? How much should the state tax and how to use the revenue flow from taxes for welfare measures? Vitally, what constitutes welfare? Impractical economic policy formulations by the state have serious implications for democracy as the voting pattern by single unwed African-American women to the Democratic Party demonstrate.

This is not to argue that we must not have any form of taxes. On the contrary, we must have taxes for defence, maintenance of law and order, judiciary, and other sovereign functions of the state. But is providing welfare a sovereign function of the state? Surely, if liberals have to engage in any further dialogue in economic policy formulations in future, they must first identify a process of privatising welfare measures which have in effect nationalised the traditional responsibilities of families. One cannot endlessly argue for privatisation of state enterprises and simultaneously in the same breadth also bat for nationalising the filial responsibilities. Indeed, Rutgers University sociologist David Popenoe suggests that the term 'welfare state' no longer does justice to this form of total personal dependence on the government. Instead, he uses the label 'client society' to describe a nation "in which citizens are, for the most part, clients of a large group of public employees who take care of them throughout their lives." Do we at least now realise the extent of the damage? Do we realise the rot that has set in? More to the point, do we realise the fundamental issues confronting the respective national economies? Worse still, the fact of the matter is that we have unleashed a virus for which we seem to have no economic answer.

Economics of Blacks Matter Too

Daniel Patrick Moynihan, assistant secretary of labour to Democrat President Johnson, warned the US establishment way back in the sixties that the black family was on the verge of a 'complete breakdown' because of growing illegitimacy. Inspired from the book *Slavery* written by Stanley Elkins, Moynihan's research demonstrated that even as fewer people were unemployed, more people were joining the welfare rolls. These recipients were families with children but only one parent (invariably the mother). In 1963, he estimated that out-of-wedlock birth rate for whites was a mere three percent, but for blacks, it was approximately a whopping 24 percent. Moynihan was part of a generation of Democrats who actually cared about lifting blacks up into the ranks of equal opportunity with whites. In his 1965 book *The Negro Family: The Case for National Action*, Moynihan observed that because more blacks were being born into unmarried homes, more blacks were becoming dependent on welfare to survive. Moynihan's report fuelled a debate over the proper course for government to take with regard to the economic underclass, especially blacks. Critics on the Left attacked it as 'blaming the victim,' while others suggested that Moynihan was propagating the views of racists. Expectedly, the press coverage of the report focused on the discussion of children being born out of wedlock. But that was over five decades ago. The problem has only accentuated since then.

The net result is that today, a majority of black babies are being born to single mothers – a prescription for a life of poverty and crime. Despite the warnings that have been sounded off loudly for over half a century, Democrats have done precious little to stop blacks, their most steadfast constituents, from having babies they can't take care of. This problem has perpetuated itself for over two generations now, producing generational poverty among blacks. If black lives truly matter, as Democrats claim, why don't they promulgate policies that encourage blacks to get married before they have kids? Blacks' voting overwhelmingly for Democrats over the past half-century is the quintessential definition of political suicide. But what's bad for blacks translates into a high rate of return on investment for Democrats. Marketing this 'no baby daddy' syndrome to blacks has translated into votes, lots of votes, approaching near 100 percent from black women over the past half-century.

No greater or more glaring example of liberals' profiting politically from black people's misery can be seen than the Democrats' refusal to address the illegitimate birth rate spiralling out of control among blacks. Thanks to the liberal policies of the Democratic Party (and possibly the Republicans too) in the US, approximately 75 percent of the black babies are born out of wedlock today than into married homes. That's dramatically worse than when Moynihan initially raised the issue. In short, it is becoming increasingly rare for black babies to be born to married parents in the US. Black fathers are simply not part of the black family equation. It would seem that it is far easier for us to spot a black swan than a black father with his family in the US. Women having babies without fathers isn't just a sign of the moral collapse of culture in US, it is equally hazardous to the child. When a child is born into a single-parent home, the chances of that child's growing up in poverty are much greater.

According to a Brookings Institution study published in 2009, if a person graduates from high school, works a full-time job, and waits until 21 to get married and have children, his or her chance of succeeding in life and becoming a member of the middle class rises to 76 percent. In direct contrast, if a person does not finish high school, does not marry, and has a baby before the age of 21, his or her chance of becoming poor soars to 74 percent. One of the anti-poverty solutions the Brookings study recommended was for the federal government to advocate policies that strengthen families, such as programmes "to reduce unplanned pregnancies for teens and twenty-somethings." The Brookings researchers seem to have understood that the breakdown of the black family has been the main driver of the chronic wealth gap between whites and blacks over the past five decades. The lack of families among blacks leads to a lack of education and jobs, which translates into higher rates of crime and government dependency among blacks.

Also, spare a thought for the unmarried black men in the US who have fathered a child. Like the 'excess men' in a polygamous society discussed in the previous chapter, these men too in a nanny state are condemned to being single life-long, without the support of a family and the benevolent touch of a woman. The psychological scar of being single life-long is far too deep that puts these men into a perpetual downward spiral. That implies over a period of time, these single men turn to crimes, peddle drugs, and indulge in violence against women. Sadly, at times they are victims of their own violence.

Despite all these empirical evidences that are available with the American establishment, and anecdotal references available with their policy framers, the uniform conclusion within the American establishment is that not much can be done to deal with the extent of the malaise, and hence nothing needs to be done. This is simply because, within American society, one is no longer embarrassed when a 16-year young girl is pregnant before marriage and is ready to spend her entire life without a husband. Simultaneously, no longer is a boy considered an embarrassment in American society if he tries to run away from being the father of an unmarried child. When human emotions like guilt and shame become irrelevant in a society, it is obvious that the society is unravelling. In a scenario when an individual loses his sense of shame, the state cannot be expected to step in and legislate for the lack of it. This demonstrates the limitation of the state in dealing with humans and their emotions. More pertinently, the human emotion 'shame' has a spectacular value in macro-economic management. But does anyone care?

Former US President Obama was fully concerned about this phenomenon of missing fathers in American homes, especially black families. In a 2008 speech, made in the run up to the US presidential elections, he chastised black fathers and their escapist attitude of shirking their responsibilities of raising the family. Too many black fathers, he said, are missing from too many lives and too many homes. "They have abandoned their responsibilities, acting like boys instead of men. We know the statistics – those children who grow up without a father are five times more likely to live in poverty and commit a crime, nine times more likely to drop out of schools, and 20 times more likely to end up in prison," Obama said. "They are more likely to have behavioural problems, or run away from home, or become teenage parents themselves. And the foundations of our community are weaker because of it."

The challenge to American society quoted above is merely a reflection of the challenge facing most governments the world over. If they usher in thoughtless welfare measures, like what the Americans have done since the 1960s, they are in effect providing incentives to those who are breaking societal norms or the other. The operating words are thoughtless welfare. And if they do not do, they stand condemned in the world of competitive welfare politics. Geographies such as Britain, most of Euro areas, Scandinavian countries etc. are all wedded to a socialist order, where they have significant welfare policies and programmes that probably assists deviant individual behaviour. Not all of these governments are economically sound. Some of them are economically unviable. With a falling population (a direct consequence of the breakdown in the institution of families in most countries), most governments have an unsustainable balance sheet and are on the verge of declaring themselves bankrupt. The gargantuan debt accumulated over the past two decades by countries like Portugal, Italy, Greece, and Spain (called PIGS by some, with pun fully intended) are a case in point. Ominously, having weakened their society through their recklessness, most of these countries are now facing an existential crisis, both as a society and as a political entity. Do we realise our collective folly? Do politicians recognise their perfidy? Do we realise how the Left-Liberals have caused incalculable harm to the economics of nations?

The Impact on the US and by Extension, Global Economy

The proliferation of unfettered rights (under a liberal ideology that continues to fashion the global socio-politico-economic discourse) had a two-fold impact on the global economy: one, it led to the governments assuming significant responsibilities of an individual that would normally be in the hands of the family in traditional societies, and, two, without the salutary effect of family and family values, it led to increased and reckless spending by individuals. As the role of the government increased, it began to collect more taxes to fund its ever-increasing social agenda, which it never was designed to deal with in the first place. No wonder, the government spending in the West ranges from a third of the GDP, as in the case of the US, to a much higher number in the case of some Scandinavian countries.

Noted scholar John Perazzo traces these developments to the date when President Lyndon Johnson in 1964 launched the so-called war on poverty, he actually ended up enacting an unprecedented amount of anti-poverty legislation, adding many new layers to the American welfare state. Of particular concern to Johnson was the disproportionately high rate of black poverty. In a famous June 1965 speech, the then US President suggested that the problems plaguing black Americans could not be solved by self-help. Thus began, argues Perazzo, modern liberalism's vicious and unrelenting assault on black Americans. Dressed up as 'compassion' and 'social justice,' this assault took the form of an unprecedented commitment of federal funds to a wide range of measures aimed at redistributing wealth in the US. Since 1965, more than $22 trillion of taxpayer money has been spent on welfare programmes for the poor. To put the figures in the right perspective, let us note that the Gross Domestic Product of India for 2016-17 would be approximately $2.2 trillion. To say in a measure that we can relate to, just about 10 times the GDP of India has been spent in the past five decades in the US on just such measures. The net result? Between the mid-60s and the mid-70s, the dollar value of public housing quintupled and the amount spent on food stamps rose more than ten-fold. From 1965-69, government-provided benefits increased by a factor of 8; by 1974, such benefits were an astounding 20 times higher than they had been in 1965. Also, as of 1974, federal spending on social-welfare programmes amounted to 16 percent of

America's Gross National Product, a far cry from the eight percent figure of 1960. By 1977, the number of people receiving public assistance had more than doubled since 1960.

But did the American poor, notably the American Blacks benefit? Perazzo provides answers to these questions succinctly when he points out that the most devastating by-product of the welfare state was the corrosive effect it had on American family life, particularly the Black American community. The cataclysmic destruction set in motion by such policies is there for all to see. As George Mason University professor Walter E. Williams puts it: "The welfare state has done to black Americans what slavery couldn't do, what Jim Crow couldn't do, what the harshest racism couldn't do. And that is to destroy the black family." Hoover Institution Fellow Thomas Sowell concurs: "The black family, which had survived centuries of slavery and discrimination, began rapidly disintegrating in the liberal welfare state that subsidised unwed pregnancy and changed welfare from an emergency rescue to a way of life."

As provisions in welfare laws offered ever-increasing economic incentives for shunning marriage and avoiding the formation of two-parent families, illegitimacy rates rose dramatically. For the next few decades, welfare programmes such as food stamps, public housing, Medic-aid, day care, and Temporary Assistance to Needy Families, in effect penalised marriage. At an individual level – a mother generally received far more money from welfare if she was single rather than married. Once she took a husband, her benefits were instantly reduced by roughly 10 to 20 percent. More importantly, a husband's income was uncertain while the welfare measures were not. Given this paradigm, it was but natural for every young girl to marry the state and its consequential welfare programme than marry a person and face certain uncertainty.

William Galston, who served in the 1990s as Deputy Assistant to the President for Domestic Affairs, estimated that the welfare system, with its economic disincentives to marriage, was responsible for at least 15 to 20 percent of the family disintegration in the US. Libertarian scholar Charles Murray has placed the figure at somewhere around 50 percent. By Murray's reckoning, the growth and increased liberalisation of the 'welfare complex' have eroded the traditional ethos of working-class communities that once held people who worked even at low-wage jobs, and men who married the mothers of their own children in much higher esteem than unwed parents who became wards of the state.

It is in this connection a Cato Institute study noted, welfare programmes for the poor incentivise the very human behaviours that are most likely to perpetuate poverty. Another Cato report observed: "Of course, women do not get pregnant just to get welfare benefits, but by removing the economic consequences of out-of-wedlock birth, welfare has removed a major incentive to avoid such pregnancies. A teenager looking around at her friends and neighbours is liable to see several who have given birth out-of-wedlock. When she sees they have suffered few visible consequences, she is less inclined to modify her own behaviour to prevent pregnancy. Current welfare policies seem to be designed with an appalling lack of concern for their impact on out-of-wedlock births. Indeed, Medicaid programmes in 11 states actually provide infertility treatments to single women on welfare."

Perazzo argues that the results of welfare policies discouraging marriage and family were dramatic, as out-of-wedlock birth rates skyrocketed among all demographic groups in the US, but most notably African-Americans. In the mid-1960s, the out-of-wedlock birth rate was scarcely three percent for whites, eight percent for Americans overall, and 24 percent among blacks. By 1976, those figures had risen to nearly 10 percent for whites, 25 percent for Americans as a whole, and 50 percent for blacks. And by 2016, the numbers stood at 29 percent for whites, 41 percent for the nation overall, and 73 percent for blacks. He concludes rightly that "the entire country is moving rapidly in the wrong direction, but Blacks, in particular, have reached a point of veritable catastrophe."

Strangely, economists and policy-framers within governments do not realise the consequences of all individual irresponsibility and its impact on economic policies of every government, especially a welfare state. Individual deviant behaviour does go on to destroy social norms and families. A dysfunctional family, in turn, allows the proliferation of deviant individual behaviour. Surely, when families are destroyed and men become irresponsible in sustaining their families, the state, it is argued, is compelled to take over the functions of the families. This is what is referred to as the 'nationalisation of families.' This gives birth to a nanny state where the state becomes your nanny. Of course, the idea of individual welfare stems from an important assumption that the individual will be irresponsible to himself, and the state is responsible in great measure towards maintaining and sustaining an individual and his family. Tax is the mechanism by which the states, through a fiat, funds itself to take care of welfare programmes for such delinquent families and irresponsible individuals. Taxes, we are told, are the price we pay for civilisation. My guess is it is precisely the other way around. We pay taxes, unwittingly as a cost for destroying our culture and our precious civilisation. We will be dealing with this issue in Chapter 7. When we destroy families, and with it the responsibilities possibly undertaken by an individual, the state is compelled by force of circumstances to step in and take over the functions of an irresponsible individual and his dysfunctional family.

That ushers in a vicious cycle of a welfare state (as it attempts to mimic the family) which in turn exacerbates individual irresponsibility. Welfare programmes by the state, may on first blush seem like a great idea to help single mothers. But in reality, these programmes make it absolutely easier for men to leave the women. It absolves him of all responsibilities of raising a family and sucks out morality in any social equation. All these programmes have a crushing impact on a man's practical responsibility to stay with his woman and raise their child. Moreover, modern ideas like feminism now provide absolute legitimacy for the man to desert his lady. The liberals provide the intellectual cover by rationalising such behaviour. The judiciary sees greater virtues in such irresponsible action. And finally, the state rushes to provide an insurance in the form of individual welfare. What more could an irresponsible man want?

Children in single-parent households are burdened not only with economic, but also profound social and psychological disadvantages. For example, Perazzo argues that youngsters raised by single parents in the US, as compared to those who grow up in intact married homes, are more likely to be physically abused; to display emotional disorders; to smoke, drink, and use drugs; to perform poorly in school; to be suspended or expelled from school; to drop out of high school; to behave aggressively and violently; to be arrested for a juvenile crime; to serve jail time before age 30; and to go on to experience poverty as adults. According to the National Fatherhood Initiative, 60 percent of rapists, 72 percent of adolescent murderers, and 70 percent of long-term prison inmates in the US are men who grew up in fatherless homes. This is an unending downward spiral as these men are never going to be part of families and shoulder their responsibilities. With regard to girls, in particular, those raised by single mothers are more than twice as likely to give birth out-of-wedlock, thereby perpetuating the cycle of poverty for yet another generation. Remember all these after spending $22 trillion in the past five decades or so. The state can never be your nanny.

The Quixotic Cradle Scheme

The US is not an exception to the modern economic belief that a societal disorder has to be at best addressed through a benevolent intervention of the state. On the contrary, it is a perfect example of the rule as to how the state cannot remedy a societal disorder, while it can at best accentuate the same. India too is no exception to this universal rule. In the previous chapter, we saw how Indians preferred a male child over a female. In the process, large sections of the Indian population were guilty of female foeticide – a gory process by which female fetus are identified even as they are in the womb of their mother and aborted. Female foeticide and infanticide became the ugly and earliest manifestation of discrimination against the girl child in Indian society. Female foeticide refers to "aborting the female in the mother's womb" whereas female infanticide is "killing the girl child after her birth." This is a social malaise that afflicts large parts of India, and is reflected in falling sex ratio indicators. Sex ratio in India stood at 940 in 2011, showing more continuous decline since 1961, but more alarmingly after 1991. In 1992, following a public outcry, the then Tamil Nadu government acknowledged the prevalence of this malaise and announced several schemes to eradicate it. These included the most popular one, The Cradle Baby Scheme (CBS) which allowed women to hand over unwanted babies to the government. Under the CBS, instead of resorting to female infanticide, parents who were unwilling to bring up their female babies could place them anonymously in cradles located in certain pre-determined centres. Subsequent to their placement in these centres, babies were to be placed for adoption. As per the statistics submitted by the Director of Social Welfare, Tamil Nadu, before the Madras High Court Bench, 4,969 new born babies, including 4,032 baby girls and – hold your breath – 937 baby boys had been received under the Cradle Baby Scheme between 1992 and October 2016. If female infanticide and foeticide justified the CBS, why should the centres have baby boys dropped in their cradles? The answer to this chilling question is obvious - the CBS ended up providing incentives to young girls to become pregnant without getting married in the first place and drop their child, whatever be its sex, without much remorse.

Shocked by the fact that the CBS introduced by the Tamil Nadu Government in 1992 for new born girls, remains active even after 24 years - with as many as 260 new-borns abandoned in the cradle placed at the government hospital in Madurai alone in the last six years – the Madras High Court's Madurai Bench in 2016 summoned the Directors of Social Welfare and Social Defence departments to find out if any study had been conducted to contain the trend by educating people. "The issue is really heart-rending and serious. It is not known what steps are taken by the government to educate people and curb the menace of abandoning or selling new born babies. We are also not informed about any study undertaken by the government to prevent this evil. We are pained to state that despite cognisance taken by this court with respect to illegal child care homes, no appreciable action has been taken so far," the court said, passing certain interim orders. Interestingly, it was during the hearing of these very cases related to illegal child care homes that the Madurai District Social Welfare Officer told the court that even that month, two babies were abandoned in the cradle outside the maternity ward of some hospital. Pertinently, she stated that most of the babies were abandoned by unwed mothers. And that is the point – unwed mothers.

Tamil Nadu, unwittingly, has been sucked into providing an incentive for young unwed mothers to abandon their children instead of addressing the abhorrent practice of preventing female foeticide and infanticide. What else would explain as to how and why even male children were abandoned under the CBS when the original plan was to take care of female infanticide.

Naturally, the state having created a programme is far too reluctant to withdraw it. Over two decades later, it is apparent that this practice of female infanticide has neither waned, nor the disgusting tradition of female foeticide stopped. The CBS has at best provided incentives to unwed mothers to abandon their children, with the state becoming a surrogate parent for all those children. The problem with the liberals is that they assume that the state has a solution to every societal disorder that can be remedied through state interventions. The CBS scheme is a perfect example of how it is not. Deviant behaviour by members of a society is best left to society to tackle, and the state is best advised not to interfere. In the most compelling of circumstances, if it is felt that the state has to interfere, it may do so, only after ensuring that it does not end up exacerbating the problem like it has done in the US through the social welfare programme or the Tamil Nadu government for their respective unwed mothers. These are the compelling lessons of welfare economics.

When Bahuka taught Economics

Writing on the issue of an ever-expanding welfare schemes in the US, Shri S Gurumurthy, one of India's foremost political and economic thinkers, stated that these schemes which were theoretically framed to protect families, practically ended up breaking them, besides bankrupting public finances of the US. According to him, even as far back as 1970, the perverted effect of social security and welfare schemes on families did not escape the watchful eyes of certain analysts. Pointing out that The National Bureau of Economic Research (NBER) in the US, which brought out a book titled *The US Economy in Transition*, in 1980, which he claims to contain the prophetic views including that of Milton Friedman, on US social security. Accordingly, Shri Gurumurthy quotes Martin S Feldstein, Professor of Economics at Harvard University, and President of NBER, extensively who wrote in his introduction to the NBER work that "welfare programmes introduced and expanded to help poor families might weaken the family structures;" that "in more subtle ways, government programmes that substitute the state for the family, cause behaviour that weakens the development of future population; fewer births, more unmarried individuals, more unmarried couples and more divorced parents; that medicare and medicaid introduced to help the elderly and poor might lead to an explosion in health care costs."

Milton Friedman, according to Shri Gurumurthy, declared that "as children stopped contributing voluntarily to the support of their parents and began contributing through a system of government fiat, a serious erosion of family values became inevitable" and saw "social security system as a detrimental influence on social patterns." The NBER work also pointed out how "family functions such as production of food, clothing and fuel, and some other staple items were taken over by business firms, and responsibilities such as education, childcare, and social insurance have been assumed by the state." What the NBER meant here is that business firms and the state had together robbed the families of their functions, leaving them functionless and therefore, dysfunctional. The NBER study pointed out that the market itself "doesn't provide for the organisation of society" but its "success" during the last 200 years is attributable in good part to the existence of strong non-market institutions such as the family; also adding that the "decline of the family and the growth of the government will jeopardise the market system and associated social, political and cultural freedoms." In conclusion, the NBER study stated that "In the long run, a healthy economy requires a healthy society."

This complete meltdown of families had a profound impact on the US economics. According to Shri Gurumurthy, US homes had an average of 4.5 persons in 1930; this came down to 3.5 per home in 1950, and now to 2.6. This breakdown of families meant additional dwelling units were required to be built, and as per some estimates some 88 million additional houses valued at $16 trillion at current prices were built. Whatever NBER had prophesied 30 years ago – less marriages, more divorces, more unmarried women, more unwed mothers, more single parent homes have indeed come true. While social security programmes caused the decline of families first, and subsequently such decline, in turn, led to more and more social welfare spending to support the weakening families, thus feeding on each other.

The net consequence of the breakdown of the families meant higher debt, both at an individual level and at the national level. The US families reel under debt. So does the government. The home loans of households are estimated to be in excess of $10 trillion. More than a third of these loans according to Shri Gurumurthy were not incurred to buy houses but were spent on consumption. This reckless consumption by individuals in the US on the one hand and a simultaneous welfare programme designed by the US Government has the calculated effect of condoning such deviant individual behaviour with a tremendous economic cost, not only for the US but also for the rest of the world. We will look into the economic impact of the same in subsequent chapters, especially the gargantuan debt of the US (estimated to be in excess of $21 trillion as of 31st March 2018 of which the external debt is estimated to be in excess of $6.5 trillion), and the manner such external debt is funded by the rest which includes Japan ($1.13 trillion), China ($1.25 trillion) and a host of developing countries.

Interestingly, Shri Gurumurthy brings about parallels to the modern-day economic situation prevailing in the US with a near equivalent paradigm from ancient Indian epic – the economics of Bahuka from the *Mahabharat*. Bahuka also figures in the *Bhagawata Purana* and was the advisor of Jarasandha, who was Kamsa's father-in-law. Kamsa, who regarded Krishna as his enemy, asked Bahuka's advice on how to make his subjects state-dependent. Bahuka, it is believed, told him: "Open your treasury to the people. Make the people eat, drink, and enjoy themselves. Bring up children to look upon parents as old and useless. That will make them laugh at those who talk of duty, love, and compassion. Like well-fed cattle at the mercy of the cowherd, the people will be completely dependent on you." That is modern economics for you – one where we can be reckless at the individual level, and it will be incumbent on the state to profess and practice welfare economics to protect you from your own recklessness. It is this repeated subsidisation of the undisciplined and submission to the bizarre role of the state that is the bane of modern economics.

More importantly, responsibility is the bedrock of discipline, be it at the individual, the national, or the international level. When a society is built purely on individual rights – as the American society has been – it encourages indiscipline. Oddly, this is called progressive economics by the Left and their partners in perfidy, the Liberals. Of course, individual rights have a place in a society, but cannot be paramount. Nor can it be absolute.

We need to set the precise balance between individual rights and duties. We have dealt with this delicate issue in chapters 6 and 7 in greater detail. When a society is sought to be built purely on rights and not on duties, the results can indeed be discomforting. What is forgotten in the melee is that the family was a natural way of caring for individuals for centuries, balancing in the process individual rights and duties. Liberals forget this crucial point. Do the liberals ever try to comprehend what happened to the old people, handicapped, orphans, and widows before their prescription of a 'welfare state, social security, and progressive economics?' Did the old, handicapped, orphans and widows just starve to death? The answer to this question would be a resounding no. There is no instance in recorded history of mankind where societies eliminated their old, weak, and the infirm. On the contrary, the society or more pertinently the family took care of them usually without much ado. It was the most natural thing for every society to do. And that is what societies across continents over the millennia did. Of course, every society devised its own norms to ensure certain rules and regulations to ensure that society and more particularly the family was not overburdened, while at the same time it ensured it took care of its members. There was a balance; a trade-off. One of the cardinal rules of these societies – termed conservative in modern jargons – was never to approve of pre-marital sex and childbirth out of wedlock. Such norms were obviously in the supreme self-interest of society, and more particularly the family, as it would not like to add unnecessary burden on itself! That explains, if not rationalises, the refusal of the Americans and American society to the granting of visa to the Swedish actress Ingrid Bergman in the fifties.

Importantly, conservative societies had a basic principle. The family was central to the smooth functioning of society. Parents took care of their children with a fond hope that their kids will take care of them in their old age. In a way, having children – especially a son – was an investment for their future, especially in old age. In the process, parents instilled certain work ethics and duties to their children. If parents failed to instil good work ethics or adhere to good values, they were most likely to fail as parents. To do so, they needed to be disciplined and hence be an example to the next generation. That ensured life-long investment in their children. Per contra, if parents failed to bring up their children, their insurance for old age could implode. Put pithily, disciplined children were an insurance for the future, but this insurance was highly privatised and left to be determined by the children and their parents. When children failed their parents, the parents would blame themselves. This was privatisation of the retirement benefits at its very best – left solely to the hands of the parents, their children, and the society they lived in.

Of course, there was an embedded selfishness for the parents in all these. But this selfishness was couched in a larger social requirement, for such children were most likely to be the cause of an orderly functioning of the society too. Responsibility to the family ranked explicitly high as much as it was implicitly to the society. A responsible family by this design created a peaceful society. A peaceful society acted as an effective regulator for the families and their smooth functioning. But with the advent of a 'welfare state,' this delicate arrangement between the family and the society as well as within the family, was given a complete go-by. The net result: when society could no longer discipline an individual or regulate the family, the individual became unwittingly the victim of his own lack of discipline.

Pointedly, the issue is when states set their policies to reward such indiscipline, especially in democracy, it is a race to the bottom. Politicians compete with each other to absurd levels to bring about welfare policies. In the process, they quickly degenerate from a welfare state into a populist state – a point of no return of sorts. Thus, the progression of the role of a government begins ideally with minimalist role, expands into a welfare role, and then degenerates to a populist role. This necessitates further levy of taxes and newer avenues of raising resources. At some point in time, it becomes virtually impossible to raise any further resources as these become inelastic and cannot be increased any further. States inevitably begin to take the next step to ruination – they begin to borrow to finance their never-ending welfare programmes. Governments borrow gigantic sums of money, of course with a clear agenda that it never has to repay them. In the process, welfare economists compete with each other in suggesting newer programmes for governments. Fiscal economists then step in to provide alternative routes to raise finance. Monetary economists then mark their participation by prescribing loose monetary policies. Market economists oblivious to the entire debate prescribe how the state should get out of crucial activities and privatise its responsibilities without explaining how the state will privatise the functions of a nanny!

Contrary to the popular belief that this nanny state is a by-product of the 20th-century thinking and modern welfare economics, let us hasten to add that it is not. Weirdly, Western philosophers for over 2,000 years believe that this institution of family needs to be abolished or in the least marginalised. Plato's collectivist state (it is this idea of collectivism and primacy of the state of Plato that resonates as modern-day communism), for instance, involved three classes: philosopher-rulers; guardians, who upheld the laws of the *Republic* and those below who engage in labour and commerce. Bizarre as it may seem, Plato suggested abolishing private property and family in the first two classes as he was of the firm opinion that both private property and family divided their loyalties towards the state. Of the class of Guardians, Plato suggests that women and children should be, believe it or not – 'held in common' and "no parent should know its child, or child its parent."

Weird as it may sound, the fact remains that the Platonic thoughts more or less resonate in a modern welfare state and its economic policies. One of the standard prescriptions of communists is to bat for equality of sexes by seeking equal job opportunities for women and want to set up communitarian crèches for children – where the state and not the mother will rear children. In short, all these are calculated and constant attempts to purge men (and women too) of their natural instincts. Ludwig von Mises, the great Austrian Economist explains this phenomenon – "Free love is the socialist's radical solution for sexual problems. The socialistic society abolishes the economic dependence of a woman which results from the fact that the woman is dependent on the income of her husband. Man and woman have the same economic rights and the same duties, as far as motherhood does not demand special consideration for the woman. Public funds provide for the maintenance and education of the children, which are no longer the affairs of the parents but of society. Thus, relations between the sexes are no longer influenced by social and economic conditions. Mating ceases to found the simplest form of social union, marriage and the family. The family disappears and society is confronted with separate individuals only. Choice in love becomes completely free. Men and women unite and separate just as their desires urge. Socialism desires to create nothing that is new in all this, but would only recreate on a higher level of culture and under new social forms what was universally valid on a more primitive cultural level and before private ownership dominated society."

Like Plato, the 19th century social and economic thinker Karl Marx too considered family, motherhood, and traditional gender roles to be a hindrance in their stated objective of creating an ideal society. Therefore, communists and other sundry socialists invariably sought the destruction of the institution of family. Let us hasten to add that the nanny state is not alone in seeking the destruction of family as an institution. There are several competing forces including free marketers, globalists, feminists, and liberals, all acting in tandem making a combined assault on the institution of family repeatedly. Somehow, the single point agenda of this extraordinary yet diverse alliance seems to be to liberate men from women, women from men, both men and women from family, and family from children. We will look into this grand alliance in Chapter 3 that seeks to dynamite the institution of the family.

Nothing exemplifies this failed idea of destruction of families in China under the leadership of Mao. Commenting on this, Steve Tucker points out that "the greatest and most grotesque attack on the family in China came, of course, from the communist regime of Mao Tse-Tung. Like all radical intellectuals since Plato, Mao saw the family as a strong rival institution to this plan for a totalitarian state," charging the communists of atomising the society till everyone was solely a creature of the state with personal and family identity obliterated. If the communist China thought destruction of families was a necessity to achieve its ideological goals, so do economists in the US. Whatever be their apparent differences in the socio-economic-political underpinnings, the fact remains that when it comes to the destruction of families, the Left and the Liberals invariably unite. Tucker points out that "at the height of the communists' farm collectivisation, children were taken from their parents at birth and raised collectively. Parents were not even allowed to know which children were theirs." Well, this is what Plato argued over 2,000 years ago. This is what happened in Communist China. This is what is happening in the US today!

Despite this failed experiment of over 2,000 years, economists do not realise the net effect of their deleterious prescriptions – the present generation is borrowing from the future generations or taxing the disciplined and funding its undisciplined. Either way, common sense tells us that this is not sustainable. That, in short, is modern economics. But this 'modernity' as we saw is over 2,000 years old. The rhetoric changes. So do the language and the phrases. The philosophers and thinkers do vary. But the relentless attack on family as an institution does not. We will revisit this discipline or more precisely, the lack of it, in the following chapters. Modern economic policies and thinking have spawned an unfair competition between the state and the family. The more an individual depends on the state, the more he justifies its existence.

When a society gets hooked on to the welfare state, it virtually becomes impossible to get rid of the habit of relying on the state and its welfare measures. As a result, the state becomes decisively bigger and necessarily coercive, as Bahuka opined. The idea that people can provide things for themselves either individually or through the family is anathema to modern economic thinking. One would be tempted to state that it would seem that there is concerted attempt by academicians, establishment, social thinkers, political scientists, economists, politicians, commentators, and writers to legitimise the state and delegitimise the family – as it attempted to do so since the days of Plato.

If the history of 'modern' governments is any indication, when the state sets in a welfare programme, it is virtually cast in stone. It can get bigger, encompass more beneficiaries and have higher budgetary allocations, but it can never be scaled down. Several heads of governments have attempted scaling down governments at various times in different continents, but with little or no success. The genie of welfare measure once uncorked by the government simply refuses to get back into the bottle. Rollbacks are simply impossible and hence unheard of. The women in the US seem to have seen the writing on the wall. As a net result of these machinations, it would seem that the West had devised a new institution of marriage where the women married the state and its welfare schemes and not one from the opposite gender. If Islamic societies pose a risk to the rest of the world through polygamy, the Western world poses a risk to the outside world through their complete destruction of the very institution of marriage. As welfare programmes expand in the West, they run gargantuan budgetary and trade deficits. To fund the same, they borrow from the rest. In the process, there is a transfer of wealth from the developing world into the developed world. The net consequence of all this is that the world remains exceedingly imbalanced between polygamous societies and societies where there is virtually no need for marriages. The third option of monogamous marriage – the one that is sustainable in the long run and one that provides balance – the core idea of this book, seems to have been lost on most economists of the world.

References

1. http://www.indiaculture.nic.in/mission-statement
2. Why the US is an economic burden on the world By M R Venkatesh – Dated June 23, 2008, www.Rediff.com
3. Trust: The Social Virtues and the Creation of Prosperity – By Francis Fukuyama.
4. The puzzle of monogamous marriage By Joseph Henrich, Robert Boyd, Peter J. Richerson- Published 23rd January 2012.
5. Affidavit of Joseph Henrich dated July 15th, 2010 filed in the Supreme Court of British Columbia.
6. Francis Fukuyama in his celebrated book – Trust: The Social Virtues and the Creation of Prosperity.
7. Marriage and Civilization: How Monogamy Made Us Human – William Tucker
8. https://en.wikipedia.org/wiki/Daniel_Patrick_Moynihan
9. How Liberal Policies Destroyed Black Families – The Daily Signal; March 29, 2016 By Crystal wright.
10. How the Liberal Welfare State Destroyed Black America – By John Perazzo.
11. https://www.brookings.edu- An analysis of out of wedlock births in the united states By George A. Akerlof and Janet L. Yellen.
12. 'How long will cradle baby scheme continue?' – The Hindu – November 2016.
13. Economics of Bahuka and Greenspan By S. Gurumurthy – The Hindu Businessline Dated 04th November 2011.
14. What has Government Done to Our Families By Allan Carlson -Misis Institute Dated 01.05.2003.
15. Socialism- An Economic and Sociological Analysis By Ludwig von Mises; New Haven Yale University Press, 1962.

16. Abolishing the Family — Primary Obstacle to Tyranny By Kerry Bolton in www.Altright.com
17. The dangerous myth of the 'missing black father' By Mychal Denzel Smith – The Washington Post – January 10, 2017.

3. To Destroy Family, Marx goes to Market

Reason has always existed, but not always in a reasonable form

– Karl Marx

When the family is destroyed, society eventually disintegrates

– Billy Graham

In the middle of 1993, *Foreign Affairs* published an article titled *The Clash of Civilizations?* authored by Samuel Huntington. Huntington was, at that point in time, and even to this day, the most cited political scientist in America on international relations. No other article, according to the editors of that distinguished journal, had generated more discussion in their publishing history since the 1940s. Huntington subsequently expanded this article into his most famous work – *The Clash of Civilizations and the Remaking of World Order* (1996) arguing pointedly that the conflicts of the future would not be between political ideologies but between 'civilisations' – yes, civilisations. Anything to do with civilisation, culture, and the interplay between the two, naturally holds our attention. In the said article, he posed a hypothetical question as to whether the relationships between civilisations would dominate the future of world politics. In his book, he attempted to precisely answer this intriguing question, demonstrating not only how clashes between civilisations, especially those rooted to religions, are the greatest threat to world peace, but also sought an international order to avoid this clash. According to him, such an international order was the best safeguard against such future civilisational conflicts.

The argument on an international order put forth by Huntington in *The Clash of Civilizations* is of extreme importance. Can we establish such an international order as suggested by Huntington? Is it desirable? Is it within the realms of practicality? If yes, what should be the ideal model for any such futuristic international order? How should it be fashioned? What are its basic ingredients? What should be the theoretical framework for such an emerging order? What should be its broad contours? What are its pre-conditions? Is there a functional prototype available for ready reference? Has it been successful? Has such a model been sustainable? We will seek answers to some of these questions in this chapter and also in subsequent chapters of this book. Remember, should we establish an international order as suggested by Huntington, it will be one of the grand experiments conducted on mankind. Naturally, we need to tread on this issue of an international order with great caution. But first, let us examine the viability of his idea.

The greatest upside of this seminal work was to shift the overall discussion of the post-cold-war world from ideology, politics, and economics to culture – and especially to religion, the basis of culture – a subject generally ignored in contemporary political discourse. In this work, Huntington listed out about eight civilisations of the world: Western, Islamic, Orthodox Christianity, Latin American, Chinese, Hindu, Japanese, and African. Based on a study of all these civilisations, he predicted that the most likely future conflicts would, in all probability, be between the West on the one hand and Islam, or for that matter China, on the other. In this connection, he observed, "Western intervention in the affairs of other civilisations is probably the single most dangerous source of instability and potential global conflict in a multi-civilisational world." Since then, Huntington and his work have been the source of several serious discussions within establishments worldwide. "The dangerous clashes of the future," Huntington predicted, "are likely to arise from the interaction of Western arrogance, Islamic intolerance, and Sinic (Chinese) assertiveness."

Expectedly, his work set off a huge debate in academic and intellectual circles where he predicted divisions within the world, in which the West would at best be probably one of the several competing civilisations, with the fault lines with the Islamic and Chinese civilisations repeatedly challenging the hegemony of the West, notably the US. The subject that Huntington has put on the table for discussion is the 'clash of civilisations' involving predominantly the Western, Islamic, and Chinese civilisations. Significantly, according to Huntington, other civilisations like the Hindu, or for that matter the Japanese civilisations, do not carry the potential for any future conflicts. He warned that the West may one day have to fight for its most cherished values of liberty and democracy, and, indeed physical survival against extremists from other cultures. For him, people from other civilisations despise the West, and will sooner than later embroil the West in a civilisational war. It was his hypothesis "that the fundamental source of conflict in this new world will not be primarily ideological or primarily economic. The great divisions among humankind and the dominating source of conflict will be cultural. Nation-states will remain the most powerful actors in world affairs, but the principal conflicts of global politics will occur between nations and groups of different civilisations. The conflict between civilisations will be the latest phase of the evolution of conflict in the modern world."

The Emerging World Order

Beguilingly, Huntington assumed (and given the history of mankind, rightly so) that most civilisations, based on major religions, are pregnant with potential for conflicts. What if this assumption is structurally flawed? Are civilisations so designed across the globe? What if civilisations, for instance, arrange themselves systematically to avoid conflict with other civilisations? Restraint thy name is civilisation, isn't it? Is it possible by design for civilisations to allow cohabitation and co-existence with other conflicting ideas? What is the fundamental source of such future civilisational conflict? Is it purely religious, meaning that which is mandated by religious tenets that govern interpersonal relationships between two persons – especially in cases where one believes in 'one god,' while the other does not? Crucially, is religion the bedrock of culture? What if religious (probably cultural and civilisational) fundamentalism gives way to plural thoughts where a philosophical outlook to every question is accepted and every idea, including its negation, given equal importance? The billion-dollar question remains – Is the 'clash' as suggested by Huntington inevitable? Or can it be avoided? If so, how?

Rose McDermott and Jonathan Cowden in an essay titled *Polygyny and Violence against Women* precisely raise these issues. According to the authors the clash, "whether derived from politics, economics, religion, or history," was to an extent reflective of "some degree of resentment towards the West and Western values, no doubt fuelled by struggles over land, resources, power, and preferred institutions for political and economic structures." Put differently, the authors raise another dimension to this debate – can the potential clash be so simply decoded? Encapsulating the entire imbroglio, the authors opine that "if these were the only sources of enmity, the search for peace would be hard enough. But the problem is worsened by a fundamental clash of values, specifically surrounding the appropriate role of women in society, that emerges entirely independently of economic and political contests, although such issues often serve to fuel such conflicts."

Before we proceed to discuss inter-civilisational clashes and the manner of eliminating them, let us first examine how various civilisations have sought to eliminate intra-civilisational clashes. One of the primary sources of conflict, as Huntington argues, within every civilisation has been the separation of spiritual power and temporal authority. In short, what should be left to the church and state and their exclusive domain has been one of the key points of conflagration even within the Western civilisation for several centuries. Huntington points out that throughout Western history, many churches existed apart from the state. God and Caesar, Church and State, spiritual authority and temporal authority, have been a prevailing dualism, and hence a perpetual cause of conflict in Western culture. In Islam, God is Caesar; in China and Japan, Caesar is God; and in Orthodoxy, God is Caesar's junior partner. The recurring clashes between the church and state that typify Western civilisation have in fact existed for time immemorial. Fascinatingly, Huntington points out that only in Hindu civilisation are religion and politics distinctly separated. Yet, in modern India, the constitutional assertion in the Preamble of the Indian Constitution of the separation of powers of the state and religion – which drawing on Western experiences and modelled on the West goes by the convoluted appellation of secularism, interestingly, has been the source of several ideological conflicts in post-independent India. Islamic societies, it may be noted, have not yet culturally matured enough to accommodate differing viewpoints even of an Islamic sect which believes in the very same Prophet, his life and his teachings, but do not believe in the said Prophet being the last Prophet. Likewise, Western civilisations are still in an embryonic stage. Hence, expecting the Western civilisation to participate in an international order, much less be its standard, suffers from the vice of excessive expectation. Probably, Huntington missed this basic point.

This is a fundamental lesson for all who want to design a global order to avoid civilisational conflicts in future in these historical narratives of various civilisations put forward by Samuel Huntington. Traditional Hindu civilisation over time immemorial saw a potential conflict between religion and politics, which was not foreseen by Western civilisations. In fact, the West was oblivious to this idea itself, and probably took over 2,000 years to resolve this basic conflict within their own civilisation. Islam is still grappling with this issue and has not yet defined the problem, much less attempted to solve it. Yet, people like Huntington want an international order modelled on the West, and sees it as a responsibility of the West. In contrast, sensing the potential conflict from the intercourse of politics and religion, Hindu civilisation traditionally arranged itself by practically separating the two, obviously without diminishing the value of either.

And one way of ensuring that this separation was sustainable was to systemically abhor absolutism in the first place. It may be noted that nothing was absolute in the traditional Indic societies. There was a place for everyone and accommodating even seemingly conflicting ideas. Consequently, what was carnal was also sacred, and what was sacred was well and truly carnal. The secular and sacred blended effortlessly within the traditional Indic societies and thereby eliminated potential future conflicts. Absolutism, it may be further noted, is the cause of imbalance and hence unsustainable. And imbalance is the anti-thesis of balance. Therefore, any dogma, belief or idea that is anchored on absolutism needs to be eschewed. This is the crux of the issue – the ability to balance contrasts and accommodate each other lies at the soul of culture. Is there a message from the Indic society to the non-Indic ones? Probably yes.

Understanding Huntington's predicament

Clearly, the West, which has taken over 2,000 years to resolve a fundamental conflict within itself, naturally fears conflicts with other civilisations at every turn. And the solution? An international order modelled on the Western civilisation with a fundamental assumption as Huntington suggested that the West is best for the rest to follow. Unfortunately, this idea is indeed a non-starter for cultures that are based on monotheistic religions like Christianity and Islam, holding a potential for all present and future conflicts. That has been our experience from distant and recent history. Monotheistic religions invariably hold that my God is the true God, my way of communicating to that only God is the only true way of conversing with him, and my Prophet is the only true Prophet – are, by every account, provocative, as much as such ideas demean every follower of other religions. Critically, an exclusive thought can be anything but not culture. Inclusiveness is the quintessence of world order. Culture, by definition, sets the terms of dealing by one individual with another individual or group of individuals, irrespective of the fact whether the former and the latter belong to the same religious denomination or otherwise. In fact, culture is much more than interpersonal relationships. Culture is the manner in which man associates with other men and includes the manner in which he deals with the environment, rivers, lakes, seas, hills, mountains, plants, flowers, fruits, rodents, reptiles, birds, insects, fish, animals, children and of course person from the other gender – for that matter include anything and everything.

Ideally, culture sets the terms to the extent that there should be no terms or pre-conditions while dealing with another person. It cannot be contractual or legal and surely not pre-conditional. It should be voluntary and obligatory. Indeed, when one sees the merit in the viewpoint of the other, even as he does not believe in the same, it is culture at play. In contrast, when one has a bigoted viewpoint or is prevented to do so by his religious beliefs or ideology or dogmas, one cannot claim to be cultured. Thus, when one deals with the other fellow human being without any terms, preconditions, or diktats, it is culture pure and simple. The very existence of any pre-conditions, terms, or diktats in dealing with another person, more so, if he is of any other denomination, dynamites the very idea of culture.

That implies that culture by description has to be inclusive and not exclusive, even if it militates against one's basic beliefs or religious tenets. That is easier than done, especially in the context of the Abrahamic faiths, their beliefs and tenets. For instance, what if a culture based on religious orthodoxies and dogmas prevent one person to even associate, much less deal with, the other? What if any human intercourse is grounded on the premise that it has to be within the four corners of my and not your, religious beliefs? What if I set rules for you, your beliefs and the manner in which you could, for instance, pray or trade? What if a religion sets rules not only for its followers, but also for non-believers? Awful as it may sound, the fact remains that this is the imperial demand as well as design of some major religions, especially Abrahamic faiths.

For the past two millennia, especially since the advent of the Abrahamic faiths, the world has been unable to find solutions to this vexatious issue - especially one where some religions arrogate themselves of setting rules not only for followers, but also for non-followers. Provocatively, some interpreters of these religions claim that their religion mandates optionless punishment to non-believers of their god, while some others claim that there is an explicit mandate to convert every non-believer into a believer of their religion. Cultures, premised on nihilism of other religions, on one hand, cannot attempt to design an international global order on the other. Such an approach is highly incompatible, especially given the underlying fact as brought out by Huntington is that most cultures are rooted to one major religion or the other. If that be so, how can an international order as suggested by Huntington resolve this fundamental issue?

Perfect Diagnosis, Imperfect Prescription

Huntington, in a way, was perfect with his diagnosis but probably wrong, given the cultural incongruity amongst various cultures, with his prescriptions. For instance, can an international order homogenise our religious beliefs or harmonise the way we pray? Obviously, it cannot. Then pray why such an audacious proposal? Shorn of all the jargons, let us not forget what Huntington suggests as 'The Remaking of World Order' is nothing but the original homogenisation agenda of Abrahamic faiths expressed differently, possibly more subtly and definitely with greater eloquence. More to the point, the Abrahamic faiths of Christianity and Islam have been precisely attempting this homogenised world order through a planned, systematic programme. Homogenisation is a shorthand for a unipolar world and an anti-thesis to a plural world. One way of achieving homogenisation is to follow an agenda of conversions. Remember conversions, especially of non-believers and pagans, are at the core of Abrahamic faiths. Implicit in their argument for conversion is that the world filled with Christians, or for that matter Muslims, lends itself to durable peace. Historical evidences suggest exactly the opposite. Islam is yet to find peace with itself, and the Christian world is in the process of attaining peace only after 2,000 years of blood-letting, that too after significantly reforming itself in recent times. The veneer of modernity attained by the West has been possible only after it had substantially de-Christianised itself. The conversions attempted by both Christianity and Islam on non-Abrahamic societies has indeed been violent and bloody. While conversion is one of the fundamental religious doctrines of both Islam and Christianity, the fact remains that conversion, in turn, negates the very idea of culture. Unless both Christianity and Islam give up conversions, one must conclude they are exclusive, and hence intolerant. Monotheism, religious fundamentalism, and conversions are a trinity that has caused most of all violence in the past, and contain the seeds for many future conflicts. This is the problem that Huntington correctly recognises in his work, but probably suggested an outlandish solution and more importantly, never explained how to make his solution workable.

This is just one dimension of the problem. The lack of equality between the sexes is another. For instance, Rose McDermott and Jonathan Cowden argue that Western values often encourage a foundation of legal equality between the sexes. Rather than counterposing East against West, arguing about the clash of civilisations in the proto-typical Huntington sense, the authors argue that the question should actually revolve around the sources and consequences of violence by men towards women as the root of conflict both within and among nations. What are some of the origins of the violence that men direct towards women? Is it simply rooted in male sexual desire for women, and the anger and frustration that may result when men hold women responsible for their own drives? Or do men seek to control women simply because they are physically and financially stronger, and because they are able to get away with exerting power over those with fewer resources? Or does male violence emerge from a much broader array of social incentives and permissions? And what are the consequences of such violence, not only for women and children, but also for the men who instigate it and for the societies that sanction it? These patterns of violence often begin in the home and more broadly, serve as models for the assumed hierarchical relationships between the sexes as well as implicit endorsement for dominance, coercion, and violence as the proper form of conflict resolution in society. Does that mean that the international order, as suggested by Huntington, is a non-starter? Probably yes, if viewed from the narrow prism of religion and culture based on religion. Probably no, if viewed otherwise – that is, if culture is premised as a way of life and divorced from religion. Ideally, any international order that accepts plural thoughts and ideas in religion, and that accepts multiple gods and multiple ways of praying to their respective gods will, by its very definition, be culture at play. But do the Abrahamic faiths that are dogmatic have within themselves to accept this fundamental fact? Do they have the ability to reform themselves from within? Can they allow plural thought to flourish? We will deal with this vexatious subject of culture and the manner in which it affects economics, both at the national and global levels, in subsequent chapters of this book.

However, the prescription of an international order as suggested by Huntington must be viewed from the limited context of his candid diagnosis – arrogance of the West, intolerance of Islam, and increasing assertive of the Chinese. Coincidentally, we have dealt with these three societies in some detail in the first two chapters of this book in the context of the institution of family. On first blush, there is nothing to link these three societies. They have nothing in common. In fact, nothing unites them, and probably they are differentiated by every imaginable denominator. An Islamic society is definitely distinct from a Western society, which is different from the modern Chinese society modelled on the ideals of Mao and his teachings. But on deeper examination, one fact unites the three – none of these societies are inherently monogamous. None of the three societies believe in the institution of a monogamous family and the fundamental laws of nature and economics associated with it. They are probably united in their beliefs that societies are malleable and can be fashioned and repeatedly re-fashioned. While one is avowedly polygamous, the other has virtually destroyed the institution of marriage in the name of upholding individual rights of its citizens, and the third probably is willing to sacrifice the institution of marriage in the pursuit of a revolution.

That brings us back to the issue of monogamous marriage. Questions naturally arise. Do societies hold a potential threat to global peace in the future simply because they have weakened their families as an institution? Is all this at the root of their aggressive behaviour? Have these societies become what they are and developed fault lines, as they have domestically become inherently unstable after destroying the institution of family? Is the absence of family as an institution in these societies preventing the germination of a workable international order? Does destruction of families in these societies implicitly mark the destruction of culture? Or is it that the lack of culture ultimately led to destruction of the families? Let us flip the argument – can the West be less arrogant, Islam be more tolerant, and China less assertive if only they are strictly monogamous with all its attendant traits? Let us examine it from other dimensions too.

Culture flowers when there are no pre-conditions within the dealings of men and their worldly affairs. It is acceptance of others as they are in their natural pristine state. Marriage between two opposite sexes is a case in point, the first decisive step to culture. The central idea of this book in sustaining the institution of a monogamous marriage is to leverage this institution as a primary building block of culture and subsequently, economics. This was discussed in greater detail in Chapter 1. Nevertheless, the importance of culture in moulding a society, and the role of society in shaping, de-shaping, and reshaping national economics is probably one of the most under-studied areas of modern times. The consequences of this neglect are indeed cataclysmic as events that unfold before us demonstrate. A society that does not believe in the potency of culture and the institution of a monogamous marriage will obviously be in a state of constant boil. This is simply because it will be unable to set a balance between a man and woman. Such an imbalanced society cannot be logically expected to partake in any international order. If Huntington's prescription of an international order is to be taken seriously, should not these societies begin by setting their house in order? That implies societies need to revisit the terms and conditions of how men relate to women, and women to men, and both to families. More particularly, it is all about how various cultures (read religions) have traditionally viewed women. Since the fault lines are admittedly with the Western and Islamic societies, let us at the outset examine the collective psyche of these societies, and how these societies traditionally viewed woman and her equation with man since the days of Adam and Eve.

Original Sin and its Impact on the West

As is commonly believed, the Judaeo-Christian conception of the creation of Adam and Eve is narrated in detail in *Genesis*. God accordingly prohibited both of them from eating the fruits of the forbidden tree. The serpent, the belief goes, seduced Eve to eat from it, and Eve in turn seduced Adam to eat it with her. When God rebuked Adam for what he did, Adam evidently tries to place all the blame on Eve. "The woman you put here with me, she gave me some fruit from the tree, and I ate it." Though God cursed both, the reader of this Biblical story is generally led to believe how Adam was innocent and how Eve is the real villain of the piece. More to the point, this creation story shared by Christians, Muslims, and Jews is fundamental to the historical bias of Abrahamic faiths against women. To an outsider, it would seem that good and evil acquired genders in Christian theology – man was distinctly associated with the spiritual and godly, while woman was linked to flesh and the world. Needless to emphasise, this image of Eve as an evil temptress in the Bible has, in effect, created a negative image of women throughout Christianity. Successive generation of women are believed to have inherited from the Biblical Eve, both her guilt and her guile, as part of original sin.

Accordingly, it is firmly embedded in Christian thought that all women are devious and morally inferior. In the *New Testament*, according to St Paul, "A woman should learn in quietness and full submission. I don't permit a woman to teach or to have authority over a man; she must be silent. For Adam was formed first, then Eve." It is commonly said that women were accorded far better treatment by Jesus than they were accorded subsequently by his male followers, as it is experienced that the attitude towards women in

Christianity seems to have degenerated since the days of Jesus. The Catholic Bible states explicitly that: "The birth of a daughter is a loss" (*Ecclesiasticus 22:3*). Further, according to the Bible, a man must fulfil any vows he might make to God. He must not break his word. On the other hand, a woman's vow is not necessarily binding on her. It would seem to an outsider that even God cannot take women seriously. It has to be approved by her father, if she is living in his house, or by her husband, if she is married. If a father or husband does not endorse his daughter's or wife's vows, all pledges made by her become null and void: "But if her father forbids her when he hears about it, none of her vows or the pledges by which she obligated herself will stand. Her husband may confirm or nullify any vow she makes or any sworn pledge to deny herself" (*Num. 30: 2-15*). The original sin and the perceived role of Eve somehow seem to have dominated and simultaneously disturbed the collective Western thought, especially its women, since then.

James Boyce captures this demented psychology of the Western world for over 2,000 years in his scholarly and exhilarating work *Born Bad*, where he points out that the Western mind has been distinctly shaped, de-shaped, and constantly reshaped by the dominant view within Christianity that "human beings were born sinners, subject to the just wrath of God." The Western view – which corresponds and is proximate to the Christian view of the world – is that Adam's defiance did not affect him alone. In fact, his defiance wrecked successive generations forever in the eyes of God. Since then, everyone is consequently 'born bad,' offensive to the Creator, and this taint can be washed away only through His grace and "the unearned gift of God's forgiveness," in the form of baptism. More to the point, the idea of original sin conveys the thought that the human race does not begin afresh with each new person. Thus, according to the Christian beliefs, we are all, in effect, born with a historic burden, caused by the sinful behaviour of Adam and the guile of Eve, and we carry it from our first breath. Thus, a Christian is born in sin, lives in sin and an impure state, and cannot redeem himself by his own inner resources, but only through an intervention of Christ. Therefore, salvation for a Christian is centred on an external entity – Christ. Evidently, Christianity is grounded in a deeply personal emphasis on the 'broken self,' and "a corresponding reliance on an external divinity to provide salvation."

Boyce concludes that the doctrine of original sin "has always been central to the Western experience of what it means to be human." Put pithily, absent the original sin, there would be no need for a saviour – the Christ. Belief in Christ as a saviour is of primary importance to Christians. No amount of confession, charity, or repentance can save Christians. Only Christ can.

Interestingly, according to Boyce, for centuries the debate about original sin has been a mainstay in the thought and argument of philosophers, economists, and thinkers in the Western world. For instance, Thomas Hobbes viewed man in the state of nature as vicious and brutal. David Hume argued that reason was always a slave to wilfulness and passion. Adam Smith's economics was theorised on people's elemental selfishness. Benjamin Franklin believed that men were ruled by "the love of power and the love of money." It is the collective thought of these men that forced the founding fathers of the American Constitution to recognise the fallen nature of men, and charted a government that would 'rationally manage' man's inherent sinfulness. Fascinatingly, many other countries who draw their inspiration from the US Constitution, invariably end up with a sub-conscious idea that the state has to be 'supreme, omnipresent, and omnipotent' to rationally manage men and their inherent sinfulness. Even Rousseau, in his *Confessions*, revealed that our inner selves were cauldrons of emotion, perversity, and paranoia. By the 20th century, Freud argued that men and women were moulded "by instinctual drives, especially sexuality and aggression, which exist in tension with morality and conscious thought." That we are all bad to the bone seems to be the overarching thought that permeates the Western world since the original sin. Boyce, in effect, argues that the very idea of original sin has got so far under the skin of Western culture that even in the modern age, it remains the dominant paradigm for discussions in every new discipline. "For in a sense," he concludes, "the history of the West is an account of what happened when a people were brought up to believe that their deity had turned his back on his own creation."

Thus, this idea of original sin since the days of Adam and Eve has impacted several ideas within the Western civilisation. More to the point, the cause of the original sin – Eve – and all women after her are held as fallen souls within the Christian world. But by borrowing ideas, thoughts, and ideologies, the non-Western world is inadvertently subscribing to the idea of the original sin that is deeply embedded in the collective Christian psyche. Importantly, this imposes the two millennia-old guilt complex of women in the West on its own unsuspecting people. Yet, women in the non-west world in turn then believe that the solution for all their problems stems from the very same solutions devised by Western women for the problems faced by them in Western societies.

That also explains why it is easier for a Black American to become the President of the US than for a lady to ever become its President. Contrast this with two important developments in the evolution of Constitution Law in independent India – one, there was virtually no debate in ensuring universal adult suffrage and two, there was virtually no theological bar to any lady becoming the Prime Minister in as early as 1966.

Absent Feminine Divine and Divine that is Feminine

There is yet another fault line within the Abrahamic faiths – patriarchal theology. God is He, in all three Abrahamic faiths, and not She. Having held women as evil and the cause of all evil, it was beyond Abrahamic theological construct to have a feminine divine. In the absence of a God of the opposite gender or what is essentially Goddess, women in every congregation constantly hear such phrases as 'God our father,' 'sons of God,' 'men of God,' and the 'brotherhood of man.' Nowhere do they ever hear or for that matter ever will hear in future 'Mother God' or 'daughters of God.' American feminist Rosemary Ruether puts it succinctly: "The male is taken to be the normative representative of the human species, the norm for imaging God, and for defining anthropology, sin, redemption, and ministry." But the female? Well, there are three options for women – play a secondary role to man, be silent, or remain absent. The net result is that women have, of late, begun to question this Judeo-Christian tradition of Eve and her role in particular, and the role of women in general. In the process, a 'Goddess' movement is slowly but surely emerging in the West, in which women are attempting to reform ancient worship and celebrate a woman's creative power. Spiritual feminism has to become, sooner than later, an important aspect of the women's movement in the West, more to fill the theological void of the absence of a feminine divine or what can be termed as 'Goddess.' Absence of a feminine divine and a divine that is not feminine is an unprofitable thought, which the West is in the process of learning in its 2,000-year-old tryst with monotheism. Restoration of divinity in feminine, and seeing feminine as divine is an idea in Christianity whose time has well and truly come. Restoration of a theological balance, it is argued, will at once ensure balance in society, politics, and of course economics in the West.

Expectedly, and as a prelude to this development, more and more women are challenging this fundamental theological assumption that religion should be the sole preserve of men. This challenge goes on by the appellation of women's movement, and is at the root of the feminist ideas that is currently sweeping the Western world for some time now. It is now no more acceptable to the West and their women to blame women, at least in the theological sense of the original sin. Of course, one is appalled to hear horrendous stories of persecution of women in the medieval times. As many as nine million women are estimated to have died in the witch-hunts between the 14th and 17th centuries. The resultant pain and grief have brought stringent criticisms of male bias in religious practice and thought. Absent the feminine-divine, the ordinary feminine in the West finds it increasingly difficult to relate to the divine. This realisation, albeit belatedly, resulted in the germination of the women's rights movement – where the pendulum swung from one extreme of persecuting and belittling women to the other viz., women's liberation and feminism and women movements. In the process, modern societies in the West lost the requisite balance in their society – a subject that lies at the core of this book. Nevertheless, the shift was tectonic – from a persecuted class to a class that insists on its rights and rights only. This resulted in a society, especially of women, who cared too little for anything else, especially duties.

This focus on women's rights from a historical perspective of women in the West may well be justified, but has created a gargantuan societal imbalance. Largely originating in the West, women's movements had come to represent their rights and interests in diverse fields, including but not limited to politics, economics, society, and of course religion too. Throughout the history of the West, women were invariably viewed as second-class citizens. The reason obviously stems from the original sin viz., Adam and Eve discussed earlier. The *Encyclopaedia Britannica* points out that even as late as at the end of the 19th century in France, women were compelled to cover their heads in public, and, in parts of Germany, a husband still had the right to sell his wife. Even as late as the 20th century, women could neither vote nor hold elective office in Europe and in most of the US. Women were prevented from conducting business without a male representative, be it father, brother, husband, legal agent, or even son. Married women could not exercise control over their own children without the permission of their husbands. Moreover, women had little or no access to education and were barred from most professions. This is in sharp contrast to several Asian civilisations and even among tribal cultures where women were never accorded such inferior status. In many parts of Africa, for example, the status of women had begun to erode significantly only with the arrival of European colonialism. In all these regions then, the notion that patriarchy is the predominant problem seems absurd. Strangely, in a country like India, Indian feminists, parrot these very same lines of patriarchy without realising that women in a country like India face a different set of problems. And their problems have nothing to do with the problems faced by women in the West, where the problems are indeed rooted to patriarchy, which in turn can be traced to the original sin.

The impact of the original sin seems to have lasted well into the 20th century so much so that Western societies had come to some sort of belief that women were indeed vile creatures. Resultantly, a powerful and possibly an intellectually militant women's movement, originated in the West, challenged certain fundamental theological beliefs and social dogmas to exorcise the ghost of the past 2,000 years. While this transformation ensured women as an individual retained their status within the family and society, it also set the stage perfectly for everyone to wreak havoc on the institution of family through the very same women.

The Persistent Attack on the Family

This classical status of women, rooted to the original sin, in Western society gradually underwent tremendous reformation over the millennia. These reforms were sporadically carried out over the past few centuries and climaxed in the first half of the 20th. In retrospect, and on a simple analysis, it is obvious that women in the US progressively acquired their natural space, both within the family and society, especially in the early part of the 20th century. That was substantially because of the simultaneous evolution of family as an institution of social importance, and hence acceptance of women. This progress, along with the arrival of monogamy as a just, equitable, and acceptable social order made an ocular demonstration of the virtues of trust, culture, and probably sustainable peace. That explains, if not rationalises, the average American abhorrence to the grant of visa to Swedish actress Ingrid Bergman, even as late as in the 1950s. This was discussed in greater detail in Chapter 2. But by a quirk of fate (and possibly by confluence of circumstances), this evolution of social status for women in the Western societies 'progressed' far too much. Women who, in effect, craved for equality over the millennium, now challenged the taboos of the very same society that had denied justice to women over the millennia. In the process, women liberalised themselves of the society, probably to correct the historical wrongs perpetuated on them over the millennium. But before matters spiralled out of control (as they seem at present), and after women regained their social status in the West, there was a 'sweet spot' – a well-defined structured balance between individual rights and duties. The 'sweet spot' included respect to women, practice of monogamy, and regarding family as a dominant institution. All these social developments ensured the spectacular economic growth of the US. As we now understand, the 'sweet spot' in American economic history coincided with its spectacular, sustained, balanced economic growth. Is there a lesson for economists here? Is the answer to sustained economic growth rooted to organising families, especially women? The answers to these questions are obvious: if an economy is socially balanced, it is sustainable. We will revisit this sweet spot in the economic history of the US, which approximates to its cultural sweet spot in subsequent chapters too.

In his book *Democracy in America*, published in the 1800s, Alexis de Tocqueville heaped praise on the 19th-century American family. "There is certainly no country in the world where the tie of marriage is more respected than in America," and wrote, "or where conjugal happiness is more highly or worthily appreciated." Today, as we saw in Chapter 2, the American society has redefined morality that has turned the institution of marriage into an almost laughably inconsequential arrangement. Surveys now show that two-thirds of Americans view divorce as a 'morally acceptable' way to escape an inconvenient union. Most Westerners have not only accepted the plague of divorce, but many now see it as the morally right thing to do in most circumstances. As divorces increased, the state was compelled to intercede and legislate divorce laws. The lower tolerance to a marriage partner and increasing the legal cost of divorce has virtually made marriages economically unsustainable. That has, in turn, brought the idea of a live-in relationship to the fore, which neatly symbolises the collapse of the family as an institution.

Tocqueville lauded the 19th-century American family for accentuating the 'diverse' roles men and women undertook in marriage. "They have carefully separated the functions of man and of woman so that the great work of society may be better performed," he said. The roles of husband and wife, he explained, perfectly complemented one another. "You will never find American women," Tocqueville wrote, "in charge of the external relations of the family, managing a business or interfering in politics; but they are also never obliged to undertake a rough labourer's work or any task requiring hard physical exertion. No family is so poor that it makes an exception to this rule." This was probably true for the American family even in the first half of the 20th century. According to him, Americans understood that while men and women were made to fulfil different roles within the family, each role was equal in importance. Today, these unique roles have been reversed. Men have forsaken their responsibilities in the home as the family's primary leader, provider, protector, and educator, which as we saw in Chapter 2, was taken over by the state. Meanwhile, American women have, by force of circumstances, ceased to be the loving mother of young children that they were a few decades ago. In 1950, for example, one in four married women between the ages of 25 and 44 were employed outside the home in the US. Today, three in four are. As a consequence, children are largely left to themselves – growing up without proper parental care or a clear code of ethics upon which they can build their future families.

And without a strong parental influence at home, children have become easy prey to drugs or unsafe sex, usually both. What should have been a primarily filial responsibility of taking care of children has gradually shifted outside the family. In view of the emerging paradigm where neither the father nor the mother is available at home to take care of the children, the society and the government in most countries have now virtually accepted delinquency in children as a given. As a net result, pre-marital sex is seen as inevitable for teens, and quietly governments have – as a net consequence – shifted the focus to 'sex education' and 'safe sex.' This approach, of course, encourages further sexual activity among teens, which in turn increases the frequency of illegitimate births, sexually transmitted diseases, and abortion. As sexual morality decreases in each individual of the family, the institution of family comes under a severe onslaught. Naturally, to address these and in the absence of an instrumentality of the family to tackle the problem, the state is compelled to step in through various programmes and to fund them by levying higher taxes. This triggers a vicious cycle of state-sponsored individual irresponsibility leading to a downward spiral, from where it becomes virtually impossible for the individual, family, or the state to recover. Therefore, women and women's rights are central to sustaining the idea of family. We will deal with this subject in greater detail in Chapter 10.

Communism and the Hatred for Family

But this assault on women and by extension family is not limited to Christendom or Abrahamic faiths. In fact, every ideology, as it seeks to expand seeks to destroy family. To do so, it specifically targets women. Targeting family and carrying out a relentless war on morality, especially sexual morality, has been vital to the idea of Communism for over several decades now. Communists abhor the idea of family, chastity of women, and issues like filial piety that binds the family. And pray, what is the pre-condition for Communism to proliferate? The answer to this convoluted question is not far to seek – it is annihilation of the institution of family. It is family and family alone (more specifically, women in the family) which stands between communists and their ideology. Men and women without the safety net of the family are easy pickings for communists. For instance, the notorious Red Guards who were a group of students at the Beijing University owing allegiance to China's communist dictator Mao, firmly believed that in order to build a new world, they had to wipe out the old one. So, they travelled around the country, eradicating anything representing China's past: old customs, cultures, habits, and ideas. Museums, temples, shrines, heritage sites, including Confucius' tomb, were defaced, ransacked, or even totally destroyed. One of the worst instances of destruction took place in the Ming Dynasty (1368-1644) tombs as the Red Guards dug up the remains of Ming emperors and empresses and burned the remains with treasures, including priceless ancient books and manuscripts. Several personal properties, including some family's genealogy book containing 50 generations of information was confiscated and burnt. Such drastic efforts to erase the influence of the past and remake society in a revolution was all done with a naked objective of destroying culture, and with it the family. Let us remind ourselves that the sequence can always be a subject matter of debate, not the intent of the communists.

One of the most important works on this subject is a book authored by Paul Kengor, provocatively titled *Takedown: From Communists to Progressives, How the Left Has Sabotaged Family and Marriage.* According to him, for nearly two centuries, from the 1800s to the 1960s, leftists have based all their arguments on the *Communist Manifesto,* where Marx and Engels wrote of the abolition of the family. "Blessed is he who has no family," Marx wrote to Engels, and termed marriages as 'bourgeois claptrap,' in effect smashing the idea of monogamy, approximately a century before the 1960s New Left adopted the idea in the US. And these efforts to destroy family through a planned, sustained, and ideological effort was not limited to Marx and Engels. Kengor, in fact, traces the effort to 'revolutionise family and marriage' from socialist utopians like Robert Owen, Charles Fourier, and Albert Brisbane to cultural Marxists such as Herbert Marcuse and Wilhelm Reich to 20th-century leftists and progressives ranging from the Bolsheviks – Lenin, Trotsky, Alexandra Kollontai – to Margaret Sanger, Betty Friedan, Kate Millett, and 1960s radicals Bill Ayers, Bernardine Dohrn, and Mark Rudd.

Explaining the reason for their war on marriage and family, Kengor brings about how communists in their desperate pursuit have even begun to celebrate homosexuals and same sex marriages. One is unable to fathom the cause for their celebration when such deviant behaviour, if at all, are at best personal choices and left to the individuals concerned. Let us never forget that it is not their love for homosexuals or the belief in individual liberties that compels them to back same-sex marriages, as much as their desire to abolish families that makes them to back the former. Communists will do whatever they need to destroy the family, and in this quest for what they seek to achieve, gay marriage becomes one obvious choice. It is the long-sustained belief of the Communists that family as an institution is a huge stumbling block for carrying out their agenda of 'revolution,' whatever it may mean. To effectuate their idea of revolution, annihilation of families becomes necessary. For them, it is family that protects culture and harbours civilisational values. Both culture and civilisation are anathema for communists. It is their considered view that unless families are completely destroyed, tradition and culture cannot be demolished. To demolish tradition and culture, women had to be liberated from families. To liberate women, families had to be destroyed. Unless all three – families destroyed, culture and traditions demolished, and women liberated, Marxism cannot succeed. 'Smashing monogamy' was merely one manifestation of blowing up coveted traditions. Kengor summarises the communist paradigm succinctly: "As communists over time broke down barriers in sexual relations and the covenant of marriage, many moved towards acceptance and advocacy of homosexuality and bisexuality."

Wittingly or unwittingly, intentionally or otherwise, led either by the spirit of the times or by more sinister forces that have long led communists, the communist priority is less of gay rights than it is a continued assault on the family. The assault means a rejection of older and more established and despised enemies for communists: morality, tradition, religion, and religious beliefs. What else would explain that even the once militantly anti-gay places like Castro's Cuba are stridently embracing same-sex marriage now? Kengor places the entire communist agenda vis-à-vis the family when he points out to the clear pattern of abolishing marriage. He states: "We see, among other things, a fanatical push to abolish all right of inheritance, to end home and religious education, to dissolve monogamy in marriage, to pursue pre-and extra-marital sex, to foster and tolerate (as Engels puts it) the "gradual growth of unconstrained sexual intercourse" by unmarried women, to nationalise all housework, to shift mothers into factories, to move children into day care nurseries, to separate children into community collectives, apart from their natural parents, and, most of all, for society and the state to rear and educate children." Unconstrained sexual intercourse by women seems to be the sole objective, the cherry on the cake at every twist and turn of the socio-political underpinning of the Left! Fascinatingly, for over two centuries, they have successfully made the world to believe, that what they believe, is indeed an ideology.

Destroy Family and Sustain Ideology

Remember that all this is not 19th-century communist ideology, as professed by Marx and Engels. Alexandra Kollontai, a leading communist ideologue of the early 20th century, sought to provide some answers as to what the communists thought of the institution of family. According to Kollontai: "These questions are troubling many women of the working class and worrying their menfolk as well. Life is changing before our very eyes, old habits and customs are dying out, and the whole life of the proletarian family is developing in a way that is new and unfamiliar and, in the eyes of some, 'bizarre.' No wonder that working women are beginning to think these questions over." And the communist prescription to deal with the proletarian family? The answer is to purge the women of her family by first setting up crèches, while simultaneously demolishing the household kitchen. Kollontai begins with the sweeping declaration that the individual household is dying, without realising that the household is the first known institutional construct set up by man. This is followed by yet another sweeping assertion that women's work is becoming less useful to the community as a whole, as it is becoming unproductive. And the solution – collective housekeeping. That implies that instead of the working woman cleaning her house, the communist society can arrange for men and women whose job it is to go around in the morning cleaning rooms. In short, while the lady in the house will go to work, the communist society will arrange for someone to clean her house. Meanwhile, for all you know, the lady may be employed by the communist society to clean her neighbour's house. And that is communism for you – do not clean your house but clean your neighbour's. Meanwhile, your neighbour will clean yours. In the process, the communists could claim complete employment for their poor masses. No wonder with such 'scientific thinking and understanding' communism had such an abrupt downfall the world over.

Kollontai does not stop here with such outlandish prescriptions. More is yet to come. "Under communism", it is declared, "everyone will be able to eat in the communal kitchens and dining rooms. The working woman will not have to slave over the washtub any longer." But in their eagerness to pull the woman away from her family, the answer to the question on how the economics of the community kitchen will work was never answered. Of course, the very same women may be employed by the state to prepare food for the entire community. Fascinatingly, what was held unacceptable by the communists for the lady to do in her kitchen for her family was held perfectly acceptable for the lady to do for the entire commune. At this distant point in time and the death of communism, obviously, it looks hilarious if not downright foolish. But do we realise that this thought dominated the political discourse well and truly into the last decade of the 20th century? Several countries even to this day follow and practice some form of communism, even without realising they are doing so. That is the tragedy of our times.

The Chinese Communist Revolution also initiated certain structural reforms pertaining to women. In fact, the first official act passed by the new government under the Chinese Communist Party was the marriage reform law. The new law sought to address the most prominent issues faced by women by abolishing forced marriage, protecting women from feudal practices, as well as the equal right to seek divorce. While apparently, this idea seems 'progressive,' the fact remains that there was a deeper economic agenda of the communists – all these were carried out so that women can more easily enter the workforce. Mao believed that women had been a wasted reservoir of labour, and were to be co-opted in communes until China had the necessary mechanical means of production. In essence, the state-sponsored feminist movement had less to do with the women, but more to do with the grand economic development of communist China. As things did not pan out as was announced, and fearing backlash from its own people, the Chinese government abandoned the marriage reform law in 1953. Shorn of the jargons and the rhetoric, the fact remains that the communist party sought to over-ride traditional authority of the family with its own authority and destroy family so that commitment to the party exceeded all other ties. This too failed, and the communists were caught 'red-faced.'

Finally, Kollontai concludes: "But even if housework disappears, you may argue, there are still the children to look after. But here too, the workers' state will come to replace the family, society will gradually take upon itself all the tasks that before the revolution fell to the individual parents." Pray how? Since all these thoughts were quintessentially dialectical, Kollontai had a ready answer to this too. "Just as housework withers away, so the obligations of parents to their children wither away gradually until finally, society assumes the full responsibility. We already have homes for very small babies, crèches, kindergartens, children's colonies and homes, hospitals and health resorts for sick children. Restaurants, free lunches at school, and free distribution of textbooks, warm clothing, and shoes are given to school-children. All this goes to show that the responsibility for the child is passing from the family to the collective." But Kollontai never answered the most basic question – how will these programmes be funded and by whom? After all, what was being offered by communism was nothing but shifting the work of the women from the family to the communes. Did this idea put the women on a higher pedestal? How will an infant bereft of the emotional bonding with its mother survive? How will the economics of all these sustain itself in the long run? The answers to these questions never mattered to Kollontai. Neither it did to the several communists who lived and died by this rhetoric.

What is indeed worrying is the absolute similarity in the prescription of Kollontai in the early 20th century and those of Plato. Writing in his *Republic*, Plato commented "no one man and one woman are to set up house together privately, wives are to be held in common by all, so too are the children, and no parent is to know his own child, nor any child his parent."

Apparently, some of the core ideas contained within Plato's *Republic* had resurfaced under the guise of Communism. Though over 2,500 years separated them, the idea of abolishing the family by destroying the family kitchen and setting up community crèches continues. Importantly, the nationalisation of women seems to be an important recurring idea in the history of mankind that simply refuses to die. Women as a property who are capable of being nationalised is repugnant to the very idea of culture and civilisation, as much as it is to condemn women to the family kitchen or the commune kitchens. We shall specifically look into this issue in Chapter 10. Monogamy is antithetical to these ideas. It is based on equity and equality. It ensures certain natural (not artificial) rights of women are automatically protected. It preserves her dignity as much as it protects her self-esteem. No wonder communists hate monogamy and all those cultures and traditions that bind a man to a woman and a woman to a man.

Likewise, Leonid Sabsovich, the leading Soviet urban planner under Lenin and Stalin, in a series of influential writings published by the Kremlin in the late 1920s, argued for a total separation of children from parents starting in the earliest years of child development. Sabsovich denounced those who disagreed. Those who found his suggestion of full child-parent separation unnatural and unwelcome were termed as un-progressive cretins "soaked in petit bourgeois." Sabsovich insisted that because the child should be and was the property of the state, rather than the family, the state had the right to compel parents to turn over their offspring to specially designed 'children's towns' – read creches. These towns were to be built "at a distance from the family." Such extreme proposals by him were to be incorporated within his plans for creating the ideal 'socialist city.' Pertinently, the sinister idea of creches was obviously not only to separate the children from the family but to create a vast army of future citizens who would have no emotional bonding with others including their own parents. Such a 'designer citizenry,' bereft of filial loyalties was expected to owe its loyalty to the state and the communist ideology!

It is indeed strange that despite its chequered past, crèches always find favour with policy-framers even today. For example, the Ministry for Women and Child Welfare, Government of India, had introduced a crèche scheme for the children of working mothers. Named after former Prime Minister of India, Rajiv Gandhi, the scheme probably innocent of the history of the development of crèche and the sinister idea embedded within it, claims that the "past few decades have shown a rapid increase in nuclear families and breaking up of the joint family system. Thus, the children of these women, who were earlier getting support from relatives and friends while their mothers were at work, are now in need of day-care services which provide quality care and protection for children. Children who used to grow up in the secure and warm laps of their grandmothers and aunts are now confronted with an insecure and neglected environment. Therefore, women need a safe place for their children in their absence. It has become necessary to provide support to the young children in terms of quality, substitute care, and other services while the mothers are at work."

The solution? What else but crèches administered by the Government of India? Never mind its efficacy. Never question its origins or its consequences. The Ministry for Child welfare itself points out that "The Steering Committee on Women's Agency and Child Rights for the 12th Five-Year Plan (2012-17) under the aegis of the Planning Commission has, in its report, stated that the Rajiv Gandhi National Crèche Scheme (RGNCS) has so far fallen short of its target of providing quality day-care services for children." And the solution? A new improved crèche scheme. It is in this connection that the Ministry for Child welfare points out: "In the above background and based on the experience gained/feedback received from the implementation of the Rajiv Gandhi National Crèche scheme and recommendations of evaluation study conducted by National Institute of Public Co-operation and Child Development (NIPCCD), the present scheme has been revised for strengthening the existing programme components, and thus making the services more effective in achieving the envisaged objectives." This too will fail as most schemes sponsored by the government have failed. Sooner than later, because of the shoddy implementation, the revised scheme shall be revisited, rejigged, and rearranged. But the idea of state-run crèches is entirely different. It contains with it the toxic idea of destroying the family, of separating mother from her child and to create a designer citizenry. Does the Government of India realise it?

Inheritance Anathema to Leftists

Communists also seek to terminate all rights of inheritance. Both Marx and Engels saw inheritance as a menace that perpetuated the role of traditional family, and hence needed to be abolished. Of course, inheritance was about private property, which Marx and Engels detested. Let us not forget that abolition of private property is fundamental to the communist idea. The desire for property was in their view unacceptable also from their ideological standpoint. In Engels' view, private ownership of property was the drive that preserved the idea of monogamy. Men with property wanted heirs with a legitimate title, and for this, they also wanted legitimate heirs. Probably, in the calculation of both Marx and Engels, monogamy and family as an institution will cease to exist once properties are nationalised. With no right to property and no possibility of handing over an inheritance to their legitimate heirs, men it was suggested, will no longer care to identify their offspring. Or it may be the other way around – with no legitimate identifiable offspring, men may not care about properties getting nationalised. At the end of history, they opined, sex will again be unfettered. In the socialist future, Engels opined that "the single-family ceases to be the economic unit of society," which will result in "the gradual growth of unconstrained sexual intercourse." The central idea of this book is to oppose this thought and simultaneously seek to explore as to how to restore family as the basic economic unit of the society.

There is yet another aspect to this idea of abolishing private property. Family, and therefore inheritance, was perceived to be a stumbling block in their pursuit to create a classless society that guarantees equality of income. Private property was intrinsically linked to the idea of family. It is a communist imperative that families must be destroyed to nationalise property. Nationalisation of properties is crucial for classless society. For the communists, ideas such as private property, inheritance and classless society somehow seem to be ideologically intertwined with the idea of destruction of family, which, as explained earlier, is seen as a stumbling block. Whatever be the flaws of his theory, Engels was precise about the endgame: as socialism advances, family recedes. As the tasks of raising children and caring for the old begin to disappear, fewer and fewer reasons will remain for a man and a woman to form a lasting bond. This is precisely what is happening in America, as we saw in the previous chapter.

Interestingly, in the Indian context, the idea of communism somehow dominated the Indian political and economic thinking for the four decades beginning from 1950. In the process, unlike other Fundamental Rights, which were constantly expanded in sweep and scope both by the legislature and the judiciary, the Right to Property in the Indian Constitution was somehow subject to innumerable attacks, where its scope was continuously sought to be diminished by various amendments. Successive governments in India between 1950 and 1975 had brought in a series of constitutional amendments that had the calculated effect of diluting Article 31 (which dealt with the Right to Property) of its soul. Subsequently, in 1978, the then government eliminated the Right to Property altogether from the list of Fundamental Rights in Part III of the Constitution of India. Thus, an aggrieved person has no right to approach the Supreme Court under Part III of the Constitution, as right to property is no longer a fundamental right, though it is still a constitutional right. The net consequence of this amendment is that it empowered the state to appropriate property, provided it was for larger social welfare purposes. In other words, the amendment bestowed upon the Indian socialist state a licence to indulge what Fredric Bastait termed as 'legal plunder' and where the law has been amended to make plunder look legal, sacred, and conscionable.

Significantly, India adopted a new economic policy in 1991 by jettisoning the socialist ideas of the previous four decades. Since then, several political parties from the Left to the political Right have been in power at the Centre. Most have constantly disowned the socialist economic ideas that dominated the political and economic landscape for the four decades beginning 1950. Yet, not one government since 1991 has ever initiated a serious public debate seeking to restore the Right to Property as a Fundamental Right under Part III of the Constitution. It is time for future Indian governments to declare property as a fundamental right, comprehend the link between property and inheritance, while simultaneously looking into the association between inheritance and family, monogamy and culture.

The reason for the same is not far to seek. Contrary to the popular belief, the stranglehold of the Leftists even to this day on the Indian establishment is indeed stunning. Though they do not occupy political power, the Left in India is admittedly a dominant ideological force even to this day. Bureaucracy, judiciary, academia, media, intelligentsia, and of course political parties in India are invariably manned by persons who owe their allegiance to the Left and its ideology. And India is no exception to this institutional capture by the Left. Worldwide, it is a standard operating practice of the Left to control the establishment, which includes the following steps:

- The Left understands that colleges and schools are prime catchment areas. To do so, they seek control of the educational institutions and indoctrinate students at an early age. Then, they make rebels out of students, and encourage general indiscipline among them. They encourage students to question even morning prayers in educational institutions in the name of secularism. There is a consistent call for moderation of the curriculum in the name of benefitting poor students. In the process, they ensure that their ideology somehow worms its way into the textbooks.
- Ensure teachers are ideologically correct and owe allegiance to the Left thinking, who in turn promote students who are 'appropriately inclined.' This is to be followed up through the academic establishment that projects and promotes teachers who are ideologically compatible. The triad of teacher-taught-teachings are too important for furtherance of the Left ideology worldwide, more so in India.
- Continue discrediting all forms of traditional culture, including arts and science. Question all of history, select and accept only those which suits the Left narrative. Use mass media, especially popular arts like television serials and cinema, to question family as an institution. Show women as perennial rebels and dissenters – one with or without a cause, but never without a pause. Encourage those who present homosexuality, degeneracy, and promiscuity as normal and natural.
- Promote writers and thinkers through international awards (ably executed with international connections), followed by national recognition by domestic institutions. Eulogise them. Take their work

to be gospel, provided it questions civilisational moorings, culture, and family. Another standard plan is to recognise writers who challenge traditions, and then promote them. Once a writer is 'recognised,' the eco-system will automatically take care of him.

- Brand anyone questioning the Left as illiberal, dogmatic, or antediluvian. Control all sections of media and lampoon anyone who questions the Left. Troll ideological opponents to such an extent that they must break and give up. This is to ensure that no ideological opponents exist to question the Left and their ideology. And even where they exist, they must be thoroughly discredited.
- Seek to eliminate all laws governing obscenity by claiming it to be a 'challenge to freedom of expression.' Hold freedom of expression as sacrosanct if it suits the Left. Question the government when it bans access to pornographic and adult sites as an assault on individual rights, freedom, and choice. Seek continuation of all such laws by claiming to fight against "any form of censorship", and demonstrating allegiance to free speech and press. In the process, break down cultural standards of morality by promoting pornography and obscenity at every turn.
- Discredit the family as an institution. Portray every member of the family as selfish and promiscuous, especially women. Lower tolerance levels in mass media of husband and wife towards each other. Make them intolerant of the other and consistently emphasise on their rights (and never on their duties). Encourage divorce. Divorces are vital instruments in destruction of families, and every possible encouragement must be laid for both husband and wife to seek divorce at the drop of a hat. Constantly underline the need to raise children away from the influence of parents. Portray parents as suppressive and outdated.
- Make divorce proceedings complex and costly, so that men and women shudder at the very thought of marriage. Once divorce becomes traumatic, encourage live-in relationship where men and women live together in the very same house but without formally getting married. That would imply no abiding loyalty of one partner to the other, which in turn would 'normalise' adultery over the times. As both men and

women are encouraged to be promiscuous, they would be applauded and hailed for being 'liberal.'

- Advocate solutions through the state and its coercive machinery for every issue confronting the family or society. If anyone questions this idea where the solution at times may be far worse than the problem, term them as 'anarchist' or 'regressive.'

Naturally, given this hostile environment, governments do not get the necessary political traction to deal with such vexatious subjects like culture and family, much less on inheritance. In the face of such heavy headwinds, most governments buckle. Inheritance of property is merely a case in point. In fact, to address these convoluted issues, India requires a complete re-calibration of her political, legal, and economic arrangement. But that is easier said than done, for the stranglehold of the Leftists on the Indian establishment is simply astounding. Nevertheless, till the time it is done, Marx and Engels would be laughing in their respective graves as to how their thoughts continue to dominate the Indian political and economic discourse even to this day. The restoration of right to property as a fundamental right is a test by fire for current and future Indian governments. The earlier it is done, the better.

As more and more population depended on the state, the more it justified its existence, its policies and programmes. It then becomes a self-fulling prophecy. The idea that people can provide things for themselves either individually or through the family is unacceptable to the Marxists and socialists, as it delegitimises the very existence of state. A movement away from the welfare state is a well-defined movement towards better family values and greater family cohesiveness. But that is unacceptable to the Marxists, liberals, and socialists. Put bluntly, the extinction of the family in effect rationalises the existence of the state.

But champions of Free Markets Fare no Better

For long, the idea of free markets has been held to be an alternative to the socio-economic-cultural thoughts as put forward by Marx. Strange as it may seem, if you thought Marxists were the only villain of the piece in seeking destruction of the family, let us hasten to add that the champions of free markets despite their outward differences with Marxist thoughts are no less hostile to the very idea of family. The destruction of families is as much the primary unstated objective for the champions of libertarian values as it is for Marxists, with the sole exception that the former is too sophisticated about it, while the latter, as is their wont, are crass. While the Marxists seek annihilation of the family to let the proliferation of the state and its coercive agencies, the champions of libertarian values seek to place the individual and individual alone at the centre of all their arguments. In the process, to let the family to be damned seems to be the ulterior motive. Under Marxism, if destruction of the family was a prerequisite for the state to prosper, under the idea of free markets, destruction of the family was an inevitable prelude to its success. The distinction, if at all there was one, was between prerequisite and prelude.

Markets, let us not forget, operate multi-dimensionally and at multiple levels. It is a complex term. As market economics by itself is a vast subject which provides a mere context to the current text, we shall limit the study to merely two aspects – global and the local in that order. The idea of globalising markets, rooted as it were to the economic principles of free markets and libertarian values, were marketed by its champions with a missionary zeal beginning in the early 1970s, more specifically after the implosion of Soviet Russia in 1990. Free markets (and its political twin, democracy) were seen by many scholars as the sole, surviving, successful, and the only alternative to the idea of Marxism, Communism, and totalitarian regimes. Little did we realise at that point in time that the implosion of Soviet Russia by itself was a powerful, yet an inconclusive argument in favour of these ideas, especially free markets. Remarkably, the history of the 20th century has witnessed a partnership between Marxist ideas of managing the economy, and the Communist ideas of a totalitarian state. More to the point, the correlation between the Communist totalitarian state and Marxian ideas in managing the economy was near perfect in several countries. Marxism and totalitarian regimes went hand in hand for a greater part of the 20th century as much as free markets and democracy. Naturally, when one collapsed in the weight of its own internal contradictions within a country, the other limb, too faced an existential crisis. As the clash of these two contrarian ideas in economics and politics – popularly termed as the Cold War – dominated every single decade of the 20th century, the collapse of Soviet Russia signalled the "ultimate triumph of democracy and free markets." But was it a fact? Francis Fukuyama, the acclaimed American political philosopher, captured the global imagination precisely at the end of the Cold War when he prophesied the *End of History* – a belief that, after the fall of communism, free-market liberal democracy would win inevitably become the world's 'final form of human government.' His argument was too simple: Democracy would eventually win out over all other forms of government because the natural desire for peace and well-being set nations on a path to progress, from which it was impossible to divert. If a state – even if it were a Communist state – wished to enjoy greater prosperity, it would have to embrace some measure of democracy and capitalism. Since wealth creation depends on the protection of private property, 'creeping capitalism' would invariably demand greater legal protection for individual rights, and hence usher in democracy and with it, probably rule of law.

Now, at this moment when liberal democracy seems to be at a crossroads, Fukuyama, too, wonders about its future. "Twenty-five years ago, I didn't have a sense or a theory about how democracies can go backward," Fukuyama was quoted by the *Washington Post* in 2016. Nevertheless, his facile argument of the *End of History* probably created the framework for an international order for the past two decades. Globalisation, it was suggested, was the vehicle by which liberalism would spread across the globe. Liberalism would, in turn, lead to explosion of markets. The rule of law and institutions would create a new world order run on the twin engines of democracy and free markets with international bodies providing the necessary oversight in ensuring durable peace. The very same Fukuyama now recognises the extent of global crisis merely two decades after he foresaw the *End of History*. In the interregnum, something somewhere has gone horribly wrong. "Globalisation really does seem to produce these internal tensions within democracies that these institutions have some trouble reconciling," he confessed. Combined with grievances over immigration and multi-culturalism, it created room for the 'demagogic populism' that has Fukuyama deeply concerned.

Where did Fukuyama go wrong? The fault probably was at the outset – the idea that free market and democracy triumphed for eternity was probably a fallacious assumption. But weren't Marxists and Hitler equally guilty of such a sweeping assumption just a few decades ago, and as subsequent events turned out, were comprehensively wrong even in their assessment of contemporary events? Was Fukuyama as guilty as Hitler, Stalin, Mao, and Marx in their assessment of the future based on current events? As Mao's China is experimenting with market economics administered through a totalitarian regime with some degree of success – an idea that has probably never been attempted on such a grand scale and sweep anywhere in the history of mankind – 'Marxist Capitalism' is fast emerging as a fault line (or a viable socio-political-economic idea, depending on your political inclination) in the emerging global order. If the prediction of Fukuyama were indeed correct, the success of market economics in China must have accelerated its march towards democracy. Unfortunately, it has not. Neither is the seeming success of market economics enough to prevent the continued rise of the ISIS – which is probably aiming for an Islamic caliphate, and surely not for a democracy within the Islamic world.

That implies that the fundamental assumption of Fukuyama – that democracy is an inseparable twin of free markets, and both thrive on ubiquitous libertarian values has come under greater challenge in the first two decades of the 21st century. Events since the implosion of Soviet Russia has demonstrated that economic prosperity is not merely an outcome of free markets or democracy. In fact, in some societies, given their state of existence, free markets and democracy may not figure for some inexplicable reason in the aspirational chart. Crucially, even in countries that embraced free markets and democracy, questions are increasingly raised about the efficacy of these systems in delivering larger goods for a greater number of people. As Thomas Piketty argues in his seminal work *Capital in the Twenty-First Century*, free markets have not only enlarged the gap between rich and poor, but have also reduced average incomes across the developed and developing worlds. We will deal with the issue of inequality subsequently. It is in this connection, Timothy Stanley and Alexander Lee note in their column with great concern "Across Europe, economic interventionism, nationalism, and even open racism have exerted a greater attraction for those casting their democratic votes than the causes of freedom, deregulation, and equality before the law." The net result they conclude: Liberal capitalist democracy has not triumphed. Instead, the failures of capitalism have turned democracy against liberalism. In turn, liberalism's intellectual self-identity has been left in tatters.

Understanding Globalisation

But what about globalisation? It may be recalled that globalisation was essentially an idea to establish a global order. To understand what has been stated here, it is necessary that we understand the fallout called globalisation – the mother of all economic and political ideas in the 20th century. Technically, globalisation is defined as a socio-economic process of interaction and integration among the people, corporates, and governments of different nations, a continuous process driven by international trade, investment, and aided by information technology. This process has effects on the environment, on culture, on political systems, on economic development, prosperity, and on human physical well-being in societies around the world. The idea that drives this concept of globalisation is not an innocent one. In fact, there have been several waves of globalisation – read homogenisation of the world – attempted in the history of mankind. And at least, there are three prominent attempts since the beginning of the common era. The first attempt to globalise was in the first millennium after Christ through religious intervention, with the army and commerce playing a distant secondary role. The second attempt, in the second millennium, was through the army, with religion and commerce playing a supplementary yet purposeful role. The third wave of globalisation, coinciding with the end of the last millennium and the beginning of the third, has been through commerce, which has emerged as the chief driver of modern-day globalisation. In this third wave, both the army and the religion have played an influential complementary role. Critically, the thin dividing lines between the three are increasingly getting blurred in this wave of globalisation. Distinguishing this current wave of globalisation from earlier ones, author Thomas Friedman has opined that "today, globalisation is farther, faster, cheaper, and deeper."

Whatever be it, the current wave of globalisation has been driven ceaselessly by policies that have prised open domestic economies to international trade and commerce. During the past two decades or so, many governments adopted free-market economic systems – some compelled by the diktats of multilateral lending agencies, and some by force of circumstances, but mostly the former. This, in turn, obligated governments to reduce barriers to trade, both in goods and services, as well as allow foreign investments. This opening of economies in effect benefited multi-national corporations, but at a tremendous cost to local enterprises, cultures, and common people – all of which, in turn, negatively impacted the institution of families in these countries. This has also given rise to a deeper concern – that globalisation has a tremendous impact on the collective psyche of the people where people's life and livelihood have become tradeable commodities. Even if we assume for a moment that globalisation has made economies more efficient, the questions remain: are the economic gains worth the cultural cost? Is globalisation resulting in destruction of family values? Is it leading to the triumph of individualism over community? And to greed instead of sharing? Materialism rather than relationships or spiritual values?

The answers to these questions cannot be answered in binaries and requires deeper examination. But that is not all. Even in the case of commerce-led modern-day globalisation – the global economy is being increasingly confronted by an enormous challenge by what is innocently termed as 'global imbalance.' And this requires no great seer to either explain or understand the issue on hand. In fact, this imbalance is a direct consequence of a mere two decades of interplay between the profligate and the prudent, between savers and spenders, between interest rates and the index, between exporters and importers, between the reckless and the cautious, and between countries that have a strong currency and those who have a weak currency. How does this impact families and destroy their culture? Let us examine in greater detail the very idea of globalisation.

The experience of the past few decades or so point out to the fact that there is a distinct dichotomy in the approach to economics by Asian countries on the one hand, and the Anglo-Saxon world led by the US on the other. But what makes economics in Anglo-Saxon world to work, behave, or react in contrast to their Asian counterparts is something that is far beyond the radar of any meaningful debate even at the global level. The fundamental distinction between these economies are the diminishing family values of the Anglo-Saxon world. Naturally, this has turned everyone in these Anglo-Saxon countries into reckless consumers. It is the breakdown of the institution of family that has atomised the individual, leading to this consumption binge that is having a profound impact on both the national as well as global economics.

Let us put the entire issue in the present context. The whole of Asia exports goods and services to the West, notably the US. But being family-based economies and conservative societies, the Asian nations are unable to absorb their export surplus (read savings). The net result: they park their export surplus into those very countries that import from them in the first place. In effect, they finance the West to import from these very Asian countries that produce them in the first place. This one-way export of both savings as well as goods remains at the core of the imbalance in the present wave of globalisation. In the process, it is capital from the 'poor developing Asian countries' that is flowing uphill into the developed, rich West. The reason for this uphill movement of capital is not far to seek. Asian countries being rooted in traditional family values have been parsimonious in their consumption, and hence enjoy a far higher rate of savings which fuels their domestic investment. In this third wave of globalisation, this correlation between family and economics is fast emerging as the latest frontier of economics. Importantly, economists may now well understand that while Asian countries may not be engines of global growth caused by reckless consumption, they are surely not the cause of global instability either. At best, they can be guilty of producing more, saving more, investing more and exporting more, and yet many of them are termed as 'poor developing countries.'

Surely, economics has been turned on its head, when it is the poor who lend and the rich borrow. Nevertheless, it was this mindless consumption by the West that acted as an engine of global growth, including for several Asian countries for the past several years. In the process, it ushered in a great amount of prosperity at the macro-level, never mind the consequent imbalance associated with it. Yet, not many have analysed the intrinsic instability of this model. As Western countries imported, Asian countries exported. As the latter piled their export surplus, they needed to park the same. Once again, the West came to the 'rescue' of the Asian countries as they borrowed this excess, lying in the hand of the Asian countries. How long will this continue – where the Asian countries ceaselessly produce and continuously export for some of the Western countries to import and consume, for the Asian countries to lend their export surplus and for the Western counterparts to borrow? What if the Asian countries suddenly turn around and request the West to return their borrowed monies? Well, that would be accelerated economic apocalypse. The lenders know that it would be perilous to demand back the money, just as the borrowers know that it would be impossible to return the sums borrowed. That is globalisation for you.

The Withering of Discipline in Economics

The net result of a mere two decades of globalisation has ensured that the US is the world's most indebted country. This is not a mere accounting problem or a transient trade policy issue, as it seems to most economists. The core issue that seems to be missed in the melee is that blatantly, the developing world has transferred its hard-earned wealth to the developed world without the latter firing a bullet when such wealth could probably be put to better use by the very same developing countries. These billions of dollars held by developing countries as foreign exchange reserves are lent in the global markets which ultimately find its way to the developed world. That explains why the US is highly indebted. To be fair, it has been taking the responsibility of absorbing the excess savings of the modern world by its reckless and gargantuan consumption. The collapse of the institution of family and the concomitant increased consumption within the US has been the recurrent theme of this book. The correlation between the two – which we have dealt in the previous chapter of this book, and will continue to explore in the subsequent chapters – is far too obvious to be missed by any.

Importantly, we are facing the unthinkable prospect of the US defaulting on its debt obligations. Naturally, this prospect raises fundamental questions.

How could the world's sole superpower run the risk of defaulting on its debt obligations? Crucially what happened to the economic theories developed by Nobel laureates no less and marketed with missionary zeal by various multilateral institutions led by the US Treasury? Or does the malaise run far deeper? Honestly, the issue is not as simple as it seems on first blush. It is not a purely a legal issue as the political fraternity in the US would like us to believe. Nor is it merely political or ideological. And definitely, it is not simple economics as most believe and would like us to believe. It is legal, political, economic, and possibly much more.

To appreciate what is stated above, it is important to visit the root assumptions that govern modern economics in the three-decade period beginning in the mid-1980s. In fact, this is a subject of great debate among macro-economists in recent times. According to one economist from Harvard, the past 30 years of macroeconomics training at American and British universities were a "costly waste of time." Yes, a costly waste of time! *The Economist* put the entire issue in proper perspective in 2009 when it stated that "The macro-economic crisis of the past two years is also provoking a crisis of confidence in macroeconomics." The article goes on to add, "These internal critics argue that economists missed the origins of the crisis, failed to appreciate its worst symptoms, and cannot now agree about the cure. In other words, economists misread the economy on the way up, misread it on the way down, and now mistake the right way out." We will deal with the issue of the degeneration of economics as a discipline in Chapter 8.

At the core of the present conundrum in global economics are certain fundamental theories of macroeconomics – much of which was debated, celebrated, and even imposed on others – without even considering the possibility that such ideas could be plainly wrong or unworkable in entirely different circumstances, countries, or cultures. Call it confidence or blame it on arrogance. Call it economic fundamentalism or blame it on some conspiracy. The fact remains that most of the macro-economic theories of the past three decades ensured cannibalisation of alternative ideas in the discipline of macro-economics, so much so that since the 1990s, the economics of the Democrats in the US was virtually undistinguishable from the 'free market economic thought' of the Republicans. In the process, any contrary economic ideas were put down ruthlessly all over the world. It all began in the early eighties with the advent of Ronald Regan as the President of the US that spawned a new brand of economics – Reagonomics – which placed supply at the centre of economics. And to effectuate this idea, tax cuts were proposed so that an individual could have more money in his hands, and tariff cuts were carried out, which allowed global access to goods at competitive rates. Finally, interest rates were significantly lowered to provide the last mile connectivity.

All this is good economics, except for the fact that this was overdone. And that can be simply explained. We need to produce to keep the wheels of economics moving. Out of the production that is generated, we need to consume a portion and leave the balance as savings. Savings are vital for investment. And investment must result in production. All this was turned on its head during the past thirty years or so by mainstream economists. Consumption was by design turned into a virtue. Economic theories are created using consumption as the leveraging force in all economic theories. In the process, explained through models, economics became extremely complex, complicated and jargonised.

Simultaneously, in a remarkable coincidence, the advent of Reaganomics timed well with the rise of East Asia. Several East Asian countries had over the 80s and 90s, thanks to their economic policies, became huge suppliers of cheap yet quality goods to the global – read the US markets. Further, in the aftermath of the Asian currency crisis of the late 1990s, many Asian countries discovered the virtues of a weak currency and engaged in 'competitive devaluation.' Under this scenario, many countries simply leveraged their weak currency vis-a-vis the US dollar to gain access to global markets. While Asian countries continue to export, the US continues to import. Obviously, the current account deficit of the US becomes the corresponding current account surplus of other exporting countries, viz. China, Japan, as well as other oil producing and exporting countries. Naturally, this arrangement – where some countries continue to export and a few who continuously import and consume – has created serious imbalances within the global economy. Has the third wave of globalisation achieved what it sought to, viz., transfer of wealth from the Asian countries to the West without firing a single bullet? A question that will probably never be answered.

Commenting on this paradigm, the then Reserve Bank of India Governor D Subbarao stated in a lecture in New Delhi on July 31, 2009: "Global macro imbalances got built up because of the large savings and current account surpluses in China and much of Asia in the wake of the East Asian crisis a decade ago. These were mirrored by large increases in leveraged consumption and current account deficits in the US." In short, "Asia produced, and America consumed. Despite a raging debate on what was the cause, and what the effect – the US consumption boom or the Asian savings glut? – Subbarao posed a fundamental question. "Regardless, the bottom line is that one was simply the mirror of the other, and the two share a symbiotic relationship," he concluded. The key words here are 'symbiotic relationship.' It is to be noted that this symbiotic relationship also goes by the sexed-up appellation of globalisation – a mechanism that translates national imbalances into global imbalances; national crisis into global ones. It is therefore a matter of time that the US debt crisis spirals into a global one. Sensing that this macro-economic model has run its full course, the Chinese in their approach to the 12th Five-Year Plan (2012-17) had sought to rebalance their economy by increasing domestic consumption and simultaneously placing less reliance on exports. In short, they seem to distance themselves from what are the main causes for their seemingly spectacular economic growth over the past three decades.

In this scenario, economists have now sought to blame Alan Greenspan, the former Federal Reserve chairman, for the extant global economic imbalance. According to many, the 'irrational exuberance' exhibited by the US financial markets during the period leading to the 2008 financial crisis was an outcome of a lax monetary policy and extremely low interest rates. Greenspan, in turn, seeks to defend himself. In a paper, titled *The Crisis*, and presented in April 2010, Greenspan states: "A large segment of the erstwhile Third World nations, especially China, replicated the successful economic export-oriented model of the so-called Asian Tigers: fairly well-educated, low-cost workforces joined with developed-world technology, protected by an increasing rule of law, unleashed explosive economic growth." Further, Greenspan says, "In the developing world, consumption restrained by culture and inadequate consumer finance could not keep up with the surge of income and, as a consequence, the savings rate of the developing world soared from 24% of nominal GDP in 1999 to 34% by 2007, far outstripping its investment rate." But the moot point is, if the culture in developing countries is the cause of excessive savings, as Greenspan argues, then should not culture (or the lack of it) be the cause of excessive consumption in the West too? Inexplicably, Greenspan remained silent on this issue.

While excesses in consumption is creating its own imbalances in the West, the Asian countries too are facing certain imbalances. In fact, the Chinese are equally facing significant difficulties in rebalancing their economy. Used as they are to excessive savings; it is as difficult to make the Chinese spend more as much as it is difficult to get a thrifty American. Now, the world of macro-economists would see for itself that excessive spending is as much a challenge as excessive savings. Macro-economists who had marketed economic theories as models, and models as gospel, are loathe to realise this fundamental truth. Naturally, they stand discredited, even in their own eyes. The global imbalance is merely an extension of the crisis of modern economics – a discipline that seems to have lost respect for discipline. Certainly, the US will shortly face the music because of its excessive debt. So, will those countries that saved excessively and blindly lent to the US. The world is divided even to this day over the role of Greenspan in triggering the economic crisis of 2008. Nevertheless, he needs to be congratulated, at least for one issue: he has linked economics to culture for the first time in 30 years. And that is crucial.

This present conundrum was succinctly put forth by my teacher who brilliantly explained the extant economic model as hereunder:

- Atomised individuals
- This led to the collapse of the institution of families
- Result is reckless individualism
- Finally, leading to nationalisation of families.
- This, in turn, had the following inevitable consequences:
- A pauperised state is unable to carry on the responsibility of the family

- This, in turn, leads to privatisation of the functions of government
- Naturally, that demanded a corporatised economy; and
- Finally, that necessitated a globalised market for the survival of these corporates.

This is economic globalisation in brief. In the process, the markets mechanism as conceived initially by Adam Smith was suspended, and the invisible hand as conceived by him, chopped. And when corporates too failed as it has happened recently with unfailing regularity, one wonders what is next. Yet, those who swear by globalisation failed to demonstrate as to how a model that is created by the West for itself – and that becomes dysfunctional even in the West – can claim it to be a success elsewhere. At best, it can be a grand experiment of the West. It may be noted that the internal imbalance within the US economy, thanks to the atomisation of individuals as explained above, has led to the fall in family values that led to gargantuan internal deficits within the US. And to fund this deficit in the US, the world has been sucked into a vortex called globalisation. Experts are slowly veering to a view that it is the internal imbalance within the US that remains at the root of this global imbalance. We need to have a quick rethink on the issues concerning globalisation. Obviously, the intent of globalisation - to homogenise and standardise the world through commerce and finance – probably with an unstated view to dominate others is surely facing troubled times. Apparently, the recent slide of the West, notably the US, calls for greater introspection. Communism with all its internal contradictions and monstrous manifestation was bound to fail. Reckless capitalism too is taking the Titanic route.

Is there a third way? Is there an alternative to this destructive model of mindless Communism and reckless Capitalism? Or were all these an aberration with an economic model rooted in family values the only way to sustain the economy? Economists, unmindful of all these, even to this date assume that most economic crises are technical issues caused by a lax regulatory mechanism caused either by excessive demand, supply, investment or supply. They are sadly and comprehensively mistaken, for economics is not a simple subject of analysing demand and supply and the resultant equilibrium. It is often a collective psyche of a billion minds at work, each one incentivised by innumerable variables – all of which make the study of economics fascinating. The West has failed to diagnose the cause of volatility in modern economies, and continues to treat symptomatically rather than diagnostically. Yet, it is this symptomatic treatment of the economic malady that has indeed become the economic standard for economists in the rest of the world. Hence, economists continue to prescribe superficial financial remedies to a rather comprehensive socio-economic-cultural malady. In fact, to fix the economics of the world, one needs to fix this disorder. The fact of the matter is that all these issues are interlinked and interdependent. Unless all of these are recognised, rectified, and reversed, the global economic crisis will continue to haunt national economies. Importantly, corrosive economic thoughts will continue to dominate sombre economic policies. We need to address these challenges afresh, as ideas that surround globalisation have been found to be unworkable.

Markets misfire at the national level too

If market economics has spawned serious discontents at the global level, destabilised its classical twin 'democracy,' and devalued libertarian ideals, it has fared inadequately when it came to national economics too. At the root of the present consternation in the era of individualism is the excessive obsession about individual autonomy, that has reduced every single individual into a rootless wonder although it must be conceded that globalisation brings about a sense of being part of a larger world, while simultaneously providing wider and greater access to goods and services. However, it brings along certain downsides on society, community, and particularly the family. Forced opening of domestic markets, especially in less developed countries, often on the advice or suggestions of multilateral agencies and through economists of great repute, has devastated local industries as multi-national corporations have replaced indigenous businesses. Even as goods flooded the markets and economists saw the virtue in de-regulations and greater integration of markets across nations, people lost their jobs and saw their personal economic fortunes slip dramatically during globalisation. These changes are adversely affecting individuals and families, even as there is a widening gap between the rich and the poor.

As poverty engulfs societies, individuals are forced to distance away from their traditions and culture in search of jobs. Individuals migrate, often in the process abandoning their culture and traditions, in search of greener pastures. Naturally, tradition and culture are often the first casualty of biting poverty. Therefore, uprooted from their traditional homes, many suffer from an identity crisis. Economies, that were vibrant till recently, have been destroyed by people who have seized the opportunity to finish the business that was being carried on for long. In the alternative, the manner in which the business was carried out was significantly altered. The twin attack on individual identity and on his traditional business has been far too brutal. In the absence of any meaningful study, it is presumed that all is indeed well and damages if any are at best collateral.

If large multinational corporates entering local markets, competing with local players, and destroying jobs is one aspect of the problem, robbing people of their hard-earned savings systematically by mis-pricing domestic interest rates is another aspect of the entire problem. Lower interest rates, classical economists explain, boost current consumption, while also shifting savings from bank deposits into stock markets. On both counts, the biggest beneficiaries of such policies are large multinational corporates. Artificially lowering the interest rate is nothing but mis-pricing of capital. This allows flab by way of excess capacity to accumulate within the economy. Factories are set up anticipating higher future demand at lower interest rates. But even a partial upward adjustment of interest rates as witnessed in the past few years has dynamited this assiduously built plan.

Alan Greenspan goes on to explain how he, as chairman of the US Federal Reserve, cut interest rates in dealing with various economic crises and instantly triggered growth. In a way, he could afford to do so as Americans do not have much savings (barring the mandatory ones). And such savings were predominantly linked to the stock market. That explains why rate cuts suited most Americans, and how the US economy responded positively to such rate cuts in the first place. Crucially, as explained in the earlier part of this chapter, Americans depend on the savings of the rest of the world even for their domestic needs. In effect, a depression of interest rates, albeit artificially, benefits the US, as it is the single larger borrower at a global level, and of course, at a concomitant cost to the rest of the world. Put differently, the poor of the developing world not only fund the richest country of the world (the US) but also subsidise such funding. Paradoxical, isn't it? And it is this internal contradiction in national economics that is increasingly widening the fault lines at a global level.

The events unfolding in decade between 2005 and 2015 in a developing country like India is a classic case in point. In a country where there are millions of depositors who deposit billions of rupees each year into the bank as deposits, the standard practice in the past decade or so has been to shift the debate in favour of lower interest rates for the borrower. In the process, little do we realise we are hurting small savers to favour the popular narrative of economists from the West, stock market sentiments, and multi-national corporates. In India, in the absence of a social security mechanism (and good governance), bank savings have emerged as a viable – and will continue in the foreseeable future – an effective social security mechanism. Savings, in the Indian context, are an insurance against a rainy day – old-age pension, health care, education for children, and a host of other things, all rolled into one. Needless to emphasise, savings in banks are held by most as being liquid and reliable. This is one crucial differential – that interest in India also doubles as a social security that most analysts miss when it comes to dealing with rate cuts in India. Consequently, lower interest rates rob ordinary Indians of his returns, makes him unsure, and consequentially nervous about his future. That makes the prudent Indian probably become irrational all under the idea of the most rational of economic policies – market economics. And when large number of men become irrational, it becomes extremely dangerous for any nation and its economy.

Naturally, when inflation overtakes interest rates as it often does in India, the average Indian responds by improving his aggregate savings. This has unintended consequences that most economists are unable to comprehend. Lower interest rates in an emerging economy like India, lowers consumption, and does not increase it as they theoretically imagine.

Worse, Indians shift their savings from banks to avenues that offer better and probably safer returns. In the Indian context, that happens to be gold. This, in turn, leads to imports of gold and surge in currency account deficit. Whenever savings get parked in unproductive assets, as it happens repeatedly in the case of gold, it dynamites the macro-economic balance in India. What is a perfect investment avenue for the individual probably ends up as a cumulative disaster at the national level. Crucially, the Indian rupee takes a hit, as continuous current account deficit leads to depreciation of the rupee. This, by itself, leads to the inflation of gold purchased, and becomes what is technically called a self-fulfilling prophecy. Importantly, a weaker rupee leads to higher fuel costs (approximately 80 percent of the Indian crude requirement is imported). Higher fuel cost in turn leads to higher inflation. This again has a debilitating impact on the economies.

Interestingly, most believe that lower interest rates will instantly revive growth in all economies. But the fact remains, mis-pricing interest rates by artificially lowering interest rates in the context of developed countries has a debilitating impact on the national economy. Indian experience demonstrates that lower interest rates are no guarantee for sustained economic growth, and probably could lead to asset bubbles. On the other hand, lower interest rates are generally perceived to favour the corporates at the cost of the individual. The idea of a soft interest rate regime lends itself to some perception that all that matters in the balance sheet of the corporates, rather than the balance sheet of the nation. Naturally, artificial lowering of interest rates is seen as an assault on families to benefit corporates and business houses. This transfer of wealth from the hands of the families to the corporates under a toxic economic regime is at the centre of the modern economic conundrum. In the process, economic policies seem to have divorced families, their desires, anxiety, and fear. That explains partly, if not wholly, why there is an opposition to market economics from those who feel that their culture is under some sort of threat.

Modern Economics and its fixation to Consumption

'Shop till you drop.' This was the clarion call of President Bush in the aftermath of the tragic events of September 11, 2001. It was a terrorist attack of unprecedented scale. The global war (remember whenever a tragedy strikes the US, it is always global) on terror had just begun. For a citizen of India (who has been a victim of terror for over 1,300 years), this appeared not only comical and farcical, but also tragic. But that is less relevant to the extant discussions. The issue is why did the President of the US in the aftermath of a gruesome attack suggest that every American should shop till he dropped dead. "Get down to Disney World in Florida," he urged just over two weeks after 9/11. "Take your families and enjoy life, the way we want it to be enjoyed." The suggestion that a large section of the population should "go to Disney World" while the US administration was fighting terror was downright funny. More to the point – even as families of those who were killed in this terror attack were in a state of mourning, the President of the US wanted the rest to behave as if nothing happened.

And this is not an isolated event. Half-way around the globe, the city of Mumbai has been a victim of repeated terror attacks. Thousands of its citizens were either killed or maimed in those dastardly attacks. Yet what matters the very next day was whether the Bombay Stock Exchange index went up or fell as a consequence to those attacks. What mattered was whether the suburban trains in Mumbai – the lifeline of Mumbai – had begun to function. The functioning of this public transport is vital for the functioning of the city. And when it did begin to function, the common refrain was "look at the resilience of the city." Media would repeatedly whip up passion of a Mumbai that had ignored the terrorists, and how it had returned to normalcy even as the number of dead in every such attack would increase by the hour. All this was hailed as conclusive evidence of how the city of Mumbai had thumbed at the nose of the terrorists. This is Mumbai's equivalent to the profound stupidity of President Bush's call for 'shop till you drop' post the terror attacks in September 2001. On first blush, there is nothing to link between the call of President Bush and the narrative built around 'Mumbai's resilience' after every successive terror attack. But on deeper analysis, there is an umbilical cord that links the two. Why should it be business as usual after such serious terror attacks? Who scripts such profanities? Who orchestrates such a line of thinking? How does the media respond in unison to such ideas? Who controls the collective thinking of every media? Why are the intellectuals silent and fall for the bait?

The answer to these questions is easy – it is the corporates that seek to declare that it is business as usual. It is in the interest of corporates to ensure that terror should not paralyse their businesses. More specifically, corporates seem to believe that they must remain irrelevantly neutral in the war on terror. To them, all that matters is money and markets. Life must go on. Isn't it? As advertisements and sponsorships flow from corporates, media is compelled to toe their line of thought. President Bush could not have suggested anything else. His corporate sponsors would not have allowed him otherwise either. In the era of globalisation, where corporates dominate markets and market economics, let us face a simple fact: President Bush never had a choice. Neither does the global media have any after a terror attack. Having prised open markets through the idea of globalisation, having built factories with huge capacities, large multinational corporates now know that they need to push their goods at a feverish pace. That puts them in direct conflict with families and their culture. For consumerism to flourish, families need to resort to borrow, sometimes way beyond their means to buy. But that is merely an issue of facilitation – sorted mostly by the exponential growth of credit cards. But what if families refuse to get sucked into the vortex of consumerism? What if families practise restraint – the quintessence of culture? What if families believe in the need to live within their means and do not wish to be co-opted into what they consider a mad race? The answer is plain and simple – destroy families to let corporates profit.

It is precisely for this reason that multinational corporates and modern economic thinkers consider family as a stumbling block to economic nirvana. Modern market economics does enable people to indulge in a lifestyle marked by the illusion of radical individual autonomy and a slave to all personal passion. Nothing else matters. Nothing else should. In *Born to Buy*, Professor Juliet Schor details the marketing and advertising techniques that bypasses parents, and points out to corporate attempts in trying to market their products directly to children as young as three and four years old. Companies spend millions in marketing research and advertising to every age category, beginning from, believe it or not, toddlers. Benjamin Barber, in his book *Consumed*, discusses the troubling trend of individuals defining themselves by the brands they use. Brands, he argues, have frighteningly replaced families, religion, and communities as a source of identity. He writes, "The boundary separating the person from what she buys starts to vanish, and she starts to become the products she buys." These are serious problems. As several commentators including William Leach in *Land of Desire* have noted, America has seen a cultural shift from productive capitalism, with a focus on savings and investment to a consumerist society where Americans consume on borrowed money. The reasons, according to Leach, are a complex interaction of cultural shifts, education, increased individualism, and centralisation, much of it driven by modern economic policies which have encouraged consumerism and borrowing. Little do we realise that consumerism is a toxic malady that will undermine a free society. Wilhelm Röpke – the Swiss economist who was instrumental in rebuilding Germany after World War II, and an ardent free marketer – once asked if there was "any more certain way of desiccating the soul of man than the habit of constantly thinking about money and what it can buy? Is there a more potent poison than our economic system's all-pervasive commercialism?"

A market economy with an abundance of goods is well and truly welcome. This idea of market economics is distinct from consumer-driven economics where the idea is incessant supply will create its own repeated demand. Naturally, in this toxic scenario, economic policies alone cannot put fetters on anyone to limit consumption. Like the ecosystem of the Left, liberals too hunt in packs. Any contrarian viewpoint is put down with ruthless force. Consumerism is ultimately a 'spiritual quotient deficiency syndrome' that cannot be remedied by mere economic policies alone. We need to realise that it is family and family alone with its ability to restrain individuals from reckless consumption and ensure balance in economy and society. It is thus the destruction of family that has emerged to be the meeting point of Liberals and Marxists.

Nothing illustrates the meeting point between the Liberals and the Left, other than the idea of taxing inherited wealth. Recall the discussion on the issue of inheritance earlier in this chapter, and how the Left is traditionally against it? Interestingly, one of the issues that unite the Liberals and the Left is the idea of taxing inheritance. The rationale for the Liberals is that such a tax incentivises the wealthy to live lavishly during retirement years. The broader calculation is that such spending aids current consumption, so there is little left at their death for the government to tax. Dying broke surely beats the taxman, but is terrible for the next generation, who instead of building the inherited business have actually to begin from the scratch.

Free market economists realise that having unleashed the genie of consumerism; they must necessarily allow the institution of family to wither. As families wither, consumerism flourishes. These economists also realise that even as it seeks to maximise profits in the short run, they increasingly have made their economic model unsustainable in the medium and long term. There is an increasingly, albeit belated, realisation within the pantheon of economists that there is indeed a missing quotient in their entire theory. And that is restraint. Restraint in turn flows from families rooted to culture and civilisation. But having declared their theories to be absolute, economists are now caught between a rock and a hard place. If they jettison their theories, they are doomed, and if they accept the missing quotient in their economic thoughts, they are damned. As long as the party lasted, everyone was having a ball. Now, everyone is asking a fundamental question – who will foot the bill? Remember, economics works on the four ideas of demand, supply, savings, and investments. It is the family that ensured that the four ideas were constantly counter-balanced. As families were under a frontal attack, first by the Leftists, and subsequently by the Liberals, the counter-balancing mechanism, so very vital for the functioning of the macro-economy, went sorely missing. That explains why the discipline of economics has turned into a study of indiscipline.

References

1. Samuel Huntington – US political scientist who foresaw future conflict arising from a clash of cultures By Godfrey Hodgson – The Guardian – Jan 1, 2009.
2. Looking the World in the Eye By Robert Kaplan – The Atlantic – December 2001 Issue.
3. The Clash of Civilizations and the Remaking of World Order By Samuel P. Huntington.

4. The Three Abrahamic Religions and their Image of Woman By 2016 By Emanuel L. Paparella- Modern Diplomacy – May 26, 2016.
5. How American Anarchy Parallels China's Cultural Revolution By Helen Raleigh – The Federalist dated August 23, 2017.
6. 'Born Bad': How the idea that we're all sinners has shaped Western culture By Michael Dirda in Washington Post – Dated May 20, 2015.
7. Cultural Marxism and the War on the Family – Bill Muellenberg- Culture Watch Dated April 8, 2016.
8. Communism and the Family – First Published: in Komunistka, No. 2, 1920, and in English in The Worker, 1920; Source: Selected Writings of Alexandra Kollontai, Allison & Busby, 1977; Translated: by Alix Holt.
9. Americans buy into Marxist Family Planning By Paul Kengor – The Federalist dated June 29, 2015.
10. www.wcd.nic.in
11. The Long War Against the Family By Ryan N. S. Topping.
12. The man who declared the 'end of history' fears for democracy's future – By Ishaan Tharoor Washington Post, February 9, 2017.
13. It's Still Not the End of History – By Timothy Stanley and Alexander Lee, www.Atlantic.com- SEP 1, 2014.
14. What We Mean by Individualism By Adam Martin – Mises Institute.
15. The Economist – The State of Economics dated July 16, 2009.
16. Does Capitalism Destroy Culture? By Michael Matheson Miller.

4. Culture – Emerging Frontiers of Economics

A *nation's culture resides in the hearts and in the soul of its people*
– Mahatma Gandhi

After the conversations about Indian philosophy, some of the ideas of Quantum Physics that had seemed so crazy suddenly made much more sense
– W. Heisenberg

It was seemingly an innocuous statement made by an actor in the autumn of 2005 – probably with a calculated intent of remaining in the spotlight. *India Today*, a respected weekly, at that point in time, conducted a survey from various segments of society on the sexual habits and preferences of people residing in the cities of India, including issues centred around virginity, premarital sex, and chastity. These remarks were published alongside a survey, the relevant extracts of which are reproduced as hereunder:

> "Will you marry a person who had relationship with others?
>
> 18% – Yes, 71% – No 13% – Do not know/Cannot Say
>
> Is it necessary to be a virgin till the time of marriage?
>
> 65% – Yes, 26% – No
>
> 82% women had given an opinion that a girl should be a virgin at the time of marriage."

Khushboo, the actor in spotlight, responding to the queries posed to her by the magazine, opined on the issue. Pointing out to the increasing incidence of pre-marital sex, the actor added "According to me, sex is not only concerned with the body, but also concerned with the conscious . . . Our society should come out of the thinking that at the time of the marriage, the girls should be with virginity (sic) . . . But when having sexual relationship, the girl should protect themselves (sic) from conceiving and getting venereal diseases." As these statements received more than their usual share of attention in the media, especially local media, all hell broke loose. In retrospect, sex and opinion on sex by an actor seems highly inflammable, at least in the south Indian state of Tamil Nadu.

Almost on cue, several criminal complaints were filed against the actor under Sections 499, 500, 509, 153-A, and 292 of the Indian Penal Code read with Sections 4 and 6 of the Indecent Representation of Women (Prohibition) Act, 1986, in multiple locations in the state of Tamil Nadu. To escape from multiple prosecutions, she approached the High Court of Madras to quash these complaints. Given the sensibilities involved and that the society was on a boil at that given point in time, the Madras High Court refused to step in. The actor vehemently defended herself by provocatively adding: "The persons who are protesting against my interview – which culture are they talking about?" Therein lies the rub – Which culture? And what is this Culture? Was Khushboo referring to Tamil culture in her defence? Assuming it is indeed a reference to culture and Tamil culture at that, the moot point is whether marriage and sex are linked to Tamil, or for that matter Indian, culture? By extension, does culture mean remaining a virgin before marriage, and chaste thereafter?

Culture, as we briefly discussed in the previous chapters, is all about restraint. Absent restraint, there is no culture. No to pre-marital sex i.e., retaining virginity till marriage is a self-imposed restraint, and hence, culture. Likewise, to remain chaste after marriage, and be faithful to one's partner is also culture. It is this restraint that is at the root of every cultured individual, which in turn sustains a society. Bluntly said, there is nothing called an uncultured society, as society – by its very definition – must be cultured. If that is so, what happens to the idea of individual liberty that has assumed central stage in modern socio-political-economic discourse? Isn't the modern narrative all about individuals, that too without societal fetters and artificial restraints? The symbiotic link between monogamy and how it elevates the animal *homo sapiens* into Man was discussed in greater detail in

Chapter 1. Absent this restraint, the animal instinct takes over us, and we instantly become polygamous. More to the point, absent the restraint, we collectively no longer retain the characteristics of a civilised society. Once we become polygamous, we lose the moral-cultural-civilisational software to function as a society, which by its very definition is organised. When this restraint ceases to exist, the conventional thinking within every 'civilian' is that a society, built and nurtured over several centuries based on such assiduously crafted restraints, degenerates. This fear of societal degeneration – and we will explore more of it from the macro-economic standpoint in the following chapters – is more pronounced in cultural-civilisational-nations like say India or China, than in a modern nation-state like the US. When culture degenerates, people fear as we would see shortly, that it is a road to nowhere, more particularly in the sphere of national economics.

This restraint is practiced by individuals, tempered by families, and overseen by societies, mostly under trying circumstances. Traditional icons, especially women, who lived and even died for this restraint (read discipline) are deified in such societies, including Tamil society. Practitioners of restraint are venerated and held as examples for future generations to follow. It is their life and lifestyle that is sought to be emulated, for good reason, by the future generation. Forget saints and seers for a moment, our society recognises even ordinary men and women who practice such restraint and are held in high esteem within society. Self-esteem is an aspirational goal more for those who may not be economically prosperous. To paraphrase Chairman Mao, it is glorious to be restrained and cultured. Naturally, when someone speaks her mind on the convoluted issue of culture (or the lack of it within society), people get incensed, as it disturbs the assiduously built idea of self-esteem. It psychologically disturbs the society at a granular level. It conjures the picture of a bleak future – of illness, ignorance, and poverty. That explains, if not rationalises, the spontaneous outrage in society to such statements that mock or questions its collective psychological underpinnings. It may even be conceded that those who opposed the actor's statement may well be practicing what Khushboo preached at the individual level, yet do not accept it or subscribe to her thoughts as the acceptable societal norm.

Khushboo, after realising the extraordinary opposition from Tamils to her statement, shifted her focus from pre-marriage virginity to post-marriage chastity. Concluding on the subject, the actor added, "Is there anyone who does not know about sex in Tamil Nadu? Is there anyone who does not know about AIDS? How many men and women do not have sex before marriage? Why are people saying that after marriage, husband and wife should be honest and faithful to each other? One should have confidence in the other, only to avoid mistakes from being committed. If the husband, without the knowledge of the wife, or the wife, without the knowledge of the husband, have sex with other persons, if a disease is caused through that, the same will affect both the persons. It will also affect the children."

Like Khushboo who sought to diffuse the issue of virginity with chastity, the legal fraternity mixed up the issue of freedom of speech of an individual with societal norms and taboos. Of course, Khushboo, the citizen of India, had the fundamental right to free speech under Article 19 of the Indian Constitution. In fact, it might be the case that her statement was her opinion, but never intended to hurt Tamils and their culture. But the moot point remains – Is pre-marital sex an accepted and acceptable norm within Tamil society? Or is it an exception? Is chastity, for both men and women, a non-issue among Tamils? Even assuming for a moment that both virginity before marriage and chastity after marriage are a non-existent societal norm, pray what is the accepted societal norm? Do societies have one? Is it desirable? Who decides what is right and what is wrong? And pray why? The answers to these questions are not possible in simple binaries.

As the actor approached the Hon'ble High Court of Madras for quashing the criminal complaints against her, the court while refusing to do so in 2008, commented on the conservative societal norms prevailing in Indian and Tamil society. "In this country, though cultural heritage, customs, usage, languages etc. differ from state to state, in so far as sex is concerned, throughout the country, certain conservative ideas are adopted." Underlying these conservative values and its umbilical link to the issue of virginity, and chastity to the idea of family life, the court opined: "Chastity is considered here to be a lifestyle that brings freedom, respect, peace, and even romance without regret, and it liberates a couple from selfish attitudes of using each other as objects, and makes them capable of their love. No one questions his would-be whether she is a virgin or not, because everyone faithfully believes and has a good point of view about his bride or her bridegroom as the case may be that she or he would be chaste and modest."

This refusal to objectify women in the process, according to the court, elevated her status both within the family and in society. Needless to emphasise, the court was talking of age-old virtues of self-restraint – the core building block of culture. It is a societal norm created with great care over millennia and zealously guarded by its very participants viz., men and women so that deviants are corrected and not celebrated. The court rightly pointed out that the trade-off between individual restraint practised by a woman and the concomitant respect earned from society by that woman has the calculated effect of elevating such women and not demeaning her, as it is commonly believed. Thus, there is a two-fold responsibility on every individual – one to practice restraint, and two, to cognise and respect social restraints. Absent one of the two, culture or respect for women, a society goes into a downward spiral. In this connection, the court opined: "In India, chastity and love are explicitly regulated, and that is why, women are assigned an elevated position in society ordinarily not approachable by men except through legal means viz., marriage. In the other situation, where love and chastity are implicitly promoted but not regulated, one could witness women's position is subject to the utter tedium of placing themselves at the disposal and protection of their men."

Distinguishing between the two approaches by society – one that is conservative like Indian society that even to this day culturally values virginity before marriage as well as chastity after marriage, and the other one being a permissive society like many in the West, the court explained the contrast rather eloquently. In this connection, the court observed: "Incidentally, it is notable that the so-called open or permissive societies, blindly lauded by the petitioner, are ipso facto incapable of promoting conditions for any deep and intense love relationships. Their conditions lead to waywardness and wantonness, in the process of seeking transient affairs, if not while indulging in momentary and lustful pleasure."

Further, the court went on to differentiate the idea of something as carnal as sex in the West and in India. In this connection, the court elaborated the difference in the viewpoint of sex in permissive societies, and a civilisation like India, and added: "No doubt, sex has been eulogised in many ways, both in the West and in India. Yet, there has come to be a difference between the Indian and Western conceptualisation of sex. Unlike Indian society, in the West, in particular, sexual relationships are generally viewed as the private preference of each individual as perceived by the petitioner. No one has the right to determine with whom, or how one conducts one's sex life. What occurs between consenting adults, no matter what sex or how many, is usually condoned. Pre-marital sex is considered quite acceptable and normal, well within the bounds of morality, and indeed desirable. Dating begins at a very young age, and every socially well-adjusted youngster is expected to have several girlfriends and boyfriends by a certain age. Use of condoms by school-going children has become a common phenomenon there. Thus, those who grow up in the West are weaned on sex in both subtle and not so subtle ways. That is why, to many Westerners, sex can be worthwhile as long as it embodies the sweetness mutually attainable by lovers. Individuals of opposite sex there prefer the desirability and enjoyability of living together in mutual love and comfort, to the constant annoyance and boredom of living as singles. They aim at maximising enjoyment of life." With due respect to the court, one may hasten to add that this is a sweeping conclusion and gross generalisation on the moral values practiced by Western societies. But the differentials between the Indian and Western societies on the convoluted subject of sex is indeed palpable.

The court did not stop there. It went on to explain the distinct approach to virginity, chastity, sex, and marriage in Indian societies, by stating: "In quite contrast thereto, in Indian society, sex is regarded as something inexorably desirable in itself only through marriage and one would pray while entering conjugal life that the marital relationship should continue even after death in the world of souls. If such a social set-up, strengthened by moral and ethical ideology, is criticised, it would result in adverse impact. Both emotional and consequential." In finality, the court said: "Morality is not old-fashioned or irrelevant in the modern world, for, morality is not simply a creation of religion, but rather a necessary underpinning of a healthy and successful society. While many things have changed a great deal over the years, some things have not changed and other things should not change viz., moral and ethical values. There would be no purpose in hiding the fact that today's society is running backward, turning away from ethical and moral norms, and sexually inciting materials are in prevalence everywhere." On this point, did the court hit the nail right on the head? Let us explore.

Arjuna's Concern and his Dilemma

Old-fashioned as it may sound, the fact remains that the Hon'ble Madras High Court raised certain pertinent issues on culture, marriage, chastity, and of course sex. These issues have been raised intermittently by mankind since time immemorial. Arjuna in Chapter I of the *Bhagavad Gita*, for instance, raises precisely these questions to Lord Krishna. Unfortunately, in the current social debates encompassing the issue of sex, marriage, virginity, and chastity, the seemingly caring observations of Arjuna may seem to be patriarchal and even, misogynist. To the uninitiated, the *Gita* unfolds even as two factions of the Kuru clan are lined up for a war to inherit the kingdom. The Kauravas, one of the two factions, have allegedly usurped it from the other faction, Pandavas. Negotiations have been attempted between the two factions and abandoned as the differences have reached a point of no return. War, therefore, was the only option that remained to settle the issue of inheritance to the kingdom.

But even as the war is about to commence, Arjuna – one of the Pandavas - loses his composure and becomes extremely reluctant to fight the war. It does not appeal to him at the eleventh hour – even as the armies of both sides are ready for the war – to kill his own cousins, uncles, teachers and friends to regain his kingdom. This dilemma of Arjuna is contained in Chapter I of the *Gita*, more specifically in the ten verses beginning verse 36 and ending with verse 45. How Lord Krishna who doubles as his charioteer as well as his friend, guide, and philosopher counsels him, removes his dilemma, and demonstrates the right path contained in the next 17 Chapters of the *Gita*, making it one of the highly recommended philosophical works of mankind.

While explaining his dilemma, Arjuna raises some pertinent questions to the Lord. "In the destruction of family, the immemorial clan traditions perish, and on the loss of tradition, the whole clan comes under the sway of lawlessness," laments Arjuna, who adds "yet, why should we not learn to turn away from this sin of the destruction of family?" Worried that war will lead to the "women becoming corrupt, and when women become corrupt, mixing of clans arises," Arjuna points out to the consequences of war as to how war ultimately led to the destruction of the "immemorial traditions of clan and family." According to him, the destruction of these traditions was 'a great sin' that was not worth committing even for the rightful inheritance of the kingdom. Overcome by a kaleidoscope of emotions, he concludes that it would be better even if the Kauravas kill him, unarmed and unresisting. Arjuna's fear on how the war would ultimately destroy families and corrupt women, which ultimately destroy immemorial traditions is probably logical, quintessentially sensible, and definitely humane. Despite the compelling nature of these questions, the fact remains that the Lord has apparently not answered these questions directly, despite labouring in the next 17 chapters in attempting to remove the confusion of Arjuna. Probably, the Lord has answered them indirectly. We would not know.

However, the questions raised by Arjuna requires some amplification. It may be noted that the commentary by the Gita Press, Gorakhpur, is considered as an authentic one. Let us capture in brief the dilemma of Arjuna referred to and well-chronicled by this commentary. Elaborating Arjuna's point of view, the commentary notes that every good family is a reservoir of many good and beneficial customs and usages, which are handed down from generation to generation. These help in maintaining the high standard of conduct of the family and prevent its men and women from going astray. These beneficial and uplifting customs and usages are known, according to Arjuna, as 'family traditions.' The commentary further notes that there are five incentives, which compel a man to be virtuous. They are fear of God, command of the scriptures, fear of violation of family traditions, state laws, fear of physical injury or pecuniary loss. Among these, God, though absolutely real, and command of the scriptures, though representing truth, depend on man's faith. These are not direct or perceptible incentives.

State laws govern only the subjects of the state, but those who wield power generally do not respect them. Fear of physical injury or pecuniary loss affects only individuals afflicted. It is family traditions and family traditions alone that link up the individual with family and society. It is obvious that once the family tradition gets obliterated, the individual becomes undisciplined. Therefore, the society and family too become unruly and wayward. When the members of a society or family throw off every form of restraint (and remember restraint is culture), he becomes uncultured.

With the disappearance of family traditions, as men and women lose all forms of restraint, their activities, in most cases begin to be tainted by vice. The net consequence is that sin becomes predominant and spreads itself over the entire society. Given this possibility, where individual and collective restraint ceases to exist, moral values begin to be treated as outworn formulas and rapidly lose their import. Far from observing the rules of morality and practising restraint, men and women even remain oblivious of them to the extent of making fun of those are disciplined and hence cultured. In that state, the sacred law of conjugal fidelity, which is the very root and foundation of the social code, loses its hold on society. That ideal being lost, women get corrupt and tainted with the vice of adultery. In effect, the commentary brilliantly draws the symbiotic link between family traditions and restraints, between restraints and moral values – one of the core themes of the book. Of course, we also explore how a functioning of the family with culture ensures the orderly functioning of the society and how such a society is a sine qua non for a sustainable economic growth of the nation. Moral values, the commentary concludes, superscribed by conjugal fidelity lies at the root of social functioning.

Arjuna's concern was that war could destroy family traditions which in turn destabilise the assiduously built social order of those times. According to him, nothing was more precious – not even the kingdom – than the social order. Remember war leads to killing of men, mostly young men. Obviously, Arjuna calculated that a war, just or unjust, will skew the men-women ratio decisively in favour of women which in turn will upset the natural gender parity. In Chapter 1, we saw how a polygamous society where one man takes multiple wives was inherently unstable and volatile. Arjuna's fear post-war were virtually the same. As women post- war were bound to exceed men in numbers, conjugal fidelity was bound to be disturbed. Family was the basic structure of the society and Arjuna feared it could get negatively impacted by war. Implicitly, Arjuna was arguing that this social order was inviolable, whatever be the overarching personal or just compulsions.

Arjuna, in conclusion, declares that he would not be involved in the war and consequently would desist in committing the great sin of destroying family values and in turn had the calculated effect of disturbing the sacred social order. Arjuna was clear in his mind that his death without any show of resistance would lead to, in the least, the protection of the family traditions. As stated briefly above, while the Lord provides a detailed answer to several questions posed by Arjuna, He does not precisely answer the questions raised by Arjuna on the specific issue of disturbing the social order. Despite being a philosophical treatise, the questions raised by Arjuna and lack of direct answers to the same by the Lord in the entire *Gita* haunts some readers to this day. We are one of them.

Now, let us revert to Khushboo's tryst with our judiciary. Even as the Hon'ble Madras High Court rejected her plea, it, in order to prevent the inconvenience of litigating the same subject matter in multiple locations directed that all the cases instituted against the actor be consolidated and tried together by the Chief Metropolitan Magistrate, Egmore (Chennai). Aggrieved by the aforesaid judgment, Khushboo approached the Hon'ble Supreme Court of India. In relation to the issue of the societal acceptance of pre-marital sex, the Supreme Court conceded that the predominant view within Indian society is to permit sexual contract only between marital partners, but also found that there was nothing within the legal framework that prevents willing adults from engaging in sexual relationships outside the marital setting with the sole exception of adultery (which too, as we saw in chapter 1, was subsequently de-criminalised in a separate judgement in 2018). In this connection, it observed – "While it is true that the mainstream view in our society is that sexual contact should take place only between marital partners, there is no statutory offence that takes place when adults willingly engage in sexual relations outside the marital setting, with the exception of "adultery" as defined under Section 497 IPC." Drawing reference to another judgement given by the very same court in the context of legal tenability of live-in relationship between two consenting adults of heterogenic sex, it had observed such acts do not amount to any offence even though it may be perceived as immoral. It added as a matter of fact that a "major girl is free to marry anyone she likes or live with anyone she likes." But this observation is limited to the legal domain. Obviously, a court cannot outlaw a live-in relationship in the absence of such a law in the first place. But without a law, society actually frowns on such relationships. Obviously, when it comes to culture and legislating morality, the viewpoint of society on one hand and the legal framework circumscribed by the limitation of the Constitution on the other, shall necessarily have an unbridgeable chasm. This can never be filled by the best of legal minds or social reformers. Nevertheless, on the issue of legal charges, the court held that Khushboo neither intended to cause harm to the reputation of complainants, nor could any actual harm be discerned from her remarks. As she had not suggested that all women in Tamil Nadu engage in pre-marital sex, but had merely addressed how pre-marital sex was viewed in society at that time, the court directed quashing of all complaints against her.

Constitutionally speaking, the issue certainly remains one of fundamental rights of Khushboo. But is it one merely of intolerance as it was sought to be canvassed in the courts by her lawyers? The fact that political parties in Tamil Nadu were seen at the forefront of the protests did raise genuine questions on the 'spontaneity' of the protests against the actor. Thus, there were two questions – one, the individual rights of Khushboo to opine and two, whether her opinion in respect to pre-marital sex and chastity, was legally untenable. On the first point, the court correctly upheld her right, while on the second rightly opined that it did not have a legal benchmark to hold the actor criminally liable.

Nonetheless, both the Madras High Court and the Supreme Court flagged certain pertinent points on the issue of morality, individual discipline, and the resultant social order. Possibly, it was not within the realm of the courts to explore the morality associated with virginity before marriage and chastity after marriage for the simple reason that morality cannot, and in my considered view should not, be legislated. And once it cannot be legislated, it naturally does not fall within the realm of courts. But the courts did express its concern on the vexatious subject of individual morality, the High Court did so emphatically while the Supreme Court did so ever so subtly. And both High Court, as well as Supreme Court, merely mirrored the views expressed by an overwhelming majority regarding the subject as evidenced by the survey. The findings of the survey and the subsequent turn of events culminating in the verdict of the Hon'ble Supreme Court leads to three inescapable conclusions – (1) That the societal impulse, including that of courts, is overwhelmingly in favour of self-restraint (2) The fear is that this discipline is increasingly being violated by individuals and the state, its institutions or the society is unable to provide the necessary oversight and (3) The moral code is a necessity and needs to be maintained and if in case it ceases to exist, needs to be restored.

The reason for this concern stems from the eternal understanding by the Indic society about self-restraint – that every discipline or order has within it, seeds of destruction and once it is destroyed, a divine force will decisively intervene to restore a new order. The Indic society believes that this cycle gets repeated. Remarkably, every member of the society also believes that it is his duty to protect and maintain this order, albeit its inevitable destruction over time to the point of complete chaos till a new order is restored through divine intervention. It might, on superficial examination, seem to be an exercise in futility to protect something that is designed to be on a downward spiral. But in the Indic tradition, this is not. Thus, protection and maintenance of any order, by an individual, designed and approved by the society is as divine in Indic tradition as the divine intervention to restore order after its collapse. Did the refusal to understand this fundamental fact lead to the outcry against the statement of Khushboo in Tamil Nadu? Or was it a grand design at protecting the existing order, even as it is broadly understood to be on a downward spiral? Either way, there seems to be some angst in society even today against what is perceived by it as moral decay in individuals. All these questions require greater examination.

Social Entropy

Simply put, the concept of entropy originated around the mid-19th century, from the study of heat, temperature, work, and energy, collectively known as thermodynamics. That was the era of the steam locomotive. The study of how heat could be most efficiently converted to mechanical energy was of prime interest. It was understood that there was a relationship between heat and temperature. The more heat you applied to an object, the hotter it gets. It was also understood that heat and work represented different forms of energy and that under right circumstances, we could convert one into other. Furthermore, it was observed that the only time the heat would spontaneously flow out of one body was when it was in contact with another, colder, body. That is, heat always flowed from a hot to a cold body.

Entropy, slightly distanced from the idea of thermodynamics or physics, also explains a tendency for systems to move from order towards disorder. Order is having everything in its proper place, behaving as it is expected. Disorder is exactly the opposite – either a thing is not in its proper place, or when it is in proper place, does not perform as expected. Order is a well-tuned machine with all its parts moving in perfect coordination with all other parts. A machine with parts not behaving as they should, is obviously out of order. Importantly, scientists observed that it is the natural tendency of things to lose its order. Left to its own, life will always become less structured, unsystematic. The inevitable fact of life is that, over time, things become less organised. It is one of the fundamental laws of our universe. The pull of entropy is relentless. Everything decays. Disorder prevails. Chaos reigns.

Entropy explains why heat flows from warm objects to cold ones. This dissipation of heat is natural; it arises on its own. Nothing can stop this. In direct contrast, solutions always require our attention, energy, and effort. Heating an object requires some effort. Leaves falling in autumn is entropy. Collecting them into heaps is a way of countering them. But this requires effort. Solving a jigsaw puzzle requires effort. Cleaning a room requires effort. Successful offices require maintenance and effort. Organising individuals into a cohesive team requires effort. Successful relationships require care, attention, and effort. Effective teams require communication and effort. Creating music out of cacophony requires labour. So does writing poetry. Or for that matter any form of art, invention, or innovation. A disease striking a body is entropy; a surgeon intervening and curing it, puts in effort. Training, practising, educating, co-ordinating, caring – all are examples of efforts that counter entropy. Without effort, things will decay, or in the least remain disorganised.

Obviously, all efforts require energy. What should not be missed in the melee is that to expend energy, we need to have it in the first place. That energy which converts disorder into order must be extraordinary to counter the relentless force of nature. Put differently, a shuffled deck of card has probably a one-in-a-trillion chance of falling into a neatly arranged pack. It will never happen unless there is an extraordinary effort and a calculated decisive intervention. Should it happen, it will be an astonishing level of energy in action. Likewise, we are comprised of billions and billions of cells that could probably be arranged in a virtually infinite number of ways. All but just one arrangement, just one arrangement, lead to a form of life. Statistically speaking, the odds are overwhelmingly against our very existence. Yet we exist. Isn't our very existence proof of an extraordinary effort and energy – call it divinity if you can – in action? Do we realise we are a highly improbable combination of cells that is arranged and working efficiently? Mathematically speaking, we should not exist, and yet we are here, living, breathing, and analysing. Isn't it truly remarkable? In a universe where entropy rules, the presence of life with intricate organisation, structure, and stability is well and truly stunning. Only the blessed realise such subtleties of life.

The idea of entropy is no longer limited to the discipline of physics. It is now borrowed by social sciences and put to gainful use. The idea of social entropy has proven to be a convenient framework in the study of social systems to explain the tendency of structures – especially artificial constructs - to degrade over time from order and cooperation towards disorder and conflict. Every system, it is well understood, will naturally incline towards self-destruction. So, will any system put in place by the government. Or, for that matter, any social order. Each one of them left unattended will decay naturally. Hence, conventional wisdom lies in recognising the fundamental fact that it is as much an effort to create a system as to maintain it.

This insight – that disorder has a natural tendency to increase over time, and that we can counteract this only by expending spectacular levels of energy – lies at the core of evolution. Fascinatingly, does all this carry an uncanny resemblance to the eternal understanding of the Indic society about itself, self-restraint that assiduously creates a social order, the overarching need to preserve the same, and one that inevitably will go on a downward spiral over a period of time? But what about the spectacular energy that is required to put a degenerative system into order? Where does it come from? What impels it to act and put a completely degenerated system into order? And why? What if the spectacular energy fails to deliver or act? In the alternative, what happens when a system is put into order by such spectacular energy? What is our role in all this?

The Lord, Entropy, and Gita

"Arjuna, whenever righteousness is on the decline, and unrighteousness is on the ascendant, then I manifest" says the Lord in Verse 7 of Chapter IV of the Gita, and adds assumingly in the following verse "For the protection of the virtuous, for the extermination of evil-doers, and for establishing *Dharma*, I will re-create Myself from time to time." To some, this statement of the Lord represents the final denouement of the Gita. To others, it represents the quintessence of Gita. To us, it is a tacit admission of the power of social entropy that will eventually triumph any social order, and therefore, at some point in time will require divine intervention for the reconstruction of a new sustainable order, which is otherwise humanly impossible. This divine intervention – to the agnostic might well be a spectacular flow of energy – that is required to put the house in order. Without this spectacular flow of energy, life does not move on.

To comprehend what is stated above, a reference once again to the commentary by the Gita Press shall be in order. Accordingly, it is apparent that first, the downward slide – read entropy – of any arrangement is inevitable. Secondly, it is the Lord and Lord alone who can set right the order, albeit the fact that the timing shall be of his choice. It is not possible for the faithful to judge the time or for that matter the extent of damage which compels His manifestation. According to the Gita, this divine intervention, resetting of the order and the downward spiral of the order so created even by the Lord over a period of time till it reaches a tipping point where the Lord once again is compelled by his own inviolable law of intervention to reset the order is the quintessence of Gita. This inexorable sequence of resetting of an order, degeneration of the order over the efflux of time, and to a point where the Lord is compelled by the force of circumstances and His own inviolable law to intervene is a fascinating idea in the Gita that contains the natural rhythmic flow alternating between social entropy and what we call, spectacular energy. To the faithful, this is a divine guarantee that has never defaulted to honour its commitment.

Alternatively, ignore for a moment what the Lord promised in the Gita. Let us take an agnostic view of life too. On a daily basis, we witness widespread physical destruction caused by fire, earthquakes, tsunami, floods, diseases and other causes. And in the process sometimes lives, cities, countries, civilisations, powers empires, and even species get wiped out. Fascinatingly, man has not been a mute witness to such natural devastations. On the contrary, history of man has been replete with examples of how man picked himself and others from the nadir and reconstruct whatever was destroyed. Of course, this rebuilding requires humongous quantum of energy. The history of mankind is the story of its remarkable ability to rebuild repeatedly from the ruins. It is not the fall that matters, the ability to rise that defines the character of our species. And in every rise, there must be considerable flow of energy. The sinking of the Titanic did not deter man from designing bigger and better ships. Cities devastated by natural calamities get rebuilt by spectacular bouts of energy provided by leaders, civil society and its residents. Lives shattered by torturous events get re-created, of course through dedication, devotion, and discipline. Without destruction, the beauty of creation will be lost. Equally, creation without destruction would create its own share of imbalance that would be humanly difficult to remedy. Destruction followed by creation and creation followed by destruction in a neat rhythm is mother nature's own way of ensuring a neat balance. This continuous yet alternative march of destruction and creation, fall and rise are akin to two pistons of a giant machine that are in relentless action.

It is not that every twist and turn need the divine to intercede. In fact, divinity manifests when ordinary men and women perform extraordinary feats. It is this extraordinary feat that transformed an ordinary lawyer in Mohan Das Karamchand Gandhi into a Mahatma, for organising millions of his countrymen, battered by over a thousand years of invasion, war, foreign rule and consequential ill-effects, manifesting through poverty, ignorance and disease, by a simple yet potent weapon of non-violence. This divinity was in action when Nelson Mandela, despite being in prison for over 27 years was able to demolish the scourge of apartheid. This divinity was yet again in action when Mikhail Gorbachev, leader of the erstwhile Soviet Union who oversaw the transition from Communism to Democracy in the Soviet Union and Eastern Europe while allowing the collapse of the Berlin Wall. The history of mankind is essentially the history of such extraordinary men who have shaped, de-shaped, and reshaped the flow of events during their lifetime, and probably in case of some, after it. Time might well separate the actions of these men. Their achievements might be different. Their methods are indeed diverse. What unites these extraordinary men is the extraordinary efforts that required spectacular levels of energy. Sadly, what they achieved in their lifetime or after it, is bound to dissipate in the near or distant future.

The reason for the same is simple. Entropy, like death and taxes, is inevitable. Whatever be the state of our preparation and forewarning, the march of entropy will be relentless. Does that mean that we allow things to drift? Does that imply that we can be supinely indifferent to the scheme of things and surrender ourselves to this unceasing flow, doing precious nothing? Do we wait for divine intervention to restore order? The answers to these questions are once again available in the Gita. If the assurance of the Lord to manifest referred to above is all about resetting the order through a divine intervention, the Lord also mandates something simpler and practical at the individual level. In Chapter II Verse 47, the Lord exhorts that everyone has a "right is to work, but never to the fruit thereof" and sagaciously adds "Do not be the cause of the fruit of action; nor let your attachment be to inaction." Is there a lesson for all of us here even if it were a relentless march to ruination? Of course, the answer is an emphatic yes. There is a definitive role for the divine. Yet, we have no alternative but to continue with our own individual efforts to restore order while also be prepared for the eventual onset of entropy. Seeking balance between the two is the central idea that dominates this work.

Let us put these arguments from a different perspective. The Black Swan will arrive when you least expect it. A preventive drug for cancer will be discovered when you have virtually given up hope on it. A leader will appear from nowhere and deliver. The phoenix bird will surely rise from the ashes of its predecessor – an allegory of resurrection and life after death. The resurrection of Lord Jesus, after being crucified by the Romans, should appeal not only to pious Christians, but also to those who believe in the power of the unexpected. Nassim Nicholas Taleb explains these events as 'Black Swan theory' in his much-acclaimed work, which goes with the same name – *The Black Swan* (2007). Taleb focuses on the impact of rare and unpredictable outlier events (and the human tendency to find simplistic explanations for these events, retrospectively). Mathematically speaking, all these can be explained too. For instance, the Sine Function has this wonderful up-down curve when plotted in a graph. At sine 0 degrees, it is 0, at Sine 90 it is 1, at sine 180, it is again 0, at sine 270 it is -1 and again at sine 360 it is once again 0. To the naked eye, the sine graph alternates between 1 (sine 90 degrees) and -1 (sine 270 degrees). The cosine graph too alternates between cos 0 at 1 to cos 180 at -1.

Indic society sees the world as these up-down graphs – alternating between the heights caused by human efforts and endeavours to a decisive divine intervention when everything is down and out. For all that you know, we may have just escaped a catastrophe, or a screw driver turn away from greatness. Amazingly, we may be ignorant about both. The story of life alternates between the providential escapes and lucky breaks, at times without our knowledge but never without our own efforts. The traditional understanding of life in all its hues in Indic societies is that the final leap to success is ordained by the divine, but is assiduously built on sustained hard work. Thus, in more ways than one, the Gita does place the individual effort on par with the divine intervention – probably making it one of the rare texts that elevate individual efforts to that of divine intervention. Simply put, the Gita does not believe in the idea of an indifferent individual awaiting divine intervention. On the contrary, it guarantees divine intervention only on top of sustained efforts, individual or collective. This is the traditional Indic position where the Lord is supreme, but not the sole determinant of one's fortunes. To move to Sine 90 from Sine 0 requires human intervention, and at Sine 270, it requires the involvement of the divine to rise once again.

Nonetheless, this crafting of balance between belief in divinity on one hand, and in self on the other, is one of the major challenges of life. If polygamy, as discussed in Chapter 1, is the mother of all societal imbalances, achieving this is the mother of all balances. Let us hasten to add that attaining and retaining this balance remains at the core of life as it is of society, and for governments. This is the initial building block in creating a sustainable economic model. Without balance between belief in self and in divinity, no economic model is sustainable. For instance, a society that is pious, but has little or no faith in sincere, sustained, intelligent hard work is bound to be only pious and not prosperous. This lack of emphasis on prosperity while being pious contains the seeds of self-destruction. Indic values, while respecting such pious societies, never approved of the same. The lack of emphasis on material success in Buddhism, in direct contrast to traditional Indic societies, is a case in point. Such a pious society is not sustainable in the long run, as in the absence of the grand stimulation of prosperity, a society is bound to implode, sooner than later. This is our experience since the dawn of civilisation. Renunciation or becoming an ascetic is not the best way to handle poverty. Nor is it the route to progress. Prosperity, let us not forget, is one elixir of life that cannot and should not be ignored. But prosperity without the countervailing force of piety is equally self-destructive. When the quality of life improves, it is often seen, individuals do not find it necessary to adhere to their core cultural values. What holds true for individuals, holds true for societies too. Prosperity, thus in more ways than one, also contains seeds of cultural self-destruction. The challenge, therefore, lies in being prosperous while retaining core cultural values. We will confront this issue of balance between prosperity and piety as we proceed further.

Under Indic beliefs, prosperity without individual hard work is virtually impossible, unworkable, and assuredly unsustainable. Unrestrained prosperity or consumption is never approved. Likewise, unrestrained prosperity, it is believed, will invariably lead to individual excesses, which in turn are bound to have a debilitating impact on family, society, government, and of course the environment. In pursuit of our individual successes, we cannot trade the quality of life of our future generations. Do we comprehend the damage that we have inflicted on the environment in the quest of our material happiness? Do we realise that the damage we are causing to the environment is probably irreversible? Do we have the right to abuse mother nature to the point that we are virtually ensuring the end of mankind? Again, modern economic models with their singular focus on material prosperity seem to have an inbuilt self-destruction program. At least, under the Indic beliefs, it is well and truly unsustainable. The reason for the same is not far to seek – under the Indic beliefs, in the long run, creeping entropy will provide an answer to every excess – possibly in a gradual manner, but more likely in an abrupt fashion.

There is yet another dimension to this entire debate. Individual dignity and liberty have their own place in any sustainable socio-economic order. Those are eternal values and cannot, in my considered view, ever be altered. Let us not forget that an individual without self-esteem has very less to contribute in any economic order. Such persons are invariably a burden on their family, society, and the state. However, by chasing self-esteem as an end in itself without any self-restraints, either by the society or family, an individual is more likely to commit one form of excess or the other. By excess, we simply mean the lack of discipline. This lack of individual discipline results in the collapse of family traditions, which in turn results in breakdown of culture, and ultimately results in social entropy. The arguments put forth by Arjuna in Chapter I of the Gita and briefly discussed above are valid even today. Equally, it is important that every individual must comprehend the impact of such discipline at a collective level on the economy.

That restates the importance of individual and his efforts in sustaining an order. The breakdown of individual discipline is the first decisive step to social entropy. This needs to be cognised at the earliest and prevented.

Enchantingly, it is self-restraint and self-restraint alone that tempers individuals from committing such excesses. An individual without excesses ensures a disciplined family, and a disciplined family tempers an individual. A disciplined family ensures an equitable, functional, and sustainable society. Simultaneously, both the family and society prevent an individual from committing excesses. This paradigm ensures an order, which is a pre-requisite for sustained economic progress. Let us not overlook the fact that these individual restraints (read culture) resulting in a social order are crafted by individuals, practised by their family over a period of time, and implicitly approved and overseen by society. Culture is the operating system on which the software of macro-economics is eventually and successfully run. This is the crucial missing link in understanding modern macro-economics.

Economic Values and being economical with values

The *Mahabharat* is one of the two major epics of ancient India, the other being the *Ramayana*, that dominate the collective socio-cultural psyche of India. The *Mahabharat* is estimated to have more than one lakh verses, of which the Gita contains only about 700. We referred to just two of them in our discussions above. Commenting on the epic, several experts opine that the original epic was called *Jaya*, then it was called *Vijaya*, then Bharata, and finally Mahabharat. *Jaya* had about 25,000 verses, while the final form had over one lakh verses. *Jaya* was about spiritual victory, *Vijaya* was about material victory, Bharata was the story of a clan, and Mahabharat included also the wisdom of the land called *Bharatvarsh*. The renaming of *Jaya* to Mahabharat by itself is a fascinating tale. While the epic talks and probably provides philosophical answers to several questions that confront us in daily life, most scholars are near unanimous in their view that the story is all about re-emphasising the importance of conquering self before conquering the world. Conquering self is all about being self-restrained, disciplined, and having the ability to introspect one's own action. Unlike certain other religious texts, the *Mahabharat* is not about infidels, pagans, or converting the non-believers, or for that matter punishing them. On the contrary, it is all about self and self-realisation through self-restraints. No wonder, in

Chapter VI, Verse 5 of the Gita, the Lord adds sagaciously that one should lift oneself by one's own efforts and should not degrade oneself; for one's own self is one's friend, and one's own self is one's enemy. Nothing can be more pointed towards self-introspection than this. Several philosophers worldwide, and across time spans have alluded to this point of self at the core of every solution.

Despite the overwhelming tilt towards individual liberty, the conservative idea of self-restraint has received some attention in modern times too. The self-control theory of crime, originally developed by criminologists Travis Hirschi and Michael Gottfredson, is a theory about the lack of individual restraint as the chief drive behind every criminal behaviour. The self-control theory of crime by these two noted criminologists suggests that individuals who were ineffectually parented before the age of 10 develop less self-control than individuals of approximately the same age who were raised with better parenting. Of course, this theory has been subjected to a great deal of debate in the field of criminology. The authors hypothesised that a child's level of self-control, which is heavily influenced by child-rearing practices of its parents, stabilises by the time he reaches the age of eight. Thus, they identified parenting as the most decisive factor in determining the likelihood of a person turning out a criminal. Children reared in settings of neglect or abuse, for example, will be more likely to commit criminal acts than children raised in supervised homes with appropriate parental care.

But just recall what was discussed about the destruction of families by Marxists earlier in Chapter 3. Naturally, destruction of families leads to decreased parenting, which in turn leads to increased crimes. Marxists love this weird idea of purging a child from the natural comfort of its mother, and if possible, parents. To them, the answer to such a scenario would be to increase policing, more laws, and greater state intervention. And to fund such activities, Marxists advocate higher and newer forms of taxes to justify their interventionist ideology. Thus, what should have been a natural task of parenting at childhood (which, in turn, prevents crimes at a later stage) is converted through ideological fundamentalism into a complex set of economic policies – all to prevent deviant individuals, who are more likely to transform into criminals, in a scenario of no or low parenting. Remember

Plato's suggestion (explained in greater detail in Chapter 3) of "no parent should know its child, or child its parent?" Recall how Kollontoi, the communist ideologue, sought to purge women from her family by setting up crèches, while simultaneously seeking to demolish the household kitchen. Refer to the Communist Manifesto where Marx wrote of the 'abolition of the family,' and famously added "Blessed is he who has no family." To Marx, marriage was 'bourgeois claptrap.' But do Marxists know of the socio-economic consequence of their idea of destroying families? Do we realise the costs of such grand social experiments conducted on us? Plato or Marx, the ordinary man continues to be a guinea pig in the hands of such ideas and intellectuals even to this day. Modern day macro-economics, sans the idea of culture, is yet another grand experiment.

Now, let us look at the other end of the spectrum – liberals and their economics (discussed in greater detail in Chapter 3). Do we now understand the implications of the marketing and advertising techniques of corporates in trying to reach out their products directly, at times, even to very young children, as explained by Professor Juliet Schor? Gradually, corporates saw consumers and only consumers in individuals. Globalisation converted individuals, even of distant lands, into consumers of multinational corporates. The process of doing so is very simple. Constantly, individuals are to be bombarded with advertisements of goods and services. The power of allurement is unleashed on the hapless individual, whereby the natural failings of men are exploited to the hilt. Advertisements are designed to ensure people have brand recall. In the process, individuals without branded products are made to feel inadequate, small, and incomplete. Such individuals are made to feel low on their self-esteem. As families traditionally counter-balanced such individual inadequacies, lecherous corporates and liberals turned against the very institution of family, for in their view, family and family alone was the stumbling block in subjugating the individual. Brands, as we saw, are increasingly replacing families, religion, and communities as a source of identity. Once brands step in to fill such individual inadequacies, family as the traditional emotional stabiliser becomes defunct. The 'complete man' – as the tagline of an Indian fabric manufacturer goes – is well and truly intended for the 'incomplete man.'

Marx or market economics, the demonic idea is to break the self-restraints of an individual, purge him of all his dignity, and exploit him to the hilt. These ideas continue to proliferate since the dawn of civilisation. The ideas of Marxists or market economists are not new either. It may have acquired newer forms in the 19th, 20th, and 21st centuries. But these are age-old ideas, recycled with modern clichés, that continue to haunt us. Remember both Marxists and champions of free markets see family as an ideological adversary that deserves to be eliminated. That, explains why individual restraints – *Jaya,* if you permit – remains a countervailing force to both Marxists and free market economists even to this day. Modern economists and their economic theories aim precisely to demolish individual restraints, family values, and social norms. Marxists and Liberals, no wonder, frown on all these.

David Brooks, a noted political and economic columnist (with the *New York Times*) as well as author, comments precisely on this point when he says, "what the US requires today (given its macro-economic instability) is a restoration of economic values; a return to financial self-restraint." Pointing out to the fact that wealth and power lead to affluence and luxury, which in turn lead to decadence, corruption, and decline, Brooks notes with immense pride, and rightly so, to the fact that "despite its amazing wealth, the United States has generally remained immune to this cycle." He rationalises this phenomenon when he points out that despite its notorious materialism, there has always been a countervailing stream in the US of sound economic values. Brooks is clinical in his diagnosis when he refers to the "erosion in the country's financial values." He disappointedly notes: "Executives and hedge-fund managers began bragging about compensation packages that would have been considered shameful a few decades earlier. Chain restaurants went into supersize mode, offering gigantic portions that would have been considered socially unacceptable to an earlier generation." The moot point is whether the US, or for that matter any government, can reverse this phenomenon.

The net result of all this is stunning. Brooks notes that in the three decades between 1950 and 1980, personal consumption was remarkably stable, amounting to about 62 percent of the GDP. In the next three decades, it shot upward, reaching 70 percent of the GDP in 2008. As a direct consequence of this gluttonous consumption, personal debt exploded. In 1960, Americans' personal debt amounted to about 55 percent of the national income. By 2007, Brooks points out that it had surged to 133 percent of the national income. If his diagnosis is spot on, his prescription leaves everyone – possibly with the sole exception of modern economists – stunned. "If there is to be a correction, it will require a moral and cultural movement," he concludes. Morality and economics? Well, if the arguments of Brooks are in order, this is the new emerging frontier in modern economics.

To Brooks, this transformation within the US society from a conservative to an unrestrained one, all within a generation or two, is worrisome on two counts. First, he is worried about the decline of moral and cultural values within the US, and on the second, he is worried that excessive and unrestrained consumption – the cause – is being celebrated by economists, administration, and academics. On the first point, Brooks need not worry. Like all economic and political superpowers before it, the decline of the US as an economic, political, or military superpower is inevitable. Superpowers before the US have collapsed earlier. Superpowers in future too will collapse. What is being witnessed is entropy in action, about which nothing much can be done. But on the second point, Brooks is undeniably spot on. The cause of his consternation is the carnival of the undisciplined by economists. People indulging in ostentatious consumption are celebrated. Spending, not saving, has become a virtue. These undisciplined instantly become role models for future generations. Remember how Americans, not so long ago, denied a visa to Swedish actress Ingrid Bergman because she had a 'love child' born outside of wedlock with Italian director Roberto Rossellini, as discussed in Chapter 2? Brooks fittingly laments about this fall in moral values in American society, and its consequence on the American economy.

Economic values rooted to hard work, discipline, self-denial, savings – all that he calls 'Calvinist Restraint' – are regrettably no longer the touchstone of economic, political, or social discourse within the US. Financial sobriety has been virtually replaced by a celebration of excesses, especially of consumption. In the process, the US – which was traditionally a 'producer economy' has now been turned into a 'consumer economy.' As a direct consequence, economic policies that originally were designed for producers are now increasingly replaced with theories that focus on consumers. Recall the suggestion of the then US President to continued shopping in the aftermath of 9/11, as discussed in Chapter 3. As society increasingly turns into a collection of atomised individuals leading their lives with gay abandon and indiscipline, the discipline of economics was turned on its head. Classical theories of economics, let us not forget, were designed for individuals, families, societies, and governments – each one inter-dependent on the other. It was not intended for atomised individuals leading their personal lives without any social fetters. The net result: Individuals now wallow in huge personal debt. Switzerland – with a household debt of 128 percent of the country's GDP – tops the global list, followed by the United Kingdom at 86 percent, and America at 77 percent. Interestingly, India is at a mere 11 percent, far lower than the global average.

The state, by its very design, is not made out to counter-balance such recklessness of the individual. In the process, it too gets sucked into the quagmire of debt or more taxes, but usually both. For instance, the governmental debt-to-GDP ratio is a whopping 180 percent for China, 103 percent for US, and 50 percent for India in 2017. Is there a positive correlation between individual debt and governmental debt? Do economists ever correlate personal debt and government debt? Do they realise increased individual debt also corresponds to increased governmental debt? In fact, a superficial examination of personal debt and governmental debt suggests that both are positively correlated. This increased debt at both levels obviously results in macro-economic instability.

Given the inherent instability at the individual, family, and social levels, it is but natural that there would be macro-economic instability. The impact of how the US runs gargantuan trade and fiscal deficits, and their collective contribution to the global economic imbalance was discussed in greater detail earlier in Chapter 2 and Chapter 3. It is therefore natural that the sub-prime US crisis of 2008 had transformed into a full-fledged global economic crisis. What is happening within the US is the lack of restraint at the individual level, which is transmuting itself – in the absence of filial restraints and social oversight – into national and possibly global imbalances of an unprecedented level. Strangely, modern economists are repeatedly advocating the economic model of the US on the rest as the very best for others to emulate. Do economists realise the inherent imbalance within the US economy? Do they realise that increasingly, the US is becoming a burden on the rest of the world with its gargantuan consumption? Do we realise the risks associated with the grand experiment? Champions of markets economics are remarkably silent on this imbalance.

In contrast, Americans in the first two generations of the 20th century emphasised on the dangers of excesses. Like all successful societies before it, Americans constructed useful social institutions to encourage virtuous self-restraints. These social institutions, in turn, ensured financial values, which in turn created sustainable economic models, both at the individual and the national levels. Remember, the creation of the US economic miracle was not merely divinity in action, but also the sustained hard work of individuals tempered through self-restraints. All these changed even within the US in the past few decades, probably after the 1960s, as we saw earlier in Chapter 2. Since then, sociologically, politically, and of course in the discipline of economics, it has been a continuous narrative of the celebration of the unrestrained self. As individuals become self-centred, narcissism becomes the order of the day. Factoring the nation, community, corporate, or even the family or spouse is old fashioned in any such modern thought, much less in deed. Put pithily, the story of modern economics is the story of the shift from values in economics to being economic with moral values itself. Worse, modern economics cognises, nay, legitimises all these by crafting newer economics theories that encourages, instead of discouraging deviant behaviour. We will revert to this issue in greater detail in subsequent chapters of this book. Is 'Self, selfie, and selfishness' thy name, modern generation? Daniel Brooks surely has a point – Calvinist Restraint or *Jaya* are crucial elements missing in modern economic discourse.

Importance of Balance

All these take us once again to certain fundamental questions – how important are individual restraints? Do restraints achieve macro-economic stability? Is stability crucial to efficient and sustainable economics? How can individual restraints be encouraged, especially by economic policies? Recall that we discussed how the element of discipline was lost in the discipline of modern economics in Chapter 3. Macro-economics, simply reiterated, is an interplay between its four limbs viz., production, consumption, savings, and investment. Is that why Goddess Lakshmi – the Hindu goddess of wealth – is portrayed with four limbs? Virtually, every modern economic theory implicitly postulates the imbalance between these four limbs of economics. Modern economics seeks to address this lack of balance between the four limbs of economics, and are constantly on the lookout for the remedying the situation, of course at a superficial level. Let us amplify. Excess of production, for instance, leads to depression; consumption leads to deficits; while excessive savings and investments leads to a glut. In real life, most economies are in a perennial state of imbalance, requiring constant external intervention to restore balance. There is either an excess or a shortage of production, consumption, savings, or investment. Modern economists fully cognise this paradigm and are professionally tuned to addressing the resultant imbalances. Crucially, they assume they have the responsibility to set the house in order. Experiences of the past century or so demonstrate that as economists restore balance in an economy, a newer set of imbalances germinate. What is forgotten in the melee is that modern economic theories focus more on treating the symptoms rather than the disease itself. Of course, they cognise the imbalance and seek to address the same, but in the process, create a newer set of imbalances. But the root cause of economic imbalances is never sought to be addressed by any economic theory, but the fallouts of such imbalances are superficially sought to be addressed, especially through intervention of either markets or the government. Modern economic theories alternate between fiscal policies and monetary policies, with the former dealing with taxation and government spending, and the latter dealing with central bank actions regarding money supply and setting of interest rates. In fact, the entire gamut of economic policies relating to taxation, industrial growth, export-import, currency, interest rates, money supply, agriculture, exchange rate management, in the aggregate, fall in either of the two buckets discussed above. The third bucket is yet to be announced. The discipline of economics, thus, revels in a narrow compass of addressing excess or shortage of production, consumption, savings or investments, and thereby excels in dealing with the consequential imbalances arising out of a mismatch between these four limbs. Put differently, if there is a natural, harmonious, and sustained balance between production and consumption, savings and investments, economic theories put forth by modern economists would be virtually redundant.

This can be explained through a reference to the self-sustaining, balanced, and inter-dependent forest ecosystem. In a forest, the ecosystem first ensures a balance between living (biotic) organisms and non-living (abiotic) features in the environment. Abiotic features of a forest ecosystem include precipitation, temperature, landscape, sunlight, soil, water, and moisture. Biotic factors in a balanced forest ecosystem include primary producers such as plants, primary consumers such as herbivores animals, secondary consumers such as carnivores, consumers such as omnivores that consume both plants and animals, and detritivores that eat decaying organic matter. Biotic factors rely upon abiotic factors to survive. For instance, plants require a certain temperature, moisture, water, and soil chemistry to thrive. Animals rely on those plants for their food. A precise balance of all participants ensures sustainability of an ecosystem. Any imbalance within the forest ecosystem would trigger mass extinction of one or more biotic participants. When an ecosystem is self-balanced, of course, there is no need for intervention by external forces. This is the first crucial lesson.

A balanced ecosystem works centrally through energy and material cycling. The chief energy source of ecosystems is sunlight. Photosynthesis of sunlight by plants creates oxygen as a waste product, which in turn is used in respiration by animals. Animals, in turn, create carbon-dioxide as a waste, and that is used by plants. Interestingly, even the waste of one biotic set is consumed and becomes vital for the survival of another biotic set. The conversion of the sun's energy to chemical energy for photosynthesis requires the sun to exist in the first place and perpetuate the energy cycle. Ecosystems do have both a top-down that is predator-related as well as a bottom-up control that is reliant on primary producers such as vegetation. Top-down control by a predator means that predators control the grazers, who in turn control growth of vegetation. When a predator is removed from an ecosystem, the entire food chain is affected, as primary consumers increase, leading to a greater competition for food, probably leading to the collapse of the ecosystem. Thus, an intricate natural balance first between biotic and non-biotic factors, as well as inter-se between various biotic players ensures the sustainability of a forest ecosystem.

Dianne Dotson, a well-known science fiction author explains how the hunting of sea otters by humans led to the collapse of the Kelp Forest ecosystem in the Aleutian Islands, as sea urchins overtook the kelp forests. Once sea otters returned to predate the sea urchins, the Kelp ecosystem returned to balance. Likewise, Dotson argues how prey animals such as krill fuel the ecosystem in the oceans surrounding Antarctica. These tiny animals not only serve as grazers of phytoplankton, but also comprise the primary food source of many other animals, such as seals, penguins, whales, squid, fish, petrels, and albatross. Krill is therefore considered a keystone species, essential to the survival of the Antarctic ecosystem balance. Without krill, the Antarctic ecosystem would collapse.

Is there a lesson for modern economists in all these? Does the discipline of economics, as it stands today, lend itself to such delicate yet all-encompassing idea of balance? Do economists realise that their prescriptions are more to deal with specific or superficial imbalances rather than creating and sustaining balances within national economies, and if possible, the global economy? Ecologists who have intensively studied forests and the associated ecosystems have invariably noticed that big cats hunt herbivores and others down the food chain only to satisfy their needs. Obviously, the animal instincts work, but within the canons of a natural order. There is an expected restraint in their behaviour. What if the big cats in a forest go on a killing spree of all herbivores? What if the birds no longer feed on the insects? Though the phenomenon of excessive hunting by animals has been observed by some, albeit rarely, the fact remains that animals instinctively desist from committing such excesses. They feed on the others in the food chain only to such an extent that sustains the forest ecosystem. Excesses of all hues are naturally shunned and abhorred in the forest. When excesses are committed, it is the unrestrained who are the biggest losers, as they would be disturbing the delicate imbalance within the forest ecosystem. Probably, nature has a way of conveying this subtle yet powerful message to these animals. Surely, animals understand this completely and demonstrate absolute obedience to this natural order. Their restrained behaviour is a conclusive evidence of the power of self-restraint at play in the forest, which ensures balance, which in turn makes a forest sustainable in the long run. While the phrase 'jungle law' suggests exactly the opposite, let us not forget that 'jungle law' is a law well and truly respected by its participants.

In contrast to such disciplined behaviour, economists talk of 'Animal Spirits' – a term popularised by renowned economist John Maynard Keynes – to explain irrational human emotion that drives consumer confidence, especially in conditions of uncertainty. Keynes described 'animal spirit' as "a spontaneous urge to action rather than inaction, and not as the outcome of a weighted average of quantitative benefits multiplied by quantitative probabilities." In simple terms, it means irrational behaviour born out of individual indiscipline. In his magnum opus *The General Theory of Employment, Interest and Money* published in 1936, Keynes went on to elaborate on this subject: "Even apart from the instability due to speculation, there is the instability due to the characteristic of human nature that a large proportion of our positive activities depend on spontaneous optimism rather than mathematical expectations, whether moral or hedonistic or economic." Researchers have since then traced the usage of this term as far back as 300 BC, when the term was believed to have been used in the fields of human anatomy and medicine physiology. In effect, it then referred to the fluid or spirit present in sensory activities and nerves in the brain. Economists have, since the 1930s, used this term first during the downturn, debating how to revive the 'animal spirits,' and then subsequently during the economic boom, discussing how to control the very same 'animal spirits.'

Interestingly, the modern version of the term is used in finance to describe investor psychology, including fear, pessimism, and confidence. For instance, if spirits are low, then confidence levels will be low, which will drive a promising market down, even though the fundamentals of the market or economy remain strong. Likewise, if spirits are high, confidence will be high among participants in the economy and market prices will soar, notwithstanding the fundamentals. Subsequent to the economic crisis of 2008, the idea of animal spirits once again began to resonate among the pantheon of the world's leading economists. In 2009, George A. Akerlof (a Nobel laureate and professor of economics at the University of California) and Robert J Shiller (professor of economics at Yale University), in their book, *Animal Spirits: How Human Psychology Drives the Economy, and Why it Matters for Global Capitalism*, argue that the governments should not allow the market to function on its own. Rather, they opined that the government's active role in economic policy-making is required to control these 'animal spirits.' They believe that these spirits are important, but it is equally imperative to control them because left on their own, capitalism will go too far and may lead to the kind of over-indulgence as seen in 2008, leading to a global economic crisis. In short, what economists accept as gospel is that animal spirits are essential for any economic growth, yet they need to be tempered by constant interference of the government, or by markets themselves – both during exuberance and downturns. It is this assumption that lies at the core of the successive economic theories put forward by the economists. The most 'liberal' amongst economists believe that, by nature, society is prone to cycles of depression and exuberance, which in turn results in economic instability. This instability, according to modern economic thought, can be addressed only through the intervention of markets or governments. Thus, the three assumptions – the inexplicable mood swings of society, the resultant economic volatility, and restoring economic stability only through state intervention, has come to be held as sacrosanct in modern economic theories. This inviolable hypothesis lies at the core of all modern economic theories.

The reason for the same is not far to seek. Economists believe that human nature, collective or otherwise, is intrinsically irrational, and hence requires to be constantly monitored, interfered, and tempered. Surely, the idea put forth by James Boyce in *Born Bad*, and discussed in greater detail in Chapter 3 acquires greater relevance now. Critically, they rationalise that such tempering can be done only through governments or markets with very little or no third alternative. But is it not precisely what animals instinctively desist – irrational behaviour – whatever be the temptations or compulsions? Ever heard of big cats killing deers in excess of what it requires to satisfy their hunger? Or ever heard of vultures turning into a monk and desisting from playing its natural role of clearing the remains of a carcass? In animal kingdom, excesses are virtually absent. So is abstinence. Everyone revels in his given role and performs it to their fullest. No one is irrelevantly neutral. Animals in the forests, it would seem, have taken the teachings of Lord Krishna in Chapter II Verse 47 of the Gita far too seriously than we humans. They continue to perform their assigned role by mother nature to near perfection. Is that why there is no government or markets in the forests, and yet remain stable and hence sustainable? By sheer restraint and without any external intervention, the forests continue to ensure balance and hence sustain themselves. Apparently, there is a subtle yet powerful message from the animals in these forests – the power of balance and the importance of restraints. Balance is achieved within the ecosystem by practicing restraints over a period, not otherwise. Animals, or for that matter any living being rooted to nature, instinctively cognise, respect, and profit from it. Sadly, we as humans do not. This is yet another aspect that lies at the core of this book.

The shift in Modern Economics – Back and Forth

But this shift in economics – originally tempered by individual restraints with a reasonable oversight by the family and society, to the unrestrained – is of recent origin, probably after the Great Depression in the first part of the 20th century. Simultaneously, the traditional role of restraining the individual excesses were transferred from the family and society to the state, and declared to be modern economic thoughts. So, what was a cost-effective supervision of the individual by his family or society, became over a period of time a rather cumbersome means of restraining an individual through the state or its agencies.

This classical position was explained by the father of economics, Adam Smith, in his 1776 treatise titled *An Inquiry into the Nature and Causes of the Wealth of Nations*: "It is not from the benevolence of the butcher, the brewer, or the baker that we expect our dinner, but from their regard to their own interest. We address ourselves, not to their humanity but to their self-love, and never talk to them of our own necessities but of their advantages.

Nobody but a beggar chooses to depend chiefly upon the benevolence of his fellow citizens. Even a beggar does not depend upon it entirely. The charity of well-disposed people, indeed, supplies him with the whole fund of his subsistence. The greater part of his occasional wants is supplied in the same manner as those of other people – by treaty, barter, and by purchase. With the money which one man gives him, he purchases food. The old clothes which another bestows upon him, he exchanges for other old clothes which suit him better, or for lodging, or food, or money, with which he can buy either food, clothes, or lodging, as he has occasion." The butcher, baker, or brewer (together, what may be called the 3B economy) doing their respective jobs is restraint at play. By doing so, they place restraint at the core of their economics. Implicitly, Adam Smith argues that it is in their supreme self-interest to be restrained. Neither are they passively irrelevant to the scheme of society.

This classical position continued for over 200 years since the days of Adam Smith, where the fundamental assumption in postulating any economic theory or policy by the then governments was that the supreme self-interest of an individual will temper his behaviour, and therefore, will be restrained in his behaviour, requiring little or no intervention. Economic theory was intrinsically designed for this rational person. Consequently, till the early 20th century, the role of the government was limited, and government finance was primarily concerned with pure allocative function. The job of the government was to raise revenue as cheaply and efficiently as possible to perform the limited tasks that it could do better than the private sector. In effect, the government was in direct competition with the private sector, leading to greater efficiency in the respective national economies. Remember, what gravity is to physics, competition is to economics. As competition flourished between the government and the private sector, efficiency increased, leading to greater economic growth.

But all this classical economics was turned on its head in the events leading to and in the aftermath of the Great Depression in the first half of the 20th century. The Great Depression and the resultant worldwide economic downturn began in 1929 and lasted until 1939, sparking fundamental changes in economic thought, theories, and policies. The economic impact of the Great Depression was enormous, including extreme human suffering. Although it originated in the US, the Great Depression caused drastic declines in production, severe unemployment, and acute deflation in almost every country of the world. Needless to emphasise, the Great Depression left an indelible mark on the collective psyche of governments and economists. Economists, since then, at every twist and turn, fear another great economic depression of the 1930s. Expectedly, a great deal of economic thought has gone in, since then, to avoid another Great Depression and address turbulence in economies.

The billion-dollar question, therefore, was how to make economies stable. Modern economists assume it is a given that economies will be in a constant state of 'turbulence' (a term popularised by Alan Greenspan, former chairman of the US Federal Reserve) and would need constant external intervention to stabilise them. The fundamental assumption is that economies will be perennially cyclical – irrationally exuberant or inexplicably in a state of doom. This has overturned the classical approach to economics where every individual was balanced and expected to make rational decisions. But questions remain: Are economies inherently volatile and turbulent? Why are economies in a constant state of boil? Is it a given that we shall constantly witness alternative bouts of booms and bursts? Or is this cyclical behaviour exaggerated in the first place? Are economists fixated on this idea of addressing the cyclical behaviour, especially after the Great Depression? In the process, is the discipline of economics missing the woods for the trees? If so, what is the solution to stabilise the economy? What are the pre-conditions that stabilise an economy? And assuming everything is indeed stable in an economy, is it durable? To answer these questions, we shall have to revert to the ideas expounded by John Maynard Keynes yet again.

To the uninitiated, *The Time* magazine in 1999 included Keynes among the most important people of the 20th century, and opined that "his radical idea that governments should spend money they don't have may have saved capitalism." This was almost five decades after his death in 1946. Better still, *The Economist* in 2013 described Keynes as 'Britain's most famous 20th-century economist.' What made Keynes an important economist of the 20th century, to be quoted several decades after his death? More to the point, what was his contribution to the discipline of economics whose ideas seem to resonate long since his demise? To answer these questions, one needs to comprehend Keynes's magnum opus, *The General Theory of Employment, Interest and Money* which was published in 1936 in the backdrop of the Great Depression. This work served as a theoretical justification for the interventionist economic policies which Keynes favoured for tackling a recession. In effect, it was an extraordinary prescription for an extraordinary event – the Great Depression. Keynes, through his magnus opus, successfully challenged the then prevailing economic paradigm, which had held that markets unfettered by government interference, as prescribed by Adam Smith, would naturally establish full employment equilibrium.

Alan Greenspan puts its succinctly when he states that the views of John Maynard Keynes, the great British economist, had replaced those of Adam Smith and his classical economics, when the Great Depression of the 1930s failed to follow Smith's model of the way economies were supposed to behave. Greenspan notes that Keynes "had provided the intellectual underpinning for Roosevelt's New Deal", and explains how Keynes "argued that free markets, left to themselves, do not always deliver optimal good to society, and that when employment stagnated, as it did disastrously in the Great Depression, government has to step in." That the government had to step in during the Great Depression is understandable. But that it had become a template to address even mild volatility in every economy is indeed questionable.

Yet another idea of the seminal work of Keynes was that if savings exceed investment, unemployment will rise. Keynes was of the view that when interest rates are high, people tend to save more, leading to this anomalous situation. At the height of the Great Depression, in 1933, Keynes also published *The Means to Prosperity*, which contained specific policy recommendations for tackling global recession, which were predominantly counter-cyclical public spending. *The Means to Prosperity* contains the first reference to the multiplier effect. While it was addressed chiefly to the British government, it also contained advice for other nations affected by the global recession. A copy was sent to the newly elected President Franklin D Roosevelt and other world leaders. The work was initially taken seriously by both the American and British governments, and paved the way for the global acceptance of Keynesian ideas. Subsequently, President Roosevelt created the Works Progress Administration (WPA), which was the largest government programme of its time, and which was funded by Congress by an amount of approximately 7 percent of the national income of the US. During each year of the remainder of the Great Depression until the US joined the Second World War in 1941, the WPA hired approximately 6 percent of the workforce of the US as relief workers. This was the only time in US history that the US Government hired such large numbers of people in an attempt at economic stabilisation. Keynesian economics became firmly part of American economic policy in 1938, when Congress passed the Pump Priming Act. *The General Theory* is often viewed by the pantheon of economists as the foundation of modern macro-economics and dominated the collective economic thinking in the post-World War II era. Such was the contribution of Keynes to the discipline of economics that Milton Friedman (latter echoed by US President Richard Nixon) – another great economist of the 20th century – unabashedly declared in late 1965 that "We are all Keynesians now."

The reaction of Britain in response to the economic crises and busts of the business cycle was more or less on similar lines. The response was to place a greater reliance on the government toward its citizens, and the beginning of the British brand of socialism. Much of this was articulated by the Fabians, including celebrities like George Bernard Shaw. These immensely influential intellectuals sought to replace the "scramble for private gain" with the achievement of 'collective welfare.' Their method, instead of those suggested by Marxists, was incrementalism, not revolution. For inspiration, the British obviously looked to experimentation and interventionist reforms of Franklin Roosevelt and the New Deal. Yet, others were drawn more to the Soviet Union and accomplishments of communism, socialism, and central planning, which seemed to make the USSR the exception to global stagnation. A segment of the British intelligentsia maintained its romance with Soviet Communism for all too long till World War II, which had vastly enlarged the economic realm of the government. The British government took over the economy and ran it far more efficiently, on a much larger scale, than had been the case in the 1930s. All of these historical currents led to a rejection of Adam Smith, laissez-faire, and traditional 19th century liberalism as an economic philosophy. In the immediate post-war years, there was scepticism and outright disbelief in the idea that the individual's pursuit of what Adam Smith defined as self-interest would add up, in the aggregate, to the benefit of all. As Attlee put the matter succinctly, a belief in private profit as the motive for economic progress was in those heady times "a pathetic faith resting on no foundation of experience."

Post-war, the Labour Party had a blueprint at hand. It was in the Beveridge Report, prepared by the British government during the war under William Beveridge from the London School of Economics. The report's influence would be global and far-reaching. It not only gave a blueprint for Britain, but also the idea of social welfare to the entire industrialised world. In line with its recommendations, the government established free medical care under a newly constituted National Health Service, created new systems of pensions, promoted better education and housing, and sought to deliver on the explicit commitment to 'full employment.' All of this added up to what the British were to call the 'welfare state.' Interestingly, the national insurance for pensions and illness had been pioneered by German chancellor Bismarck, as early as the 1880s. In contrast, Britain introduced the first state insurance schemes for unemployment and health, and old-age pensions in 1906. These initial steps of what was at the time called the 'ambulance state' were quite modest, yet critiqued. By contrast, William Beveridge transformed Britain from an ambulance state into the first major welfare state. Obviously, too much water had flown in the Thames between the first and the fifth decade of the 20th century, obviously on account of the war.

Thus, what was a unique prescription for an unprecedented event in the history of mankind subsequently became the default position for future economic policy formulations. Alan Greenspan brings about this tectonic shift in economic thinking away from markets to the interventionist ideas of Keynes when he states that economics students in the late 1940s were on a mission: "What really bound us together was the sense that economics was undergoing a transition, and we were there at the frontier. Anyone who was studying economics at that time was determined that there would never be another major depression. The depression of the 1930s had led to World War II, and so we were imbued with the sense that we could not let this disaster visit us again. It was hard to find anyone who was not strongly influenced by the Democratic Party and John Maynard Keynes, and his idea about the very strong role that the government could and should play in dominating economic affairs."

The natural fallout of all this was that the Keynesian presumption held sway in world capitals, and the overarching idea in the management of the economy was that it could be actively done through governmental intervention. In practical terms, governments and bigger governments became the norm worldwide, both as a regulator of men and (as a net consequence), of their affairs. In the process, governments ended up occupying the commanding heights of the world economy. In view of this, a constant challenge to policy framers was to work out programmes that ceaselessly involved the state or its instrumentalities, and raise revenues for such programmes. Thus, governments became central to our lives and, of course, to our economic thinking. First, we are taxed. And subsequently, in the net of the gargantuan expenditure of governments, we became the targeted beneficiary of these programmes drawn by it. Thus, money flow from people through taxes (or borrowings) to the government, and once again back to people as governmental welfare (or investment) programmes was intermediated by the government and its agencies. This is how the Keynesian idea of government intervention during depression degenerated over time. To a dispassionate observer, it would seem that not many have demonstrated the required courage to question the prevailing conventional wisdom of the omnipotent and omnipresent role of governments in the post-war era till date. Of course, involving the government was not the most ideal or cost-effective way. But who could question? Who could dare question?

And to those who did, unregulated markets were the only alternative. Given the bitter experiences in the first four decades of the 20th century, the alternative ideological framework to Keynesian ideas initially never got the necessary traction. But not for long. Call it as entropy in action in global economics, the fact remains those Keynesian ideas became outworn within two decades of World War II. To illustrate, Keynesian economics was officially discarded by the British Government in 1979, but forces against it had begun to gather against Keynes's ideas over 30 years earlier, though never recognised officially or academically. Friedrich Hayek, an Austrian economist (along with Ludwig von Mises and Milton Friedman, who are considered contemporaries of Keynes) had, since the days of Keynes, nurtured alternative economic theories to Keynes. The idea of 'big government,' that had appeared to be dominating post-war economics, was slowly but steadily yielding space to the dominance of markets in the 1960s. Two noted journalists Larry Elliott and Dan Atkinson point out that by 1968, the economic power shifted decisively in favour of private players and markets. Elliott and Atkinson picked out America's suspension in 1968 of the conversion of the dollar into gold as the beginning of the breakdown of the Bretton Woods system, and by extension of the Keynesian ideas. In 1968, Milton Friedman and others began challenging economic dogmas that were rooted to Keynesian ideas. Friedman suggested that sustained Keynesian policies could lead to both unemployment and inflation rising at once – a phenomenon that soon became known as 'stagflation.' In the early 1970s, stagflation appeared in both the US and Britain just as Friedman had predicted, with economic conditions deteriorating further after the 1973 oil crisis. Aided by the prestige gained from his successful forecast, Friedman led increasingly successful criticisms against the Keynesian consensus, convincing not only academics and politicians, but also much of the general public with his radio and television broadcasts. The academic credibility of Keynesian economics was further undermined by criticism from the Chicago School of Economics. So successful were these criticisms that by 1980, Robert Lucas, a prominent economist, claimed that economists would take offence if described as Keynesians. All this, when merely 15 years ago in 1965, officially and academically, it was declared that "We are all Keynesians now."

Crucially, what should not be forgotten in the melee is that to this extent the ideological underpinning of economic thought alternated in the whole of 20th century between two extremes – one that presumes a significant role for the government, and the other, without it. *The Commanding Heights for the Battle of World Economy*, authored by Daniel Yergin and Joseph Stanislaw, captures this apparent tectonic shift in economic ideas, and explains in simple language the economic history of the 20th century. A riveting account of both history and politics of the post-war years, *The Commanding Heights* is a compelling story of politicians, thinkers, policy-framers, and businessmen who brought these changes. It is a story of how the marketplace came about to occupy the commanding heights of the world economy in the last two decades of the 20th century, which was originally occupied by the governments in the first two decades following the World War. It is the story of how Margaret Thatcher, Ronald Reagan, Deng Xiaoping, and Bill Clinton effectuated at the political level the economic ideas of Friedrich von Hayek, who at that point in time was believed to be destined to win the "battle of ideas." Written with unique access to many of the key players, *The Commanding Heights* brought about an understanding of the tumultuous economic events that happened in the second half of the 20th century. Thus, *The Commanding Heights* is all about what the authors termed it as "the epic struggle between government and the marketplace" and the manner in which the shift from government to markets have influenced and dramatically transformed our lives then. Interestingly, this economic transformation – as chronicled by *The Commanding Heights* – coincided with the re-drawing of political maps in the aftermath of the collapse of the Soviet Union. Naturally, the authors declare authoritatively that this shift was good for all times to come.

And pray why not? By the dawn of the 21st century, it would seem the ideas of Hayek had conclusively triumphed the ideas of Keynes. The word 'globalisation' had virtually come to dominate the socio-economic-political lexicon. Market economics dominated Keynesian ideas of intervention. *The World is Flat*, declared Thomas Friedman, the award-winning *New York Times* columnist. Friedman, like Daniel Yergin and Joseph Stanislaw, went on to once again declare triumphantly how the flattening of the world happened at the dawn of the 21st century; what it meant to countries, enterprises, communities, and individuals; and how governments and societies can, and must, adapt to the new flat world. Like Yergin and Stanislaw, Thomas Freidman too fell into the trap of premature triumphalism. Most economic policies designed and celebrated in the 20th century, let us not forget, were predominantly symptomatic, and probably never diagnostic.

No wonder all this euphoria on markets, globalisation, privatisation, and deregulation lasted a mere decade or two. It was as if economic theories were never eternal ideas – one that withstood the test of time. On the contrary, they seem as fashion statements intended for a particular period of time or for a specific situation. The 'ultimate triumph' of economic ideas of Hayek over Keynes as put forth by Daniel Yergin and Joseph Stanislaw, and so eloquently argued by them in *The Commanding Heights* perhaps lasted a decade or so. Their work traces the forces and individuals most centrally involved in the rise and fall of socialist policies around the globe. The authors have painstakingly listed the key names and ideas associated with the drama. Their history of each nation's sorry experience with socialism is simply brilliant. The anecdotes and damaging quotations from the now-discredited proponents of socialism make the read worthwhile. The book reveals an amazingly consistent pattern of political connivance with which politicians and their coterie of 'economic advisers' across continents systematically capitalise on fear and gullibility among the masses to replace freedom and property rights with central planning and bureaucracy. The authors illustrate how eagerly totalitarians have and, in future, will pounce on every economic crisis as an opportunity to grasp more power.

While all this, and the inevitable fall of socialism and consequences thereof is well understood, the authors had virtually declared market economics as a triumphant destination point for the entire world by the end of the 20th century. Similarly, the world indeed became flat, as announced by Thomas Friedman. But the world did not remain flat for long. Likewise, recall the declaration of Francis Fukuyama in Chapter 3, and how within a decade or two of his prophecy of *End of History and The Last Man*, Fukuyama was compelled by the turn of events in the first decade of the 21st century to revisit his own theory. Yet, these very authors, economists or commentators themselves declared triumphantly as they put forth their idea or theory. Implicit in their declaration was that their idea was eternal, when subsequent events – all within a few years – demonstrated the mortality of the same.

The financial crisis caused by toxic derivatives within the US in 2007-08 subsequently transformed itself into a full-blown global economic crisis. Naturally, this raised questions about the free market consensus even from its champions. In March 2008, Martin Wolf, a well-known commentator at the *Financial Times*, announced the death of the dream of global free-market capitalism. This was just a few months even before the crisis was full-blown. In the same month, macro-economist Galbraith launched a sweeping attack against free-market consensus and crucially argued that Keynesian economics was far more relevant for tackling the emerging financial and economic crises. Robert Shiller, another economist of great repute, had begun advocating robust government intervention to tackle the extant crises, specifically citing Keynes. Nobel laureate Paul Krugman also actively argued the case for vigorous Keynesian intervention in the economy in his columns of *The New York Times*. Others who then argued for government intervention based on the ideas of Keynes to mitigate the financial crisis include George Akerlof, J Bradford DeLong, Robert Reich, Joseph Stiglitz, Hyman Minsky, Robert Skidelsky, Donald Markwell, and Axel Leijonhufvud – all of them economists of great repute, and some of them, till then, champions of free markets. Hayek who was the darling of these very pantheons of economists till then made an abrupt unceremonious exit. And the exit of his ideas marked the re-entry of Keynes. And, of course, we all become Keynesian yet again in 2008.

Now, let us look at the responses of the US Government to the 2008 crisis. As a first step to the financial crisis, the US Federal Government along with the US Federal system announced a series of major bailouts. The first step was to immediately 'nationalise' (a dirty word since the 1980s) the two government-sponsored enterprises which oversaw most of the US sub-prime mortgage market – Fannie Mae and Freddie Mac. In October 2008, Alistair Darling, the then British Chancellor of the Exchequer, referred to Keynes as he announced plans for fiscal stimulus to deal with the recession. Similar policies were adopted by other governments worldwide. Much of the post-crisis discussion reflected Keynes's advocacy of international coordination of fiscal or monetary stimulus, and of international economic institutions such as the IMF and the World Bank. By the end of December

2008, merely three months into the crisis, the *Financial Times* reported that "the sudden resurgence of Keynesian policy is a stunning reversal of the orthodoxy of the past several decades." In December 2008, Paul Krugman released his book *The Return of Depression Economics and the Crisis of 2008*, arguing that economic conditions similar to what existed during the earlier part of the 20th century had returned, making Keynesian policy prescriptions more relevant than ever. In February 2009, Robert J Shiller and George Akerlof published *Animal Spirits*, a book where they argue that the current US stimulus package is too small, as it does not consider Keynes' insight on the importance of confidence and expectations in determining the future behaviour of business people and other economic agents. In a March 2009 speech titled *Reform the International Monetary System*, Zhou, the governor of the People's Bank of China, came out in favour of Keynes's idea of a centrally managed global reserve currency. Stimulus plans were credited for contributing to a better-than-expected economic outlook by both the OECD and the IMF, in reports published in June and July 2009. Both organisations warned global leaders that recovery was likely to be slow, so counter-recessionary measures need not be rolled back too early.

The lessons of all this are obvious. First, economic policy made during an unprecedented crisis cannot be a prescription model for all times to come. Secondly, most economic ideas come with a shelf life – probably for a decade or two. Third, most economic theories are designed for normal times, and fail in the face of unprecedented crisis. Fourth, economic crisis is invariably caused by one form of excess or other, and is bound to happen sooner than later. Fifth, even without excesses, most ideas including economic theories are subject to laws of entropy. Sixth, economists constantly seek durable stability which remains elusive. Seventh, economic stability is not desirable through governmental interventions nor attainable through market intervention. Eighth, most ideas in modern economics deal with the symptom than the disease. Ninth, the search for the ultimate stabiliser in economics is incomplete. And finally, tenth, the discipline of economics needs to outgrow the ideas of both Keynes and Hayek.

Undoubtedly, one of the great unresolved debates in economics is what should be done to prevent bubbles in the first place, and what should be done after the bubble is burst. Many economists believe that monetary policy can be used by central banks to stabilise the economy through a counter-cyclical monetary policy. Reducing the money supply and raising interest rates during a boom would slow down the investment during the boom. The reversal of these policies is prescribed to tackle periods of bust. Either way, there is a near consensus view among economists that the market economy is inherently unstable, and that left to itself, it will repeatedly undergo through periods of costly booms and busts. The only point of contention among economists, as already pointed out, is how to tackle them.

It is now obvious that between Keynes and Hayek, there is a missing middle in the discipline of economics. Economic policy formulation for too long has reduced it to a simple binary position. On the contrary, the subject of macro-economics is an interplay between the markets, governments, and a third dimension. Experiences of the past century, which were briefly discussed above, demonstrate that for too long, economists have ignored this aspect completely – what one may now call it as the missing middle. Is this missing middle family and culture? Is there a symbiotic link between culture, family, and economics? Do economists realise now that the discipline of economics is incomplete without factoring in the stabilising influence of family and culture? Do we appreciate the fact that the biggest challenge is sustainability in modern economics? If not for family, what else? Put differently, are the laws of economics unsustainable or unworkable in a society that is culturally challenged? Laws of entropy seem to work overtime on economic theories than otherwise. Is that why ordinary men and women realise that it is the combination of family, and by extension culture, that ensures stability in society, and by extension, in the economy? Is that why Arjuna lamented in Chapter I of the *Bhagavad Gita* on the potential collapse of family in the aftermath of a war? Is that why Tamils got incensed with the statements of Khushboo that seemed to question their culture in the first place? Does the common man instinctively understand that without the hydraulic yet invisible force of culture, ideas in economics are merely theories? In effect, are economic ideas unworkable without the benign presence of family? Is family and culture the emerging frontier of modern economics? We will answer these questions as we proceed along in the following chapters.

References

1. Excerpts from "Trials of Truth: India's Landmark Criminal Cases" By Pinky Anand and Gauri Goburdhun; Published by The News Minute with permission of Penguin Random House India – January 10, 2018.
2. Judgement of the Hon'ble Madras High Court in S. Khusboo vs Kanniammal dated 30 April 2008.
3. Judgement of the Hon'ble Supreme Court of India in S. Khusboo vs Kanniammal & Anr dated 28 April 2010.
4. Entropy Is Not Disorder by Steve Donaldson – January 4 2011 – Science 2.0.
5. Entropy: Why Life Always Seems to Get More Complicated By James Clear - www.jamesclear.com
6. Gita Press, Gorakhpur.
7. https://www.nytimes.com/2009/09/29/opinion/29brooks.html
8. Describe a Balanced Ecosystem By J. Dianne Dotson; April 10, 2018 - https://sciencing.com/describe-balanced-ecosystem-5761235.html
9. Animal Spirits -www.investopedia.com
10. Saurabh Kumar -https://www.livemint.com- October 3, 2012.
11. Government economic policy by WRITTEN BY: Assar Lindbeck John Anderson Kay Charles Nicholas Morris Kenyon Edwards Poole John F. Due - https://www.britannica.com/topic/government-economic-policy.
12. https://tradingeconomics.com/country-list/households-debt-to-gdp
13. https://en.wikipedia.org/wiki/List_of_countries_by_public_debt
14. The next culture war: economic restraint, September 29, 2009 By David Brooks, The Seattle Times.
15. https://en.wikipedia.org/wiki/John Maynard Keynes.
16. The Age of Turbulence By Alan Greenspan.
17. The Commanding Heights: The Battle for the World Economy By Daniel Yergin, Joseph Stanislaw.

5. A Case for the Missing Middle

The family is one of nature's masterpieces – George Santayana

A great civilization is not conquered from without until it has destroyed itself from within – Ariel Durant

In the previous chapter, we had argued that there is a missing middle in the discipline of economics, more so in our understanding of the repeated cycles of economic booms and busts. More to the point, the modern approach to the study of economics has been oversimplified that it has excluded an undefined, unexplored, and probably a misunderstood core. We regard this exclusion of the missing middle fatal to the very understanding of the discipline of economics. This has, in our opinion, reduced the very understanding of economics into a reductionist exercise and examination of possibly the fringe. Consequently, economic theories developed in the past few decades are constantly subjected to cataclysmic resets with the solutions alternating seemingly at a wide spectrum, but, inexorably only between the grand ideas of Keynes and Hayek in realistic terms. Liberalise or nationalise seem to be the only two possible ways to deal with the tumultuous issues confronting the national, or for that matter, the global economy. To an alien, it would seem that there is no third way and the world of economics is condemned between the ideas put forth by these two undoubtedly great economists. Nevertheless, this over-simplification meant that the economic theories by Keynes are debunked at some point in time (as demonstrated in the previous chapter) only to resurface and gain currency a decade or two latter, even as theories of Hayek adopted as an alternative to Keynes, fail. Likewise, when the ideas of Keynes are no longer the flavour of the season, instinctively and invariably governments find virtues in the economic thoughts of Hayek. The solutions by Hayek to the challenges contained in Keynesian ideas, and answers by Keynes to the problems sought to be created by the economic thoughts of Hayek, by themselves, contain the seeds of cyclical booms and busts.

Governments increasingly realise, that in alternating between the ideas of Keynes and Hayek, the biggest challenge in macro-economics is the lack of stability, and hence absence of sustainability. If markets collapse, let the government step in, and when governments fail, unleash the power of markets seems to be the mantra. In fact, it would be obvious that economies are extremely skewed without any force to counter the imbalance inherent in every economy. It is this lack of countervailing force – the central idea of this book – that makes economies inherently unstable, volatile, and hence vulnerable to extreme gyrations. With no solution in sight to this rather vexatious issue of having a natural (or for that matter even contrived) counter-balance to prevent or neutralise the economic volatility, economists have signalled those modern economic theories do not seek to address economic instability in the first place. In fact, volatility is a given in most modern economic theories. In the absence of a stabilising and calming influence, it is but natural that the economy is constantly in a state of boil. If the repeated cycles of boom and doom are a norm, and given the fact that we do not seemingly have any instrumentality to stabilise it, do we then have to inevitably live through the world of irrational exuberance and exaggerated lassitude? Therefore, the question is whether modern economists are side-stepping a crucial fact – is the lack of understanding of the missing middle, much less dealing with it, the cause of these recurring cycles of boom and doom?

Crucially, we put forth this question: Is this missing middle the institution of family? Is the family the eternal countervailing economic force that naturally and effectively counter-balances economic cycles? Put differently, can governments ensure that we can get over the repeated cycles of boom and doom by nurturing the institution of family? Can we offset this cycle by empowering the institution of family? Do families have the inherent strength of absorbing economic crises and providing antidotes to such problems, while simultaneously offering the means to sustain economic growth? Contrary to popular belief, the answers to these questions are not complex. In fact, it is our viewpoint that the discipline of economics has been deliberately made complex to overcome the fundamental lack of understanding of the missing middle.

Family, the Homeostasis at play

In the previous chapter, we had referred to the idea of entropy, borrowed from thermodynamics. Entropy, as we saw earlier, is the downward spiral from order to disorder. But even as a system goes on a downward spiral, from order to disorder, from command to chaos, there is a marked tendency of every system to re-stabilise at the earliest possible occasion. This is because every natural system invariably comes with a self-regulatory or a self-balancing mechanism. The phenomenon of any system attempting to balance all by itself, even as it may be on a downward slide, can be explained as 'homeostasis' in action. Put differently, the natural resistance to change by a system, when already in the optimal conditions, and balancing naturally through a regulatory mechanism where this pre-set equilibrium is disturbed, is expressed through a biological term called 'homeostasis.' The concept of homeostasis is widely used, in physiology, to identify what seems to be a general attribute of living organisms – the ability and tendency to maintain and restore the state of natural or desired equilibrium. An obvious example is that of body temperature, which in humans tends to fluctuate only in a narrow range of 98.5 to 98.7° F. When this temperature rises above the normal range, corrective reflexes (perspiration, reduced metabolism, etc.) go into synchronous action to restore the desired state of equilibrium. Likewise, if body temperature drops, several systems within the body get automatically activated, and corrective actions are naturally carried out.

How does this homeostatic mechanism work? This requires some explanation. Classically speaking, all homeostatic mechanisms have at least three inter-dependent components – detection of significant change, instant reaction to change, and setting of a new equilibrium. To explain further, the dynamic state of equilibrium of a human body is occasioned by the optimal functioning of many variables, such as body temperature and fluid balance being kept within certain pre-set limits. Other variables include the concentration of sodium, potassium, and calcium ions, as well as that of the blood sugar level. Obviously, these need to be regulated on account of changes in the environment, diet, or physical activity of the individual. As the equilibrium is disturbed, the homeostatic mechanisms instantly and instinctively come to play. It ensures that the body is appropriately regulated to ensure an acceptable equilibrium is attained at the earliest.

Naturally, a robust homeostatic mechanism will ensure that it detects any change, reacts at the earliest, and sets up the new equilibrium seamlessly and constantly. Given the fact that economies are in a constant cycle of boom and doom, do economists realise that there is an urgent need of a homeostatic mechanism in macroeconomics – one that continuously detects deviations, instantly reacts to correct deviations, and effortlessly sets a new equilibrium. Is the lack of a vigorous homeostatic mechanism, the missing middle in modern economics? Is the lack of missing middle the family? But before we proceed to answer these questions, let us first understand why economies are volatile and subjected to such extreme swings as we have witnessed in the past century or so.

Hyperbole as a Solution

The repeated cycle of boom and doom in modern economics and the absence of a serious study in understanding its causes and addressing remains at the core of this work. In fact, events of the past 50 years or so have demonstrated that economists have been reluctant to diagnose the issue beyond a point. When diagnosis is itself a non-starter, what to speak of the prescription? This lack of serious thinking on the part of the pantheon of economists to tackle the issue of boom and doom through 'economic reforms' is probably the bigger problem.

Therefore, the biggest challenge, one suspects, is that the answer to this convoluted problem in macro-economics, has over the past decade or two, in the absence of fresh thinking allowed the solution to degenerate into mere clichés without much of ideas, contents, or policies. Nothing illustrates the lack of new ideas in modern economics on this cycle of booms and busts than the fact that most economists agree that this is the time for 'structural reforms,' without specifying what is meant by this universally abused, highly persuasive, yet superficial term called 'structural reforms.' In the absence of even a precise definition, the term 'structural reforms' lends itself into multiple interpretations and manifold explanations. No wonder when the term is explained even by any high priest of any global economic organisation, one is left mostly in the dark and not any wiser. For instance, in her remarks delivered on June 10, 2013, at the 19th Conference of Montreal International Economic Forum of the Americas by Angel Gurría, the Secretary-General of the Organisation for Economic Co-operation and Development (OECD) admitted that there were serious flaws in our present-day economic thinking. More to the point, she adds: "It has highlighted the need to look at economic policy with more critical, fresh approaches. It has also revealed the limitations of the existing tools for structural analysis to factor in key linkages, feedbacks, and trade-offs – for example between growth, inequality, and the environment." While this may be the first step in realising the fact that there are inherent limitations in the modern economic thinking, the fact remains that not many want to take the next tentative steps of any structured analysis, or for that matter detail out what does she mean by 'fresh approaches.'

Angel Gurria encapsulates the collective thinking (or the lack of it) within the OECD on the issue of 'structural reforms.' But pray what is this animal called structural reforms? Will it be in any position to address the issue of cyclical booms and busts, or for that matter poverty, inequality or growth? "At the OECD, we are convinced that the best way forward is through the implementation of a comprehensive package of structural reforms," she declares and explains that these reforms "can boost long-term growth and welfare, but also underpin confidence and reduce the pressure off monetary and fiscal policies to buttress the recovery." Explaining that OECD had simulated the effects of 'structural reforms' on potential output across the OECD area through 2060, she further adds to the issue on hand – "Our analysis shows that moving to best practice across a number of policy areas like education, innovation, competition, deregulation, labour, and product markets, taxes, health systems, R&D, and infrastructure would raise per capita incomes by some 20 percent in the median OECD country." Claiming that this would be 'huge,' her clarion call to achieve this quantum leap in economic growth was to "Go Structural! It is good for growth and prosperity, and it is good for the public finances." Stunningly, the economic policy blueprint is well and truly ready for the next few decades. When hit by slowdown, downturn, recession, or depression, economists begin to revisit the drawing board and explain the past with no reference, much less assurance of better economic prosperity in the future.

'Structural reforms,' Angel Gurria, claims "will also increase our government's ability to address the social crisis. Indeed, that's why our second advice is to 'Go Social.' The impact of this crisis on families has been devastating, and there is still significant room to improve social policy in many countries (in taxes, education, youth, health, social security, migration, gender)." She did not stop here and the third limb of her 'structural reforms' included a reference to the environment where she elaborated the OECD position as seeing this moment as an opportunity to 'Go Green' and added, "We are on a collision course with nature and cannot continue to promote an economic growth based on highly polluting energies and overconsumption. Instead, we can move towards greater energy efficiency by implementing smart structural reforms." Behind all these 'structured speeches' is the simple fact that the idea of 'structured reforms' is still in its embryonic stage. And in conclusion, she also added in good measure: "We also believe that this is the time to apply reforms to strengthen the institutional capacity of our countries. It's time to 'Go Institutional.' It is crucial that we reinforce the capacity of our governments, and our institutions, to deliver better results, to be more effective, and to communicate better the positive effects of reforms and policies. The crisis has had a very strong impact on public trust on governments and we urgently need to reverse this trend."

Thus, the entire issue of structural reforms as broken in its entirety consists of four limbs – structural, social, environmental, and of course, governmental. This urge to place the government as the dominant force that can stabilise an economy and provide solutions for every challenge confronting an economy is an outworn prescription, probably even a flawed idea to begin with. In the world of economics, governments have often been found to be the villain of the piece. And where governments have not been the villain, they invariably are without the requisite tools to tackle the extant economic crisis. Nevertheless, that is what OECD seems to have done and probably fallen into the very same trap that the economic policy framers had fallen into for the past few decades, viz., placing too much reliance on formal institutions, regulations, and in the government. Interestingly, strengthening the institution of government to achieve 'structural reforms' remains at the core of this approach of OECD and based on this assumption, it has gone on to draw economic simulations for over the next 50 years, and arrive at certain definitive conclusions! Do we at least now understand the extent of the sclerosis that has set into our collective thinking? Surely, when the next economic crisis hits us, OECD will be as clueless as most of us about its cause and of course, solution. The OECD prescriptions are not mere exceptions to the issue. In fact, they would form part of the policy prescriptions across continents. Of course, even the jargons would be the same.

Eating Crow as Economic Policy

The reason for such scepticism stems from the fact that global economic institutions, economists and politicians have often declared that they have put in place a robust economic management system, institutions, and policies which will ensure that there never be a return to 'boom and bust' economics, only to eat crow within a few years. It is not that none of us are unaware of the potential boom and doom in the national and possibly, global economics. It is only that not many have a solution to the repeated cycles of 'boom and bust.' The challenge for every policy framer is therefore to claim complete knowledge of the same and proffer solutions, when in fact, he has none.

In the process, most of them recycle their own templated speeches and clichés on the subject without a sense of remorse of repeating themselves. Gordon Brown, the former Prime Minister of Britain, for instance, has repeatedly expressed his views for approximately a decade between 1997 and 2007 on the need for the British economy to fight the issue of boom and bust. Interestingly, the view of Gordon Brown seems to be static for nearly a decade. At least for the sheer consistency, one must indeed applaud him. But apart from the clichés there are not much takeaways from his ideas, or for that matter details except for the fact that stability in economy seems to be his destination point. These have been meticulously chronicled by noted columnist Deborah Summers in the *Guardian*. Let us quote the same from what Deborah had reported:

> **May 20, 1997:** Speech by the chancellor to the CBI: Exploiting the British genius – the key to long-term economic success: "Stability is necessary for our future economic success. The British economy of the future must be built not on the shifting sands of boom and bust, but on the bedrock of prudent and wise economic management for the long term. It is only these firm foundations that we can raise Britain's underlying economic performance."
>
> **April 28, 1998:** Speech by the chancellor to the British American Business Council in London: "Now, it is true to say in Britain that the last 40 years has been characterised by stop-go, boom-bust instability in economic policy. And so, I can tell you that the first objective of the new government has been the determination to ensure monetary and fiscal stability, in place of stop-go, and to do so in an economy far more open than the sheltered national economies of the past."
>
> **June 10, 1999:** Speech by the chancellor at Mansion House: "The way forward is for governments to consciously pursue monetary and fiscal stability through setting clear objectives, establishing proper rules, and requiring openness and transparency – the new rules of the game. Particularly important for a Britain which has been more subject than most economies to the instability of boom-bust cycles and constantly changing policies.
>
> Indeed, the economy of 1997 was set to repeat the same cycle of boom and bust that had been seen over the past 20 years. There were strong inflationary pressures in the system. Consumer spending was growing at an unsustainable rate and inflation was set to rise sharply above target; there was a large structural deficit on the public finances. Public sector net borrowing stood at £28 billion.
>
> So we put in place a wholly new long-term framework of monetary and fiscal policy based on: first, clear objectives: price stability through a pre-announced inflation target – a symmetrical target – and sustainable public finances through tough fiscal rules: the golden rule that requires that over the cycle, we balance the current budget, and the sustainable

investment rule requires that, as we borrow for investment, debt is held to a prudent and stable level; second, well understood rules: a new system of monetary policy-making, at the heart of which is the independence of the Bank of England, and its open letter system, and an equivalent and equally important set of fiscal procedures legally enshrined in the code for fiscal stability; and third, transparency in policy-making: an open system of decision-making in monetary policy through the publication of minutes, a system of voting and full reporting to parliament; and in fiscal policy the same openness and disclosure with key fiscal assumptions independently audited."

April 5, 2000: Speech by Gordon Brown to the British Chamber of Commerce National Conference: "In a global marketplace, with its increased insecurities and indeed often volatility and instability, national economic stability is at a premium, the precondition for all we can achieve, and no nation can secure the high levels of sustainable investment it needs without both monetary and fiscal stability together. And it was to avoid the historic British problem – the violence of the repeated boom and bust cycles of the past – that we established the new monetary framework based on consistent rules – the symmetrical inflation target; settled, well-understood procedures – bank independence; and openness and transparency. And side by side with it and as important, a new fiscal discipline with, again, clear and consistent rules – the golden rule for public spending; well understood procedures – our fiscal responsibility legislation; and a new openness and transparency. My vision is of a Britain where there is not stop-go and boom-bust, but economic stability; a Britain which is business-friendly, and where there is enterprise, opportunity for all; a Britain which rewards the innovator and risk-taker and encourages a new generation of entrepreneurs, a Britain which, because opportunity is open to all, is enterprising and fair."

June 20 2001: Chancellor's speech at Mansion House: "Every time in recent decades when the British economy has started to grow, Governments of both parties have taken short-term decisions which too often have created unsustainable consumer booms, let the economy get out of control and sacrificed monetary and fiscal prudence. And everyone here will remember how quickly and easily boom turned to bust in the early nineties. So, Britain did need a wholly new monetary and fiscal framework that went beyond the crude Keynesian fine tuning of the 50s and 60s, and the crude monetarism of the 70s and 80s and, instead, offered a modern British route to stability."

March 28 2002: Speech to the TGWU conference, *Manufacturing Matters* – "With Bank of England independence, tough decisions on inflation, new fiscal rules, and hard public spending controls, we today in our country have economic stability, not boom and bust, the lowest inflation in Europe, and long-term interest rates – essential for businesses planning to borrow and invest – lower than for 35 years. So, while many have claimed Britain was worst placed of any to withstand the global slowdown, the OECD and IMF have both shown that Britain last year had the highest growth of any of the G-7 countries. So, nothing we do will put at risk the fundamental stability on which manufacturing depends. There will be no return to the short-term lurches in policy that would put long-term stability at risk. No relaxing our fiscal disciplines as some would like."

November 18, 2003: Speech to the CBI national conference – "But, for the first time in 50 years, Britain has not only avoided recession but has continued to grow in quarter after quarter, year after year, in all six years of our government since 1997. Remember the old days, what was called the British problem: stop-go, boom-bust, unstable cycle. Britain, the country usually first-in, worst-hit and last out of any world downturn; invariably hit by an inflation problem that prevented interest rates falling when they needed to come down, and usually then by wage inflation that could not be afforded and prevented you making long-term investment.

So I want to explain to you today the policy we – and the Bank of England – will continue to pursue to ensure the British economy entrenches our new won and hard won stability and continues to grow – ensuring we take no risks with inflation or stability generally, or with the fiscal position."

April 21 2004: Remarks at the British Chambers of Commerce Annual Conference: "Now, by working together, we can see a Britain that has a new-found and hard-won stability with: the lowest inflation for 30 years; and the lowest interest rates for 40 years; the lowest unemployment for a generation; and a Britain that is seen today as the most stable of all the major economies.

And it is important we understand how and why it is Britain – once the most stop-go of economies – which has avoided the recessions that hit America, Germany, Japan, Italy, and most other industrial economies during the world downturn of the last few years, and has enjoyed sustained and sustainable growth. So, let me just explain the long-term difficult decisions that had to be made and what I know we must also do to entrench that stability for the future."

September 13 2005: Speech the Trades Union Congress Annual Conference: "And I also tell you straight – in the face of that global challenge from which there is no hiding place, no safe haven other than equipping ourselves better for our future – if we are to succeed, there must be no return to the fiscal irresponsibility, the economic short termism, the inflationary pay deals and the old conflicts and disorder of the past; there can be no retreat from demanding efficiency and value for money, as well as equity as we renew and reform public services; there is no future for a global trading nation like ours in trying to erect protectionist barriers with the rest of the world. And just as we need stability in inflation and interest rates, we need stability in our industry policy, stability in industrial relations, and stability in our trading relationships with the rest of the world, and we build this stability for a purpose: for it is the one sure route to full employment for our generation and prosperity for all. And at every time, we must act to tackle the risks to stability and growth, risks that are today already reducing European growth rates to one per cent and raising European unemployment beyond 20 million, risks that now have risen from the doubling of world oil prices."

May 5 2007: Speech at the CBI annual dinner – "Exactly 10 years ago, when I first spoke to you as Chancellor, the country had spent a whole era wrestling with inflation and volatility and quite frankly, the havoc stop-go visited on long-term investment. Thinking back to my words to you then, I set out my pledge to make stability the central pillar of my economic and business policy. I was convinced that having the strength to take the long-term decisions to ensure Britain's competitiveness meant developing a shared national purpose that economic stability

> came first. Now tonight, I am here speaking to you 10 years on to say that we need to forge that same shared national purpose for the years ahead, this time to meet and master the new and even more profound challenges ahead – mastering the pace of change and the relentless competition we face from every part of the world in every area of our economy, now affecting every area of your business.
>
> And building on our hard-won stability, our mission now and for the years ahead is to make Britain the dynamic and competitive enterprise economy we all want it to be."

In more ways than one the speeches of Gordon Brown between 1997 and 2007 reflects the challenges faced by most economic policy-framers of our times, including their speech writers. In fact, these economic ideas of Gordon Brown could well have been repeated by most economic policy-framers in the ten-year period between 1997 and 2007. Surely, his hyperbolic speeches reflect the economic thinking (or the lack of it) of our times. Funnily, it could as well be any finance minister handling the economy in any country across continents, a decade prior to 1997 or a decade after 2007, or for that matter during that point in time. That in more ways than one, summarises the challenge to the repeated cycles of boom and bust – everyone seems to recognise the problem, but consciously duck it when it comes to providing solutions to the same. Remember in 2008, the whole world once again became Keynesian, as we saw in the previous chapter. So, the 'hard-won' battle of Gordon Brown against economic instability in 2007 was at best pyrrhic, and essentially, short-lived. At the end of the day, all his speeches quoted above were nothing but prayers repeated at regular intervals - prayers without conviction; plans without details.

Balance between Markets and Government

The classical role of government and markets have been repeatedly redefined in the past three decades or so to the extent that they are seen at best as 'evolving.' The relationship between the two is at best in a state of dynamic equilibrium. While it is indeed true that neither the role of government nor markets can be cast in stone in any economy, the fact remains that at every boom and bust, both their roles have been repeatedly reset to the extent that both are increasingly marginalised in the economic policy formulations. In the process, we have weakened governments and undermined markets, alternatively, after every cycle of booms and busts. This, in short, is the challenge that is confronting us – after every crisis, we are blunting the very instrumentality that is supposed to provide us solutions. The downward spiral seems to be irreversible and relentless.

In a paper titled *A Broad View of Macro-economic Stability*, José Antonio Ocampo captures this frightening shortcoming in the discipline of economics when he states "Over time, fiscal balance and price stability moved to centre stage, supplanting the Keynesian emphasis on real economic activity. This policy shift led to the downplaying and even, in the most radical views, the complete suppression of the counter-cyclical role of macro-economic policy. Although this shift recognised that high inflation and unsustainable fiscal deficits have costs, and that 'fine-tuning' of macro-economic policies to smooth out the business cycle has limits, it also led to an underestimation of both the costs of real macro-economic instability and the effectiveness of Keynesian aggregate demand management." The net consequence of all this is that the role of the government was remarkably reduced even as the role of markets was repeatedly reworked – from regulated to the unregulated. As a result, when the world moved away from the classical Keynesian ideas of countering economic cycles caused by deregulation, the cost and consequences of which were originally underestimated. Ocampo puts this cost of pro-cyclical policies when he explains succinctly that this shift was particularly sharp in the developing world, where capital account and domestic financial liberalisation exposed developing countries to the highly pro-cyclical financial swings. These are characteristics of assets that are perceived by financial markets as risky, and thus subject to sharp changes in the appetite for risk. Put differently, when markets do lack the idea of constraints or, for that matter, self-restraint – the quintessence of culture – players in every economy in their search of insatiable appetite for obscene returns, turn irrational. Likewise, when markets explode, the ability of players to take risks goes down substantially, so much so that bare minimum risks required for a functional market is absent. That makes markets dysfunctional. Either way, it is mass irrationality at play.

Economists might even get their timing of such irrationality right (as the National Bureau of Economic Research has done it in the US since 1857) but have never got the root cause of such mass irrational behaviour across continents. Why do assets that get traded multiple times its real value at the peak of a market boom remained untraded even at a fraction of its value when the markets collapse? Why does collective euphoria get displaced by aggregate despondency in an economy, sometimes with great alacrity and even without any provocation? If it was irrational behaviour during the boom, it remains so even after the collapse. Most economic theories do not have a precise answer for this collective insanity and resultant mood swings. Is the missing middle – read filial restraints – the solution to such irrational behaviour? Should markets depend extensively on families rooted to culture to prevent players from turning irrational? Is the breakdown of families or their extraordinary dependence on governments, the reason, why macro-economic stability is eluding us? Experiences tell us that formal regulatory oversight, even it was all encompassing, is insufficient for markets to function smoothly. Whatever be the institutional oversights introduced to oversee the functioning of markets, nothing works better than self-imposed restraints. Restraint, as we have repeatedly seen is culture. And it is decidedly family and family alone that establishes, recognises, nourishes such restraints. Even for markets to function smoothly, probably there is a pre-condition. Is family, the platform on which the software of economics is expected to function better? We will examine this as we proceed.

Ocampo is not alone in this analysis. Stiglitz went a step ahead and pointed out that we replaced Keynesian automatic stabilisers with automatic destabilisers. But the world has first experimented with the Keynesian idea only to find it unworkable beyond a point. This necessitated the shift to market economics, which was mistakenly assumed to have an in-built stabilising factor. But contrary to the popular view that markets had an in-built disciplinary mechanism, excessive dependence on pro-cyclical market-friendly policies encouraged macro-economic instability and the accumulation of risky balance sheets during periods of financial euphoria.

This led, in several cases, to financial meltdowns. And when markets collapsed, governments clamped down on the markets making them ineffective. Ocampo concedes that the menu of macro-economic policies had broadened over recent years, though, in our considered view, not fully enough to encompass the natural oversight functions of the missing middle viz., the family. And wherever we have introduced oversights, we have done ever so tentatively. According to Ocampo, macro-economic stability involves multiple dimensions, including not only price stability and sound fiscal policies, but also a well-functioning real economy, sustainable debt ratios, and healthy domestic financial and non-financial private sector balance sheets. This is the ideal destination point in macro-economics, no doubt. But the trillion-dollar question is how to achieve this and crucially sustain the macroeconomic stability so achieved? Needless to state, Ocampo opines that a well-functioning real economy requires, in turn, smoother business cycles, moderate long-term interest rates and competitive exchange rates, all of which may be considered intermediate goals of the ultimate economic objectives.

While all this is putative, why they may even be a pre-requisite in every economy, one needs to ask the question – whether an economy grounded firmly on the institution of family would by itself probably lend to meeting these ultimate economic objectives. What Ocampo and other scholars probably miss is the point, that there is no self-balancing mechanism in an economy between its various conflicting limbs. Consequently, attaining macro-economic stability remains fleeting at best and illusionary at worst. The net result is that everyone is conscious of the fact that assumptions matter in macroeconomic predictions. All economic models do make simplistic assumptions. The billion-dollar question is – whether the macro-economic models are obnoxiously simplified? Whether there is an appropriate weightage provided to families and their decision-making process? The danger is that the simplifications bias the answers, significantly, sometimes in ways that we cannot fathom. Whatever be it, economists concede that macro-economic stability requires significant trade-offs, dextrous management and deal with any excesses (i.e., production, consumption, savings and investment) on a real-time basis. Governments, or for that matter, markets, are either too inefficient for this role or too corrosive in their approach. Governments or markets are genetically unsuited for the purpose of achieving and much less sustaining macro-economic stability. In fact, markets thrive on greed. Greed leads to recklessness. Recklessness in turn makes it volatile. Volatility leads to collapse. Governments too, as experiences have taught us are unsuited to sustain macro-economic stability. Consequently, in the absence of a third alternative, no wonder we cyclically rely on either markets or governments for macro-economic solutions only to delude ourselves. And by default, whenever markets fail, governments suddenly find their relevance.

Whatever be it, both markets and governments are significantly opposed to the idea of sustaining the institution of family. That is a question that was answered in substantial parts in Chapter 3. We will continue to look into this aspect in greater detail now. But let us first examine the overarching link between family and economy.

Family – the First Building Block in an Economy

The existence of a family is to a very large extent is dictated by nature. According to Aristotle "there must be a union of those who cannot exist without each other; namely, of male and female, that the race may continue and this is a union which is formed, not of deliberate purpose, but because, in common with other animals and with plants, mankind has a natural desire to leave behind them an image of themselves." However, families are also basic economic units that share consumption, coordinate work activities, accumulate wealth, and invest in children.

We believe that this primordial instinct of families is the engine of economic activity that in turn drives the national economy. It guides the four limbs of economics – production, consumption, savings, and investments. Yet, the study of contemporary economics is more inclined towards individual tastes and preferences, than otherwise. Individual-centric economics could probably be true in case of societies where family as an institution is weak or absent. Empirical studies suggest that the behaviour of an individual towards all the four limbs of economics mentioned above would be different in societies where the family as an institution plays an important role in fashioning the individual decisions, than otherwise.

Let us elaborate. Traditionally, families have certain disciplines in all aspects of life, most of which have profound impact on economics. For instance, there are communities in India who have traditionally eschewed from investing in stocks of companies that deal with liquor, tobacco, or meat. More particularly, the latent discipline of these traditions in the family supersedes every blatant investment opportunity. Whatever be the market opportunities, it is discipline that compels investors from making investments in such companies. Likewise, the rise or fall in the prices of pork is of little or no consequence to a devout Muslim as is the price of beef to a devout Hindu. Discipline, in this context, implies restraints and restraints which transmutes into culture over a period. Some of these are obviously determined by mother nature as they are by geography or religious beliefs. For instance, people in coastal areas will necessarily tend to have fish as their staple diet. It is natural that fishing and culinary preferences based on sea food becomes a family habit for all those who live along the coast. But over period, this transforms into a certain culture where fish and fishing occupy a pride of place resulting in families desisting from fishing during certain time of the day, month or year, or fish or sea being revered as per local customs. All these traditions are handed over from one generation to the other so much so that these restraints become an integral part of the family and hence sacrosanct. Anyone in the fishing community is instantly ostracised – sometimes to the point of ex-communication – that no one dares to break this unwritten code within these communities. Markets do not fathom this. Nor do they appreciate this. In their sole pursuit of the insatiable, nothing matters. And if anything comes in their way, it has to be per force exterminated. It may be pertinent to note that markets, in the above cited example, will be stable and hence sustainable when handled by fishermen and local communities. They have innate knack of handling excesses over the millennia. The tools of handling distortions are subtle and this wisdom is passed on from one generation to the other. What distorts the markets is when large corporates with ownership completely divorced of the sensitivity involved in each and every particular coast, attempt to make profits as the sole drive and ruthlessly eliminate competition. In the process, the local fisherman community get destroyed. So do species of fishes in the sea. This is what Arjuna briefly alluded to in opening verses of Chapter 1of the *Bhagavad Gita*. It is this discipline that sustains families over extended period and disturbing the discipline, as we briefly saw in Chapter 4, could have all round cataclysmic consequences, including the national and global economy.

When culture is near-perfected with a self-balancing homeostatic mechanism – primarily family and to a small extent community – economies become sustainable over a longer period. This idea of family as the centrifugal force that controls the economic decision-making remains at the core of this book. Economic policies must be dovetailed factoring this paradigm. The question is – do governments and markets cognise this paradigm? In fact, it is our view and we argue right through this book that the government must not only cognise the role of family and the discipline associated with it, but must fashion economic policies that encourage families to be disciplined. This would make every national economy, workable. To illustrate further, when families believe that their children have to be cultured – a natural instinct of parents – and hence necessarily educated, the investment in education will be to that extent higher in an economy, than otherwise when parents do not take the responsibility of the educational needs of their children. Naturally, this urge to educate their child will drive the young parents to save more. In the process, a choice is exercised between present consumption for themselves and a future consumption for their child i.e., higher education. This suppresses current consumption and favours future consumption. Naturally, this infuriates the market players who revel in instant gratifications.

Therefore, governments must cognise these basic impulses of families (which may be distinct from individual impulses and may well be in line with market expectations) and fashion our economic policies. In the instant case, governments need to channel the saving impulse of family on account of their natural urge to educate their children towards investment in institutions that provide quality higher education. What is the financial instrument that provides a long-term investment plan to young couples for the education of their child, the regulation to monitor the educational sector, subsidy for higher education, educational loans, and of course whether higher education should be a government monopoly or should the private sector be allowed, is a matter of greater detailing in the macro-economic policy framework - some to be decided and done by the government and some, necessarily by the family. What is missed in the melee is that we forget the fact that the state cannot step and supplant, though it can supplement, the natural collective instincts and consequential decision making of parents. This must be true of several issues including housing, clothing, old age-related financial security and of course health-related matters of every family member. In all these matters the root assumptions in modern economics is that it is the individual who decides, and therefore, the individual alone matters in the decision making forgetting for a fact that it is the family and family that is the basic socio-economic unit that determines several of the economic decisions that in the aggregate makes or mars the economy.

Therefore, it is family impulses that cumulatively shape, de-shape and reshape the economic policy formulation at a national level on several issues, and not the individual as popularly believed. If families, and not individuals, are placed at the centre of our economic policies, the world of economics will be entirely different. Do we recognise this? Let us amplify. The natural urge of mankind to leave behind an imprint of themselves, as pointed out by Aristotle, is the biggest trigger for savings (and hence acquiring and bequeathing property) in an economy. It is this instinct that is the genesis of the idea of savings and the resultant property that Marxists seek to destroy. Liberals too seek to do so, for the simple reason as family brings along with it, restraints – a virtual spoiler in their quest for unlimited profits.

In contrast, it is often noticed that societies with higher filial ties do tend to have a higher rate of savings. When families do not have the natural economic drive, or when families wither away, the engine of economic growth naturally splutters and gives away. To illustrate further, the natural impulse of young couples to educate their child will be obviously lower if they are engaged in the legal process of divorce. Naturally, in such cases, the child would suffer, and the government must necessarily step in to fill in the vacuum caused by the withering of the family by spending much more on the education of that child. This implies lower savings rate in an economy by the households and higher current expenditure by the government. This distorts the current income in favour of current consumption and not towards investment and potentially future consumption. Demonstrably, this is the singular impact of couples who divorce or have children outside of their wedlock. If society permits couples to have children outside of their wedlock while steadfastly refusing to take care of them, the macroeconomic policies would have to be necessarily different. Economic ideas riveted to simple GDP computation and computing quarterly growth rate will not be able to fathom the structural and qualitative difference between an economy where filial ties are strong and where it is not. To fund such higher current spending as explained above, governments resort to higher taxes from those who work, save and are disciplined! We would deal with the vexatious subject of taxes in the subsequent chapter too.

Re-working the Trade-Off

But we also concede all these are classical socio-economic viewpoints. The role of the family has changed drastically in recent times, say in the past five decades or so. In modern societies, thanks to codified divorce laws, individuals can enter marriage and exit out of it almost at will. The average household size in the US has dramatically dropped from 3.4 people to less than 2.5 people between 1960 and 2015. Several developed and developing countries too have seen a similar drop in the same period. Likewise, due to medical advancement, avoiding pregnancy is easy; child mortality is low. Importantly, thanks to technological changes, it has become much easier for both the husband and wife to work within the traditional framework of family. Notwithstanding these developments, non-marital fertility has risen dramatically in the past quarter-century. According to the National Centre for Health Statistics, approximately 40 percent of births in the US are outside-of-wedlock. Of course, the percentage of non-marital births differs by race and ethnicity: 25 percent of non-Hispanic white births, 48 percent of Hispanic births, and 70 percent of non-Hispanic black births were non-marital. The share of US children living with an unmarried parent has more than doubled since 1968, jumping from 13 percent to 32 percent in 2017. That trend has been accompanied by a drop in the share of children living with two married parents, down from 85 percent in 1968 to 65 percent.

Some three percent of children are not living with any parent, according to a Pew Research Centre analysis of the US Census Bureau data. These children also experience many transitions in where and with whom they live, since most unmarried mothers eventually marry, and the divorced re-marry. With multiple serial partnerships between parents, families have become more complex, with uncertain implications for parent-child relationships and investments in children.

Though fertility outside legal marriage has become commonplace in many developed countries, especially in north-Western Europe, this emergence of non-marital child-bearing reflects, to a large extent, the decline of the social imperative that pre-marital pregnancy should lead to marriage. For many men, paternity has been separated from parenting responsibilities. Financial obligations are increasingly, as we saw in Chapter 2, enforced by the state. This, we note, has disastrous downsides. While this made women economically independent, it had its downside, as it has made men emotionally vulnerable. The classical trade-off that went on to create monogamous family as an institution – where the alpha male curbed his natural instincts towards polygamy for the sole attention (read emotional dependence) of his female partner towards him – was decisively broken in the second half of the 20th century. Put pithily, in the present times, thanks to the advancement of science and law, the institution of marriage is now in a search of a new equation (read trade-off) between the man and his wife. Alarmingly, the withering away of the man-woman equation has the calculated effect of dynamiting the assiduously built societal consensus on monogamy. Unless this trade-off is once again reworked and settled between men and women, the institution of marriage – more specifically monogamous marriage – will not attain its desirable primacy in the near future. Naturally, these developments will have consequences for both national and global economics.

In the absence of this traditional trade-off, there is bound to be higher turnover in the marriage market. Accordingly, some individuals transit through several marriages, and intermittently remain single during a larger part of their lifetime. All these factors have combined to increase the heterogeneity of families, and to decrease the stability of the living arrangements in which children are brought up. While these developments may seem innocuous and possibly trivial even for an individual, these have profound impact on the national economy and economic policy formulations. As marriages break and new marriages are formed, the traditional division of labour between husband and wife, especially in taking care of the children or savings by the family, is under greater pressure. Crucially, this breakdown of the family breaks the natural filial impulses.

Several experts have traced the evolution of the family from primitive societies to the present. They rightly conclude that many of the functions that families performed in traditional societies are now performed by the market or the state, or a combination of both. Markets, they opine, have largely displaced the family in some activities, such as food production, and continues to encroach on other activities, such as food preparation. Likewise, the state has become more important than the family as guarantors of security for persons and property, insurance, age-old care, and education of children. The instrumental value of children to their parents has continued to decrease. A rapid expansion of government and market means that the elderly no longer need to depend on their own children. All these have been achieved by relegating family to a point of irrelevance in macro-economic policy formulations. Nevertheless, the sustainability of all these ideas is indeterminate now. And the question that needs to be repeatedly asked – are these changes viable, sustainable, and hence eternal? Or are they merely transient? Can we now, given the tectonic shift in our thinking and resultant developments, announce the end of family as an institution? Are we to understand that family as an institution is on a terminal decline that has no scope for revival in the near future? Importantly, can government and markets be an efficacious substitute for family? We shall look into these questions shortly.

When families are destroyed and filial impulses are broken, individual responsibilities are given a go-by. Economic policies rooted in certain traditional, rational, and legitimate behaviour of men and women too collapses. Economic policies, in the classical sense, are fashioned by a man who places his and his family's interests supreme while taking any decision – and hence would be prudent, disciplined, and balanced. This balanced decision-making at the individual level remains crucial to balanced decision-making, in the aggregate, at the national level. Put differently, the imbalance in the fundamental equation between a man and his wife has far greater consequences than is possibly imagined. When men or women become irrational, or curb their natural filial instincts, or for that matter give away their specific responsibilities to maintain their family at the altar of individual rights (which in modern nation-states is paramount, and hence virtually become non-negotiable), their personal economics cannot be expected to be rational. When a society is filled with such irrational or irresponsible individuals seeking only rights with little no adherence to duties, the skew in the national economy gets that much more pronounced. Markets or governments lack the instrumentality to address individual irresponsibility, though, at best they can punish such deviant behaviour. And even to punish such behaviour, it is often seen that it is the disciplined lot who bear the resultant cost. This, in short, is the conundrum confronting modern economics.

Global Imbalance, Savings Glut, and Globalisation

It is one of the most important debates within the pantheon of economists – whether savings in an economy is a virtue or is it a vice that needs to be clinically avoided. Some economists, and rightly so, assume that it is indeed a virtue, while others feel that savings prevent present consumption, and hence is a burden. But there is yet another aspect to this debate. Savings fuels investments (though not necessarily at all times), which in turn leads to production at a later date, which ensures (though again not necessarily at all times) future consumption. Mathematically, if present production equals present consumption, leaving nothing as present savings, present investment and consequently future production will necessarily get impacted. On the other hand, if there is a marked bias towards savings with no incentive to consume at present, economies could run the risk of an irretrievable downward spiral. Thus, economists ideally seek to achieve a delicate balance between savings and investment.

John Maynard Keynes, who published his influential work, *The General Theory of Employment, Interest, and Money*, in 1936, noted that savings can ultimately be detrimental to the economy because of the paradox of thrift. He argued that if everyone individually cuts spending to increase saving, aggregate saving will eventually fall because one person's spending is someone else's income. Surely, Keynes was indeed referring to the trade-off between savings and consumption, as increased saving, by definition, decreases current consumption. But what if a large number of people decide to save and only save without consuming? Of course, this could lead to a savings glut (a term popularised by Ben Bernanke, the successor of Greenspan at the US Fed), which implies excessive savings. Or what if there is an excess of savings within an economy, with little or no avenue to invest or the reasons to invest? What would be the consequences where people have extraordinary bias towards savings and hence towards investment, future production, and consumption? We will try and answer these questions.

Most economists are near unanimous in their opinion that economic growth in America in the past three decades was sustained by high levels of American consumption (which in turn allowed the growth of the Chinese economy through an increase in their production). This was explained in greater detail in Chapter 2. While consumption as a chief drive in an economy is of a recent origin in the discipline of economics, the fact of the matter is that there is a high co-relation between savings and investments (as it is between growth and consumption), a fact lost on many. Yet, the thrust seems to be to fashion modern economic policies that signal the virtues of consumption, not savings.

Nevertheless, the paradox of thrift, as argued by Keynes and noticed in many circumstances, is invariably a short-run phenomenon. Americans, for instance, have historically saved about eight percent of their income and experienced sustained economic growth. Over the long-term, a higher savings rate provides capital for entrepreneurs to invest. That enables entrepreneurs to access capital at moderate rates for investment, which in turn feeds growth. Thus, the virtuous cycle of growth has created within the US a delicate balance between production, consumption, savings, and investment, (remember the four arms of the Hindu goddess of wealth Lakshmi referred to in the previous chapters?) caused through a variety of factors including interest rates, financial intermediation, regulatory oversight, governance, and of course tempered entrepreneurial spirits. That, in short, is the American growth story where American savings historically funded American investments; American production feeding American consumers. All that is history now. The delicate balance within America has well and truly been disturbed in the past few decades – probably for all those reasons discussed in Chapter 2. America currently runs gargantuan current account deficits to fund its equally monstrous consumption with very little domestic savings.

Alan Greenspan, the former chairman of the US Federal Reserve, points out that the US current account deficit is at the root of concerns about the American economy. By 2006, the financing of that deficit – that is, the inflow of money from overseas into the US siphoned off more than three-fifths of all cross-border savings of 67 countries that ran corresponding current account surpluses in that year. Developing countries, which accounted for half of those surpluses in that year, were apparently unable to find sufficiently profitable investments at home. According to Greenspan, Americans in 1995 could not have run up a nearly $800 billion annual current account deficit, as they ran it in say 2006, for the simple reason that the US could not have attracted such huge foreign savings to finance its deficit, as there were not much global savings in the offing. In 1995, for example, cross-border savings flows were less than $350 billion. The collective thrift and the spectacular economic growth of several of these 'developing countries' were, in effect, funding the gargantuan US consumption by 2006. Thus, the exports caused by sustained diligent hard work in these developing countries led to the build-up of current account surplus in these countries, only to be matched by current account deficit of a handful of countries – notably the US. This surplus was parked in the US by these countries, which in turn was used by the US to finance its imports. In effect, the US continues to be dependent on the rest for the goods as well as finance for its imports. This continuous flow of exports from a set of countries to the US, and then the parking of surplus arising out of such exports of goods and services once again back into the US – goes on with a rather innocuous appellation – global imbalance. This, to us, is a greater paradox than the paradox of thrift, as it is the poor developing country that has been funding the developed country for the past two decades or so. One question that needs to be repeatedly put forth in this context is why do developing countries believe in maintaining reserves that are invariably invested in developed countries? Crucially, is this model sustainable?

Greenspan explains this paradox and points out that the spectacular economic growth of developing nations since the early 1970s increased global income and concomitant savings. The result has been the shift of a significant share of the world's gross domestic product to the developing world, a trend with extraordinary consequential effects. Developing countries, Greenspan explains, typically have much higher savings rates than do industrialised nations – in part because developing nations' social safety nets are weaker, so households naturally set aside more money for times of need and retirement. Other factors also played a part. In the absence of well-established consumer cultures, for example, households have less inclination to spend. This shift of shares in world GDP since 2001 from low-saving developed countries to higher-saving developing countries, especially in Asia, has increased world saving so much that Greenspan argues that the aggregate growth of savings worldwide has greatly exceeded planned investments. Or to put it another way, savings looking for a safe return with a positive yield has grown faster than global investor demand. The market process that equalises actual global savings and investment, according to him, has driven real interest rates markedly lower. Of course, we have a contrarian take on the issue of low interest rates in Chapter 9.

This lowering of returns gave rise to the new phenomenon of savings looking out for newer cross-border investments that provide for higher rates of returns. Traditionally, saving was directed almost wholly towards domestic investment, that is, plant, equipment, inventories, and housing within investors' sovereign borders. However, Greenspan points out that since the 1990s, home bias began to decline perceptibly as countries began dismantling of restrictions on cross-border capital flows. This is where the difference between economics and finance became increasingly blurred, so much so that the discipline of economics becomes fully integrated into the undisciplined world of finance. This blurring of difference coincided with the broader idea of globalisation, but in effect was rooted to financial integration, where cross-border investments were allowed and foreign ownership significantly liberalised in several countries. This is also the precise point where water moved uphill – i.e., from poor, capital- starved, developing countries to rich, developed nations. We have dealt with this convoluted issue in Chapter 3. In short, vast improvements in technology and governance have expanded investors' geographic horizons since the 1990s. And as rightly pointed out by Greenspan since 1995, the greater rates of productivity growth in the US apparently produced correspondingly higher risk-adjusted expected rates of return that fostered a disproportionate rise in the global demand for US-based assets. This, according to Greenspan, explains why such a large percentage of cross-border capital movements have been directed to the US. But this is not as simple as it seems. Why does the world even today sees investment into the US as less risky?

Unlearnt Lessons of Asian Economic Crisis

Any reference to global capital movements, especially to the US, cannot ignore the momentous happenings in the global financial markets, and particularly the Asian markets during 1997-98. In fact, it provides the necessary context to the textual references on global imbalances. These cataclysmic events in the capital markets have been well documented by many in the past two decades, capturing as to how the Asian contagion erupted, unfolded, and in the process disrupted economies in the region, and perhaps economies in other regions too. Was the Asian currency crisis a conspiracy of some grand plan? Did the US seize the political opportunity in the mid-90s in a unipolar world, grappling after the political implosion of Soviet Russia, by triggering the Asian crisis? Was it aimed at torpedoing the spectacular growth of Asia? Was it a grand design to suck out capital from Asia to other countries, especially the West? Was it a plan by Western countries, which were experiencing very low domestic savings to get more capital into their countries by forcing the Asian countries to export their capital, thanks to the culture of savings in these Asian countries? Or was it merely a ruse to ensure devaluation of currencies across Asia, and force every country to engage in competitive devaluation? Was the idea to encourage Asian countries to export a part of this grand design? In the process, did the export of these countries control inflation in developed countries, and the simultaneous export of savings provide capital – both for unbridled consumption, and subsequently, investment. Finally, did this arrangement aid and abet the consumption binge of the Western countries?

The answers to these questions are not readily available for the simple reason that there has not been much comprehensive analysis of the issue on hand. The crisis erupted when the government of Thailand, facing a shortage of foreign exchange reserves, devalued its currency, thereby breaking the fixed-rate peg to the US dollar. The instigating factor for the devaluation was the build-up of short-term and often poorly secured borrowings from abroad. Faced with such huge repayment obligations because of sudden devaluation, the Thai economy went into a tailspin. As the crisis reverberated through the Thai economy, it rapidly led to bankruptcies and layoffs. The crisis also spread through the region almost immediately and with great speed. Within weeks, the Malaysian Ringgit, the Philippine Peso, Korean Won, and the Indonesian Rupiah were all under siege. The stock markets collapsed dramatically as did real estate markets. The Asian contagion spread from market to market and from country to country. Asians saw the currency attacks wiping out 20 or 30 percent of the national wealth in a matter of days what had been laboriously built over several decades.

The immediate economic trigger for the speculative attacks was attributed to unsustainable deficits in the current accounts of these countries. These deficits resulted from years of fuelling their rapid growth through imports (mostly of capital goods and equipment to feed higher domestic investment, which in turn resulted in rapid output and income growth) in overvalued local currency. The resultant current account deficit was funded through inflows of foreign capital, both through short-term and long-term capital flows. This arrangement allowed these countries to maintain their exchange rates to be pegged to the US dollar. Significantly, this pegged exchange rate attracted more and more investment into the region as the pegged rate provided the necessary insurance against exchange fluctuations. Insured of exchange risks the region naturally began attracting huge capital. However, when China devalued its currency by 34 percent against the US dollar in 1994, it made exports from these countries uncompetitive. This widened the deficits, and in turn, increased the cost of foreign capital. Expectedly, countries were forced to attract capital through higher interest rates to tide over the shortfall.

Originally, the absence of currency risk and the large spread between high domestic interest rates and lower rates abroad, encouraged foreigners to lend and local companies to borrow, especially loans denominated in dollars. Easy availability of loans fuelled domestic booms, more specifically in property and contributed to widening current account deficits by stimulating import demand and increasing external debt-service payments. They also led to grand plans for huge government infrastructure projects, which earn revenues in local currency over an extended period of time. The cumulative effect of all these meant that the Thai central bank which continued to support the Baht by selling US dollars from its foreign reserves, finally gave up and floated the currency on July 2, 1997. This signalled the beginning of the Asian currency crisis. After the Baht was floated, speculative selling triggered similar falls of the Philippine Peso, Malaysian Ringgit, and Indonesian Rupiah, whose economic fundamentals were similar to, but not as bad as, those in Thailand. The initial 10 to 25 percent fall in these currencies (in comparison with the 35 percent fall in the Baht) was on expected lines. As the financial crisis that began in Asia in the middle of 1997 spread to the rest of the world, it left a trail of devalued currencies, shattered stock markets, confidence-battered banks, and bankrupt financial institutions. While these are the disaggregate pictures of the crisis, the net aggregate of this crisis saw savings of nearly a generation get wiped off within weeks in some Asian countries. But worse was yet to come. Post this crisis, most Asian countries predominantly led by China have been voluntarily parking their savings in developed countries through an arrangement of devalued currencies, improved market access, liberalised capital flows and of course a seemingly sustainable economic model little realising the consequential global imbalance. Crucially, the answer to the question whether thrift is a virtue or not, at least in the context of the Asian savings is very obvious – their own savings do not belong to them, production is meant for consumption by someone in a distant land, and so are investments. Is this the unlearnt lesson of the Asian crisis?

But why do we harp on the issue of thrift more than the other three arms of goddess Lakshmi – consumption, production, and investment? Are we partial to the convoluted subject of savings? While we do not plead guilty to this charge, we must confess that savings is more rooted to filial values than probably the other arms of Lakshmi. The reason for the same is not far to seek. Savings signal assumption of responsibilities for any possible future liabilities by families. Through savings (and concomitant investment), they signal the assumption of personal responsibilities for any contingency that may arise in the future. And when future liability is secured by the contemporary conduct of families, where is the role for the government, or for that matter markets? It is this conduct that makes families far too important than we realise. It may not be out of place to reiterate that responsibility and discipline are anathema to modern economists. That explains why the ideas of individual discipline and filial constraints that lead to savings are given a short shrift by modern economists. Let us now once again revert to the convoluted issue of the Asian currency crisis.

Family, Savings and Economics

In retrospect, the Asian financial crisis was definitely the outcome of clashes between different financial systems. At the heart of the matter was a systemic imbalance – a mismatch between global capital markets and national financial systems. In hindsight, it seems that many countries did not have the necessary regulatory and surveillance machinery to cope with the sudden surge in inflow as well as the abrupt outflow of funds. This crisis, as we saw, was a result of a sudden reversal of capital flows in the international capital markets, caused by the contagion and the herding behaviour of international financial investors. Why did these investors who praised these countries till the middle of 1997 suddenly turn hostile and act in tandem? Or were they forced to behave thus? Was 'crony capitalism' – a charge levelled against the Asian countries to indicate the poor quality of investments discovered overnight by these investors? It is these questions that continue to haunt us without appropriate answers.

Some economists do not define this as a mere clash of different financial systems – but also a clash of cultures, values, social structures, function of families, as well as the differing role of markets, regulators, and governments. To illustrate, the risk-taking ability of an entrepreneur in a developed nation is significantly enhanced, as it is considerably subsidised by an elaborate social security system that provides a huge safety net for an individual, should something go wrong in his venture. However, in the absence of a social security mechanism, risk-taking ability is restricted, or at least tempered in developing countries by societal and filial considerations. That substantially explains why people save in first place in developing countries. Savings, it is often seen, comes with an attendant package – tempering risks of entrepreneurs. This, in turn, makes markets sustainable in the long run. Let us flip the argument – filial piety as a mechanism ensures that entrepreneurs do not turn reckless in their pursuit of profits. It is this reckless pursuit of profits by entrepreneurs that is at the root of several booms and dooms. Once filial piety is ensured, markets become sustainable. We look at the role of family in greater detail in Chapter 9. But without the restraining effect of family, much of all these become impossible – a fact lost on Gordon Brown and his ilk.

This tempering of risks undertaken by the individual is the fundamental difference in the approach to the market by entrepreneurs in developed countries and in others. Family, culture, and civilisational values are a crucial differential that economists fail to cognise. Again, this arrangement is not without a downside. On the flip side, this social arrangement in the developed countries enhances the quantum of risk capital in an economy and thereby leads to enhanced economic activity by providing the necessary impetus to an entrepreneur. Nevertheless, the financial viability of the social security system, as we discussed in great detail in Chapter 2, is increasingly known to become unstable and hence run the risk of an economic collapse. Put pithily, the developed countries have privatised profits and simultaneously subsidised the attendant entrepreneurial risks through an elaborate social security system. And to fund the social security system, they have laid out an intricate structure of collecting direct and indirect taxes. In contrast, countries like India that do lack social security systems, obviously have benign tax-GDP ratios. Nevertheless, the Asian currency crisis brought home the fundamental fact that the role of the markets, social security system, family and societal pressures on families have a tremendous bearing on the functioning of economy in different countries. This differential approach to capital, markets, and risks has been eloquently captured by Daniel Yergin and Joseph Stanislaw. Commenting on this vexatious issue, the authors state: "People in a number of countries may not believe that their cultural life should be dominated by satellite-borne media images from the West that globalise the values of Hollywood, and the 'Anglo-Saxon cult of shareholder value,' which would ruthlessly cut away what are seen in other societies as social obligations and responsibilities." This explains substantially, if not fully, why there is huge opposition to the idea of globalisation.

There is yet another fascinating dimension to the Asian currency crisis – one that is immediately relevant for us to understand the crucial interplay of family, culture, and economics. It is indeed remarkable to note that the Asian growth story of the two decades preceding the financial crisis, was labelled as a 'miracle' by many developed countries and multilateral financial institutions. The use of the phrase 'miracle' was singularly pejorative, if not downright offensive. What was probably lost then, and had become increasingly apparent subsequently, was that the word 'miracle' suggested that these Asian countries were incapable of a sustained growth, and that their economic growth, as witnessed by the developed countries, was nothing short of a 'miracle.' What is forgotten in the melee is that the Asian countries had a huge population, value systems in place, and simply worked hard when the opportunities presented. It is this virtue that ensured they could rebound after the world wars as they did after the Asian economic crisis. Importantly, economists worldwide realised that these countries had now reached a stage where they could export capital – as against the popular belief (that exists even to this date) that these 'poor' developing countries require capital from the developed economies for their growth. The contrasting position – where it is the developed countries that require capital, and it is the sustained export of capital from the developing world to the developed world that is sustaining the latter is lost on many, including noted economists like Ben Bernanke and his illustrious predecessor, Alan Greenspan.

Triumphant Capitalism

This is simply because most believe in the theory that modern capitalism, especially of the successful triumphant variety, is germane to Western civilisation. This theory was first espoused by Max Weber, a German economist and sociologist in the early 20th century, through a series of essays. In his celebrated work *The Protestant Ethic and the Spirit of Capitalism*, Weber puts forward this thesis that influenced the development of modern capitalism in the 20th century. To this date, it is this theory of Weber that provides the basis for a broad understanding to most economists of the impact of religion on national economics. With the publication of Max Weber's work in 1905, the idea that religion and culture matter quite a lot even to a worldly issue such as economic growth, became widely recognised, probably for the first time. Weber's work demonstrated how economic growth under capitalism had to wait for the concomitant rise of Protestant religion, which had a positive attitude to the creation of wealth and prosperity, and to capital accumulation. Protestantism, as rightly pointed out by Weber, valued worldly success. It had a positive worldview, which Weber thought was congenial to innovation and investment, which in turn enabled the industrial revolution and the rise of capitalism and economic growth under it. Protestantism may not have lauded the profit motive, but it valued hard work and thrift, and did not look askance at the accumulation of wealth, which led to investment. It emphasised asceticism, which meant a thrifty way of life, and the resultant savings. We did deal with the issue of Calvinist values in Chapter 4, and how by the turn of the previous century, it had been virtually given away.

Weber did not stop there after merely linking Capitalism to Protestantism. In fact, he goes further to suggest that Hinduism (or for that matter, virtually every other religion) is incompatible with capitalism, particularly in his subsequent book, *The Religion of India: The Sociology of Hinduism and Buddhism* (1958). Similarly, the term 'Karma Capital' is not a celebratory term, as it is commonly understood in India. Rather, it seems to suggest that an Indian Hindu entrepreneur is incapable of being successful at the global level because of his belief in fatalism, and would preferably subject himself to fate than carry on with his business in a professional manner. The modern and more sophisticated version of Weber's analysis of the Protestant work ethic manifests in a new idea – 'Savings Glut' – implying as well as conditioning the world to believe that it lacks the necessary confidence in investing elsewhere other than in the developed countries. This theory implies a very high level of savings in the surplus countries, mostly Asian, with disproportionately lower domestic investment avenues to park their savings. The global 'savings glut' theory, as we saw, affirms that the excess saving in emerging economies, mostly Asian, flows to other countries, mainly to the US. This has the calculated effect of keeping the long-term interest rates in the US (as availability of funds increases) at reasonably low levels. It is this low level of interest rates which in turn has allowed it to absorb imports from various countries into the US, leading to a construction and consumption-driven boom in the US, and an export-led growth in other countries. This routing of the export surpluses, due to the lack of investment avenues in the developing countries back to the US, is the origin of this theory of 'savings glut.' Implicit in the argument is the failing of the developing countries to handle their export surpluses – a sure sign of their success – a fact that probably Weber did not visualise would probably happen within a century of this prophecy.

But Weber was not alone. Albert Schweitzer had similar views on Indic religions as earlier in 1936 in his work *Indian Thought and Its Development*. Subsequently, Kapp in 1963 too held more or less identical views. The essence of their criticism of Indian religions was that they were so much philosophical in their approach, which made every follower of these religions accept every twist and turn of life. India's economic backwardness and poverty were blamed on this philosophical approach, which was taken to have also accounted for slow economic growth. The tepid rate of economic growth in India since 1950 until around 1980 (at 3 percent per annum) was even called the Hindu Rate of Growth by Raj Krishna, a Marxist economist. It is fascinating to note that even as the economic policies in India were based on the then fashionable Soviet model, economists blamed Hinduism for her growth rate, and not Marxism. But since 1980, as India slowly jettisoned the Nehru-Marxian economic policies, she has seen a spectacular growth rate in excess of six percent per annum. The liberalisation of the economy (away from the Nehru-Marxian ideas) in the early 1990s has put India on a robust economic growth, so much so that by 2020, India is seen as an emerging economic power. We will examine the reason for the same in the subsequent chapters of this book.

It is obvious that Weber's understanding of Hinduism was limited and his resultant criticism was probably flawed. The first was to limit Hinduism to a unitary idea or a singular philosophy. The second was to distance it from material success. Though on the whole, within all strands of Hinduism, there is a definite priority for one's spiritual upliftment, a substantial weightage was surely given for material progress too (*Jaya* and *Vijaya*, again as we saw in Chapter 4). Different strands of Hindu philosophy have repeatedly emphasised at arriving at this delicate balance between spiritual progress and material gains. This is one aspect of life that most Westerners fail to recognise while critiquing Hinduism.

Most religions grapple with this seemingly irreconcilable thought of balancing between spirituality and materialism. However, this is not the case with Indic religions. This balance between spirituality and material success is also explicitly listed out as one of the goals of human life – popularly called as *Purusharth*. Material success is acknowledged as an aim of life, as is spirituality. Within Hinduism, most philosophers have concluded that there are four basic goals of life: *dharma* (in the absence of an English equivalent, it is extremely difficult to translate; nevertheless, loosely translated, it is a moral code of conduct in everything we do), *artha* (material prosperity), *kaama* (propensity to consume), and *moksha* (complete spiritual liberation). Hindu philosophers have neither laid out any hierarchy for these four nor have they expressed any preference. To them, all four are fully integrated to the other and one cannot exist at the exclusion of the other. However, the overarching need to ensure *Dharma* is repeatedly emphasised. In fact, the idea is an overarching idea that subsumes most actions – including, believe it or not, there is a *Dharma* for a warrior for his conduct in a war, as it is for businessmen, teachers, doctors, and even philosophers. Thus, an act of war is not prohibited for Hindus, but carrying on a war without adhering to the code of conduct is. All these imply that the pursuit of material success is not at all prohibited, but merely tempered by a certain self-determined code of conduct. This tempering acts as a restraint, which over a period of time becomes what is loosely called as Hindu or Indian culture. It is this restraint that was probably mistaken by Weber. Whatever be the truth, it is apparent that Hinduism does not approve of asceticism for everyone, though true to its broad outlook, Hinduism does not frown on asceticism either. However, *Moksha* is the final destination and is slated to be achieved only after all other goals are achieved.

Weber, it may be noted, suggested that 'Ascetic Protestantism' was one of the major 'elective affinities' associated with the rise of capitalism, bureaucracy, and the rational-legal nation-state in the Western world. By elective affinity, Weber meant something less direct than causality, but something more direct than correlation. Weber's work emphasized, probably for the first time, how culture influences economics. Although Weber did not argue that religion caused economic change, he did conclude that Ascetic Protestantism and modern capitalism often appeared alongside one another in societies. To explain these observations, Weber argued that Protestantism had redefined the connection between work and religion. Historically, Christian religious devotion had been accompanied by a rejection of mundane affairs, including economic pursuits. In contrast, Weber showed that Protestants supported worldly activities and the rational pursuit of economic gain. Therefore, believers in Protestantism expressed their piety towards God through hard work and achievement in their secular vocation. Because of this religious orientation, human effort was shifted away from the contemplation of the divine, and towards rational efforts aimed at achieving economic gain. Furthermore, the Protestant ethic, while promoting the pursuit of economic gain, eschewed the profligate. Thus, believers were encouraged to make money, but not to spend it. This is what is popularly called as the Calvinist Restraint – a dominant denomination within the Protestants. This motivated believers to work hard, be successful in business, and reinvest their profits rather than spend them on frivolous pleasures. Protestant believers, thus, reconciled and even encouraged the pursuit of profit with religion. Instead of being viewed as morally suspect, greedy, or ambitious, financially successful believers were viewed as being motivated by a highly moral and respectable philosophy, the 'spirit of capitalism.'

Interestingly, this is the nearest Christianity ever got to the Hindu idea of placing work above everything – a fact lost even on Weber, and probably every critique of Weber. Verse 47 of Chapter II of the *Bhagavad Gita*, for instance, deals with this issue, where the Lord is quoted to have sagaciously opined: "Your right is to work only, but never to the fruit thereof. Do not be the cause of the fruit of action; nor let your attachment be to inaction." At least on the charge that Hinduism does not provide enough weight to work, rewards, and success gets dynamited by a plain reading of this verse. Therefore, the criticism by Weber, especially his views on Hinduism, is probably based on a superficial analysis of its traditions. It is pertinent to note that emphasis on sustained hard work is equally present in Hinduism. Probably, as a way to prepare the worker for the unexpected, it mandates him not to take credit or blame for the outcome.

Weber, therefore, was right up to the point in tracing the elective affinities within the Protestant societies. But eventually, the rational roots of this doctrine outgrew their religious origins and became autonomous cultural traits of a capitalist society, delinked from their religious moorings. In other words, the Protestant societies currently do not have a moral-religious persuasion to ensure its stability, and hence, sustainability. Once ethical values were ignored, economic values eroded. And when economic values eroded, financial values also eroded. Thus, America which prospered by practising cultural restraints not so long ago is now a society that is well and truly unrestrained. Of the four pistons of economy – savings, consumption, production and investment, Americans are known today only by their gargantuan consumption. For the rest, America depends on the outside world to a large extent. This was not the case say a few decades ago as probably the 'Calvinist Restraint' ensured consumption could never be the chief drive of the American economy. Naturally, it would have been fascinating to examine the views of Weber today on both Protestant ethic – which has virtually collapsed, as pointed out by David Brooks and discussed in Chapter 4, and simultaneously, his views on Hinduism, given the fact that India has re-emerged as a major economic force, since it may be noted that Weber wrote about India in the early 20th century.

Let us take the idea of Weber and elective affinities forward. Why capitalism, as understood by Weber himself, is no longer in play even in the US? Why is the impact of Protestantism waning, especially in the field of economics? Why is it that Protestant society is no longer the socio-economic-religious model for the capitalistic world as Weber predicted? Why is the Protestant society fatigued? Why is American consumption seen as a risk and not an engine of growth? Why are alternative models - especially from India and China – fast emerging as a durable economic model for the world at large? Are India and China emerging, or are they re-emerging, given the fact they were an economic powerhouse for over two millennia? Is the dip in the economy of China and India, more specifically in the 20th century an aberration, and their subsequent spectacular rise, a natural order? Importantly, what fuels their rise? And what is the lesson for the world?

To understand the sustainability of an economic model, one needs to revisit the root assumptions of modern economics. One of the fundamental flaws in our understanding of economics is on the flawed assumption that an individual, not family, alone matters. The behaviour of a restrained individual is significantly different from that of the unrestrained individual. Little do we realise that it is the family, culture, and civilisational values that impel, propel, or compel an individual to be restrained. While all this is accepted universally accepted, economists argue that by its very definition, culture is broad, ubiquitous, and vague. Therefore, it does not lend itself to precise statistical tests or mathematical modelling. Any co-relational study between culture and economics faces a basic problem – the causality link is unlikely to be established in precise mathematical models. And since culture is incapable of being subjected to mathematical modelling, the study of the impact of culture has been excluded from the discipline of economics.

Classical economists were comfortable in using cultural explanations for economic phenomena. Adam Smith, for instance, viewed his *Theory of Moral Sentiments* as an integral part to the *Wealth of Nations*. Karl Marx, for good measure, inverted this direction of causality: rather than culture determining economic relations, he argued that the underlying technology determines the type of social structure prevailing, and even the dominant culture. For him, the hand-mill produced a feudal society, and the steam-mill, a capitalistic one. Whereas Marx saw religion as a by-product of relations, Max Weber – as we saw above – regarded religion as crucial to the development of capitalism and argued that the Protestantism rationalised how any pursuit of wealth should be regarded not merely as an advantage, but as a duty. Karl Polanyi, another economist of great repute not only agreed with Weber on the suggestion that religion was important to the establishment of markets, but also viewed religion and culture as a factor in moderating the excesses of the market. In the decades immediately after World War II, the work of Polanyi was enormously influential in the field of political science and in the discipline of sociology, but fell on deaf ears among economists.

As economic theory increased its mathematical sophistication, and the set of tools at its disposal expanded, economists did not feel the compulsion to introduce other potential explanatory variables like culture that were hard to measure, and be subjected to definitive mathematical modelling. Precisely on this point when mathematical modelling began to dominate economics, economics as a discipline began to disassociate with culture. As a net consequence, no explanation was sought, and none given. Strangely, non-economists in this period were seeking to explain the link between culture and macro-economic functioning. It is interesting to see that several non-economists have emphasized the links between culture and values on the one hand, and from values to economic outcomes on the other. Needless to emphasise, these arguments were rejected by the pantheon of economists. Fascinatingly, these non-economists have attempted to link cultural factors like thrift, hard work, tenacity, honesty, filial piety, and tolerance with economic performance, and contrasted it with the performance of economics in societies which lack culture in the first place. Naturally, given its potency, it is this branch of economics and its confluence with culture that is fast re-emerging once again as the newer frontiers of economics.

Asian Century?

But does all this explain the rise and rise of Asia in what is believed to be the Asian century. Economists, political scientists, and emerging market pundits have been talking for decades about the coming of the Asian Age, which the *Financial Times* opines will supposedly mark an inflection point when the continent becomes the new centre of the world. According to it, Asian economies will be larger than the rest of the world combined in the near future, probably for the first time since the 19th century. The phenomenal rise of China and the impressive growth of India explains a large part of this trend, even as other smaller Asian countries like the Philippines, Indonesia, South Korea, Singapore, Vietnam, and a host of others have kept pace with their other Asian peers. This resurgence, which began with Japan's post-war economic resurrection, represents a return to a well-researched, documented, and known historical norm. Asia, it may be noted, dominated the world economy for most of human history until the 19th century. The resurgence of the Asian economies – first by Japan and Korea, and subsequently by China and now India – is a return to the natural order of the first 18 centuries of the common era. The aberration seems to be only in the 19th and 20th centuries, where Asia lost to the rest of the world. How did the Asians dominate the world economy till the 19th century, why they fell, and how and why are they re-surging is a story probably untold from the angle of civilisation-culture-economic nexus? Is the recent resurgence of Asia linked to culture and family values? Will its resurgence be constantly under attack in future from colonial or any other monstrous ideas? Will Asian affluence itself be a risk, as we saw during the Asian crisis, and will necessarily be transferred into the hands of the 'developed West,' as we realise after the Asian crisis? What makes Asia the net exporter of capital? We will deal with these questions shortly. But the moot question is whether the resurgence of Asia is in effect triggered by traditional family values? Is savings fuelling its economic renaissance? Is this a welcome derivative of culture? Is frugality a virtue? We had argued at the beginning of this chapter as to how family comes with certain restraints. It is these restraints that make and sustain economics, not otherwise. Remember, even the spectacular rise of the US in the early 20th century, was rooted to Calvinist restraints. Sadly, by the second half of the 20th century, the US had virtually given up on these traditional restraints.

Crucially, where is the American family and its virtues of the 19th century that was discussed in Chapter 3? The answer to most questions probably lies in what Tocqueville, a French diplomat, saw in the early 19th century America and chronicled it. He wanted to know what was the crucial differential that ensured the US to emerge as the world's political and economic superpower then. His conclusion was emphatic as it was elementary. "There have never been free societies without morals, and it is the woman who moulds the morals," he wrote. This moral judgement is what Tocqueville believed brought men and women on equal grounds more than anything else. Tocqueville saw American women as the keystone of the family, the ones who held everyone else together. The women, Tocqueville saw, was not the modern, liberated women who occupied exalted positions like CEOs of any large corporates or were celebrities, politicians, or professional athletes. They were largely confined to the home, and were quintessentially the homemaker – cleaning, cooking, taking care of children. By taking primary responsibility for the home, American women allowed their husbands to fulfil their traditional roles as providers, and they both worked towards a common goal of strengthening their family. These traditional roles of men and women, maligned today as harmful 'gender stereotypes,' are precisely what helped to make America exceptional in Tocqueville's eyes. This role clarity, according to Tocqueville, within the family is what held the family, society, and economy together in the early part of 19th century US.

In effect, Tocqueville was to warn us about the feminist movement that would take shape almost a century or so later. In a startling observation, he had warned the world not to mistake equality with similarity, and prophetically added: "There are men in Europe who, confusing the different attributes of the sexes, claim to make the man and the woman beings, not only equal, but similar. It can easily be imagined that by trying hard in this way to make one sex equal to the other, both are degraded, and that from this crude mixture of the works of nature, only weak men and dishonest women can ever emerge." Importantly, the "men in Europe" that he refers to above were certain sects, which began as a socialist movement pushing for equal representation of women in public, but finally ended as embracing infidelity as a virtue, and viewing reproduction as a function of the state rather than of the private family. By making the contributions of women to the 'social well-being' similar to those of men, the traditional family, as a barrier between the state and the individual, according to Tocqueville, began to break down. The men and women he observed had different roles, but their focus was the same: filling the needs of the family. "Progress," he wrote in conclusion, "does not consist of making almost the same things out of dissimilar beings, but of having each of them fulfil his task to the best possible degree."

Similarity Mistaken for Equality

This is what has in effect been achieved by feminists – in the search for equality for women, they have ended up making women similar to men. There is a natural and biological limitation to this idea. Equality in opportunities and pay is definitely possible and surely welcome. But would it be prudent to extend the idea of gender similarity to everything under the sun? We will look into the issue of this reckless idea of feminism and its debilitating impact on families in the succeeding chapters of this book. Nevertheless, feminism had the calculated effect of ensuring an unnatural competition between male and female, with the obvious destruction of families. The net result of all these is that we dynamite macro-economic stability. Remember it is the household (family) that saves, not corporates or for that matter, the government. It is these savings that are channelled to banks or stock markets as investments. It is this investment that ensures production, which is ultimately consumed by the family. When families cease to exist, savings plummet. Alternatively, consumption increases.

Either way, the balance in an economy is disturbed. Families, by their very definition, are tempered in their behaviour, be it consumption or savings. The American boom in the early part of the 20th century was a result of a stable American family. American consumption binge is predominantly on account of the destruction of its families. The resurgence of Asia in the second half of the 20th century is once again due to its families. The original growth of Asia in the first 18 centuries of the common era was due to its adherence to family values. India's spectacular rise in the 20th century is again due to its culture, family, and civilisational values.

But what is the definitive link between family and economics? The link is obvious, though not mathematically determinable. Probably, the nebulousness of the idea by itself does not lend to precise mathematical modelling. And since it is mathematically indeterminate, not much of studies have been carried out by economists. Recall, when mathematics allied with economics, culture ceased to be a factor in the discipline of economics to the point where economists began to first ignore culture, and latter to fashion their policies to even hurt it. Therefore, this is one area where one can at best quote anecdotal references and empirical studies, but never reduce it to any precise modern economic theory. Nevertheless, it can be safely concluded that culture – of which family plays a dominant role – does substantially determine the course of economics. Family, by definition, is bound by its own traditions which are rooted in culture. Culture restrains and constrains a family – restrains in doing certain negative acts, and constrains a family in doing some positive ones. What is negative and what is positive is subject to societal approval, which over a period of time when practised by families, becomes the traditions of the families. Of course, these constraints and restraints are under sustained attack since the days of Plato. Nevertheless, these acts of constraints and restraints in the aggregate have a profound impact on the national and possibly global economy. Put pithily, it is these traditions that make the family spend and consume even during times of economic slowdown, or for that matter personal economic limitations. Thus, family and its time-honoured traditions are the perfect antidote to economic recession. It is precisely why countries like India never face a recession, as it is the family and its traditions that constantly ensure demand. Once demand is ensured, where is the question of recession? Likewise, the emotional bonding of the parents towards their children compels them to save. This, in turn, ensures capital for future investments on a sustainable basis. These are fundamental lessons that modern economic theories tend to ignore.

It is not only the institution of the family that is historically under duress. It is observed that when family-based societies accumulate wealth, they too come under constant attack, physically or otherwise. The colonial rule of the 19th and 20th centuries over large parts of Asia is a case in point. And the Asian currency crisis discussed earlier in this chapter once again reiterates the basic truth of life that it is the prosperous who are always vulnerable. These are lessons from our history too. One must not lose sight of the matter that India was always a prosperous nation from time immemorial. Her prosperity was, unfortunately, her Achilles heel. She was under attack right through her history – first by Alexander, then by several others, subsequently by Islamic invaders, and finally by the Europeans. As per a recent study (we will deal with this later), and quoted by the Indian External Affairs Minister, S Jaishankar, the British loot of India over the period of their colonial rule was estimated to be approximately $45 trillion. Such waves of attackers over 2,000 years demonstrate not only the prosperity of the Indian economy, but also its sustainability over this extended period of time, despite repeated destruction by invading forces. Truly, Incredible India!

Does this prosperity and sustainability arise from its family values? If India has survived for over 2,000 years despite such intellectual hostility and physical animosity, is it not because of family, culture, and civilisational values? If not family, what else would have sustained her as a civilisation over the millennia? What is missed in the melee is that it is a classical Catch-22 situation – if a country is not rich in culture, it cannot be prosperous. But the very prosperity of a country over a period of time attracts attackers, who by definition lack restraints, as we saw in Chapter 1. It is time that economists paid attention to risks arising within an economy from its prosperity. We will deal with this issue in Chapter 9 in greater detail.

Awaiting Asianisation of Globalisation

Importantly, let us not forget that the Asian rise in the 21st century is deeply 'structural' and not 'cyclical.' It is in this connection that Indian Prime Minister Narendra Modi commented in March 2019 that the global economic gravity is once again shifting towards the Asian continent, and how Asia "has become the main growth engine of the world. In fact, we are now living through what many have termed the Asian Century." The economic reasons for this optimism are not far to seek. The Asian economic zone from the Arabian Peninsula in the west to Japan and New Zealand in the east, and from Russia in the north to Australia in the south now represents 50 percent of the global GDP, and two-thirds of global economic growth. Of the estimated $30 trillion in middle-class consumption growth estimated between 2015 and 2030, only $1 trillion is expected to come from today's Western economies. Most of the rest will come from Asia. That, in effect, signifies the importance of Asia in the forthcoming decade.

And the downside? Obviously, Asia would be witness to an elevated economic activity in the near future. This would lead to sustained wealth accumulation in the next few decades. And if history is any indication, it is this wealth that would make Asia vulnerable once again to sustained attacks. The prosperity of Asia will ultimately turn out to be its Achilles heel. If we need to prevent history repeating itself yet again, we need to understand the fundamental fact of life – that in a fight between the uncultured and the cultured, the latter have little or no chance. In a competition between the restrained and the unrestrained, the unrestrained will necessarily triumph over the former. In a war between a monogamous society and others, it is the latter which will constantly run over the former. Put pithily, the cultured are at a constant disadvantage when pitted against the non-cultured. Analysts do assess 'systemic risks' when assessing an economy. So do investors and market players. But cultural superiority as a risk is probably never recognised in their analysis, and hence never factored. This is yet another frontier of economics that needs to be factored.

If the 21st century is to be indeed an Asian century, as some prophesise and most believe, then there is one aspect which one needs to strategically considered – whether it will be an Asian century riding merely on Western ideas, institutions, and philosophies. Or will it be an Asian century constructed ab-initio with Asian values? The answer to these questions cannot be answered in a binary mode. Asia will be both Asian as well as global in her rise in the 21st century. Asia will have her share of ideas, institutions, and philosophies in shaping the emerging global order. But these have been marginal till date for obvious reasons; these are never considered global at present. In fact, the 'global' has never included Asia in substantial measure. Nonetheless, some Asian values, especially those relating to the family, have been time-tested. They have a proven track record of stability and sustainability. Asia has been the cradle to several civilisations, and has been the land of birth of quite a few religions. Strangely, they have not received the approval of a global audience, more particularly economists. The fault probably lies in the fact that Asians, barring exceptions, never believed in global dominance, in a manner which the West would believe or approve. But if Asia has to 'dominate' the immediate future, it needs to play a pan-Asian narrative, especially of family values, culture, and its impact on economics. Therefore, it is but natural that the next great leap has to necessarily be Asianisation of all that is currently global, and Indianisation of Asia. The world of geo-politics exemplifies a simple binary paradigm – dominate or get dominated. That would include the discipline of economics, and with it the primacy of family in economic policy formulations. Complex as these prescriptions may sound, it needs to be remembered that history is a mute witness to the fact that Asia has always been subjected to tremendous physical attacks, probably because of her wealth. The Asian currency crisis, as pointed out in this chapter, is a case in point. Huntington, in a scathing indictment of the Western ideas of conquest and dominance, puts it across in a devastating manner when he points out that "The West won not by the superiority of its ideas or values or religion, but rather by its superiority in applying organised violence. Westerners often forget this fact; non-Westerners never do." If Asia (more specifically, India) has to de-risk from future attacks, more specifically from the West, Asia has to ensure that culture and civilisation plays an important part in the global economy. Let us not forget what Maharishi Aurobindo had prophesied – India's rebirth will be out of the ruins of the West. The West is indeed in ruins. It is time for India's rebirth. For starters, we need to encourage and promote the monogamous family as an institution globally on a war-footing. The primacy of the family has to permeate every policy of all governments across continents. The triumvirate of misplaced belief in markets, irrational government policies, and extraordinary individualism are collectively a huge burden on modern economies. More specifically, each of these individually and collectively seek to destroy the institution of the family. We need to revisit the root assumptions of all three seemingly disconnected yet symbiotically interlinked ideas.

To do this, for starters we need to re-explore the idea of Samuel Huntington and his seminal work – *The Clash of Civilizations and the Remaking of World Order*, and referred to in Chapter 3. Left only to the West, the remaking of the new world order will necessarily reflect their view.

But as events of the past few decades indicate, that is neither sustainable nor desirable. The world can ill-afford the popular prevalent ideas, more particularly in economics, that emanate – linked to the modern triad referred to above. In its stead, Asia needs to step in and provide viable sustainable alternatives. For starters, it needs to revisit the root assumptions of modern economics. It cannot leave modern economics to alternate between the vicissitudes of the markets and the demagoguery of governments. The world is fatigued gyrating between the ideas of Keynes and Hayek. Economists are in a constant search for an effective antidote to the constant cycles of booms and busts. If Asia's time has indeed come, it must place definitive economic ideas and alternatives. This is not the time for Asians to point out that Takahashi Korekiyo (one of Japan's premier macro-economists who made certain macro-economic prescriptions that preceded Keynes) is Asia's Keynes. It is in fact and the precise occasion to point out that Keynes succeeded him and Keynes was Europe's Takahashi Korekiyo.

For all these to materialise, we need to prepare the world from the Asian point of view. To this day, and for too long, Asian perspectives are often seen through Western prisms. We need to break this orthodoxy. The West has inadvertently atomised its society completely. We need to reverse this construct. A monogamous family-based society and a set of economic policies that would reflect the aspirations of such a society would do more for world peace and the consequent good to the global economy, than probably any other policy. The earlier the world realises it, the better.

References

1. www.wikipedia.com/homeostatis
2. www.oecd.org
3. www. Guardian.com
4. A Broad View of Macroeconomic Stability By José Antonio Ocampo – DESA Working Paper No. 1 ST/ESA/2005/DWP/1 October 2005.
5. Family Economics By Martin Browning Pierre-André Chiappori and Yoram Weiss; January 2011, Cambridge University Press.
6. The American Family and Family Economics By Shelly Lundberg and Robert A. Pollak NBER Working Paper 12908.
7. The paradox of the paradox of thrift, Nov 18th 2009 By The Economist.

8. Remarks By Governor Ben S. Bernanke At the Sandridge Lecture, Virginia Association of Economists, Richmond, Virginia, March 10, 2005.
9. "The Commanding heights – The Battle between government and the market place that is remaking the modern world" By Daniel Yergin and Joseph Satinslaw.
10. Handbook of Hindu Economics and Business – By M V Nadkarni.
11. Does Culture Affect Economic Outcomes? By Luigi Guiso, University of Rome Tor Vergata, Paola Sapienza Northwestern University & NBER, Luigi Zingales, Harvard University, NBER – Paper prepared for the Journal of Economic Perspectives.
12. The Asian century is set to begin, By Valentina Romei in London and John Reed, Financial Times March 26, 2019.
13. Tocqueville: Women Made America Great By Maddie Mehr, July 11, 2017, The American Conservative.
14. British looted $45 trillion from India in today's value: Jaishankar By Dipanjan Roy and Chaudhury, ET Bureau, October 3, 2019.

6. In Search of Utopia

Liberals want the family destroyed, they want religion destroyed, because then you have loyalty directly to the state

– Ann Coulter

Power has only one duty – to secure the social welfare of the People

– Benjamin Disraeli

Mother nature, by an inexplicable genetic algorithm, has ensured that at birth, a person has as much chance of being a male as he has of being a female. A male has one X chromosome and one Y chromosome. A female has two X chromosomes. How and why the permutation and combination of these chromosomes occur and determine the sex of an individual is one of the biggest challenges confronting modern science. Sex, let us understand, is the biological identification of a person. Man (or for that matter woman) is someone more evolved than merely possessing the right combination of chromosomes. But what elevates a male or a female into a man or a woman, as the case may be? The answer to this vexatious question is determinable tentatively at best. One can possibly suggest that it is prevalent culture that elevates a male or a female into a man or a woman. The former is merely sexual identification. The latter is gender identification with each society fixing certain pre-assigned roles for males as well as females individually, and collectively for both of them in the form of a family.

Traditionally, in these 'cultured' societies, males had to ceaselessly demonstrate their masculinity while females, their feminine qualities. This was done by males and females taking to gender-specific roles. While the former was to take to military, politics, and to enforce public law and order, the latter was largely confined to parenting and home-making. Men in most religions or societies were culturally placed higher in the pecking order, especially in European societies, when compared to women. The Pharaonic, Greek, Roman, Muslim, Ottoman and even the British laws positively discriminated against women. Indian women too, over the ages, had their share of problems. Patriarchy, at least in the Western world, was the norm till the industrial revolution. This – coupled with the fact that women were seen as evil in some societies and religions – compounded matters. Obviously, this created a palpable imbalance within families and hence, societies. This was dealt in some detail in Chapter 3. Nevertheless, families operated with a defined set of goals. Social security, as we now understand, was predominantly privatised and remained in the hands of the families. Health, education and most of individual needs were taken care by the families. This left the king or the government of the day to have a residuary role which at best included either building roads or maintaining a military. As transportation and communication systems were not particularly developed till the 20th century, even collection of taxes was decentralised (as was dispensing justice) and left to local communities.

Likewise, markets were at best local where the produce of one member of the village was exchanged generally for the goods and services provided by the other members. Over a period of time, all these changed. The state first established courts to dispense justice – especially in cases of disputes involving family and those within the community. Simultaneously, they began collecting taxes. For the taxes collected, the state provided certain services like protecting a village or community from attacks by outsiders. Bereft of all sophistry, it was only protection money. Even then the family reigned supreme and did not allow the state or the market to interfere into their personal affairs beyond a point. Consequently, every individual, male or female, till the industrial revolution, was tethered in a large measure to the family and not to the state or the markets. Life was simple.

The Mother of all Trade-Offs

Yuval Noah Harari in his acclaimed book *Sapiens*, describes the inflecxion point in the history of mankind where the state and markets replaced traditional families, their role and responsibilities. Harari explains as to how the state and the market approached the people with an alluring offer that could not be refused. The trade-off was simple, according to Harari. It was to atomise a person and distance him from his family. "Become individuals," was the quintessential idea of this trade-off, says Harari, and adds this came with an attendant licence from the state to an individual to "Marry whomsoever you desire, without asking permission from your parents. Take up whatever job suits you, even if community elders frown. Live however you wish, even if you cannot make it every week to the family dinner. You are no longer dependent on your family or your community. We, the state and the market, will take care of you instead. We will provide food, shelter, education, health, welfare, and employment. We will provide pensions, insurance, and protection." In short, this atomisation was the cultural end-game at that point in time in the evolution of man since tribalisation.

Harari adds that modern literature often presents individual as somebody caught in a struggle against the state and the market. Nothing, according to him, could be further from the truth. Explaining the contours of the trade-off, Harari adds: "The state and the market are the mother and father of the individual, and the individual can survive only thanks to them. The market provides us with work, insurance, and a pension. If we want to study a profession, the government's schools are there to teach us. If we want to open a business, the bank loans us money. If we want to build a house, a construction company builds it and the bank gives us a mortgage, in some cases subsidised or insured by the state. If violence flares up, the police protect us. If we are sick for a few days, our health insurance takes care of us. If we are debilitated for months, social security steps in." More importantly, modern states, in direct contrast to the manner in which women were historically treated, see women as individuals and allows them to enjoy economic, legal, and political rights. Of course, this liberation of the individual, especially women, came with a resultant downside. While the state and market may disagree on their role, duties, and responsibilities, the fact remains that they demand too much from an individual and provide too little in return. Harari touches a raw nerve when he explains as to how this arrangement has degenerated over the years so much so that the state has come to be seen as coercive, and the markets exploitative.

But that brings us back to the original issue of the grand trade-off referred to by Harari. What was the trigger for the trade-off referred to above?

What was the underlying philosophy that triggered this trade-off? What are the attendant consequences of this trade-off? This trade-off, referred to as Social Contract Theory, is the genesis of modern constitutional law adopted by most nation-states. It is the basis on which all laws are codified and written on the assumption that diverse individuals came together collectively to give on to themselves laws to regulate their individual and collective behaviour and subjected themselves to the supremacy of the law. These were further effectuated through two unwritten but elaborately codified agreements – first by the *Pact of Unionis*, where people came together for a common purpose. As, a result, people undertook to respect each other and live peacefully and in harmony. By the second – *the Pact of Subjectionis*, people already united together by the *Pact of Unionis*, pledged to obey a higher authority and surrendered the whole of their freedom and rights to an authority viz., the state, which in turn had the basic function of protecting their life, liberty, and property. Thus, it was in essence a contract – one wherein everyone surrendered to a collective body – the government – but with a caveat that the government would protect life and liberty of every individual.

That explains why Constitutions of modern nation-states have a Preamble which explains how and why the people of a country have come together and resolved amongst themselves to constitute a Republic. This coming together of people is the *Pact of Unionis* at play where in the case of India, the people of India came together to give on to themselves a Constitution in 1950. The Preamble of the Indian Constitution as approved by the Constituent Assembly is reproduced hereunder for ready reference:

> "We, (emphasis supplied) the People of India, having solemnly resolved to constitute India into a Sovereign Democratic Republic and to secure to all its citizens Justice, social, economic and political; Liberty of thought, expression, belief, faith and worship; Equality of status and of opportunity; and to promote among them all Fraternity assuring the dignity of the individual; In our Constituent Assembly this 26th day of November 1949, do hereby Adopt, Enact and Give to Ourselves This Constitution."

It may be interesting to note that the Constituent Assembly originally took a considered decision not to include within the Preamble any particular political or economic ideology apart from that of democracy and a republican form of government. The repeated attempts by some members of the Constituent Assembly to smuggle in the word 'Socialist' into the Preamble of the Indian Constitution was wholly and roundly defeated by others at that point in time. It may be not out of place to mention that in fact Dr BR Ambedkar, the chairman of the drafting committee of the Indian Constitution, specifically explained the rationale for the non-inclusion of the word 'Socialist' in the Preamble of the Constitution, and settled the issue decisively. In this connection, he opined in the Constituent Assembly Debate on November 15, 1948: "What should be the policy of the State, how the Society should be organised in its social and economic side are matters which must be decided by the people themselves according to time and circumstances. It cannot be laid down in the Constitution itself, because that is destroying democracy altogether. If you state in the Constitution that the social organisation of the State shall take a particular form, you are, in my judgment, taking away the liberty of the people to decide what should be the social organisation in which they wish to live. It is perfectly possible today, for the majority of people to hold that the socialist organisation of society is better than the capitalist organisation of society. But it would be perfectly possible for thinking people to devise some other form of social organisation which might be better than the socialist organisation of today or of tomorrow. I do not see, therefore, why the Constitution should tie down the people to live in a particular form and not leave it to the people themselves to decide it for themselves." It is with such grand liberal values (where the ideological underpinnings of the coming together were deliberately kept open-ended by our founding father so as to keep the joints of economics absolutely flexible) that Ambedkar sought to navigate the constitutional debates as the chairman of the drafting committee, despite his personal leaning towards socialism.

Socialism triumphs, but trips India

In contrast, Nehru, the first Prime Minister of India, was determined to ensure that independent India was well and truly a socialist state. Nehru at the outset proposed tentatively that independent India will indeed be a socialist state. Moving the Objective Resolution, Nehru outlined the socio-political-economic objective of the proposed Indian Constitution to the Constituent Assembly on December 13, 1946. In this connection, Nehru expounded his personal position on a socialist form of government as: "Well, I stand for Socialism and, I hope, India will stand for Socialism and that India will go towards the Constitution of a Socialist State and I do believe that the whole world will have to go that way. What form of Socialism again is another matter for your consideration. But the main thing is that in such a Resolution, if, in accordance with my own desire, I had put in, that we want a Socialist State, we would have put in something which may be agreeable to many and may not be agreeable to some and we wanted this resolution not to be controversial in regard to such matters." Despite exhibiting such remarkable clarity on a vexatious subject and being at his persuasive best, Nehru was in a hopeless minority when it came to actually deciding this issue in the Constituent Assembly.

As a result, he had to take a tactical retreat in imposing his personal views on others. Nehru's time had not come in good measure in 1946. That explains when the inclusion of the word socialist in the preamble of the Constitution were in effect debated in the Constituent Assembly, especially on October 17, 1949, the resolutions proposed by the constituent assembly members including Maulana Hasrat Mohani, Prof Shibban Lal Saksena, and Brajeshwar Prasad were squarely rejected.

Thus, the debate at least in 1950, when the Constitution was adopted was seemingly settled against the inclusion of the word socialist in the Indian Constitution. However, while decoding the Constituent Assembly debates at this point in time, one is compelled to note that the genetic structure of the Indian Constitution was decidedly socialist. Like the leaning tower of Pisa, the Constitution of India too leaned, and leaned heavily in favour of socialism. The towering personality of Nehru combined with the overwhelming Keynesian ideas that flowered worldwide post-World War II, meant that the Constitution was essentially a socialist construct. Post-independence, the socialist state turned into a welfare state, subsequently degenerated into a populist state, and is now spiralling downwards into a reckless state.

The idea of Nehruvian socialism is best exemplified by the legislations thrust on a new nation by Nehru and after his death in 1964 by his daughter, Indira. It may be noted that by 1954 Nehru, as the sole dominant figure within the Indian political landscape, got Parliament to accept the 'socialist pattern of society.' Further, in 1955, the Avadi session of the Indian National Congress, passed a resolution promising to keep the public sector at the 'commanding heights' of the economy, "establishment of a socialistic pattern of society where the principal means of production are under social ownership or control" and "equitable distribution of the national wealth." While the Industrial Policy Resolution of 1948 was ambivalent towards private enterprises, the 1956 version permitted only the government to undertake new ventures in several sectors such as textiles, automobiles, and defence. Along with all these policy and legislative initiatives, Nehru curbed personal liberties and raised taxes. The tentative liberal philosopher Nehru of 1946 who spoke of socialism as an ideal destination for independent India had given way to an obstinate, ruthless Nehru by 1956 for whom socialism was a non-negotiable, immutable, and unassailable ideology. A decade is indeed a long time in politics, that too Indian politics.

Parallelly, Nehru had set up the Planning Commission (a body set up by a mere administrative fiat which had sweeping powers) on the lines of the Gosplan of the Soviet Union and directed it to draw five-year plans. As part of his grand design to convert India into a socialist country, Nehru amended the Indian Constitution to dilute personal property rights of citizens, allowed for the nationalisation of any industry and ushered in a licence permit raj to set up any new private enterprises. Profitable industries were nationalised. Land reform laws were legislated with a ceiling imposed on the amount of land one could own. Simultaneously, the government acquired sweeping powers to take over any land, private, industrial, or for that matter agricultural. Labour laws were legislated merely to stamp the control of the state on the national economy and stymie private enterprise. Profit, as a consequence, became a dirty word in the Indian political lexicon.

When Indira Gandhi, daughter of Nehru, became Prime Minister of India in 1966, the Nehruvian economic ideas were taken to their logical conclusion. Banks were nationalised, severe taxation on higher incomes were introduced along with wealth and gift taxes, privy purses were abolished, followed by nationalisation of coal mines, general insurance, and textile companies. Meanwhile, the Monopolies and Restrictive Trade Practices (MRTP) Act was legislated to curb potential monopolies. The draconian Foreign Exchange Regulation Act (FERA) was brought into the statute books ostensibly to regulate India's 'precious' foreign exchange, but in effect regulated the affairs of Indira's political opponents and stubborn businessmen who refused to tow the establishment line. Thus, the role of the Indian state, by the mid-1970s had transmogrified into an omnipotent, omnipresent one from that of an efficient enabler, without any ideological leanings as was originally envisaged by the founding fathers of the Indian Constitution.

Distributing Poverty, not Wealth

The cumulative effect, despite the best efforts of Nehru, of all these was indeed not very encouraging. In effect, instead of producing wealth, the Indian state concentrated on distribution of wealth. This was sought to be achieved through the crass intermediation of the state and its coercive agencies in virtually every aspect of an individual. If there was a food shortage, the response was not to produce more food but to have a Food Corporation and mandate distribution of food through the fair price shops. Not many really bothered to find out whether there was food in the place to distribute. If there was a foreign exchange shortage, the idea was to not find means to increase the availability of foreign exchange but to legislate exchange laws and regulate the use of foreign exchange. The endgame was that the assault on poverty in effect turned to be an assault on the wealth creators. Indians did not realise for long that the Indian state became relevant only when there was a shortage or a crisis. To make itself relevant, the state contrived in every possible way to create a shortage and contrive a crisis. Little did Indians imagine that as against the avowed policy of distributing wealth, the Indian state actually ended up distributing poverty. Where is the question of distributing wealth when for distributing it, someone had to produce it?

And where is the question of production when the state was against it in the first place?

Meanwhile, through the 42nd Amendment to the Indian Constitution, in December 1976, the words 'Socialist' and 'Secular' were added between the words 'Sovereign' and 'Democratic' and the words 'unity of the nation' were changed to 'unity and integrity of the nation' by the then government headed by Indira Gandhi. These insertions were made in the Preamble of the Constitution, amidst bitter criticism that the Parliament did not have the power to amend the Preamble. The statement of object and reasons appended to the Constitution's 42nd Amendment explained the rationale for the Parliament to carry out such an amendment. Accordingly, at the outset, it stated that for a Constitution to be living, it must be growing. If the impediments to the growth of the Constitution are not removed, it rationalised that the Constitution will suffer a virtual atrophy. Accordingly, it clarified that the question of amending the Constitution was for removing the difficulties which have arisen in achieving the objective of socio-economic revolution. It was suggested that this would end poverty, ignorance, disease, and inequality of opportunity, which has been engaging the active attention of the government and the public for some years now. Secondly, it made a grand announcement that the democratic institutions provided in the Constitution are basically sound and the path for progress does not lie in denigrating any of these institutions. However, the statement of object and reasons alleged that there could be no denial that these institutions have been subjected to considerable stresses and strains and that vested interests have been trying to promote their selfish ends to the great detriment of public good. Therefore, it concluded that it is proposed to amend the Constitution to spell out expressly the high ideals of socialism, to make the directive principles more comprehensive, and give them precedence over those fundamental rights which have been allowed to be relied upon to frustrate socio-economic reforms for implementing the directive principles.

Pursuant to the insertion in the Preamble, the Representation of the Peoples Act too was amended and Part IV-A comprising Section 29A was inserted, which dealt with the Registration of Political Parties. Sub-section

(5) of this section reads as follows: "The application under sub-section (1) shall be accompanied by a copy of the memorandum or rules and regulations of the association or body, by whatever name called, and such memorandum or rules and regulations shall contain a specific provision that the association or body shall bear true faith and allegiance to the Constitution of India as by law established, and to the principles of socialism, secularism, and democracy, and would uphold the sovereignty, unity, and integrity of India." Thus, every political party that seeks to register itself in the country has to swear by the political and economic ideology of socialism, even if it was wholly antithetical to this view. Thus, the views of the Constituent Assembly, more particularly Dr BR Ambedkar, were buried fathoms deep within three decades by those very people who swore by him!

But what is this beast called socialism? How does it operate? How does it differ from a welfare state? Does it differ in the first place? How and why did the welfare state degenerate into a populist state? Who will benefit? And who will not? And if it failed to deliver as promised, who will be accountable? What are its consequences? We will seek to answer these questions shortly. But first a bit of historical background to the origin of Social Contract theories.

Contract Reneged

Social Contract theories, it may be noted, had their greatest currency in the 17th and 18th centuries, and is associated with such philosophers as Thomas Hobbes and the Frenchman Jean-Jacques Rousseau. By comparing the advantages of organised government with the disadvantages of the state of nature, they showed why and under what conditions government is useful and ought, therefore, to be accepted by all reasonable people as a voluntary obligation. These conclusions were then reduced to the form of a social contract, from which it was supposed that all the essential rights and duties of citizens could be logically deduced. According to Hobbes (Leviathan, 1651), the state of nature was one in which there were no enforceable criteria of right and wrong. People took for themselves all that they could, and human life was "solitary, poor, nasty, brutish, and short." The state of nature was therefore a state of war, which could be ended only if individuals agreed in a social contract to give their liberty into the hands of a sovereign, who was thenceforward absolute, on the sole condition that their lives were safeguarded by sovereign power. Needless to state that all these evolutions in the thoughts of these great philosophers, as we saw in Chapter 3, were in turn based on 'original sin' and how to deal with it.

Likewise, Part III of the Indian Constitution deals with the delicate idea of Fundamental Rights (Pact of *Subjectionis*). By forming and surrendering to the state, every individual was, in turn, granted certain 'fundamental rights' by the state including a promise of life and liberty, absolute in some countries and subject to certain restrictions, in others. It may be worthwhile to recall that this pact suffered a serious challenge in India when the then Prime Minister Indira Gandhi imposed Emergency in 1975. In October 1976, when most of the opposition members in Parliament were in jail and censorship at its peak, a bill was passed by a truncated Parliament and enacted as 42nd Amendment to the Indian Constitution. This amendment represented the most devastating attack upon the Constitution, as it sought to nullify the eternal values (enshrined as fundamental rights) in the Constitution and holding them to be neither operational nor justiciable. The nebulous (*subjectionis*) pact between the state and its subject was fragile, to begin with. Emergency merely exposed it. The net implications of these amendments were canvassed by the then government counsel in a proceeding before the Hon'ble Bombay High Court in Bhanudas Krishna Gawde and recorded by the hon'ble courts in its judgement as under:

> "In fact, (counsel for the government) went so far as to suggest that if the Conditions of Detention Order contained a clause that detenus are not to be allowed to eat any food, it could not be challenged and the petitioner would have no remedy by way of a petition under Article 226 as long as the Presidential Order, suspending the enforcement of the fundamental right under Article 21, of which the right to eat is a part, is in force. Embolden by this proposition of (Counsel), which we cannot help observing is a startling proposition, the learned Government Pleader interposed and said that even if the Conditions of Detention Order were to authorise that the detenu should be shot,

> such a clause could not be challenged during the subsistence of the Presidential Order."

A similar proposition was canvassed even in the Supreme Court by the then Attorney General of India in the famous ADM Jabalpur vs Shava Kant Shukla Case, (popularly known as the Habeas Corpus Case). Justice H.R. Khanna, one of the judges who had heard this matter writes:

> "Mr Niren De, Attorney-General, who argued on behalf of the State, contended as has been done before the High Courts that as the rights to move the court for enforcement of Article 21 has been suspended, the writ petitions were not maintainable. I sought some clarifications about certain aspects to which Niren De gave replies. It was, however, found by me that some of my colleagues who used in the past to be very vocal about human rights and civil liberties were sitting tongue tied. Their silence seemed ominous. In the course of discussion, I put it to Mr. Niren De that Article 21 related not merely to personal liberty but also to life. In view of his submission would there be any remedy if a police officer because of personal enmity killed another man? The answer of Mr De was unequivocal: "Consistently with my arguments" he said, "there would be no judicial remedy in such a case as long as the Emergency lasts", and he added, "I may shock your conscience, it shocks mine, but consistent with my submissions, no proceedings can be taken in a court of law on that score." The above answer put the matters in plain light and left nothing in doubt so far as the position of the State was concerned."

Of course, this position could not have found the immediate approval of the founding fathers of the Indian Constitution. Fortunately, this perversity in the interpretation of the Constitution was quickly recognised and corrected by the courts themselves. Interestingly, all these were overcome by a series of judgements by the Hon'ble Supreme Court of India in the 1970s and 1980s which evolved and refined the idea of 'basic structure doctrine' expounded by some of the leading jurists of those times. Nonetheless, what is and continues to be the 'basic structure of the Indian Constitution' remains a matter of intense debate even today among parliamentarians, jurists, and judges. Neither has the judiciary explicitly defined the basic features of the Indian Constitution. By the last count, at least two dozen features that have been loosely described as 'basic' or 'essential' by the courts in numerous cases before it. Jurists believe that the list will expand in future too as it is open-ended at this point in time. The march of law has been relentless, at least on this subject, in India. What is of relevance to the discussion on hand is that the welfare state is one assumed to be one of the ingredients constituting the idea of basic structure of the Indian Constitution by courts. Since the courts interpreted the Indian Constitution and added 'welfare' to the basic structure doctrine, the question, therefore, is whether socialism is welfare or, are they different ideas? If not, how are they different? As we deal with this issue of welfare and socialism, we will have to deal with a far complex issue – balance between liberty and equality – the ideas mentioned in the preamble of the Constitution.

Balancing Liberty and Equality

Harari points out that ever since the French Revolution, people throughout the world have gradually come to see both equality and liberty as fundamental non-negotiable values while setting their public order. Yet, according to the author, the two political ideas "contradict each other." Equality, according to him, can be ensured only by curtailing the freedoms of those who are better off. Guaranteeing that every individual will be free to do as he wishes inevitably short-charges equality. The entire political history of the world since the French Revolution can be seen as a series of attempts to reconcile this contradiction. Achieving and retaining balance between these two, eternal yet conflicting values, is one of the central ideas of this book.

One of the appealing features of the Indian Constitution includes individual liberty. So is equality before law. Article 14 of the Constitution of India deals with the issue of equality, while Article 21 deals with the issue of liberty. Article 14 of the Constitution of India provides for equality before the law or equal protection of the laws. It states: "The State shall not deny to any person equality before the law or the equal protection of the laws within the territory of India." Article 21 of the Constitution of India provides that, "No person shall be deprived of his life or personal liberty except according to procedure established by law. It is fascinating to note that both Articles 14, as well as 21, are pithily worded, couched in negative language and consequently been the legal fodder for many a court room battle. That is not all. Article 38, (comprised in Chapter IV of the Constitution) also provides leeway to the government to enact laws to deal with inequality. Accordingly, Article 38(2) of the Indian Constitution directs the state to "strive to minimise the inequalities in income, and endeavour to eliminate inequalities in status, facilities and opportunities, not only amongst individuals but also among groups of people residing in different areas or engaged in different vocations." Armed with the right to eliminate inequalities, the government has often come up with bizarre ideas and convoluted legislations only to buckle under the hydraulic pressure of public opinion in India. It is captivating to note that while Article 14 guarantees equality to all citizens of India, the fact remains that Article 38 expressly directed the state to deal with the issue of 'inequality' too. Probably, this extra bit of care and concern for 'inequality' by the founding fathers of the Indian Constitution stemmed from the then prevailing fashionable idea of socialism. Between equality and liberty, the Constitution of India as a construct was skewed decidedly in favour of equality and against liberty. By a quirk of fate, the nation had to choose Nehruvian socialism over the liberal ideas of Ambedkar. Over a period of time, it chose the former.

Contemporary American politics (as it is in Britain, India, and several other countries) also revolves around resolving this inherent contradiction between equality and liberty. For instance, in the US, the Democrats want a more equitable society, even if it means raising taxes to fund federal programmes to help the poor, elderly, and infirm. Laudable as it may be, the fact remains that it infringes on the freedom of individuals to spend their hard-earned money. Republicans, on the other hand, want to maximise individual freedom, again a laudable objective, even at the cost of increasing inequality. In short, Democrats would seemingly stand for equality while Republicans for liberty. Before anyone comes to a conclusion that this debate between equality and liberty is restricted only to the US or India, let us hasten to add that this idea permeates political discourses in democracies across continents with one political party espousing the cause of liberty, while the other championing the idea of equality. Again, this debate is not restricted to political parties or politicians alone. This debate on the contradiction between the grand ideas of equality and liberty engulfs scholars, sociologists, and of course economists in most countries.

Thus, since the French revolution, liberty and equality have been considered antithetic. Liberty has been viewed as protecting the unfettered expression of individuality. Equality, in contrast, is implicitly seen as a limitation on human action. Heightened by philosophies of individualism and the resultant competitive economics on the one hand, and by periodic waves of egalitarian ideas and concomitant socialist ideas, the conflict between liberty and equality has been a continually recurrent political-economic one for the past two centuries, more particularly since 1945. This dichotomy in the construct in every Constitution of a modern-state reflects in the recurrent oscillation in our approach between the economic ideas of Keynes and Hayek. In short, the genesis of the contrasting ideas of Keynes and Hayek are in fact grounded in the conflicting constitutional values of equality and liberty. That, in itself, explains the importance of establishing a balance between equality and liberty. We will look into the battle of ideas between Keynes and Hayek in the following chapters of this book.

Theoretically and practically, the dichotomy between these two cherished constitutional values had been seemingly reconciled through the idea of a minimalist, restrained, and inobtrusive government, funded by a moderate taxation regime. This is the core idea of balance between equality and liberty. This was probably the imaginative 'basic structure' of a government, that political philosophers originally envisaged when they fashioned the social construct theory with a modest tax regime emerging as a small price to pay to organise ourselves into a modern nation-state. However, over a period of time the scope of government was constantly revised so as to encompass a vast arena of human activities, sometimes even as a monopoly, and at others as a compulsion. In the process, equality suddenly acquired greater traction in public discourse, thereby putting the other idea of individual liberty to the backseat. Simultaneously, more was expected out of government – for instance, the rise in global terrorism gave rise to the need for increased security, which the government alone could ensure to all its citizens. Funding these governmental programs necessarily meant more money was required by the government. Importantly, to ensure security, the state had to necessarily interfere into the affairs of men, including at times, his privacy. Taxation regimes and greater regulation by the state turned out to be increasingly coercive and all encompassing. As a consequence of these developments, governments have sought to progressively tax and increasingly regulate every activity of its citizens with a concomitant promise to deliver a variety of goods and services to the individual. This increased role of the state in the affairs of men has put the economy of the several nations in a tailspin. It is, therefore, desirable that any future development in Constitutional Law should necessarily balance the ever-expanding role of the state and never-ending areas of individual activity.

But did the increasing rates of taxes and greater regulation eventually reduce equality? Did taxation of newer areas of human activities finally address the issue of inequality? Could the state have expanded its scope without interfering into the affairs of men? Does the idea of a residuary or a minimalist state sound anti-diluvian in the current context, especially given the state of affairs and the expectations from national governments by individuals? We will seek to answer these questions shortly.

The Original Basic Structure

Thomas Piketty in his celebrated but controversial book *Capital for the Twenty-first Century* brings about a fundamental yet often overlooked fact that income inequality has increased sharply since the late 1970s, with a particularly dramatic rise in the share of total income going to the very highest earners. According to him, that 60 percent of the increase in US national income in the 30 years after 1977 went to just the top one percent of the earners. The only section of the US population that has done better than the top one percent is the top 10th of that one percent. The top 100th of the one percent have done even better, probably the best of all. Piketty goes on to demonstrate that this dramatic rise in income inequality has not happened simultaneously in all rich economies, and, oddly, does not really have much to do with capital. Intriguingly, the issue of inequality too had drawn the attention of the founding fathers of the Indian Constitution, way back in late 1940s.

Participating in the debate on the issue of inequality and how the new Constitution of India would address the issue, MR Masani on December 17, 1946, states "I think it is estimated that today, if our national income were to be divided into three equal thirds, 5 out of 100 Indians get one-third of our national income, another 33 get the second third, and the big mass of 62 get the remaining portion. That surely is not social or economic justice and, therefore, as I understand this resolution, it would not tolerate the wide and gross inequalities which exist in our country. It would not tolerate the exploitation of a man's labour by somebody else. It certainly means that everyone who toils for the common good will get his fair share of the fruits of his labour. It also means that the people of this country, so far as any Constitution can endow them, will get social security – the right to work or maintenance by the community." What Piketty says now and what Masani stated then are surely serious issues confronting governments across continents. But is increased taxation the solution? Is inheritance tax on wealth as suggested by some and discussed by a few, the way out to address the issue of inequality?

The historicity associated with the issue of inequality does not stop Piketty from focusing the rest of the book on capital, which he says has also become more unequally distributed since the 1970s, not just in the US but in Europe too. He believes this trend towards greater wealth inequality is very likely to continue, because the returns from capital are likely to grow faster than the economy itself, and faster than the owners of that wealth are likely to be able to spend it. All this when the world discovered newer methods of taxation and tax-GDP ratio went up significantly in most countries. The solution to address mounting inequality even as the state is expanding its role significantly, according to Piketty is taxes, more taxes, and much more taxes. Needless to reiterate, the intellectual roots of such extreme ideas go back at least as far as ancient Greek times, when the philosopher Plato depicted a type of collective society in his book *Republic*.

The storyline of Piketty is fairly on predictable lines. According to the author, over the course of the 19th century, a few hundred French families accumulated massive fortunes. The tax system, as we know it now, was still in its embryonic stage then. In 1914 however, right before its entry into World War I, France levied a tax on incomes. From a mere 2 percent on top earnings, it rose to 22 percent for corresponding incomes at the end of the war. Subsequently, it rose to 70 percent during World War II, before settling between 60 and 65 percent until the 1980s.

But inequality began to rise post-1980s in the developed countries like the US, France, and Britain. It is no coincidence that it rose along with the fortunes of right-wing political movements, headed by Ronald Reagan in the US, Jacques Chirac in France, and Margaret Thatcher in Britain. For instance, Thatcher announced as early as in 1975, when she slammed a book down on a table during a Conservative Party debate and declared, "This is what we believe." The book in Thatcher's hands was Friedrich Hayek's *The Constitution of Liberty*, in which Hayek assailed progressive taxation as inefficient and unjust. To Hayek, and to his co-believers including Reagan, Thatcher, or Chirac, inequality was an inevitable corollary of progress, and the latter was well worth the price of the former. Remember that was the time when the world, fatigued with Keynesian ideas, was jettisoning Keynes and searching for an attractive alternative. The ideas of Hayek seemed refreshing at that point in time.

In an interview after winning three consecutive elections to the British Parliament, Thatcher reflecting on her economic ideology in an interview explained: "I think we have gone through a period when too many children and people have been given to understand 'I have a problem, it is the Government's job to cope with it!' or 'I have a problem, I will go and get a grant to cope with it!' or 'I am homeless, the Government must house me!,' and so they are casting their problems on society, and who is society? There is no such thing. There are individual men and women and there are families, and no government can do anything except through people, and people look to themselves first. It is our duty to look after ourselves and then also to help look after our neighbour, and life is a reciprocal business. People have got the entitlements too much in mind without the obligations, because there is no such thing as an entitlement unless someone has first met an obligation and it is, I think, one of the tragedies in which many of the benefits we give, which were meant to reassure people that if they were sick or ill there was a safety net and there was help, that many of the benefits which were meant to help people who were unfortunate — "It is all right. We joined together and we have these insurance schemes to look after it". That was the objective, but somehow there are some people who have been manipulating the system and so some of those help and benefits that were meant to say to people: "All right, if you cannot get a job, you shall have a basic standard of living!" but when people come and say: "What is the point of working? I can get as much on the dole!" You say: "Look! It is not from the dole. It is your neighbour who is supplying it, and if you can earn your own living, then really you have a duty to do it, and you will feel very much better!"

Unarguably, it is the most candid talk about individual responsibility by any politician in the 20th century. The role of the government over the period of time, as rightly pointed out by Thatcher, had degenerated to such an extent that most people across countries have now come to assume that every problem of an individual is a problem of the government. Once it becomes a problem of the government, it is for the government of the day to solve. And this is more pronounced in a democracy where once the government is elected, people believe that it is the sole duty of the government of the day to address every problem of an individual as they believe they have elected a government precisely for that particular purpose. Employment, health, housing, environment, food, transportation – you name it – people believe it is virtually the sole responsibility of the government to ensure all these to its citizens, apart from its traditional functions of providing security and ensuring law and order. Some of these have been embedded as 'rights' in the Constitution of the respective countries. Paradoxically, the very same people also frown upon the government interfering in their privacy in the name of security or whatever, which most forget is the fundamental duty of every government in the first place. Such skew in our collective thinking has stymied our progress as more people believe that they are entitled to live on the government's dole, and hence need to do very little to sustain themselves. More to the point, individual rights as guaranteed by the law of the land is not counter-balanced by any concomitant individual duty, legally or otherwise. This has given rise to a fundamental imbalance – between guaranteed individual rights and lack of individual duties.

The political-economic ideology of President Ronald Reagan too was on similar lines as that of Thatcher and can be best described by the answer to the question on what he thought were the nine most terrifying words in the English language: "I'm from the government, and I'm here to help." Once elected as President of the US, Reagan unleashed his ideas of his war on big government by a tax reduction programme. The Economic Recovery Tax Act of 1981 was expected to return $749 billion to taxpayers over the next five years. The last Carter budget (the predecessor of Reagan) foresaw steady increases in revenue, with taxes taking 24 percent of GNP. The average federal tax burden from 1961 to 1980 was about 19 percent of GNP. In 1981, the Reagan administration predicted federal taxes would take just over 19 percent of GDP by 1984. In that sense, Reagan's tax cuts returned to the decadal average. Reagan simultaneously effectuated expenditure cuts by cutting the projected spending of the federal government by about 5 percent. Overall, discretionary domestic spending dropped about 14 percent during Reagan's first year. Several Great Society programs were sharply cut. The Community Development Block Grant program, for example, lost two-thirds of its funding. Reagan also won a 32 percent cut in mass transit spending.

Despite all this hoopla, the fact remains that Reagan eventually failed to radically reduce the size of the government. By 1989, most spending almost equalled its 1981 level, adjusted for inflation. President Reagan realised that once a government-sponsored welfare programme was rolled out, it was difficult to reverse it. How could one of the most powerful and popular presidents of America fail to renege on his promise of a small government, especially expenditure cuts? The answer for the same is not far to seek. Once the discipline of self-help and duty gets broken by doles from the government, it is humanly impossible to reverse the idea. This is universally recognised as a fundamental law of governance. Unable to raise taxes on account of his poll promise, and practical difficulties in reigning in expenditure, the Reagan era ended with the US Federal government opting for the only alternative,

Debt, to finance its ever-increasing expenditure. And national debt is a tax - both on the poor and the rich alike. We will revert to this convoluted issue of debt shortly.

Our Tryst with Socialism

"What about a camel and motorcycle?" queried Dr PS Deshmukh in jest during the Constituent Assembly debates on October 17,1949, to a suggestion by Brajeshwar Prasad, another member, who moved an amendment to certain provisions of the draft Constitution seeking independent India to establish a socialist order and to secure to all its citizens an adequate means of livelihood, free and compulsory education, free medical aid, and compulsory military training. In reply to the taunt, Prasad referred to a book titled *Liberty Versus Equality* by Muriel Jaeger and read out a passage: "It is becoming more and more widely accepted that ownership is one of those liberties that infringe the liberty of others and so must be abolished, or drastically restricted." Echoing these thoughts while participating in the debates, RK Sidhwa on August 30, 1947, commented: "In this country, Sir, there are only a few hundred or few thousands who roll in crores, while millions have no proper food. This is the state of affairs. How are we going to improve it, unless this system of inequality of wealth which has been confined to a few people in the country is to be abolished? I am sure without imposing a further burden upon the average person by various kinds of taxation, if this wealth is properly distributed, the state will have ample money to put this nation-building programme into operation very successfully. I know, Sir, our popular members of the government are alert and they may be looking into the matter." It is indeed fascinating at this distant point in time to note that the founding fathers of the Indian Constitution had such extensive debates on these economic ideas.

At the core of this socialist belief are two complementary ideas – one, the state has endless resources, and as a consequence it can take any amount of burden of its citizens; and two, socialists believe that wealth is created by the working class and wrongfully appropriated by the rich, and accordingly, the rich do not deserve their wealth, or for that matter property, and therefore such property has to, through a fiat of the government, transferred to the state. The underlying idea of socialism was that individuals or markets could not be trusted to address the issue of inequality, so the government must be mandated by law to determine where the resources of a country should be deployed, what exactly should be produced, in what location, and by whom. In short, people would be best served when they had no right to decide and most, if not all, economic decisions were best left to the government. That explains why India had such high rates of taxes in the beginning of the 1970s (and some parts of the world have even today) when the personal income tax had eleven tax brackets, with the tax rates progressively rising from 10 percent to 85 percent. When the surcharge of 10 percent was taken into account, the maximum marginal rate for individuals was a mind-boggling 93.5 percent. In 1973-74, the highest tax rate applicable to an individual could have gone up to an astronomical level of 97.5 percent. It was not only that the direct taxes regime was oppressive, but indirect taxes too were raised to obnoxious levels. High tariffs with rates up to 300 percent on certain goods, and 150 percent on capital goods, a restrictive trade regime coupled with extraordinary domestic tax on manufacturing (also called as Excise Duty) meant that domestic consumption was stymied. On top of this, people had to pay wealth tax, which effectively meant that beyond a particular income level, individuals had to work exclusively for the government. So much for the idea of liberty embedded in the preamble of the Constitution.

Obviously by the 1970s, the idea of socialism had taken deep roots within the Indian polity. The Janata government headed by octogenarian Morarji Desai that came to power in 1977 went on to amend the Constitution and removed property rights as a fundamental right. The issue, let us add, was not one of addressing inequality, but one of posturing. The question that continues to be relevant even to this day is whether socialism – through extraordinary state intervention into the daily lives of the ordinary man – was the appropriate mechanism to address the issue of inequality? Was high taxation the appropriate instrumentality in dealing with inequality? Did all these central plans, policies and programmes of the government eventually work? Did we, as a nation, address the issue of inequality as promised by the grand eloquence of the members of the Constituent Assembly? Ultimately, did socialist India meet with her promised tryst with destiny?

The answer to all these questions is a resounding 'no.' Despite all the hoopla, support by the intelligentsia and external props, India's grand experiment with socialism ended abruptly in 1991, lasting at best a mere four decades, amidst an unprecedented economic crisis. Our economic crisis in 1991 was primarily related to its balance of payments. It may be recalled that India historically had a chronic balance of payments issue. The partial liberalisation of the external sector in the 1980s allowed greater imports, even as the Indian rupee was pegged, creating a recurring current account deficit. This was further accentuated by the Gulf War when the oil prices rose sharply. All these coincided with the collapse of the ideological mentor of Indian socialists, the USSR, a year earlier. Foreign exchange reserves in mid-1991 were barely sufficient to carry out essential imports for two weeks. Importantly, there was a fear of India defaulting on her external obligations for the first time since her independence. The immediate response was to secure an emergency loan of $2.2 billion from the International Monetary Fund (IMF) by physically – yes physically – pledging 67 tonnes of India's gold reserves as collateral. This was the net outcome of our tryst with socialism - an ignominy that we neither anticipated nor were prepared for. Socialist India was well and truly brought to her knees.

India loses out on Economics Reforms too

The failure of socialism was India's 'Animal Farm' moment. *Animal Farm*, it may be noted, is a novel by George Orwell, first published in 1945, coinciding with India's independence. The book tells the story of a group of farm animals (Indians) who rebel against their human farmer (British), hoping to create a society where the animals can be equal, free, and happy. Ultimately, however, the rebellion is betrayed and the farm ends up in a state as bad as it was before, under the dictatorship of a pig named Napoleon (Socialism).

India, with more than a gentle nudge from the IMF, was compelled into a structural adjustment programme, popularly called as 'economic reforms.' The reforms process was unveiled when the then finance minister Manmohan Singh presented his first budget in the Parliament on July 24, 1991, and in effect jettisoned socialism. Quoting Victor Hugo, he said: "No power on earth can stop an idea whose time has come. I suggest to this august House that the emergence of India as a major economic power in the world happens to be one such idea. Let the whole world hear it loud and clear. India is now wide awake. We shall prevail. We shall overcome." Never in the history of post-Independent India did a speech have as much electrifying effect on the nation, with perhaps the sole exception of the *Tryst with Destiny* speech of Pandit Nehru on August 15, 1947. After all, if Nehru's speech signalled political independence from the British, Manmohan Singh's budget speech signalled economic independence from socialism. But did it achieve what it sought to do?

'Reforms' were expected to bring in new ideas into India's collective thinking. And to some extent, it did. The Indian economy took two years to stabilise since reforms were introduced in 1991, but subsequently achieved unprecedented growth of 7.5 percent per annum by 1994. Thereafter, the Indian economy has been on a sustained growth path and had clocked sustained growth rates in excess of 6.5 percent per annum in the 30-year period since 1991 till date. This is no mean achievement, given the complexity of the Indian economy. In the process, millions of people were brought out of acute and embarrassing poverty. Probably for the first time, India realised that millions of her countrymen could be brought out of the quagmire of poverty only through sustained economic growth. Reforms also brought in certain far-reaching changes to the Indian economy and the manner in which it was managed. Fiscal deficits were controlled, while interest rate distortions were addressed. Direct government control of capital markets was replaced with a regulatory framework supervised by an independent regulator. The new industry policy virtually abolished the licence-permit raj. The Monopolies and Restrictive Trade Practices (MRTP) Act was diluted significantly so as to eliminate the need for prior approval by large companies for capacity expansion or diversification. Disinvestment of government holdings in Public Sector Undertakings was encouraged. Direct tax rates were significantly cut. Simultaneously, trade policy sought to reduce the degree of state intervention on foreign trade, while tariffs were reduced and the Rupee allowed to be depreciated to reflect its correct market value. The gross domestic product (GDP) of India which was about 300 billion dollars at the commencement of reforms has seen a spectacular ten-fold rise to reach approximately 3 trillion dollars by 2020. All these developments gave confidence to the Indian government in the middle of June 2019 to fix an ambitious GDP target of 5 trillion dollars by 2024. Even as the debate amongst experts and economists shifted to whether these targets were achievable and if so, how, there are contrarian and powerful opinion that in this blind pursuit of increasing her GDP, whether India has forgotten about rising inequality. Did poverty reduce post reforms? Did inequality diminish post reforms? Did liberty flourish? Did India have her promised tryst with destiny?

These questions cannot be answered merely by applying Aristotelian binaries. For instance, it is now widely acknowledged that in the decade between 2006-16, India was able to raise 271 million people out of poverty. Nevertheless, the fact remains that although there have been significant achievements in the social sector during the reforms period, the progress has been agonisingly slow. It is obvious that while the Indian economy as a whole had a successful growth story in the three-decade period since the reforms were initiated, the fact that needs to be accepted is that there is a concomitant failure in improving social sector indicators. It is widely known that India's rank in the global human development index (HDI) is much lower compared to many other developing countries, including some of its South-Asian neighbours. This, in the view of several analysts, is on account of a telling disconnect between economic growth on one hand and our innate inability in dealing with hunger, malnutrition, skill, mortality rates, health, nutrition, education, sanitation, water and basic infrastructure on the other. Economic reforms did not, in effect, lead to a redistribution of income and distributive justice. If liberty and growth was an issue during Nehruvian era, inequality has indeed emerged as a major issue since 1991. And this inequality, let us hasten to add, is not limited to India. India merely provides a context to the larger discussion of global inequality on hand.

To understand the enormity of the challenge India faces on issue of food shortage, security and deprivation, let us look into some facts. The net per capita food availability in India in 1971 was 394 gm per day. This was just after the onset of the Green Revolution in India. Exactly 30 years later, in 2001, the net per capita of food grains availability was 396 gm per day: a princely rise of 2 gm! And by 2020, things have not improved significantly. Sadly, India ranks very high in the Global Hunger Index (GHI) published by the International Food Policy Research Institute even as several sub-Saharan and our neighbours in South Asia fare far better than us. For instance, India ranked 97 out of 118 developing countries in 2016 with prevalence of stunting among children aged below five years at around 39 percent, a serious cause of concern. In this scenario, India requires effective investments in social infrastructure in order to combat hunger.

Needless to emphasise, this comparison with other countries is crucial in understanding the extent of food shortage prevalent in India. Advanced countries, on a per capita basis, consume anywhere between 600 gm to 700 gm per day. Such healthy consumption in these countries is supplementary to the substantial quantity of meat, fruits, vegetables and milk. It is at this point that a reference to China is unavoidable. China it may be noted, is a country with approximately 1.2 times our population, produces approximately 500-550 MT of food grain every year – nearly double that of India. Does this comparison with China by itself not blow the myth of food self-sufficiency in India? Obviously, India's consumption on a per capita level is far below the world average and significantly below the average of the developed countries. It would seem that, India declared food self-sufficiency on virtually half-empty stomachs.

In a celebrated work titled *Annam Bahu Kurvita*, the authors J. K. Bajaj and M. D. Srinivas point out to the appalling fact that after the British took over the reins of India, they constituted a Commission to look into the quantity of food required in India, should India be to be hit by a famine. That was way back in the late 19th century when the British had succeeded in setting a government in India. For this purpose, the per capita food consumption was held to be 500 gm per day by the said Commission. It has to be noted that the British fixed this norm for a subjugated population and during a famine! It would seem that our colonial oppressors had a more charitable view of our basic food requirements than our own democratically elected 'socialist' governments. No wonder we have declared food sufficiency at 400 gm per day per capita.

It is in this connection it has to be noted the National Institute of Nutrition is reported to have prescribed a minimum of 2,400 calories per day per Indian. What is distressing to note is that significant sections of our population do not have access to even this minimal nutritional requirement. By the way, the average calorie intake available to an inmate at the dreaded Guantanamo Bay daily is well in excess of 4,000 calories! In effect, for over five decades India's farm growth during the much-celebrated Green Revolution has barely kept pace with our population growth. Obviously, India is not producing enough food grains or pulses on a per capita level. Yet, for the past six decades or so, we have been under the mistaken belief that distribution, not production, to be the key to the issue on hand.

The Human Development Report published by the United Nations Development Programme estimates the HDI in terms of three basic parameters: to live a long and healthy life, to be educated and knowledgeable, and to enjoy a decent economic standard of living. The HDI, like other indices, is a statistical aggregate that seeks to capture the changes occurring in a country and compares the same with the same with the changes occurring in other countries. In 2018, India was ranked 129 in the Global Human Development out of a total of 189 countries. Moreover, India also reflects inter-state disparities in regional and human development which are reflected by state-level HDIs as there are gender, regional and other related inequalities. The GHI and HDI point out to the colossal failure of our economic policies, post reforms, in dealing with inequality and poverty.

Davos: Where Inequality Meets Elitism

Davos is a small town in Switzerland. For over two decades, it has been a Mecca for all those who believe in the idea of globalisation – popularly called globalists. As a host to the annual World Economic Forum (WEF), it offers an opportunity to the global political leaders to rub shoulders with the global business elite under the watchful eyes of the high priests of global finance. In short, if you are not in Davos on an annual pilgrimage, you have not yet arrived at the international scene. Noam Chomsky, the noted political activist, captured the entire paradigm rather eloquently when he states "The WEF is a paradigm example of globalisation. It is a gathering of huge numbers of people from all over the world, from just about every corner of life one can think of, apart from the extremely narrow highly privileged elites who meet at the competing World Economic Forum." Needless to emphasise rights of people and other groups became incidental.

It is indeed a bit odd that an economic forum that has been created exclusively for the global elites invites Oxfam – a group of independent non-governmental organisations that have come together "to share knowledge and resources and combine their efforts in the fight against poverty and injustice" – to its annual meet at Davos. Oxfam International, it may be noted is an NGO formed in 1995 by a group of independent non-governmental organisations as a confederation to maximise efficiency and achieve greater impact to reduce global poverty and injustice. Its roots are found in Oxford Committee of Famine Relief, founded in Britain in 1942. It was, therefore, no surprise that Oxfam came with a Briefing Paper which was released in Davos in 2020 titled *Time to Care*. According to Oxfam, economic inequality is out of control globally. Accordingly, in 2019, the world's billionaires, only 2,153 people, had more wealth than 4.6 billion people combined. In the Indian context, the study points out that India's richest 1 percent hold more than four times the wealth held by 953 million people who make up for the bottom 70 percent of the country's population. More specifically, this study points out to policies that are fuelling the inequality crisis by enabling a wealthy elite to accumulate vast fortunes at the expense of ordinary people and particularly, poor women and girls. This great divide, according to Oxfam, is based on a "flawed and sexist" economic system. Declaring (and rightly so) that "this has to change," Oxfam comes out with a time-worn prescription of how "Governments around the world must act now to build a human economy that is feminist, and values what truly matters to society, rather than fuelling an endless pursuit of profit and wealth."

And the solution? Taxing the wealth of the richest 1 percent, according to Oxfam, by an additional 0.5 percent over the next 10 years would be equivalent to the investment needed to create 117 million jobs in education, health, and elderly care and other sectors and to close care deficits. Like existing wealth tax revenues, the additional potential revenue, Oxfam suggests, could be raised through a variety of wealth taxes, including property, inheritance, net wealth and transaction taxes. Let us not forget that these numbers put out by Oxfam are by-products of various economic models that can be twisted to suit one's argument. But what is lost in the melee is that while taxing the richest could definitely improve revenues of the government, that is no guarantee for dealing with inequality! Let us not forget that many countries including India tried and tested these policies and met with modest success. And that is the crux of the issue. While growing inequality in India is now one of the major policy challenges, the conundrum that begs the question is whether taxing the rich or levying wealth tax is the sole solution to address the extant issue. The standard outworn solutions of state intervention in improving rural sector, employment opportunities, nutrition, agriculture, health, gender disparity have been tried for over 70 years at an enormous cost, but with very limited success.

Despite such compelling evidence that successive increase in income-taxes has been unable to address the issue of poverty, Professor Esther Duflo and Professor Abhijit Banerjee, the first couple to win a Nobel Prize for Economics (along with Michael Kramer) for their path-breaking work on developmental economics and poverty alleviation, believe that the super-rich need to be taxed more. Duflo, in an interview to an Indian news channel, opined: "This is really a story like an elephant where if you look at the poorest people in the world, their income has gone up quite a bit during the past three decades; so that is the back of the elephant. However, if you are looking at the richest people in the world, their income has gone up even more. So, it is the trunk of the elephant. So, these two worlds exist. The problem is that anybody in between has been squeezed in." She said what was needed in future was to "preserve the gains for the poorest, make sure that it continues because they are still extremely poor, and at the same time see how this huge increase in top income quality can be curbed."

Duflo added "we do come up definitely in favour of wealth taxation, in favour of estate taxation if it was politically feasible; it seems to be less politically palatable. So, we could start on wealth taxation, start on higher taxation of top income and then find ways to distribute this money effectively over a longer distribution such that the very poor continue to do better and the squeezed middle also finds a way to find a productive place in the society." Advocating for wealth tax, Banerjee said it was a "very logical tax" for India to impose. "Just the value of for example the real estate that many people own is so incredibly high, there has been such an incredible windfall from India's growth and this essentially stays untaxed. Especially because the tax bracket is narrow, we should think of what are other ways to bring people in the tax umbrella and putting the value of their house as their wealth will already get a bunch of people in. If you look at the value of a house in Delhi, Mumbai, or Bengaluru, these are astronomical amounts of money. So, I think that that is a very natural way to go especially because the tax base is thin," he added.

That, in a way, sums up the conundrum facing modern economies. If a country seeks growth, there will be a concomitant rise in inequality. If a country seeks to tackle inequality, taxes will increase. In the process, growth suffers. Economists, in an attempt to balance the two, take a definitive leap of logic, depending on the audience. But we will not. We seek not only to balance the two contradictory forces but also seek to achieve an eternal balance between the two.

Back to the Basics

Duflo, is in fact right, morally speaking. Governments owe it to their citizens to bring them out of poverty. But is Duflo right, especially from the economic standpoint, when she suggests increased taxes to combat inequality? Is it the only way to tackle inequality? In fact, as countries after countries embrace democracy, the issue of inequality is seen as one of the significant political issues in the 21st century. The standard policy response, invariably to such inequality, has been plans, programmes, budgets, and state intervention – popularly called as socialist/welfare programmes. In fact, there is not much difference between the two, and if there is one, it is an exercise in semantics. Remember, all these are necessitated in a democracy where rising inequality is universally considered as an ocular demonstration of the failure of the economic policies of the government of the day. We somehow seem to conjure a sadistic idea of making the rich poorer through coercive taxes as a solution to the vexatious issue of inequality.

At this point, a reference to a certain recent political event in India would be in order. It may be recalled that the government in India headed by Atal Bihari Vajpayee lost power at the hustings in the summer of 2004, paving way for the Manmohan Singh-led administration in India. Experts, political pundits, and economists even to this day are near unanimous in their view that sustained, sharp, and robust economic growth unleashed by the Vajpayee government was paradoxically the cause of its downfall. Its perceived strength ultimately turned out to be its unanticipated Achilles' heel. As this is counter-intuitive, it requires some elucidation as to how rapid economic growth can by itself become a political liability, that too in a democracy. Modern economics has more or less come to a definitive conclusion that economic growth would inevitably first lead to inequality. This is the conundrum that was pointed out by Harari and discussed earlier in this chapter. Policy-framers, therefore are theoretically, left to grapple with the choice between growth and addressing inequality with no third alternative, much less of achieving a balance between the two. In the process, most fall within the two stools. Atal Bihari Vajpayee government was no exception. As growth accelerated in the run-up to the 2004 elections, inequality widened, leading to the build-up of extraordinary social pressures within the system. Unexpectedly, Atal Bihari Vajpayee lost the elections leaving many political and economic pundits, flummoxed.

The lessons of the 2004 general elections to the Indian parliament are compelling – macro-economic successes without addressing the sticky issue of inequality (accentuated by lack of employment opportunities) is unworkable in a democracy. In fact, it was a turning point in the management of the Indian economy and how various political parties viewed the electorate, elections, and economy. It was therefore perfectly in order that in 2004, the newly elected government of Manmohan Singh (the very same Manmohan Singh who as Finance Minister had in 1991 jettisoned socialism and found virtues in market economy) chose consciously to tackle inequality and poverty first up on assuming the office of the Prime Minister of India. Presenting the Union Budget in 2004, the then Finance Minister of India P Chidambaram observed "currently, there is a need to ensure that unemployment does not take a heavy toll on the poor people. Work has begun on the National Employment Guarantee Act. The object is to guarantee 100 days of employment in a year to one able-bodied person in every poor household." Interestingly, the Manmohan Singh administration elevated this programme into an enactment of the parliament so as to demonstrate not only its commitment to address the inequality, but also to provide some sort of durability to this programme. It is in this connection Chidambaram adds "My colleague, the Minister of Labour, expects that he would be able to introduce the bill in Parliament shortly. Pending the enactment of the new law, I propose to launch a new Food-for-Work programme in 150 districts classified as most backward and identified as areas in immediate need of such a programme. Allocations under different schemes will be pulled together to support the Food for Work programme." All these elaborate exercise in semantics were nothing but explicit admissions that the reforms of 1991 had failed the nation in tackling poverty and resultant inequality. And the polity was indeed scared of the same.

Subsequently, in 2005, true to their promise, the Manmohan Singh government introduced a national anti-poverty legislation, now called the Mahatma Gandhi National Rural Employment Guarantee Act (MGNREGA), which initially offered up to 100 days of unskilled manual labour per year on public works projects. In the process, the right of the workers to demand and get work were enshrined in a central legislation. This was supposed to be India's complete answer to the challenge of inequality. Once a programme is announced, funds allocated through budgets and an oversight process established by the administration, most policy-framers assume that they have done their 'constitutional duty.' What adds fat to the fire in the Indian context is that in 2016, a United Nations Development Programme Report (UNDPR) referred to the Mahatma Gandhi National Rural Employment Guarantee Scheme (MGNREGS) as among the best-known employment guarantee schemes providing direct jobs to the rural poor. Such international approvals put the entire political class in some grand delusion of unparalleled success.

Interestingly, even as MGNREGS gained traction, funds and attention from the government and international agencies, the Manmohan Singh government was voted out in 2014 and, in its stead, a new dispensation under

Narendra Modi was voted in. The billion-dollar question, notwithstanding the approval of UNDP Report on MGNREGS, is why was the Manmohan Singh voted out if the scheme was indeed as successful as claimed by many, including the UNDP? While a government may be voted in or voted out for several reasons, the question remained: was it because of or despite MGNREGS? Whatever be it, the fact of the matter remains that MGNREGS ceased to be an election issue, pointing to its diminishing returns in the 2019 general elections. But there is more to come. The Modi-led government, which was initially critical of the scheme, continued with this programme, even as the Prime Minister had in the past dubbed it a 'living monument' of the previous government's failure to tackle poverty. "Do you think, I will put an end to the scheme. My political wisdom does not allow me to do it. This is a living monument of your failure to tackle poverty in 60 years. With song and dance and drum beat, I will continue with the scheme," Modi had explained his position on the floor of the Parliament in a debate relating to the continuation of MGNREGS by his government. Let us not forget, in the decade between 2005 and 2015, according to official information, over rupees three lakh crores were spent on this programme, of which, approximately 70 percent was spent on wages. In the Budget for 2020-21, the annual allocation for this scheme was approximately Rs 60,000 crores. Success or no success, even for a towering political personality like Modi, MGNREGS is virtually impossible to wind up.

Apart from MGNREGS, the Manmohan Singh-led government enacted the National Food Security Act in 2013, marking a paradigm shift in the approach to food security from 'welfare' to a 'rights-based approach.' The Act legally entitles up to 75 percent of the rural population and 50 percent of the urban population to receive subsidised food grains under Targeted Public Distribution System. With an all-India coverage, out of the maximum coverage of 81.35 crore, around 80 crore Indians are believed to have been covered under this legislation for receiving highly subsidised food grains.

That is not all. For instance, the Government of India at the Union has "six core of the core" schemes for which an outlay of Rs 80,000 crores (which includes MNREGS) has been budgeted for Financial Year 20-21,

24 core schemes for which a sum of Rs 2.50 lakh crore has been budgeted and 721 central sector schemes for which a sum of Rs 8.70 lakh crores has been budgeted for the same period, in the aggregate, making it a staggering sum of approximately Rs 12 lakh crores. This is at the Union level. And if one adds the sums spent on poverty alleviation at the State level, the money spent on such 'poverty alleviation schemes' would obviously be much higher.

The increasing irrelevance of MGNREGS as a tool in tackling inequality in India, notwithstanding the UNDP Report, is demonstrated by the lack of reference to this grand idea within the political discourse in India. In fact, there is a growing realisation within the Indian establishment that MGNREGS has not addressed the issue of inequality. It may be noted that the Gini co-efficient is a commonly-used measure of income inequality that condenses the entire income distribution for a country into a single number – the higher the number, the greater the degree of income inequality. The Economic Survey of 2018-19 Volume I based on an International Labour Study notes that between 1993 and 2011, the average real wages increased in India, with the fastest growth recorded for casual labour, women's labour, and rural/agricultural labour. Despite these increases, the existing wage inequality measured by the Gini co-efficient remains very high by international standards. Likewise, the Economic Survey of 2016-17 Volume II points out that the Income Gini coefficient is 35.2 during 2010-15, which is higher than 33.6 reported during 2005-13, reflecting an increase in the income inequality.

Yet, despite such overwhelming statistical evidence in their failure to address the issue of inequality, the Modi government cannot and will not jettison these schemes. Like Ronald Reagan, Modi understands that it is easier to criticise the idea of 'Big Government' while in the opposition than reduce the size of the government, withdraw, or even reduce its expenditure. It may be appropriate to recall that his appeal of 'minimum government, maximum governance' caught the imagination of the voters in 2014. That was Modi the reformist, a man who understood the limitation of the government in fighting inequality. But nothing substantial has been achieved on that score since 2014 when he was voted to power. If MGNREGS or for that matter any of the schemes of the central government is scrapped, Modi knows that he will instantly be labelled as anti-poor – a label that neither he nor his party can ill-afford, that too in a democracy like India. In effect, Modi now realises that all government programmes are tigers which are easier to mount than dismount; easier to continue than discontinue. And this is Modi, the consummate politician, a Prime Minister who understands the limitation of democracy. That explains the tectonic shift by Modi from criticising the very idea behind this scheme, to criticising the scheme's implementation, to adopting this scheme, to celebrating it. Thanks to this transformation, while the criticism behind the scheme might have stopped, questions that drive the philosophy behind the scheme remain unanswered. What is welfare? How does it balance with individual rights and responsibility? What is the role of the government as regard to welfare? Where and what is the ideal trade-off between role of government and welfare? Whether unbridled welfare carries negative effect on economy and more pertinently on the society? How welfare needs to be administered? Where does welfare end and populism begin, and where does populism end and recklessness begin? And finally, whether we need a new welfare architecture for the 20th century? We will seek to answer these questions in the subsequent chapters of this book.

Notwithstanding the modest success of MGNREGS is dealing with inequality, Modi not only continued with MGNREGS, but also unleashed a host of flagship social welfare programmes. One such flagship programme launched by the Modi government was Ayushman Bharat Pradhan Mantri Jan Arogya Yojana (PM-JAY) in September 2018. Within a year, 46.4 lakh hospital treatments, worth Rs 7,500 crores have been carried out, and 60 percent of the amount spent was on tertiary care. Through the PM-JAY, the government aims to bring quality healthcare to around 50 crore poor and vulnerable Indians across India. Like the MGNREGS, this scheme is stunning in its scope and sweep. It seeks to give annual healthcare benefits of up to rupees five lakh for every entitled family making it one of the world's largest fully Government-funded health insurance schemes.

There is yet another grand welfare flagship scheme introduced by the Modi regime. In the interim budget for 2019, the Modi Government introduced the Pradhan Mantri Kisan Samman Nidhi scheme. Under the scheme, an income support of Rs 6,000 per year is provided to all farmer families across the country in three equal instalments of Rs 2,000 every four months. The entire responsibility of identification of beneficiary farmer rests with the state/UT governments. The fund is directly transferred to the bank accounts of about 14 crore beneficiary farmers by the union government. The budgetary outlay on account of this scheme also is approximately Rs 75,000 crores, though, the government believes that the actual outgo in real terms may be lower.

That is not all. If the Kisan Samman scheme was a basic income provider for all farmers, the Narendra Modi government has been toying with the idea of Universal Basic Income scheme for all Indians. It may be noted that the Kisan Samman scheme suffers from a fatal flaw-it is aimed at farmers who probably be far better off than the landless labour. It is in this connection the Economic Survey of 2016-17 laments that the central government alone runs about 950 central sector and centrally sponsored sub-schemes which cost about 5 percent of GDP. Surely there are rationale for running many of them. But interestingly, for the first time, the government explicitly concedes that "there may be intrinsic limitations in terms of the effectiveness of targeting" while running such schemes. For instance, the fact that nearly 50 percent of the central sector schemes continued for over 25 years, demonstrates that they were extensive and often led to wasteful use of resources and government efforts. Further, the Survey simultaneously reports 40 and 60 percent of the targeted beneficiaries were not receiving the benefits from PDS and MGNREGS respectively in 2011-12 due to exclusion errors. And as a solution, the survey argues that a serious consideration be given to the new idea of a Universal Basic Income (UBI) as a more effective way of achieving Mahatma Gandhi's objectives of "wiping every tear from every eye." And by directly transferring money to bank accounts, and circumventing multiple layers of bureaucracy, the survey asserts that the scope for out of system leakage would be low in our fight against poverty, individual indignity, and vulnerability. In short, the thinking within the Indian establishment is that such a scheme needs to be introduced to tackle the issue of inequality. Viewed differently, the idea of UBI appeals to a large section of the Indian establishment, which believes UBI is a 'great leap forward' that has the requisite potency to eliminate poverty.

But who will Bell the Cat?

The grand idea of UBI has often caught the imagination of several leaders in the history of mankind. Put simply, UBI is a universal and unconditional stream of cash income paid by the government to every member of society with an income lower than a pre-determined income level. The concept of UBI has its support from several thinkers in the 18th and 19th centuries, such as Thomas Paine. This idea of UBI can be traced to what the Englishman, humanist and lawyer Sir Thomas More who wrote in Utopia, describing an ideal society that contrasted with the highly unequal social conditions that prevailed in his time. In Thomas More's *Utopia*, published in Louvain in 1516, the Portuguese traveller Raphael Nonsenso, walking on the central square of the City of Antwerp, narrates a conversation, he says, he had with John Morton, the Archbishop of Canterbury. Such a scheme, he argued, would be a more astute way of fighting theft than sentencing thieves to death, which had the unpleasant side-effect of increasing murder rate. Referring to the routine hanging of petty thieves and larcenists over five centuries ago, the protagonist remarks: "Instead of inflicting these horrible punishments, it would be far more to the point to provide everyone with some means of livelihood, so that nobody's under the frightful necessity of becoming first a thief, and then a corpse." Hence, the term Utopian.

Yet, in recent years, the idea of UBI has gained remarkable traction in the debate on the welfare state in major market economies and democracies. It has received support from the British Labour Party, the US Democratic Party, the French Socialist Party, and the Green Parties in several European countries, Canada, and Australia. It was tried out on an experimental basis with mixed initial reports in various European countries, such as Finland and the Netherlands, and the Canadian province of Ontario. The idea of UBI also resonates with a recent policy shift in many developing countries, as well as multilateral development assistance organisations like the World Bank, towards direct cash transfers, which involve rolling all subsidies into a single lumpsum cash transfer to households.

But what is this grand idea of UBI? How does it work? Generally, universal basic income is, as the name suggests, both universal and refers to a guaranteed minimum income. It is usually defined in terms of three main characteristics – it is a regular cash income, paid to an individual directly, and without any conditionality or strings attached. Thomas Paine, for instance, advocated UBI irrespective of whether someone was rich or poor, deserving or otherwise, active or inactive, and to be unconditionally given without any prerequisite or what is called as the 'means-test.' Some of the proponents of UBI believe that the scourge of poverty cannot be fought by providing targeted welfare schemes like jobs, education, health, or housing. To most of these political thinkers, all of these welfare measures are at best 'indirect' and hence 'piecemeal,' and therefore, ineffective. Some others have opined that the idea of UBI is inevitable on account of growing automation and needs to be adopted sometime in the immediate future to tackle the issue of social unrest caused by lack of employment opportunities, and hence income. In totality, the idea of implementing UBI in developing countries is to primarily address the issue of poverty, while that of advanced economies seems to overcome the displacement of jobs and stagnant wages created by rapid automation. Put briefly, UBI is the ultimate welfare measure ever conceived by economists, political thinkers, sociologists, and futurologists. UBI, thus, is one grand idea that for one reason or the other finds traction both in developing as well as developed countries, in the past as in the future.

Therefore, it is no surprise that the Indian Economic Survey of 2016-17 had debated extensively on the same in the Indian context. The Economic Survey estimates that providing a modest basic income of Rs 7,620 per year to about 75 percent of the poorest Indians could shrink poverty from 22 percent to 0.5 percent, while simultaneously promoting social justice and empowering the poor. The survey also provides certain illustrative costs for a successful UBI, which varies between 4 percent and 5 percent of GDP and outlines a number of ideas to take UBI forward while highlighting the practical difficulties. In India in particular, it claims that a case for UBI has been enhanced because of the weakness of existing welfare schemes, which are riddled with misallocation, leakages, and exclusion of the poor. Yet, the survey discourages immediate implementation, citing the inability of the administration to deliver on several counts. In short, what plagues targeted welfare schemes will in effect plague the UBI too. Therefore, despite its abundant enthusiasm, the Economic Survey soberly concluded that UBI is 'a powerful idea' that may "not be ripe for implementation" but the concept "is ripe for serious discussion."

Strange as it may sound, world over the UBI has been embraced both by thinkers from the Left as well as the Right. Thomas Paine and possibly Thomas Jefferson were probably the earliest proponents of this idea. Thomas Paine is best known for *Common Sense*, the pamphlet he published in 1776 to argue for independence from England. In 1795, he published *Agrarian Justice*. The title page of the first edition summarised his proposal: Agrarian justice, opposed to agrarian law, and to agrarian monopoly. It was a plan for ameliorating the conditions of man by creating in every nation, a national fund. This fund was to be used to pay every person, at the age of 21 years a sum of 15 pounds sterling, to enable him or her to begin his or her life. And also, 10 pounds sterling per annum to every person living to the age of 50 years, and to all others when they shall arrive at that age, to enable them to live in old age without wretchedness. Payments were to go to every person, rich or poor, healthy or disabled. It is "a right, and not a charity that I am pleading for." He wanted the funds to come from a 'ground-rent' paid by property owners. This is just and proper, he argued, because the earth is "the common property of the human race" and everyone deserves a share. Agrarian justice, he argued, would provide that share as cash to people who had no land.

In the 20th century, this idea got further refined as slowly thinkers linked welfare and liberty. Bertrand Russell, the British philosopher wrote in 1918: "A certain small income, sufficient for necessities, should be secured for all, whether they work or not." This idea got further advanced after the Great Depression when Franklin Roosevelt in his annual Message to Congress on January 11, 1944, stated: "We have come to a clear realisation of the fact that true individual freedom cannot exist without economic security and independence. Necessitous men are not free men. People who are hungry and out of a job are the stuff of which dictatorships are made. In our day, these economic truths have become accepted as self-evident. We have accepted, so to speak, a second Bill of Rights under which a new basis of security and prosperity can be established for all, regardless of station, race, or creed."

At around the same time in 1944, FA Hayek, endorsed the idea of providing people "the security of a minimum income" and endorsed the idea of that "some minimum of food, shelter, and clothing, sufficient to preserve health and the capacity to work, can be assured to everybody." Interestingly, Hayek in his seminal work *The Road to Serfdom* had opposed most government programmes because they interfered in the market and thereby impaired freedom and security. Despite his ideological moorings, he advocated UBI. Similarly, in his 1962 book *Capitalism and Freedom*, economist and Nobel Laureate Milton Friedman considered methods to help the poor and concluded that "the arrangement that recommends itself on purely mechanical grounds is a negative income tax." Reiterating these views in a 1980 book *Free to Choose*, he wrote: "We should replace the ragbag of specific welfare programmes with a single comprehensive programme of income supplements in cash – a negative income tax. It would provide an assured minimum to all persons in need, regardless of the reasons for their need, while doing as little harm as possible to their character, their independence, or their incentives to better their own conditions." According to him, "a negative income tax provides comprehensive reform, which would do more efficiently and humanely what our present welfare system does so inefficiently and inhumanely."

After World War II, the Universal Declaration of Human Rights was enacted by the United Nations on December 10, 1948. Several of its articles imply a right to a basic income. For instance, Article 3 states "Everyone has the right to life, liberty, and security of person." Likewise, Article 25 declares that everyone has the right to a standard of living adequate for the health and well-being of himself and of his family, including food, clothing, housing and medical care, and necessary social services, and the right to security in the event of unemployment, sickness, disability, widowhood, old age or other lack of livelihood in circumstances beyond his control. In the spring of 1968, Paul Samuelson, the 1970 Nobel laureate in economics, joined four other prominent economists – John Kenneth Galbraith, Robert Lampman, Harold Watts, and James Tobin (1981 Nobel laureate) – and published a letter that called on the Congress "to adopt this year a national system of income guarantees and supplements." The letter was circulated, and more than 1,200 of their colleagues signed on.

The idea of a basic income scheme is not limited to Economists. Erich Fromm, a social psychologist and author of several books on the idea of freedom, discusses the changes that guaranteed income will bring for individuals and society as a whole. The overwhelming thought prevailing throughout most of human history, according to him, was that a man had to work to necessarily earn his bread. This threat, forced man not only to act in accordance with what was demanded of him, but also to think and feel in such a way that he would not even be tempted to act differently. In his opinion, the necessity to work, deprived man and rightly so, of his liberty. And accordingly, "Guaranteed income would not only establish freedom as a reality rather than a slogan, it would also establish a principle deeply rooted in Western religious and humanist tradition: man has the right to live, regardless! This right to live, to have food, shelter, medical care, education, etc., is an intrinsic human right that cannot be restricted by any condition, not even the one that he must be socially useful."

In short, UBI, according to Fromm would not only deal with the convoluted issue of inequality, but also be the simultaneously addressing the issue of liberty. To most of these thinkers, UBI was the ultimate balancing factor between liberty and inequality. In the process, introduction, managing and administrating these balancing factors has been elevated to become the core function of any government. Inexplicably, and notwithstanding the intellectually compelling arguments in favour of UBI, no government till date has ever ventured to implement a full-fledged UBI. It has been at this point in time limited to targeted and piecemeal welfare schemes. And wherever it has been attempted, it has at best been on a trial basis with mixed results that does not compel governments to go for UBI.

Contrast this to what Mahatma Gandhi had to say on this issue of right and entitlement to free food. Interestingly, the Economic Survey on 2016-17 quotes the Mahatma while debating the idea of UBI: "My ahimsa would not tolerate the idea of giving a free meal to a healthy person who has not worked for it in some honest way, and if I had the power, I would stop every

Sadavarta where free meals are given. It has degraded the nation and it has encouraged laziness, idleness, hypocrisy, and even crime. Such misplaced charity adds nothing to the wealth of the country, whether material or spiritual, and gives a false sense of meritoriousness to the donor. How nice and wise it would be if the donor were to open institutions where they would give meals under healthy, clean surroundings to men and women who would work for them…only, the rule should be: no labour, no meal." Despite the sublime teachings of the Mahatma, it is most likely that the UBI will be thrust on an unsuspecting nation, sooner than later.

What next? What would be the cost of UBI? Obviously, it would depend on the extent of UBI, the population involved, and the quantum of income that is sought to be transferred. Do governments have the fiscal headroom to fund UBI? Do governments have the necessary administrative bandwidth to implement UBI? Will it, even if implemented successfully, address the issue of poverty and inequality? Will equality be achieved only when we reduce all humans to have just two square meals every day? What will be the cost and consequences of such schemes? Does welfare stunt human development after a particular point? What is worrying with ideas such as UBI is that we lose sight of the fact that the human aspirations do not stop with merely having two square meals a day – the ultimate objective of UBI. On the contrary, historically it is seen that such depravations have driven humans to adapt and acquire extraordinary ingenuity.

Most governments run one or more welfare programmes. Governments seek to introduce a wide range of taxes to fund such welfare programmes. As discussed earlier, the Government of India now provides guaranteed employment through the MGNREGS. A limited UBI has been launched in 2019 for the farmers. The PM-JAY is intended to provide quality healthcare to about 50 crore poor Indians. And a Food Security Act provides targeted subsidised food to Indians. Yet poverty continues to flourish. Inequality continues to widen. India languishes at the bottom of the Global Hunger Index as well as Human Development Index. Gini Co-efficient continues to rise. At best, these schemes are working at a glacial pace. Policy framers and economists continue to blame the administrators for the limited success achieved through such schemes. Administrators, in turn, blame the very design of the schemes as being prone to leakages. As one blames the other, millions of our countrymen continue to be caught in the quagmire of poverty with no policy alternative in sight to take care of either their equality or liberty.

And even if welfare measures were to succeed there is yet another unaddressed dimension. If absolute liberty as an idea is socially incompatible and politically unacceptable to the limitless appetite of an individual for his greed and accumulation of wealth, it cannot also mean as Fromm suggests, the idea of absolute liberty to an individual to refrain from any work, yet being entitled to a basic income in equally at fault. Despite this fatal flaw in these arguments, governments will continue to toy with the Utopian idea of UBI (or some other form of welfare), especially in democracies where there will be a steady and growing demand for such 'Utopian ideas.' It is time we realise that democracy and poverty make a strange concoction. It is democracy that compels and debauches welfare into populism, and populism into recklessness. It may be recalled that one political party in a run up to the 2006 assembly elections to the South Indian state of Tamil Nadu, promised to deliver television sets to all houses in the state absolutely free. The downward spiral since then is continuous. In the following elections, another party offered certain kitchen gadgets and succeeded in the hustings.

The lessons from these are compelling. Governments, to remain in office, will necessarily pander to this growing class of people who as matter of right seek such benefits. This is a fundamental flaw in the rights-based model. And to fund this expenditure, governments would tax the industrious, productive, and the virtuous, who would increasingly find themselves in a minority. In the alternative, governments have to borrow to fund such extravagance. As taxes go beyond the tipping point, the diligent are disincentivised to carry on their activities. That in effect cripples the fiscal space. In short, welfare and populism are a zero-sum game. Taxing the diligent is no guarantee to eliminate inequality or for that matter, poverty.

Notwithstanding such overwhelming evidence of its failure to tackle poverty through the welfare route, governments will indulge in more welfare notwithstanding the cost and attendant consequences. The billion-rupee question is who will bell the cat? Where is the fiscal space for implementing the same? Can UBI be funded through an increase in tax? Is it prudent to collect taxes from the most efficient and put it to distribution through a state administrative mechanism that is admittedly 'leaky and inefficient?' What is the net consequence of all these welfare measures on the macro-economic stability?

Whatever be it, the scourge of poverty has to be tackled at the earliest. Countries world over have fallen way behind on achieving the Millennium Development Goals. The question of eliminating poverty is non-negotiable. But welfare? Well, it may not be the most efficient way of eliminating inequality but in the absence of an effective alternative, one is compelled to live by the idea of welfare. Governments are genetically socialist. To rationalise their existence, from Reagan to Modi, they need to devise bigger welfare schemes. In the case of India, as we pointed out we have subsidised food, then virtually free food, healthcare that is free, guaranteed employment for the poor. We have a basic income scheme for small farmers. It is more or less certain we will bring in UBI in a matter of years. Yet, it is the near unanimous opinion of most experts that we will not be able to eliminate poverty.

To do so, we need to revisit the mother of all trade-offs. We need to revisit the root assumptions that go into the social contract theory. We became 'individuals' as Harari suggests a few centuries ago, cutting off our relationship with our family. We have paid a very heavy price in the bargain. Cutting of our family eliminated our bargaining power with the state. We have lost our dignity. Escaping from the scourge of poverty is now subject to the success of the welfare programmes of the government, administered through a faceless unaccountable bureaucracy. And we have been made entitled by our rights. But this is of no use when the end result is not just adding up. The social contract theory needs to be reworked and made into a tripartite agreement – an agreement between the individual and the government must necessarily involve the family. For too long, we have kept the family out of the equation in our dealings with the state. In the process, we have come second best. That is because the contractual terms do not favour the individual. After several decades and worldwide experiences, we now understand the possibilities and limitations of global frameworks to address the intersection between individuals and their rights in culturally and politically diverse situations.

That is not all. Governments too have limitations. By construct, they are socialist. By design, they are interventionist. In practice they are unaccountable. Governments can at best legislate one welfare scheme after the other, but cannot make us prosperous. Budgets of government can possibly deliver outflows, not outcome. To hide this inconvenient truth, governments seek to juxtapose into every action or for that matter inaction of every citizen. They cannot be the sole arbitrator of every transaction carried on by the citizens. It can no longer be an omnipotent-omnipresent state. It has to be a residual state with the primacy accorded to the individual and his family. It is important that we as individuals also balance our rights with our duties to the society, government, and more importantly to oneself, our children and our families. For too long, we as individuals have enjoyed and lived with the luxury of extraordinary rights but without the concomitant duties. This has probably been our failing. In the process, the society is to rebalance its route to achieving both individual liberty and eliminate inequality. It is time to revisit the social contract theory all over once again. It is time to re-balance our relationship with the state with family to form a new triumvirate. It is time to work out a new equation between our individual rights and duties.

References

1. Sapiens – A Brief History of Mankind, Yuval Noah Harari, Vintage Books, 2011.
2. Social contract – Political Philosophy, Written by: The Editors of Encyclopaedia Britannica.
3. Swaran Singh Committee and 39th-42nd Amendments; July 31, 2018 By Dr Makkhan Lal; Vivekananda International Foundation.
4. Capital in the Twenty-first Century By Thomas Piketty – Review By Stephanie Flanders, The Guardian, 17 Jul 2014.
5. How higher taxes can fight inequality while promoting growth – By Paul W. Gleason, Pacific Standard, June 26, 2018.
6. Limiting Government, 1980 - 2010 By John Samples, CATO Institute, February 2016.
7. The Constitutional Assembly Debates.
8. Why Jawaharlal Nehru is the root cause of India's economic troubles By Arvind Kumar and Arun Narendhranath, July 11, 2011, DNA.

9. 1950s to 1970s: How India's economic DNA got hard-coded By R Jagannathan, 10th August 2019, Forbes India.
10. Budget Speech of Mrs Nirmala Sitharaman, Minister of Finance, February 1, 2020 in the Lok Sabha.
11. Annam Bahu Kurvita: Recollecting the Indian Discipline of Growing and Sharing Food in Plenty By J. K. Bajaj and M. D. Srinivas, Centre for Policy Studies, Chennai
12. Time to care.
13. Unpaid and underpaid care work and the global inequality crisis – OXFAM Briefing Paper – January 2020.
14. Ahead of Budget 2020, Nobel Laureates Abhijit Banerjee, Esther Duflo Bat for 'Logical' Wealth Tax – In an interaction with Shereen Bhan, CNBC-TV18.
15. Economic Survey – 2016-17; 2017-18; 2018-19 and 2019-20.
16. Budget Speech of Hon'ble Finance Minister for 2004-05.
17. UNDP calls MGNREGS best job guarantee plan for rural poor – The Economic Times – December 15, 2016.
18. Universal Basic Income: Some Theoretical Aspects By Maitreesh Ghatak and François Maniquet-www.annualreviews.org
19. Universal Basic Income for India: The Way Towards Right to Equality- A Review By A.G. Adeeth Cariappa and Apoorva Srinivas – Indian Journal of Economics and Development, December 16, 2018.

7. Taxes are a Price We Pay for Our Civilisation: Is it?

No nation has ever taxed itself into prosperity

– Rush Limbaugh

A government that robs Peter to pay Paul can always depend on the support of Paul

– George Bernard Shaw

Aesop's fables are a collection of several fables credited to Aesop; a storyteller believed to have lived in ancient Greece. The Ant and the Grasshopper is one of the most popular and instructive ones. In this fable, the ant works hard in summer, building his house and laying up supplies for the harsh winter. In contrast, the grasshopper thinks the ant is a fool, laughs, dances and plays the summer away. Come winter, the ant is warm and well fed. The grasshopper has no food or shelter, so he dies out in the cold, events triggered by his own irresponsibility. The moral of the old story: Be responsible for yourself, work hard, build your reserves and brace yourself for a difficult situation. Let us not forget that individual responsibility is the bedrock on which every successful society is built – a core idea of this work. Universally, individual responsibility – to oneself, society and country is taught by every responsible parent to their child. This moral (read economic model) has stood the test of time over the eons, and probably is relevant not only to the present but also in the distant future.

But there is yet another version, in fact – a perversion of the original Aesop's fable. In this too, the ant works hard in the withering heat and the rain, building his house and laying up supplies for the winter. And here too, the grasshopper thinks the ant is a fool, laughs, dances and plays the summer away. Come winter, the shivering grasshopper calls a press conference and demands to know why the ant should be allowed to be warm and well fed while he is cold and starving. The media latches on to a juicy story, of course for its own ratings and provides shots of the shivering grasshopper alongside a video of the ant sitting in the cool comforts of his home. The world is stunned by the sharp contrast. A deluge of questions follows. How can the ant enjoy such luxury, comfort and wealth? Why is the poor grasshopper allowed to suffer so much? Crucially, what is the government of the day doing to address this gross inequality? Such collective insanity in the media instantly converts all of us all into economists, sociologists and jurists. The resultant cacophony distorts the debate on what is already a dismal science. The net result: governments begin to understand economics through the heart, not its head.

Liberals complain that rich and privileged ants do not care about the less fortunate. The dominant view amongst them is that the ants have got rich off the backs of the poor grasshoppers. Therefore, everyone calls for an immediate tax hike on ants to make them pay for the betterment of the grasshopper. The prudent ant, let us not forget, has left little role for the government to interfere in his personal affairs. After all, by taking care of himself he made government more or less irrelevant. Expectedly, the usual suspects comprising of the media, civil society and the establishment come together to bail out the grasshopper. The Parliament immediately convenes and passes the Prevention of Cruelty to Grasshopper Act. Socialists applaud. Welfare ideologues happily approve of the same. Bureaucracy is happy as there is more money in their hands to disburse the largesse. That implies more action, more work and more pay to them. To them, the ant or the grasshopper is irrelevant to their scheme of things. Development economists come with scathing articles as to how much more needs to be done to protect the grasshopper. Government assures that it is just the first tranche and promises more in the following few weeks. A new program is launched to rehabilitate the grasshopper. And who funds all these? As we demonstrated in the previous chapter, it is the diligent, and hardworking ant, who is taxed further. Taxes, let us not forget, is a punishment for being diligent. The ant learns it the hard way. In the alternative, governments seek to borrow at obnoxiously low rates from the ant to fund its largesse to the grasshopper. Either way, tax or debt, the bill is always on the ant. Next summer, the population of ants believe that these back-breaking taxes are not getting them anywhere and hold a conclave contemplating migration to distant lands where their enterprise and individual responsibilities are well-respected. Meanwhile, the grasshoppers continue to make merry as the summer has arrived.

One must hasten to add that while the grasshopper danced and sang, economists within the establishment were happy with it as its current consumption drove up their quarterly GDP numbers during summer. Equally, they were unhappy with the ant as its decision to postpone consumption did not sex-up the relevant numbers. The diligence of the ant, its strength and responsibilities, are all perceived as its weakness in modern economics. That the ant was industrious, prudent, diligent and was ready to fend for itself are extraneous in modern economics as such a responsible behaviour makes them irrelevant to modern theories.

This book is not about the usual rich versus the poor debate. The charge that the ant being rich and resourceful, or the grasshopper as being poor or resourceless, is specious, perverted and actually distorts a serious debate. On the contrary, this is a debate between the diligent and the reckless. And recklessness is not a class attribute. The issue, therefore, is one between individual enterprise and irresponsibility. The issue is of dependency, on self, or on the government. The ant, by working hard, takes responsibility for his and immediate family members. That made him less dependent on the external assistance including the government. Further, the ant pays his tax (and rightly so) that takes care of the sovereign functions of the government. Taxing him further to take care of the recklessness of the grasshopper is increasingly having deleterious impact on the national economies. That is not all. The ant provides employment to many who in turn are able to take care of themselves and their families. It is about those who provide job opportunities to others and those who demand doles as a matter of right. In quintessence, this is between a rights-based society and a society created by conscientious duty-based individuals. While the grasshopper, is the darling of the modern media, economists and the establishment, let us reiterate that conscientious duty-based ant is the undisputed hero of this book.

Indian Civilisation – Destroyed by British Taxes

"Taxes are what we pay for civilized society." The famous quote by US Supreme Court Justice Oliver Wendell Holmes Jr. is inscribed above the entrance to the headquarters of the Internal Revenue Service (IRS) in the US. The future generation of ants wonder what is civilised society – is it the one characterised by hard work, discipline and responsibility? Or the one characterised by the individual irresponsibility, like that of the grasshopper? Over a period of time, the ants find themselves in hopeless minority. As taxes increase every year, the ants begin to migrate. The civilisation of ants, assiduously built over several generations of hardworking ants, withers away. As ants migrate what was once a thriving civilisation, characterised by the hardworking ant, falls on bad days – a classic case where civilisation is a price we pay for taxation? But what is this civilisation? How does it get impacted by taxes?

To understand all these, we need to revisit the story of the British colonisation of India. Horrifying as it may have been, it is now claimed by the apologists of colonisation that colonisation by itself did not end up with any major economic benefit to Britain. If anything, the narrative that is sought to be constructed is that the British administration of India was a cost to exchequer of the former and a grand gesture of its benevolence to latter. Let us forget this narrative by the British or their supporters for a moment. What is galling is that even the then Prime Minister of India Dr Manmohan Singh in an acceptance speech of honorary degree from Oxford University on July 08, 2005, furthered this obnoxious narrative when he conceded "Our notions of the rule of law, of a Constitutional government, of a free press, of a professional civil service, of modern universities and research laboratories have all been fashioned in the crucible where an age-old civilisation of India met the dominant Empire of the day. These are all elements which we still value and cherish. Our judiciary, our legal system, our bureaucracy and our police are all great institutions, derived from British-Indian administration and they have served our country exceedingly well." Even assuming for a moment, as Manmohan Singh concedes, all these to be a by-product of British benevolence, do we know the price that India paid for all these irrelevant intangibles? Do we as a nation realise the cost we have paid in human terms, financially and in the virtual collapse of our civilisation?

New research by the renowned economist Utsa Patnaik – published by Columbia University Press – deals a crushing blow to this narrative of British benevolence. Drawing on nearly two centuries of detailed data on tax and trade, Patnaik calculated that Britain drained a total of nearly $45 trillion from India during the period 1765 to 1938. It's a staggering sum even by modern standards. To have a better understanding of these numbers it needs to be appreciated that $ 45 trillion is 17 times more than the present annual gross domestic product of the United Kingdom today (India's GDP is estimated to be $5 trillion by 2026). To be fair to Manmohan Singh, in the very same acceptance speech he points out "As the painstaking statistical work of the Cambridge historian Angus Maddison has shown, India's share of world income collapsed from 22.6% in the year 1700, almost equal to Europe's share of 23.3% at that time, to as low as 3.8% in 1952. Indeed, at the beginning of the 20th Century, the brightest jewel in the British Crown was the poorest country in the world in terms of per capita income."

As pointed out by Manmohan Singh, researches done by historians now unanimously conclude that at the beginning of the 18th century, India's share of the global economy was approximately one-fourth, as large as all of Europe put together. By the time the British departed India, it had dramatically dropped to less than 2 percent. In retrospect it is quite evident that India was governed for the benefit of Britain and its spectacular rise for about 200 years during the colonisation of India was in fact financed by its depredations, legitimised through a corrosive taxation and trade regime, from India. The British began collecting taxes in India, and then cleverly used a good portion of those revenues to fund the purchase of Indian goods for British use. In other words, instead of paying for Indian goods out of their own pocket, British traders acquired them for free, "buying" from peasants and weavers using money that had just been taken from them. It was as brazen as that without any let or fear. And that is the issue on hand. What should not be lost in the melee is that the British colonial rule had demonstrated in ample measure that taxation is a weapon of mass civilisational destruction. In short, India literally paid her taxes for her own oppression and destruction of her wonderful civilisation. And if not civilisation at least her economy.

But how did British colonisation and its corrosive taxation regime impact Indian civilisation? When Will Durant, who co-authored with his wife Ariel, *The Story of Civilization*, witnessed what was happening in India in the 1930s, he set aside his work of history to write a monograph titled *The Case for India*. In this, the usually measured historian does not mince words, lambasting the British for their ongoing actions. The British conquest of India, Durant writes, "was the invasion and destruction of a high civilisation by a trading company utterly without scruple or principle, bribing and murdering, annexing and stealing, and beginning that career of illegal and legal plunder." Britain profited enormously from what Durant calls the "rape of a continent," so much so that on the eve of independence, the vast majority of Indians were living in poverty. It was, as Durant put it, "the most sordid and criminal exploitation of one nation by another in all recorded history."

Irrefutable historical evidences now available with us demonstrate that long before the British colonisation, India was a culturally and economically prosperous civilisation that had existed for several millennia. After all, that is why it was colonised in the first place. This paradox of prosperity is dealt with in Chapter 9 in greater detail. It had given birth to four major religions of the world – Hinduism, Buddhism, Jainism, and Sikhism, all of which peacefully co-exist with the other. India was home to the oldest university in the world and had produced countless thinkers, philosophers, poets, and scientists in several languages. By the 18th century, when India was economically prosperous, it also had certain human development indices – literacy and health for instance – all comparable at that period with the very best in the world. All these have been chronicled by several writers and do not to warrant a repetition here. By the 18th century, her fortunes had reversed: India was now one of the poorest countries in the world and thanks to the loot of India, Britain was the richest. In 1931, life expectancy in India stalled at just 27 years and the literacy rate was a mere 16 percent, with female literacy at a pitiable 8 percent. The population was severely emaciated and diseased by the time the conquerors left. Crucially, tens of millions died needlessly of policy-induced famine during the British rule. Setting the economics of plunder aside, the sheer human consequence of this is such that noted British economist Angus Deaton found that "the deprivation in childhood of Indians born around mid-century was as severe as any large group in history, all the way back to the Neolithic Revolution." The deracination and deindustrialisation of Indian civilisation was the direct consequence of British policy of loot effectuated by an elaborate tax mechanism. Even to this date, it makes a chilling read. Yes, Indian civilisation was a price Indians paid to the British for their elaborate corrosive taxation. Yet, the popular belief is that taxation is a price we collectively pay for civilisation. The trillion-dollar questions therefore are: who taxes, how much and for what reasons? We will seek answers to this question in this chapter.

Gandhiji, the consummate politician and economist realised all this when he organised a protest in 1931 against the imposition of tax on salt – a basic commodity of mass consumption – by the British. That the Dandi march or the salt protests ultimately led to the independence of India is a relevant nugget of our history having great significance for the political economy of the present times. For Gandhiji, the independence movement itself was not an end in itself; it was a subset of a grand idea of restoring our civilisation. He realised that this could not be merely achieved by continuing to feed the British through a corrosive taxation regime. That it found instant resonance across the nation goes on to demonstrate the disconnect between a corrosive taxation regime, civilisation and the citizenry.

A Live-In Relationship

Yet, despite such an overwhelming evidence of how the British rule destroyed Indian civilisation through a crude, corrosive and coercive taxation regime, there was not much of a debate in the constituent assembly on the serious issue of taxation. The debate, if any, on the vexatious issue of taxation was fleeting at best. The constituent assembly debates began with an overarching assumption that a sovereign government has a right to tax and hence will tax. The implicit logic was that if the British could tax Indians before independence, the Indian state should tax Indians post-independence, little realising that the taxation regime of the former was nothing but plunder and philander. By merely substituting the British by the Indian government, the debate on taxation was never extended to the end use of taxes, the need for such taxes and outer limit for tax rates and the primary responsibility undertaken by the government to its citizens in return for collecting such taxes. This vagueness corresponds to the discussion by the constituent assembly on the economic model, more particularly on socialism. We had dealt with this in the previous chapter. Implicit in this argument is the fact that the role of the state was indeterminate; taxation policy, being a sub-set of the role of the state too was equally unknown.

Taxes are the umbilical cord that links a citizenry to its government. Taxes, at the right rates set the delicate balance between the state and its citizens. If it is a right of the state to collect taxes and the duty of the citizens to pay the same, it must be counterbalanced with an explicit promise of certain responsibilities to be undertaken by the state qua its citizens as implicitly citizens abdicate their responsibilities towards themselves by paying such taxes. Therefore, taxes are not a matter merely of governmental revenue, but have a much larger role in setting the equation right between the state and its citizens. What is worrying is that every successive tax reform in India has merely sought to increase the revenue for the state without seeking to address certain fundamental issues. If the British did not make any promise to improve the life of Indians, the Indian taxation regime also does not explicitly promise to improve the life of the Indians. With little or no concomitant promise for the citizens, many feel, that the extant taxation regime in India is no less cumbersome, corrosive or coercive, as they were in colonial India. (To be fair to the colonial rule, taxation regimes even in sovereign countries are indeed coercive. The IRS of the US is itself a case in point).

The net result was that the provisions relating to taxation are pithily worded and negatively couched in the Indian Constitution. Article 265 of the Indian Constitution, which deals with taxation, reads "No tax shall be levied or collected except by authority of law." As a matter of further detailing, the Union Government has power under the Constitution to levy taxes and duties on the subjects listed out in entries 32 to 92B and under entry 97 in the Union list and the state governments have similar power in respect of items enumerated in entries 45 to 63 in the state list of the seventh schedule of the Constitution. A few residuary items are listed out in the concurrent list, implying both the union or the state government may tax the same. In contrast to the taxes levied by the British which resulted in extreme depredation of colonial India, it will be argued and rightly so, all these taxes are levied by a sovereign country on its own free citizens, decidedly distinct from the taxes levied by its colonial masters. On first blush one must concede it is indeed a compelling argument. But is it truly so? Is this a given? This requires some greater examination. To do so let us revert to the Constituent Assembly debates once again.

The Constituent Assembly referred these issues while drafting the Constitution to an expert committee under the chairmanship of Nalini Ranjan Sarkar in November 1947. Interestingly, the committee commenced its work on November 17, 1947 and submitted its report miraculously within a couple of weeks i.e., on December 5, 1947. In short, such a convoluted subject of taxation, the need for taxes in sovereign India, the extent of taxes to be levied, the manner in which taxes were to be levied, whether a particular tax was to be levied by the Union or the state and the manner in which the resultant revenues were to be collected and shared between the Union and the states were all distilled, discussed and presented by this committee, all in such a short span! It is this report that was discussed and adopted subsequently by the Constituent Assembly while drafting the Constitution, of course, subject to some minor cosmetic changes. Strange as it may sound, the work of these three members for a couple of weeks is the foundation of the entire taxation regime in independent India to this day. Facts sometimes are indeed stranger than fiction.

Nevertheless, the crucial question remains – how did this committee provide answers to the complex issues referred to it under the terms of reference, all within a matter of few weeks? The reason for the same is not far to seek. The Committee took the Government of India Act, 1935, (which was enacted by the British Parliament to extend its coercive and corrosive taxation regime) as its starting point of its work and did not recommend any significant changes to the same. And to be fair to the committee it need not have done anything spectacular as the terms of reference of this committee as mandated by the Constituent Assembly was simply "To examine, with the aid of the memoranda on the distribution of revenue between the Centre and the Provinces sent by the Government of India and the Provinces, the existing provisions relating to finance and borrowing powers in the Government of India Act, 1935, and their working during the last ten years and to make recommendations as to the entries in the lists and sections to be embodied in the new Constitution." Consequently, the output in the form of a report by this committee was a mere rehash of the Government of India Act. Therefore, the charge that the taxation regime of independent India is merely an extension of the taxation regime of colonial India is not entirely without any basis. This paradigm was brilliantly captured by B. Das, a member of the constituent assembly in August 1947 when he said "I was very glad to hear my friend Sir Ramaswamy Mudaliar, speak about provincial revenues and income. He was a party before 1933 to the distribution of taxation under the 1935 Act. It is galling to me that Honourable Members of this House should try to perpetuate the taxation arrangements under the 1935 Act. What is the basis of that Act? That Act gave all powers and all resources to a foreign Government. That devil of a foreign Government has quit India but the devil's system still continues. The Act of 1935 gave all resources to the Centre so that the Centre could rule and dominate and spend the country's resources as it liked. The Centre had no responsibility to the people of India except to send them to jails when it liked."

What is noteworthy is that there was no serious search for an alternative system different from the one followed under the Government of India Act, 1935. Nor was it mandated by the terms of reference by the constituent assembly. To begin with, no one asked the question – Why taxes? Who should pay? How much to tax? What is the ideal method to tax? Should the same extortionist taxation system as devised by the colonialists be continued post-independence? What is the responsibility of the states and the Union and is it the basis on which taxes are levied, collected and shared? Equally, what are the responsibilities shared between the individual and his family on one hand and the government on the other? By paying taxes what are the responsibilities of the citizens that get transferred to the state? If taxes are indeed a price we have to pay for our civilisation, then, what is the contribution of the taxation regime as envisaged by the Indian Constitution to the overall revival of the Indian civilisation that has been lost substantially to the British loot?

The net result is that the Union and the states have an unbridled power to tax its citizens with little or no explicit promise to deliver. While the right to tax was indeed secured through Article 265 of the Indian Constitution, the fact remains that there was no concomitant duty undertaken by the governments, Union or state. Interestingly this was pointed out by B Das when he added once again in August 1947: "The Central Government, including the Governor-General, or the President who will be here in six months' time, and the Ministers, must think of their primary duty of social welfare. Nowhere in the Union Constitution or even in the Union Powers Committee's report have I found any definition of the primary duty of the Central Government. Is it only to assume all powers? Certainly not. We will have to conceive of a system of administration so that the largest amount of taxation that will come from the people should go back to the people." The operating words are 'Primary Duty.'

Therefore, without prescribing any explicit duty to the government qua its citizens or by the latter to the former, the Constitution midwifed a working relationship at best between the two. While the Constitution provides an unbridled right to the state to tax its citizens, it counterbalances this right with a bouquet of rights to the citizens called as fundamental rights. Thus, the tyranny of the state was anticipated by the founding fathers of the Constitution and provided a cover against such a tyranny in the form of Fundamental Rights to the citizens. In effect, the framers of the Indian Constitution hoped that each of the "Rights" would counterbalance the excess of the other party. Thus, the "sublime" Constitution of India gave rise to a peculiar situation where everyone – the state as well as its citizens – had rights, and none had primary responsibility or duty towards the other! This was a live-in relationship at best – not marriage as it is wrongly assumed. We will deal with this issue in greater detail as we proceed along in this chapter and subsequent chapters of this book.

Rights, Duties and Karma Bhoomi

The objection to securing any rights without corresponding duty, especially in India, exists for time immemorial. This has been at the very core of Hindu civilisation. In recent times, this view was articulated and reinforced by Mahatma Gandhi, no less, in the first decade of the 20th century. Writing his political treatise *Hind Swaraj*, the Mahatma puts forth his precise views on the need for a balance between rights and duties. He opines: "We, therefore, have before us in England the force of everybody wanting and insisting on his rights, nobody thinking of his duty. And, where everybody wants rights, who shall give them to whom? I do not wish to imply that they do no duties. They don't perform the duties corresponding to those rights; and as they do not perform that particular duty, namely, acquire fitness, their rights have proved a burden to them." To us, this is an amazing piece of socio-political-economic commentary, whose implications have been strangely lost on the modern world. Rights without duties are either draconian or utopian, hence unworkable or unacceptable. It is pertinent to note that the Mahatma does not merely link rights to duties; rather he wants duties "corresponding" to those rights to be performed. Likewise, duties without rights are unsustainable over an extended period and hence unworkable. It is only on attaining a balance between rights and duties and retaining that balance that makes every social, political and economic construct sustainable and over a period, eternal.

The views of the Mahatma on this complex issue of rights and duties resurfaced over four decades later since he wrote the *Hind Swaraj*. In 1947 Julian Huxley, the then director-general of UNESCO, wrote to Mahatma Gandhi requesting him to contribute an essay to a collection of philosophical reflections on human rights. Gandhi declined. "I learnt from my illiterate but wise mother," he replied, "that all rights to be deserved and preserved came from duty well done. Thus, the very right to live accrues to us only when we do the duty of citizenship of the world." Fascinatingly, the Mahatma was educated on this idea of balance between rights and duties, not by any modern political thinkers, sociologists or jurists, but by his "illiterate" yet "wise" mother. It is appropriate that given such lucid thoughts and profound understanding of a complex subject, the Mahatma is compelled to call his mother as "wise." One is sure that this would be the position of most Hindus, literate or otherwise. Equally interesting is the fact that the Mahatma has been able to sustain this principle over four decades of public life. In this age, where politics is driven exclusively by rights, the Mahatma's emphasis on duties or responsibilities looks downright idiosyncratic, yet appealing. Attaining and retaining balance between duties and rights is an eternal idea and hence has a civilisational underpinning, at-least in the Indian context. What the Mahatma imbibed from his "wise" mother is not merely transient values but eternal ones. When rights conflict with duties as often they do, the former is usually subordinated (though not necessarily at all times) to the latter through a well-defined and widely accepted social code, thereby resolving the conflict instantaneously. We will revert to this complex issue of retaining balance between rights and duties in the succeeding chapters of this book.

Sadly, a few months after he wrote to Huxley, the Mahatma was assassinated. Therefore, he was not physically present to guide the constituent assembly and impart the wisdom of his wise mother to the constituent assembly. Bereft of such sagacious advice on civilisational values, the constituent assembly merely rehashed the Government of India Act to construct the Constitution of modern, independent India. Individual duty, the quintessence of the Indian civilisation, is conspicuous by its absence in the Indian Constitution. Cut off from her civilisational values, India that is Bharat remains only as India and does not even remotely aspire to become Bharat. This distinction is not merely an exercise in semantics but seeks to distinguish the modern rights-based nation-state from a traditional society rooted to civilisational values. It is a fine distinction, but a distinction, nevertheless.

At this point, let us appreciate that barring the Hindu civilisation and Confucianism, historically not much attention has been paid to the issue of individual duties in other civilisations. The idea of duty is rooted to the collective consciousness of this land. In fact, traditionally India is called as *Karma Bhoomi* – roughly translated as a land of dutiful. Recall the idea of *Purusharth* in Chapter 5 and the four basic goals of life associated with it: *Dharma*, *artha*, *kaama* and *moksha*. Like Mahatma's mother, most

Indians understand these eternal ideas and values, though they may lack the necessary sophistry to articulate the same. Nevertheless, such eternal ideas flow from ancient texts like the *Ramayana* or the *Mahabharat* where at every twist and turn the virtues of adhering to one's duty is repeatedly emphasised. Further, several personalities in the Indian history, including even emperors, have steadfastly adhered to the call of their duty under the most trying circumstances. Some have paid with their kingdoms, some with their properties, some with their spouses or children and some with their own lives. Yet, they have never flinched from making their life a perfect example for future generations. The morals from these stories have collectively shaped, de-shaped and re-shaped the collective Indian psyche even as such personalities have been venerated as they exemplify the value of duty. Mahatma's mother understood all this and much more. And possibly because she made her son understand this in full measure, he could become a Mahatma.

In Chapter 4 of this book, a brief reference was made to Chapter II verse 47 of the Gita, where the Lord exhorts that everyone has a "right to work, but never to the fruit thereof." The commentary of Gita Press, Gorakhpur, captures the essence of this verse when it states that a "Man has a right to action alone, not to the renunciation of action. If out of egoism, he forcibly tries to renounce all action, he will not succeed in the attempt." Most Hindus comprehend and rationalise this thought in their daily life. If one verse from any religious text dominated the collective consciousness of the entire nation for several generations, it is this. So, the idea that man has no rights, and definitely not without duties, is broadly understood by most Indians. Therefore, the inviolability of performing one's duty and the inevitability of facing the resultant consequences, is well appreciated by everyone born in this land. That explains why India is called the *Karma Bhoomi*. Mahatma's mother was only alluding to this wonderful collective consciousness.

More to the point, several stalwarts in the constituent assembly debates had placed duty to the country above self. It is their sacrifice, especially at the prime of their youth, that propelled the independence movement. Some of them, by a mere inner call, virtually destroyed themselves for the sake of the nation. It is therefore inexplicable that the constituent assembly while debating the drafting of the Indian Constitution sought inspiration from a host of other Constitutions including the Irish, French, American, Russian, Swiss, German or for that matter the British, yet, did not deem it appropriate to refer to the civilisational values, especially individual duty, that had sustained India over the millennia. Probably the long-drawn freedom struggle sapped the energy of these great men. Therefore, rehashing the Government of India Act into a Constitution was more expedient than revisiting the subject de-novo. The net result was that independence became an end in itself rather than a means to an end.

Writing a rather interesting introductory chapter in the book titled *Ayodhya and Future of India*, Dr Jitendra Bajaj brings about the net consequence of all this: "Having taken over the levers and the trappings of imperial power in India the new ruling elite quickly convinced itself that the courthouses, the circuit bungalows and the magisterial residences built by the British, as also the various manuals and codes of departmental and courtly procedure, created by them and the earlier Mughal rulers, were essential to the governance of the Indian people. Even the symbols of Indian defeat became the treasured inheritance of the Indian state." Thus, alien structures and ideas continue to dominate the Indian Constitution. Rights without corresponding duties was one such alien idea retained with all pomposity by the Constitution, post-independence, in our *Karma Bhumi*. This new arrangement within the Constitution brought about a very strange paradox – even as the Indian society is – to this day wedded to the sublime idea of duty, Indians while transacting with the Indian state instantly seem to be reminded of their "Rights!" By a remarkable twist of fate, the Fundamental Duties were introduced through the forty-second Amendment to the Indian Constitution in 1976, even as the then Union Government under Indira Gandhi had imposed Emergency. Though Article 51A, which deals with Fundamental Duties, has no judicial force and have been mere dead letters in the statute book, it is a starting point on which we need to develop.

Establishing Civic Balance

India is not only former British colony to avoid the idea of balancing rights with duties. The United Kingdom itself does not have a written Constitution, but no former British colony (including and notably the US) features a duty of the individual in its Constitution in a manner we are seeking to discuss. One is unsure whether this is a result of common law legal systems or is due to some other peculiar feature of the Anglo-Saxon tradition. As most of former British colonies (and by extension the Anglo-Saxon world) do not deal with this subject in their constitutional framework, there is hardly any scholarship focused specifically on duties and its impact on economics and politics. Nevertheless, of late there is a renewed interest about individual duties and their importance in the functioning of economy. Probably the re-emergence of Asia, more specifically India and China mark this return to renewed interest on this vexatious subject of a balance between rights and duties. The University of Minnesota Law school has done some pioneering and scholarly work on this subject. It concludes that duties and rights need not come into conflict with one another but can mutually reinforce the other. Thus, rights and duties can always coexist. But the billion-dollar question is how.

The Law school points out that duties balanced with corresponding rights emerged as an integral part of the Constitution, most prominently in Mexico in 1917. It contains the right to education in its third article. In Article 31 detailing "the obligations of Mexicans," the first obligation requires parents to send children to school. Article 4 of the Mexican Constitution also includes the right to health and adds that it is a duty of parents to preserve the mental and physical health of their children. The Mexican Constitution was the forerunner of several Latin American Constitutions of the 20th century and several countries in the region began to include lists of rights and duties in their respective Constitutions.

Contrast this with the Indian position on providing education to our children. The eighty-sixth amendment to the Constitution inserted Article 21A in 2002 to provide free and compulsory education to all children in the age group of six to fourteen years as a Fundamental Right. The Right of Children to Free and Compulsory Education Act, 2009, (RTE) which represents the consequential legislation envisaged under Article 21A, means that every child has a right to full-time elementary education of satisfactory and equitable quality in a formal school which satisfies certain essential norms and standards. The title of the RTE Act incorporates the words "free and compulsory." The official website of the Government of India explains "Free education" to mean that no child, other than a child who has been admitted by his or her parents to a school which is not supported by the appropriate government, shall be liable to pay any kind of fee or charges or expenses which may prevent him or her from pursuing and completing elementary education. Likewise, "compulsory education" casts an obligation on the appropriate government and local authorities to provide and ensure admission, attendance and completion of elementary education by all children in the 6-14 age group. With this, the government claims India has moved forward to a rights-based framework that casts a legal obligation on the Union and state governments to implement this fundamental right as enshrined in the Article 21A of the Constitution.

Now, experiences demonstrate that after two decades since this "Right" was legislated, the chronic issue of illiteracy continues to plague India. Yet, the government feels by legislating this, it has solved the issue of illiteracy in India. The poor of India too feel that the government has chalked a detailed plan to combat illiteracy. Let us not forget that the eighty-sixth amendment, by introducing Article 21A in the Constitution has at best ornamented it but not solved the basic issue of education in India. Illiteracy, poverty, hygiene, health, epidemics are all issues that cannot be wished away through mere legislation. All these require a combined effort of the state as much as the individual. A right-based society believes that the onus for dealing with these issues solely rests with the state. But by its very construct, the state has certain inherent limitations. If the parents are unwilling to send their children to school, what can the state do apart from legislating? The concomitant amendment to Article 51A of the Constitution mandating the parent to provide opportunities for education to his child between the age of six and fourteen years obviously has persuasive value at best as is evident from the results flowing from these legislative changes. Unless all these become a legal obligation on the parents, as well as the government, these age-old problems cannot be solved.

Let us once again turn to the Mexican Constitution and its influence on others. Interestingly, the Mexican model influenced the flow of events in the early 20th century as several national and international instruments sought to introduce the idea of duty, albeit in a benign manner. The inclusion of the explicit language about the duties of the state, undercut perhaps for the first time the oft-repeated argument that duties are non-justiciable. The American Declaration of the Rights and Duties of Man in 1948, also known as Bogota Declaration, was both the first intergovernmental declaration on human rights while simultaneously presented articles on individual rights and duties. The draft contained articles on rights, civil and political as well as economic and social, as well as on duties. The American Declaration is also significant because of its influence on the content of the Universal Declaration on Human Rights which was drafted around the same point in time. Delegates eventually removed all these specific discussions of state duties (while retaining most relating to individual duties) contained in the draft. Why did the final text of the American Declaration not include detailed articulation of duties that were in the draft versions? The scholarly research by the Law School comes to a conclusion that though "definitive explanations are difficult to pin down in the archival record, there is much evidence to believe that states did not want to have such detailed discussions of state duties in order to avoid potential future liability. Even states that supported rights declarations preferred to leave provisions regarding duties conveniently vague, limiting their legal responsibility in the case of non-compliance." Needless to emphasise the Bogota Declaration watered down the duties of the state while retaining those relating to the individuals. It is obvious that governments world over do not seek to be legally bound to any duty whatsoever.

Interestingly, the Preamble of the American Declaration which was adopted in 1948 reads: "The fulfilment of duty by each individual is a prerequisite to the rights of all. Rights and duties are interrelated in every social and political activity of man. While rights exalt individual liberty, duties express the dignity of that liberty." If only the Preamble to the Indian Constitution had a similar declaration! It needs to be appreciated that the idea of human rights, as well as duties, has been a long nourished and cultivated local aspiration in central America. These local aspirations reflected the region's understanding of the relationship between sovereignty on the one hand, and social rights on the other. Importantly, the general culture of these countries and regions was quite receptive to a genuine mix of political and philosophical traditions. Given our traditional adherence to duties, any introduction of duties would have been instantly accepted by the people of India. Yet, we chose not to have any civic balance while adopting the Constitution in 1950.

American Experience, Global Experiment

Even this watered-down version of the American Declaration which included only the individual duties did not survive to be incorporated in the final version of the Universal Declaration on Human Rights (UDHR). This is claimed to be a milestone in the history of human rights by the United Nations (UN) and was done within a few months of the American Declaration. It was reportedly drafted by representatives with different legal and cultural backgrounds from all regions of the world and the Declaration was proclaimed by the United Nations General Assembly in Paris on 10th December 1948 as a common standard of achievements for all peoples and all nations. Bereft of all the technicalities it is obvious that in the context of the then emerging post-World War II international order, the dominant position of the US and the United Kingdom carried a disproportionate weight in the discourse leading to and the finalisation of the Declaration. Therefore, an Anglo-American approach to rights ultimately prevailed and that did not involve duties, either of the individual or of the state.

This failure to include any detailed discussion of duties in the UDHR created a precedent where virtually all subsequent human rights treaties also failed to mention specific duties beyond a general reference. Duties, if at all, were reduced to motherhood statements. In these subsequent agreements, duties at best were implied, but never explicitly stated. As a result, over the next several decades the idea that an explicit and robust set of duties should naturally accompany rights all but disappeared from the content of international human rights law. The continuous failure to include references to individual duties in subsequent international human rights documents, has profound impact on several aspects of human life, especially economics - the core of this book.

There is yet another unexplored dimension to this issue. The UN commissioned a survey in 1976 to study the status of duties of the individual to the community under international law. To research the question, member states were requested to respond to a survey to articulate their stance toward the individual's duties to the community. The comments by both the East German government and the West German government as reproduced by the Law School gave an idea of what was at stake during the Cold War in the debate about rights and duties. The East German government wrote: "The concept of citizen's basic rights in the German Democratic Republic and the way in which those rights are put into effect are determined by the desire of the socialist State and socialist order to give individuals full scope to develop into socialist personalities, it being understood in this context that citizens' basic rights are inseparably linked with their basic duties to the community." The West German government, in contrast, expressed concern that such an understanding of rights and duties would undermine respect for human rights at a fundamental level: "The state and the community, with their inherent monopoly of power, can protect themselves against dereliction of duty and abuses of law by individual citizens. For this reason, the rights of the community vis-à-vis the individual and the individual's duties corresponding to these rights do not need to be protected and given institutionalized safeguards in the same way as human rights." In the context of the Cold War, with the shadow of fascism in the not-too-distant past, countries like West Germany probably feared that naming individual duties to the community would permit states to use an individual's failure to perform duties as a justification for denying rights. Understandable. Yet, it does not answer the point.

Now that the cold war is behind us, should we not revisit the subject of establishing a balance between Rights and Duties? Perhaps, for this reason, the initiatives to codify responsibilities were delayed until the post-cold war era where a global Declaration of Human Responsibilities was sought to be attempted in the last decade of the 20th century. The proposed Declaration of Human Responsibilities failed to make an impact and collapsed at the embryonic stage itself. The Law School points out that several legal scholars argued that the declaration was superfluous and vague. Feminists saw patriarchal motivations behind the call to balance rights and responsibilities, particularly in its insistence on family and domestic responsibilities. Amnesty International alleged that the declaration would "muddy" the understanding of universal human rights and raised the possibility that the document could provide cover to authoritarian regimes. With such varied opposition and well-entrenched interest groups, it is natural that the world is still grappling with a framework to balance rights and duties, more so that it is skewed currently in favour of rights and consequently is continuing to pay a very heavy price for a luxury that it can ill-afford. Duties must remain and retained at the core of a worthy citizenship. The next logical question to follow will be how can this be achieved?

To do so, we need to revisit the past when UDHR was drafted. Why did the US and Britain refuse to include the idea of duty in the UDHR? Why does the Anglo-Saxon world detest or in the least refuse to accept the importance of duty in their constitutional framework? Why did this momentous Declaration by the UN exclude the experiences of certain countries, most notably, the Bogota Declaration? Why did the issue of rights dominate the American Constitution and its collective political thinking since it was drafted by its founding fathers? The answers to these questions are neither straightforward nor easy. They are not fashioned by any one person or a single idea. One cannot pinpoint to any particular event in history of mankind as a trigger for such an approach. In fact, such thoughts are fertilised by several philosophers, events, ideas, experiences and of course social and religious beliefs, spread over several centuries. Some of these ideas worked in tandem with others, while some worked, we must accept that some did not. At a broad level, we can reduce the strands of thoughts into just two – political and religious, amalgam of which is popularly termed as Enlightenment that goes to dominate the American political landscape even to this day.

We had dealt with this interplay of political thoughts with religious beliefs in some detail in chapter 3 in the context of the celebrated work of James Boyce, *Born Bad*. The author, it may be recalled, argues, that the belief in original sin of Christendom has dominated every Western thought in diverse disciplines. It is in this perspective Thomas Hobbes viewed man as vicious and brutal. Consequently, he concluded that to deal with that situation there was a need for a strong leader and a powerful government. It is reiterated that this was probably necessitated by the medieval experience and the then contemporary politics, of course, aided by the dominant belief of Christendom. Rule by powerful governments brought peace and order, but at a tremendous cost to personal freedoms.

As curbing individual freedoms was an unnatural construct, things did not stop here. Along with an idea of a strong government, the concept of democracy too flowered since the 17th century. This gave rise to healthy democratic traditions and related institutions. Accordingly, the belief that an orderly society can be designed and overseen only by a strong government was now conflicted by the new democratic idea to preserve individual freedom. Western philosophers and political thinkers, even while realising that a strong government was crucial for maintaining order and cohesion within a society, also recoiled, at the very thought of sacrificing individual freedom. Political thinkers, during this march of democracy in the Western world, realised albeit belatedly the practical pitfalls in an unfettered government which could give rise to potential tyranny. The compelling virtues of personal liberty necessitated a new political instrument that intermediates between the government and an individual. This idea was to preserve the power of the state without encroaching on the liberty of the individual in any way. This reconciliation process ultimately gave rise to the Rights movement, one that also protects individual liberty. Now, this idea of a strong government and human rights go hand in hand. Thus, these rights were a necessity to counterbalance a potentially tyrannical government. This in brief is how the American experience has evolved over the years and this experience is now turning into a global experiment with probably unintended and possibly disastrous economic consequences.

Ant and Grasshopper lose irretrievably

An omnipotent government, unfettered liberty to individuals and a rights framework formed a triumvirate in the Western world. Globally, this has now come to be seen as a hallmark of modern constitutional architecture, self-balanced and secure. This development is not, contrary to the popular belief, the culmination of ideas since the days of Hobbes. In fact, this is the contemporary version of the ideas that have flowed and flowered in the Western world since the days of Plato. All these are Plato's ideas that have come to dominate the Western constructs and by extension, global frameworks. Continuing his brilliant exposition on the Western understanding of state and society Dr Bajaj states: "And with the beginning of this new phase of Western resurgence, there also arises a new interest in the ideals articulated by Plato some two thousand years ago. The ideal of breaking the society down to atomic individuals and restructuring it according to the rationality of the state begins to find a new and forceful expression in the work of Western philosophers and thinkers from around the 16th century onwards." Thus, the present conundrum of the modern world that arises from a right based Constitution, is an idea that flows since the days of Plato!

A socio-political-economic model that relies only on rights is well and truly fatigued. It is time we rebalance it with a dash of corresponding duties. Of course, there will always be a debate about the legal tenability of such duties. With the rights framework now impressively entrenched since the days of Plato, the work is long and arduous. It requires going back to the drawing board. The root assumptions of the relationship between the society, state and the individual needs to be revisited and redrawn. In the previous chapter we had dealt with the idea of balancing liberty and equality, here we are witnessing the attempt to balance order and liberty. Order, liberty and equality cannot be balanced without adding one more element into the equation – duties.

For too long, the world has been suffering from this asymmetry. It is becoming increasingly clear that a rights-based approach alone cannot address the public-policy predicaments confronting the world. In fact, they have already failed to do so, more so in macroeconomic management. The majority of the citizens of several countries are increasingly dependent on their government for their health care, education, income, or retirement. Disturbingly, at the same time, the number of taxpayers paying for these benefits are rapidly shrinking. Globally, the ants are finding themselves in a hopeless minority. Therefore, the political power is irrevocably shifting from ants to the grasshoppers. It would be naïve for the ants to believe that the grasshoppers will set it right for the ants. It is the ants who must set it right not just for themselves but for the grasshoppers too. This is the paradox of prosperity and we shall deal with it in Chapter 9. Politicians, world over, have already figured out that doles mean more political power for them. It is an unwritten yet well-known fact: a voter dependent on doles is indeed dependable. The south Indian state of Tamil Nadu is a textbook case. Such a grasshopper voter will only vote for the politicians who promise maximum doles to them from the revenues of the government and shift the cost ultimately to the ant. And innocently we believe that taxes are a price we pay for civilisation.

In the end, there is nothing compassionate about welfare – it is robbing ant to pay grasshopper. This cradle to grave welfare programme guaranteed by the government has pushed the fiscal position of several nations into the precipice. Democracy adds fat to the fire as it becomes a continuous race to the bottom as political parties compete with the other to provide more doles than the other. How can any nation survive when a good number of its citizens are hooked on to various government doles and freebies? How can a nation have civilisational aspirations when citizens no longer have the incentive to restrain the growth of government? An untrammelled government growth gnaws at the private space and therefore is not conducive for the civilisational growth. Isn't this the endgame in Bahuka's economics that we discussed in chapter 2? Mahatma Gandhi summed it brilliantly when he said "Civilization is that mode of conduct which points out to man the path of duty. Performance of duty and observance of morality are convertible terms. To observe morality is to attain mastery over our mind and our passions. So doing, we know ourselves." But can any leader in any democracy talk about duties? Does any political leader in these times have the necessary moral standing to persuade his fellow countrymen on the lines suggested by the Mahatma? Modern Constitution construct lacks this crucial ingredient in nation building. So do contemporary politicians.

A nation's economic problems are always symptomatic of a larger socio-political problem, a fact often overlooked by most economists. The challenge is to look past the symptoms and find the root cause of our problems. For starters, we need to look at economic concerns as socio-political issues too.

This will assist in providing solutions in the aggregate. Attempting to solve economic concerns alone without addressing the socio-political issues is akin to solving one edge of the Rubik cube. This compartmentalised approach shall take us nowhere. Most problems arise from government's inability to look past the symptoms. Worse still, in competitive democratic set-up, governments like to tell and do what is pleasant for its citizens to hear. In the process, governments have replaced solutions that will work in the long run with what sounds pleasing till the next election. Interestingly, the collective charges on the governments are uniform across nations – high taxes, too many welfare programs, intrusion in individual privacy and of course too much regulations in business. Governments especially in democracies respond, some rapidly and some at glacial pace. But most of these changes are cosmetic and the treatment, symptomatic.

What is lost in the melee is that we have forgotten what will ultimately make our socio-political-economic systems work? What is the end game of our government? Is it merely to provide two square meals a day to its citizens or is it to make every individual realise his full value as a human being? Is it not necessary that the government recognises the dignity of every individual? Hayek understood this idea of individual dignity rather well when he wrote, "A society that does not recognize that each individual has values of his own which he is entitled to follow can have no respect for the dignity of the individual and cannot really know freedom." Most governments assume that once they provide food and if possible, basic health and minimal shelter to their citizens, nothing more remains to be achieved. Basic guaranteed income is now emerging, as we saw in the previous chapter, as the new frontier in welfare economics. Such a welfare, that is reductionist, has the calculated effect of purging citizens of their self-esteem and their dignity. It is a tyranny of misplaced intentions at best, not welfare. This tyranny disables an individual's self-determination and undermines their core civilisational values, especially personal responsibility. The guiding principles of governments should be to help people to understand their responsibilities, build their capabilities and provide complete liberty so that they can exercise their rights to choose a life that they themselves value. Anything else is an affront to their liberty and self-esteem.

That further enables governments, especially in democracies, to rapidly expand and to occupy private spaces that are traditionally the sole preserve of individuals. In retrospect, the idea to atomise people into individuals two hundred years ago or so was part of a grand design. Once a tipping point is reached, there is no stopping the downward spiral. As government emerges as the centrifugal economic force in a national economy, it takes extraordinary efforts to place individual liberty at the centre of all policy formulations. This further crowds out the free space available to individuals, thereby curbing their freedom. Given this paradigm, the individual loses his identity. And with that the individual freedom of both ant and the grasshopper is irretrievably lost.

The Economic Impact

The tax-to-GDP ratio is a primary metric to determine the share of government's control in its economic activities. In some ways, it measures the tax-efficacy of a country. This ratio is expressed as a nation's tax collected by the government in relation to its GDP. Policymakers use this ratio to compare tax receipts and GDP growth year on year. The underlying logic is that as the GDP grows, tax revenue should increase as well. It also is indicative of the public expenditure undertaken by governments. In most cases, because taxes are related to economic activity, the ratio should stay relatively consistent over years. Yet, some changes occur at a glacial pace and are visible only across three or four decades.

New data from the Organisation for Economic Co-operation and Development (OECD) in their annual publication 2019 listed out the member country's tax-to-GDP ratio. Based on 2018 data, the publication brings about an important fact that this ratio has considerably increased across member countries over a period of five decades. For instance, between 1965 and 2017, the average tax-to-GDP ratio in the OECD countries increased from 24.9 percent in the aggregate to 34.2 percent, an increase of approximately ten percentage points. This is a conclusive evidence of the increase in activities of the government in OECD countries. Like all averages, the OECD average conceals the great dispersion in individual national tax-to-GDP ratios. In 1965, tax-to-GDP ratios in OECD countries ranged from 10.6 percent in Turkey to 33.7 percent in France. By 2017 the corresponding range was from 16.1 percent in Mexico to 46.1 percent in France. The trend towards higher tax levels over this period reflects structural changes undertaken by countries to finance a significant increase of governmental activities and outlays. As already pointed out, any increase in governmental activities boxes out the limited private space available for individuals. The increasing tax-to-GDP ratio is thus indicative of a creeping war against individual liberty and freedom – a fact lost on many.

The OECD Social Expenditure Update also brings about the composition of the corresponding expenditure undertaken by the respective OECD economies. It does not take a seer to say that the increased tax-to GDP ratio has gone on to fund enlarged governmental expenditure. Equivalent to the increase in the tax-to-GDP ratio, the social expenditure in OECD countries too have shown a remarkable rise from less than 10 percent in 1960 to more than 21 percent of the GDP in 2018. Public social spending-to-GDP ratios are highest at over thirty percent of the GDP in France, while Austria, Belgium, Denmark, Finland, Germany, Italy and Sweden also devote more than a quarter of their GDP to public social expenditure. Probably, the impact of the French Revolution is continuing to this day and is being felt not only in France but also in neighbouring countries in Europe.

In contrast, the Indian tax-to-GDP ratio has been hovering at a modest 16 percent for more than a decade or so. Several economists have been urging the government to improve the tax-to-GDP ratio. Some have suggested ideas to improve the same. Yet, India is not witnessing elevated tax-to-GDP ratios like several OECD countries. In fact, the average tax-to-GDP ratio of OECD countries is more than double the tax-to-GDP ratio of India. That naturally raises a legitimate question – how India funds its welfare programs? The answer to this question is simple. India runs significant deficits apart from having a modern taxation regime. And to fund these deficits, the Union government runs a huge borrowing program, consistently, year on year. For instance, the revenue deficit budgeted for financial year 20-21 is estimated to be rupees six lakh crores (Actually, it ended much higher due to the impact of the COVID pandemic). That implies that government borrows this sum from the markets to finance its ever-burgeoning expenditure thus crowding out the private players. The estimated revenue deficit for financial year 19-20 was approximately rupees five lakh crores and that for financial year 18-19 was rupees about four lakh fifty thousand crores. Needless to emphasise to fund this expenditure government, apart from its tax and non-tax revenues, borrows and runs a gargantuan borrowing program to finance this deficit. But this consistent borrowing is taking a toll on the Indian financial position. The net debt of the Union Government of India as at 31st March 2020 was Rs 100 lakh crores (it may be reiterated that the debt of the states is not included in this figure, which could equally stupefying, if not worse) of which the liability aggregating to Rs 55 lakh crores were not represented by any assets. Do we realise that this debt that we are accumulating is borrowings from the posterity to finance our present consumption? This upsets the inter-generational balance as future consumption are fast-forwarded to the present. To re-establish the inter-generational balance is one of the core ideas of this book. Ironically, in a country where parents consider it a sacrilege to leave any personal debt for their children to repay, collectively we are working to leave a huge public debt for the next generation. Public debt, that too without corresponding assets, is a crime against future generation. The earlier we realise and restore inter-generational balance, the better.

More specifically, this borrowing implies interest on this sum is paid without any associated income thereby skewing the already skewed Union Budget. How did this debt of Rs 100 lakh crores accumulate in the first place? The answer to this question is once again apparent: it is the more or less the accumulated balance of deficits (excess of expenditure over incomes) of the past several years. For the financial year 20-21, the Union Government has budgeted a borrowing of approximately Rupees eight lakh crores while the interest cost is rupees seven lakh crores. This implies that the government of India has virtually a low or perhaps even no fiscal headroom. Consequently, there is very little that is getting spent on capital expenditure, so very vital for India's development.

It is not as if the government is not conscious of the inter-generational imbalance. Article 292 and 293 of the Indian Constitution empower the

Union and the States respectively to borrow money within such limits as may be laid down by the Parliament or the state legislature, respectively. The Fiscal Responsibility and Budget Management Act was enacted in 2003 precisely for this reason. The preamble of the Act provides "for the responsibility of the central government to ensure inter-generational equity in fiscal management and long-term macro-economic stability by removing fiscal impediments in the effective conduct of monetary policy and prudential debt management consistent with fiscal sustainability through limits on the central government borrowings, debt and deficits, greater transparency in fiscal operations of the central government and conducting fiscal policy in a medium-term framework and for matters connected therewith or incidental thereto." Reduced to simple language, the legislation mandates the government to take appropriate measures to limit the fiscal deficit up to three percent of gross domestic product. It also seeks to ensure that the overall government debt does not exceed 60 percent of the GDP and that of the debt of the Union government does not exceed 40 percent. And since its enactment, the Union government has an impeccable track record of being in the breach of the targets set by the government under this Act. In effect, this is a legislation by the government to ensure fiscal rectitude by the government itself and the government has no recourse under this enactment to proceed against the government if the government is in breach, even when the breach is determined by the government! And inter-generational imbalance? Well, that must wait for the next generation!

Let us hasten to add, the debate is not entirely on welfare. There is yet another side to it – the cost of administering such welfare through the state machinery. For starters, if welfare is universal (like the UBI for instance) it makes the scheme prohibitively costly in a populous country like India. Moreover, there is a moral hazard of extending the schemes to economically better-off sections of the population. If it is targeted, then the cost of laying out the benchmark for welfare, identifying and administering such welfare to targeted beneficiaries takes up substantial portion of the revenues of the government. The manner in which such welfare schemes are administered in Tamil Nadu is a case in point. The salaries and pensions to government employees of the state account for approximately 46 percent of the total revenues of the state government, interest 18 percent, administration cost 6 percent and welfare, 30 percent. What is galling is that a whopping 46 percent of the total revenues of the state is spent on the state government employees, as salaries and pensions, who may at best be a small fraction (2 percent) of the state population. In comparison, the welfare distributed to the rest of the population pales into insignificance. Before we come to a conclusion that Tamil Nadu is an outlier, let us point out that it is not. In fact, the expenditure of Tamil Nadu government towards its employees is the norm, not an exception. The corresponding figure for the Union government is approximately 16 percent. Oddly, this has not received as much attention as it deserves. This cost is a millstone around the necks of respective governments. Government employees and their ruthless unions are very well conscious of the predicament of the governments and their dependence on them. This encourages them to leverage their position to extract their pound of flesh.

And this debate is not entirely on expenditure related to the salaries and pensions of government employees. There is yet another aspect – the quality of such administration flowing from such expenditures. A reference to the information received to a query made under the Right to Information Act (RTI) to the government a few years ago would be in order. The question on how many children study in the same government school where their parents are employed as teachers by the Tamil Nadu government revealed startling answers. In some of the schools in certain districts of the state, not many children (in some places not even one student) studied in the same government school where their parents were employed as teachers. It is apparent that these students were enrolled in private schools. No wonder the quality of education in public schools is abysmal to such an extent where teachers do not seek to send their children to the very school in which they are employed by the government. It must be noted that public schools are designed to make education affordable to the poor sections of our population. Understandably so as it is the only way out by which we can lift the poor and the country out of poverty. That is why taxes are collected in the first place and used for welfare expenditure such as public schools. Regrettably, there are schools and teachers, but no education and teaching.

As a result, even the poor seek to shift to private schools for marginally better education, albeit at a higher cost. Public health, as do several public services suffer from the same malaise. All these are rationalised as either welfare or salaries to the state governments in their respective budgets without any significant "corresponding" output. We have examined the outcomes relating to government expenditures in greater detail in the previous chapter. This is the endgame in every welfare program. Hard earned money by the most enterprising is paid to the government as taxes, only to degenerate as welfare and to get debased as expenditure without any significant betterment of our downtrodden. Yet we believe that taxes are a necessary price to pay for a civilisation.

And the debate does not end with the quality of administration. There is still another sideshow – as to how the government seeks to interfere in every aspect of human affairs even in the functioning of private schools and thereby prejudicing the interests of the poor. If welfare as an idea were successful and public schools functioning at its optimum best, then why RTE? Obviously, RTE is tacit admission of the government of its monumental failure on public education. Let us not forget that RTE is compulsory privatisation of education. It may be recalled that RTE provides that children between the ages six to fourteen a Right to compulsory education in a neighbouring school. The RTE further states that no child can be detained in any class till the completion of elementary education. Further, as per this act, all private and non-minority (on account of Articles 29 and 30 of the Constitution that protect that "Right" of minorities to establish and administer educational institutions) schools are required to have a 25 percent quota for students from disadvantaged groups and economically weaker sections, the cost for which is to be reimbursed by the state. Such schools, or RTE schools, also must adhere to minimum infrastructure levels, teacher-to-student ratios, and teacher qualifying requirements. While all that is the obligation demanded from the schools, the government in turn has failed miserably to perform its obligations towards the schools. One of the major bone of contention between the schools and the government, is that the managements of many a school claim that the government has not provided subsidy to them as per the provisions of the RTE. This creates enormous cash crunch on the private schools and the ultimate sufferers are the poor whose children get enrolled in these schools.

And education is merely a case in point. Most services from the government do not meet the minimal standards expected by the citizenry despite the government paying its employees significant amount of the revenue collected. The rot in the education system is further exemplified by the fact that the teachers in government schools prefer to educate their children only in private schools. Subsequently, RTE was introduced for those students who seek quality education in the private schools, with a law that mandates the government to pay to the private school providing education for such children. Even this is held in the breach making the functioning of these RTE schools unviable. As private schools become economically unviable, teachers in such schools suffer most, dynamiting the entire educational system. And finally, the cost of educating such children, RTE or no RTE, once again falls on their parents or on the society. Questions naturally arise – why do we pay taxes? What happens to huge sums of money allocated as welfare, especially education? If we must privatise education brazenly, as we are currently witnessing it being done through the RTE, why do we spend so much of our revenues on public schools? Why should government run schools and pay teachers such exorbitant salaries when their children are seeking admission in private schools?

Education is not an exception to the idea of privatising welfare, albeit on the sly. Health, public transport and public infrastructure are all witnessing some form of privatisation by stealth or otherwise with the government abdicating its duties towards its citizens. This is not a Tamil Nadu or for that matter a pan Indian phenomenon. Globally, governments are struggling to deliver on the promises made, especially relating to their core functions. Yet, they seem to have an insatiable appetite to bring greater number of private activities under its welfare fold. Put simply, the massive cost of administering an expansive welfare program is always coterminous with a mammoth bureaucracy funded by an elaborate but corrosive taxation mechanism.

This economic model has run its full course and is now imploding from within. If the Tamil Nadu government were to give up the entire welfare program (or at least a significant portion) and downsize its bureaucracy drastically, it can probably do away with substantial share of entire Goods and Service Tax (GST). Do we realise the positive impact this could have on the state of the economy, despite conceding the fact that it is an extreme example? Do we realise that it brings down prices of most goods by 18 percent (the median rate)? Do we realise that this reduction makes most goods and services affordable to that extent which will lead to a significant consumption drive by those in the bottom of the pyramid? The domino effect from here on is incalculable. When goods and services get consumed, poverty vanishes. Whatever be it, one thing is certain, taxes and welfare are not lifting people out of poverty. Nor are taxes, the price, we pay for civilisation.

Why Civilisations Fail

President Harry S Truman is reported to have quipped (though the authenticity of this quote attributed to him remains shrouded in some mystery) that he wanted a 'one-handed' economist because all his economic advisers said, "on the one hand this, and on the other hand that!" This frustration, of those unschooled in basic economics, is understandable. Economics is not a unitary discipline. It is fashioned by a multitude of factors, some macro, some micro; some global, others local. Ignoring all these and reducing the discipline of economics into a unitary one, allows most to bask momentarily in a non-existent certitude rather than to deal with practical fuzziness, triggered by real-life situations. Most human minds are not geared to fathom and trained to comprehend this complexity.

Let us amplify. For instance, at the height of Covid-19 virus pandemic, the Hon'ble Supreme Court of India passed an order directing the tests relating to Covid-19 in approved government or private laboratories and to be carried out free of cost. This is voodoo economics. Free of cost to someone means a burden for someone else. Free to the grasshopper means that the costs are paid by the ant. This is basic economics. But the highest judiciary did not seem to even realise that there are costs involved in these testing let alone answer the question who will pay for the costs? What will be the consequence if private labs, without income, file for bankruptcy? Will we not lose critical capacities in our war on Covid-19? Even the Union government does not have endless resources to test 1.3 billion people, not to speak of private laboratories. This order at best allows the Supreme Court to have a moment in the Sun and play Robinhood to full glory. Whatever be it, the Supreme Court ended up as a one-handed economist.

And this has serious implications for our public health management system. This is the beginning of the abdication of health by stealth by the government. It may be seen that making it free for any service follows virtually the same pattern as it was for education through the introduction of RTE. It may be noted that the RTE was subjected to numerous rounds of debate, both philosophical and semantical, leading to the eighty-sixth amendment of the Constitution. This amendment was the culmination of several years of judicial activism of the Supreme Court on this subject. The country witnessed an increased focus on its initiatives regarding free and compulsory education after the Hon'ble Supreme Court first recognised the right to education as a fundamental right in Mohini Jain case where the court philosophically observed that "Right to life is the compendious expression for all those rights which the courts must enforce because they are basic to the dignified enjoyment of life. It extends to the full range of conduct which the individual is free to pursue. The right to education flows directly from right to life. The right to life under Article 21 and the dignity of an individual cannot be assured unless it is accompanied by the right to education. The State Government is under an obligation to make endeavour to provide educational facility at all levels to its citizens."

In 1993, the Hon'ble Supreme Court further refined the ambit of the fundamental right to education as propounded in the Mohini Jain case (discussed above) in the subsequent case of J P Unnikrishnan Vs. State of Andhra Pradesh and observed "The right to education which is implicit in the right to life and personal liberty guaranteed by Article 21 must be construed in the light of the directive principles in Part IV of the Constitution. So far as the right to education is concerned, there are several articles in Part IV which expressly speak of it. ...Article 45 says that "the State shall endeavour to provide, within a period of ten years from the commencement of this Constitution, for free and compulsory education for all children until they complete the age of fourteen years........ The three Articles 45, 46 and 41 are designed to achieve the said goal among others. It is in the light of these Articles that the content and parameters of the right to education have to be determined." These are the genesis of the eighty-sixth amendment, RTE and the quagmire that followed. What these two judgements did to the field of education, it is feared that the Covid-19 order of April 2020 will do to the health sector.

All these point to serious imbalances – between personal liberty and economic inequality, between public order and individual liberty, public debt and intergenerational borrowings, between taxes and functions of government; between functions of the government and public expenditure and finally between outlays of government and their outcomes. These are definitely not transient issues. One cannot wish them away merely by efflux of time. Neither are these imbalances solely related to the discipline of economics. Nor are these confined to India alone. Globally, most countries are facing identical challenges. To be precise, these are civilisational challenges and each of these imbalances individually has transformed into existential crisis for the present generation across the world. Needless to emphasise, collectively, their potency is compounded. Do we have solutions to these? Are we geared to provide answers to these questions?

Much of the problems of the modern world bear an uncanny resemblance to Roman civilisation, its economic woes in its later days and finally, its fall. It may not be out of place to quote Karl Marx who famously remarked: "Hegel remarks somewhere that all great, world-historical facts and personages occur, as it were, twice. He has forgotten to add: the first time as tragedy, the second as farce." What Marx implied was that civilisational challenges repeatedly occur because we are civilisationally challenged. While the Roman empire and its grandeur continue to impress and charm us, yet, we seem to be oblivious to the reasons leading to its ultimate fall. The lessons in the decline and the ultimate fall of the Roman Empire are compelling. Rome fell simply because its dictators ruined the Roman economy and the institutions that had made it prosperous in the first place. Noted author Jeffery Harding has clinically examined the causes leading to the downfall of the Roman empire. He points out that Romans "were profligate spenders.

As emperors with absolute power usually do, they thought big infrastructure, a huge bureaucracy, and, as the key to maintaining their power they had a very large, loyal, and well-paid army. As a consequence, massive government spending far outstripped revenue. They had what today we call a deficit problem."

Does this sound eerily similar to modern day developments across continents? One could take out Rome from the above passage and substitute it with any of the modern-nation state, and yet could be completely right. Despite compelling evidence, bad ideas, simply do not die. Rather they continue to haunt us. Harding adds, "First, they kept raising taxes which became punitive. Not caring much about the consequences to the merchants, small farmers, and peasants, they came up with new ways to squeeze money out of their citizens. Onerous taxes led to tax evasion. The government's response was to double down and implement laws that restricted economic freedoms in order to raise even more taxes. Heavy taxes forced property owners, small and large, off the land. Large feudal estates run by political cronies arose in their place. Laws were enacted that forced peasants into virtual serfdom. Business owners and their children were prevented from changing jobs or towns. And, taxes had to be paid either in gold or in kind or they would lose everything. Gold became scarce. Gold money was only lawfully available to the government, army, and bureaucrats."

Modern political thinkers and economists collectively believe that government can and should cause economic growth and prosperity. They believe that government can do this by introducing various controls, regulations, spending programmes and monetary manipulation. They believe that government spending by itself will stimulate demand, generate consumer spending, kick-start production, and that we can even attain full employment and prosperity. In the process, we can solve various socio-economic-political problems. This is what Romans thought and failed. This is what several Empires in our recorded history attempted and failed. Yet, this soporific economic thought continues to inspire modern 'progressive' economists. Just as there are lessons in the fall of the Roman empire, there are also some lessons in its rise. Roman civilisation arose from a small pastoral community leading to the build-up of a vast empire spread over centuries. Crucially, there was freedom and its administration, simple and frugal. In contrast to the several luxurious and corrupt despotic regimes which it overthrew, patriotism coupled with duties was the hallmark of the Roman citizen.

After a summit of power had been reached, entropy sets in. Absolute imperial power replaced the complex checks and balances in a robust governance mechanism that took the empire to the pinnacle. The famous Senate, in case of the Roman Empire, degenerated over the years from a vigorous state council into a cabal of rich men. The Roman populace was no longer in a mood to fight for its constitutional liberties; it was lulled into complacency by the time-honoured Bahuka's economics. So long as the population received free food at public expense, were entertained by elaborate games and spectacles (does all these not have an uncanny resemblance to the football, rugby, baseball, basketball, or cricket leagues in various countries that virtually puts a large section of the population on comatose mode?), it ceased to concern itself with public affairs. Consequently, private initiatives disappeared. So did individual duties. Over time, the expenses of the Roman Empire bloated. These included salaries to administrative employees, the cost of the emperor's household and court, handouts, entertainment for civilians and soldiers, funding programmes, gifts to important individuals, foreign subsidies, and the salary and maintenance costs of the vastly expanded army. The government was expected to look after everyone and attend to everything – the original nanny state. A welfare state system taught the people of Rome and other big cities the ease of idleness. In the time of Marcus Aurelius, there was a daily distribution of bread, pork, and oil to the populace. Expenses for gladiatorial combats and other public spectacles mounted continuously to an extent that will be seen obscene by even modern standards. The once sturdy Romans showed more inclination to spend their days in the coliseum and less in serving their country. The net result: even the discipline in army eroded leaving the empire vulnerable to attacks. Finally, that is what happened.

In the opinion of the Canadian classical scholar, WG Hardy, "Even before the plague the Roman world was rotting from within. Government paternalism, bureaucracy, inflation, an ever-increasing taste for the brutal and brutalising spectacles of the amphitheatre and the circus were symptoms of a spiritual malaise which had begun when political freedom was tossed away in the interests of peace, security, and materialism. There was the canker of slavery and the equally dangerous practice of keeping a segment of the population permanently on dole. There was free labour subsisting on starvation wages because of the competition of slavery. At the other end of the scale lolled a group of multi-millionaires for whom no luxury was too extravagant. Nor did anyone perceive that inflation and rising taxation must ultimately squeeze the middle class out of being." Rome's fall, as historians are more and more inclined to agree, came about from an overwhelming pressure from internal weaknesses. This finally led to the implosion of the empire. The lessons from the fall of the Roman empire are indeed instructive to modern governments. The process of decline and ultimate fall of the Roman empire has real and urgent lessons for the US (and by extension to the entire world which is modelled on the American experience) which claims to be an heir of Roman culture and civilisation.

One would be quick to note, with alarm, certain parallels between the later Roman and modern-day developments. One of them, notably is, the willingness to barter individual rights and freedom, for a statist handout. This is what Alexis de Tocqueville had in mind in his remarkable prophetic forecast of what would be the end result of an advanced form of welfare state: "Above this race of men stands an immense and tutelary power, which takes upon itself alone to secure their gratifications, and to watch over their fate. That power is absolute, minute, regular, provident, and mild. It would be like the authority of a parent, if, like that authority, its object was to prepare men for manhood; but it seeks, on the contrary, to keep them in perpetual childhood; it is well content that the people should rejoice, provided they think of nothing but rejoicing. For their happiness, such a government willingly labours, but it chooses to be the sole agent and the only arbiter of that happiness; it provides for their security, foresees and supplies their necessities, facilitates their pleasures… what remains, but to spare them all the care of thinking and all the trouble of living? Such a power does not destroy, but it prevents existence; it does not tyrannise, but it compresses, enervates, extinguishes, and stupefies a people, till each nation is reduced to be nothing better than a flock of timid and industrious animals, of which the government is the shepherd."

The collapse of a mighty state of a well-organised, endowed society, and a fruitful civilisation of which we possess a reasonably accurate record was immortalised by Edward Gibbon's historical classic: *The Decline and Fall of The Roman Empire*. The noted historian has offered his reflections on the symptoms and causes of the decline and fall of the empire. His understanding of the situation (and mirrors the reasoning of Harding and Hardy) can be once again generalised as a twin problem that confronts most civilisations: A bureaucracy that has gone berserk; and a taxation system that has gone extortionist. Gibbons puts it philosophically "This long peace and the uniform government of the Romans introduced a slow and secret poison into the vitals of the empire. The minds of men were gradually reduced to the same level, the fire of genius was extinguished, and even the military spirit evaporated." And, describing a later phase of the decline, the reign of Diocletian (284-305 CE) for instance, Gibbon spells out this reference to oppression as the product of twin evils which always go together: a swollen bureaucracy and excessive taxation. To quote his account: "The number of ministers, of magistrates, of officers, and of servants, who filled the different departments of the state, was multiplied beyond the example of former times; and when the proportion of those who received exceeded the proportion of those who contributed the provinces were oppressed by the weight of tributes. From this period to the extinction of the empire, it would be easy to deduce an uninterrupted series of clamours and complaints. According to his religion and situation, each writer chooses either Diocletian or Constantine or Valens or Theodosius, for the object of his invectives; but they unanimously agree in representing the burden of the public impositions, and particularly the land tax and capitation, as the intolerable and increasing grievance of their own times."

The same effect of a bloated bureaucracy, an extortionist taxation system and a mindless welfare in the 6th century Byzantine Empire, under the rule of Justinian, is described by another historian George Finley, in his work *Greece Under the Romans*. According to him: "At last, the whole wealth of the empire was drawn into the imperial treasury; fruit trees were cut down and free men were sold to pay taxes; vineyards were rooted out, and buildings were destroyed to escape taxation. The increase of the public burdens at last proceeded so far that every year brought with it a failure in the taxes of some province, and consequently the confiscation of the private property of the wealthiest citizens of the insolvent district, until at last all the rich proprietors were ruined and the law became nugatory."

To most of us, governance implies appropriation of crores as taxes out of the pockets of hard working, civilisationally conscious, socially sensitive and responsible taxpayers for state-sponsored welfare programmes, hopefully, to bail out millions of our fellow countrymen out of poverty, illiteracy, ignorance and disease, intermediated by an honest hard-working bureaucracy. This we assume to be our civilisational duty. Therefore, we pay our taxes merely on this belief that taxes are a price that we pay for sustaining our civilisation. It is imagined even to this date by a vast majority of people worldwide that a welfare state, run by bureaucrats and administered through a rule of law, is the destination point in human civilisation. But the lessons of history clearly point out that it is exactly the opposite. The proliferation of bureaucracy, and its twin, the coercive taxation regime, are signs of a decaying civilisation. Historians know that both these phenomena were remarkably identifiable in the declining eras of the Roman Empire as they were visible in declining empire. Bureaucrats are an expensive breed, in two ways. They are maintained at high costs and they are fertile in conjuring schemes to commit the state to spend more public funds and therefore multiply their number. Politicians, especially in a democracy and to sustain the "constitutional structure," have no choice but to play ball with them.

Taxes are a problem as is welfare. One is the cause, the other effect. Either way, one is interlinked with the other and in the aggregate, both are ineffective. In the absence of a viable alternative, the government is indulging in the proverbial rain dance of the African tribal chief. Inequality as we saw in the previous chapter continues to raise globally as inexplicably as how tax-to-GDP ratio continues to grow world-wide. This paradox sums up our civilisational failure. We need to pause and have a relook at the root assumptions that drive our taxation and the concomitant welfare regimes.

We need to relook at the functions of our bureaucracy which have become economic black holes. Interestingly, all this wisdom did not dawn on us only in the 20th century. Nor did these come about to us through the writings of Hardy, Harding, Gibbons, or George Finley. All these were discussed by the framers of the American Constitution in the 18th century. They were arguably among the most learned men of their time. The Federalist Papers and the preserved letters of Jefferson, John Adams, Franklin, and Madison are full of scholarly references to the events of classical times and to the lessons which should be drawn from these happenings of the distant past. Within two centuries, the US has slowly let go some of the fundamental principles with which these great men came about to write a Constitution for their country. One of the most compelling lessons they drew from the decline of the Roman Empire was about its citizenry without any personal responsibility. The founding fathers of the Indian Constitution not only had the knowledge of the decline and fall of the Roman empire, the wisdom of the Federalist Papers, but also the native wisdom of the wise mother of Mahatma Gandhi. Yet, they chose to be oblivious to all these while drafting the Indian Constitution.

The West, The Rest, and the Test Ahead

At the heart of the nation-state theory is a huge paradox. The nation-state idea is itself a modern construct, though the idea is in itself a product of cross-fertilisation of the ideas of several political thinkers across centuries. The success of the US and its dominance post-World War-II (further accentuated by the collapse of Soviet Russia in the last decade of the previous millennium) ensured that this construct comes to occupy a central place in modern global socio-economic-political order. At the core of this ideology is the non-negotiable individual liberty. Yet, it ended up stealthily curtailing individual liberty in one way or the other. The French revolution, it may be recalled, began with the cries of liberty, and ended up with Napoleon's despotism. Likewise, the great march to global order fashioned on the American experience ended up with being a failed experiment on the rest. As it turns out, our collective political thinking was premised on a false belief that the Western model is a durable political idea for the rest to follow. To sovereign states, it represented an unambiguous march forward towards a universally accepted global order. Multilateral organisations were set up to further this agenda. Sadly, despite all its idealist positioning in the name of democracy, all that most nations could achieve was increased inequality, bureaucratic overreach, and a coercive taxation regime that curbed individual liberty.

As Hardy pointed out, there was nothing spiritual in the Roman Empire; there is nothing spiritual in the extant global order either. Consequently, duty or responsibility was never considered in the most constitutional arrangements. And even when it was done, it had marginal impact. Thus, all forms of individual duties – to one's own family, to society, and to government – all remain conspicuous by their absence in a formal constitutional document. And when it does, as in the case of the Indian Constitution in Article 51A, it is, at best reduced to an ornamental piece in the Constitution. This has virtually knocked us out socially, economically and politically. Further, this arrangement – of absolute rights without duties – has given a short shrift to the individual enterprise and his moral quotient. Bereft of this, citizens expect the government to do anything and everything. When government interferes in our daily life, we mock at it and call it as a nanny state. Worse still, we want the state to guard us in the interiors of our homes and decry it for robbing us of our privacy. Interestingly, the moral suasion and legal keg to seek such intervention from the government in the first place strangely comes from unrestricted fundamental rights in the Constitution! Do we realise this paradox? The damning part is that we believe once we have paid our taxes to the government, we owe nothing more to our family, society or the government.

Pithily stated, civilisations are built by duties and sacrifice, not rights and definitely not by paying taxes alone. Our history, epics, festivals, religion, duty, fine arts, social ethics, education, dealing with elders, treating women, flora and fauna, philosophies, debates, generosity, loyalty, hierarchy, literature, language, courage, charity, responsibility, restraints and concerns for the community all executed through the first institution known to man -marriage – make a civilisation. Modern Constitutions do not compel a citizen to do any of the above, not the least to maintain the institution of marriage and family. In fact, there is no compulsion even to take care of one's spouse, parents, or children. That an individual is only an individual in the eyes of law and owes his contractual obligations only to the state and no one else. Nevertheless, this idea of a modern nation-state, rooted to unbridled individual liberalism, has run its full course. The triumvirate of coercive taxation, bloated bureaucracy, and of course welfare state were supposedly to be a counterbalance to the grant of 'Fundamental Rights' to its citizens. The original imbalance, let us not forget, was triggered by this extreme liberty granted to an individual under the social contract theory. This triumvirate only accentuated the imbalance further instead of balancing the relationship between the state and the individual. The existing socio-economic-political woes of modern nation-states flow from this original imbalance caused by unrestrained individual liberty. If power corrupts and absolute power corrupts absolutely, individual liberty disrupts, and absolute individual liberty disrupts absolutely. Unless the individual is reined and his rights tethered to duties, we will continue to face this conundrum. If curbing individual liberty caused the fall of Soviet bloc countries, unbridled individualism is now fast emerging as the villain of the piece for those who accepted the post-cold war global order.

It may be recalled that after the implosion of the Soviet Union, political thinkers like Fukuyama had assumed the domination of the West over the rest created a durable socio-economic-political model for the entire world. The concerns relating to Western ideas that came to dominate modern nation-states and its apparent short comings were expressed by Fukuyama himself. This was merely 25 years after the end of Cold War and was discussed in greater detail in Chapter 3. Likewise, Huntington's call for *Remaking of a World Order* seems to be perfectly prophetic, albeit for totally different reasons. Both Fukuyama and Huntington, the most influential writers of their times, would not have predicted that the root assumptions of their respective seminal works would collapse within a couple of decades. For instance, and contrary to what Fukuyama wrote, China is more authoritarian than ever and prosperous than what it was 30 years ago. Prosperity did not push China into a democracy as Fukuyama predicted. Only the civilisational state model can rationalise this, not the Western liberal idea of a state, with pre-set contours. In fact, Chinese scholars like Zhang Weiwei, have been constantly explaining the grand idea of a Chinese civilisation state that existed over several millennia. They argue that the Chinese see their state in a different way – as a unifier and guardian of their unique civilisation and therefore have different expectations from their state. Prime Minister Modi is precisely attempting this in the case of India. Further, this idea of civilisational state comes from the sense of nationhood and is derived from collective memories of an ancient civilisation. The remaking of the world order has become a reality with the re-emergence of the civilisational state idea – where every state is attempting to re-boot to its civilisational values and rework how citizens see the state, its role and responsibilities. Implicit in this idea is that the world is culturally plural and hence is thronging for pluralism in politics and economics.

Hence, the days of spreading universal values of Western enlightenment, ideas and order have long since passed. We are currently witnessing is a penumbra where the old order has virtually given away, and the new order is yet to re-establish itself in full force. If the 19th century political thinkers and philosophers popularised the idea of the nation-state, the 21st could be the century of the civilisation state. Of late, this idea is gaining currency in Russia, India, and Turkey, apart from China. This is good augury. Most thinkers in these countries now believe that their imminent rise will not be by modelling themselves blindly on the West, but by going back to their traditions, culture, and ideas that sustained their civilisation. Countries find that unbridled individual liberalism is an idea abhorrent to their respective civilisational values. They prefer to define their countries as distinctive civilisations with their own unique cultural values and political institutions, rather than a pale carbon copy of a decadent West. They would prefer to define the role of the state according to their civilisational values, not that as seen by the West. For instance, Putin believes that Western liberal values are not universal, and do not reflect Russia's unique cultural identity. In a 2012 speech to both houses of the Russian parliament, he declared that Russia's 'civilisation state' protects the country from "dissolving in this diverse world." The West is a threat to Russian civilisation because, according to Putin, it denies moral principles and traditional ways of life. The rise of the civilisational state implies "the West may be out of the business of shaping history for everyone else, or even itself."

Inadvertently, all these recent inclinations to be a civilisational state, might have triggered something spectacular and have far reaching consequences. How about revisiting the Bogota Conference documents? We need to examine the experiences of nations like Mexico who had made duties as a workable part of their Constitution. The world needs to discuss once again the balance between individual rights and duties. To do so, we need to place the ancient and eternal institution of family at the core of our discourse. Simultaneously, we need to work out a balance between individual efforts and duties of the government. Once individual duties are defined, the role of government will inevitably become residuary, especially when it comes to dealing with citizens.

That entails India too will have a role to play in the emerging multipolar world order. We need to pitchfork the efforts and duties of an individual, not his rights, as a basic structure of this global order. We need to bring our civilisational values back to the global discourse. To do so, we need to be clear of our civilisational values and first design our Constitution accordingly. For starters, we need to deal with the emerging world order as *Bhartiyas*, not merely as Indians. This difference is not a mere exercise in semantics. Adherence to civilisational values makes an Indian, *Bhartiya*. Let us elucidate. There are several religions that have flowered and prospered in this great land. Several wonderful texts and epics have been authored by the foremost scholars, exponents and philosophers. We had the benefits of expansive thoughts of extraordinary spiritual personalities across millenniums. Of all these, as Verse 47 of Chapter II of the *Gita* – the right of man to work, but never to the fruit thereof – encapsulates the eternal durable and practical spirit of the *Bhartiya* civilisation. It is as agnostic as it can be as also spiritual. The fundamental point is that it places individual, not anyone or anything else, and his enterprise, central, to any civilisational resurgence. Gandhiji puts it eloquently when he states: "Civilization is that mode of conduct which points out to man the path of duty."

That explains why we have a civilisational connect to the ants, and not the grasshoppers. *Bhartiyas* instantly connects to eternal thoughts like 'Duties' or 'Responsibilities,' and not to alien concepts like Rights, which as saw in chapter 3 has its origins in Christianity. The quintessence of the *Bhartiya* civilisation has been performing one's duties even in the most trying circumstances. Indians speak for their constitutional Rights; *Bhartiyas* perform their civilisational Duties. This is what the wise mother of the Mahatma elucidated. And this thought would be instantaneously understood by a vast majority of *Bhartiyas*. In contrast not only was the Constitution written in an alien language – English – but also used alien phrases like 'Rights' which even the Hon'ble Supreme Court in all its majesty finds it difficult to interpret, not to speak of the ordinary citizens. It is this dichotomy that is deeply ingrained in each Indian, probably making him a split personality – an Indian while dealing with the state, and a *Bhartiya*, otherwise. This time around, we *Bhartiyas* owe it to the world to provide a new global order based on individual duties and responsibilities. That alone will make Constitutions, family and the society functional. To do so, we need to first get rid of our split personality syndrome – simultaneously between being an Indian and also a *Bhartiya*.

References

1. A modern version of The Ant and the Grasshopper By Paul W. Barada- Daily News – July 24, 2018.
2. How Britain stole $45 trillion from India And lied about it By Jason Hickel – Aljazeera – 19th Dec 2018.
3. Blighted by Empire: What the British Did to India By Omer Aziz – Los Angles Review of Book – 1st September 2018.
4. Constituent Assembly Debates.
5. Rights vs. Duties, Reclaiming Civic Balance By Samuel Moyn – Boston Review – May 16, 2016.
6. (Re)discovering Duties: Individual Responsibility in the Age of Rights By Fernando Berdion Del Valle and Kathryn Sikkink- Minnesota Journal of International Law – 2017.
7. The Coming Crisis: How Government Dependency Threatens America's Freedom – By Jim DeMint – May 8, 2001 – Heritage Foundation.
8. Tax-to-GDP Ratio By Julia Kagan – Investopedia – Jul 14, 2019.
9. Revenue Statistics 2019 Tax revenue trends in the OECD.
10. OECD Social Expenditure Update, 2019.
11. Salaries, pensions account for 71% of State expenditure' – The Hindu – January 27, 2019.

12. How The Right To Education Act Is Failing India's Children By WTD News in Education, Society, 9th November 2018.
13. Budget at a Glance – Union Budget 20-21.
14. Order of Supreme Court of India – Civil Original Jurisdiction – Writ Petition (Civil) Diary No(s). 10816/2020 – Dated April 8, 2020.
15. How to Destroy a Civilization By Jeffrey Harding – 24th June 2019 – Mises Institute.
16. Bureaucracy Kills: A Lesson from Rome – Foundation for Economic Education – By William Henry Chamberlin – January 1, 1963.
17. The decline and fall of the Western Roman Empire By Justin Ott – 2009 – Iowa State University.
18. India and the rise of the 'civilisational state' – By Hindol Sengupta, March 22, 2019, POLEMICIST.
19. China, Russia and the return of the civilisational state – By Adrian Past – 8 May 2019, New Statesman.

8. Needed: Economic Reforms or Reforms in Economics?

Economics is extremely useful as a form of employment for economists

– John Kenneth Galbraith

Economics is a choice between alternatives all the time. Those are the trade-offs

– Paul Samuelson

In an unprecedented move, the global rating agency Standard & Poor downgraded the US Government's 'AAA' sovereign credit rating to 'AA+' while keeping the outlook negative. That was in August 2011, almost a decade ago. That in turn triggered massive convulsions in financial markets across countries, including India. And pray why not? After all, the US Treasuries is the definitive benchmark for global financial markets. The Indian government's reaction to all these was on predictable lines. Terming the situation as 'grave,' the then Finance Minister Pranab Mukherjee commented: "There are difficulties and some sort of a crisis. But there is no need to press the panic button." Crucially, he added: "I do not want to worry unnecessarily. Our growth story is intact, and our fundamentals are strong." Only a seasoned politician like Pranab Mukherjee could get away by describing the situation as grave, yet not necessitating the pressing of the panic button! Some wordplay that. Or call it clairvoyance. India quickly overcame the 'crisis.'

A decade or so later, there was yet another crisis – the outbreak of the Covid-19 pandemic. At the height of this crisis, the Indian Prime Minister Narendra Modi observed that "the global economy has been going through a difficult phase but the fundamentals of the Indian economy are strong and policies are clear that will aid in reaching the target of nearly doubling the size of the economy to $5 trillion." But this was not the first time that Prime

Minister Modi was speaking of the fundamentals of the Indian economy. Nor was Covid-19 pandemic, the trigger. In fact, even before the pandemic struck the world, Modi is reported to have said: "the strong absorbent capacity of the Indian economy shows the strength of basic fundamentals of the Indian economy, and its capacity to bounce back."

This reference to both Pranab Mukherjee and Narendra Modi is not without any purpose. Though both belong to different streams of political persuasions, both are highly respected individuals with the former going on to occupy the office of the President of India, and the latter occupies the office of the Prime Minister of India. Both are communicators par excellence. They are known to measure their words, especially in a crisis. Therefore, a reference to the fundamentals of the Indian economy during periods of crisis as a reassurance to the Indian citizens is indeed well thought out. Surely, such assurances are not merely symbolic. Nor are they intended merely to ease the concerns of the citizenry without a comprehensive game plan. By drawing to such references, both leaders seek to reiterate that the economy is indeed resilient and extant crisis will blow over, leaving little or no great impact on the Indian economy. The repeated use of the word 'fundamental' by these two great Indian leaders, albeit at different times and situations, is well thought-out strategy, as the word is well-understood by the majority. It assures a rooted approach to tackling the crisis. It is philosophical yet, unambiguous. No wonder, such leaders instantly strike a chord with Indians.

Again, these two leaders have not spoken out of turn. In fact, they have a very healthy precedence. Mahatma Gandhi in 1908, when the Indian civilisation itself was gravely wounded, brilliantly explained its strength and resilience in an assuring manner: "I believe that the civilisation India has evolved is not to be beaten in the world. Nothing can equal the seeds sown by our ancestors. Rome went, Greece shared the same fate, the might of the Pharaohs was broken, Japan has become Westernised, of China nothing can be said, but India is still – somehow or the other – sound at the foundation." The emphasis was on being sound at the foundation. That was his confidence about the Indian civilisation and its impending renaissance. Moreover, the Mahatma then goes on to explain India's unique civilisational advantage: "All countries are not similarly conditioned. The condition of India is unique. Its strength is immeasurable. We need not, therefore, refer to the history of other countries. I have drawn attention to the fact that when other civilisations have succumbed, the Indian has survived many a shock." In effect, the Mahatma makes it abundantly clear in his writings as early as 1908 that India is a civilisation in perpetuity. And the Mahatma in the early 20th century implied that India had a sound civilisational foundation, a blessing that not many other countries had. Interestingly, these very thoughts of the Mahatma resonate through the two great Indian leaders, a hundred years later, in the 21st century.

The US downgrade is merely a context to a much larger discussion. As is the Covid-19 pandemic crisis. In between, Mukherjee's quote in 2011 and Modi's observation in 2020, several Indian economists, policy analysts, researchers, scholars and leaders have repeatedly hinted at the inherent strength of the Indian economy at different points in time. So have several leaders since the Mahatma brought out the civilisational strength of India in her tough times. And the Mahatma has been reiterating what several seers have stated before him, some whose historicity cannot be determined. Come any crisis, man-made or natural, economic or political, Indian economy has been by and large insulated from such negative developments. And at every turn, men at the helm of national affairs have been near unanimous in their conclusion – the Indian economy is largely protected from such crisis; the fundamentals of Indian economy are strong and by and large the Indian growth story is intact. Questions arise: What do we mean by the fundamentals of Indian economy in the first place? What is the civilisational connect to the economy? How does it manifest? How is it measured? How does it give confidence to every Indian leader to assuage the anxiety of the nation? Is it being leveraged in these troubled times? If not, how can it be done?

Economy and a Civilisational Connect

The answers to these questions require some reference to certain recent developments in the Indian economy. It may be interesting to note that liberalisation of the Indian economy since the early 1990s has not ended liberalising the average Indian. In fact, if the average national saving rate is any indication, India has achieved a higher savings rate post liberalisation than during the pre-liberalisation era. If the average savings rate was a mere 17 percent of the GDP in the 1980s, the savings rate has doubled to approximately 31 percent of the GDP in the second decade of the 21st century. Notably, this domestic savings virtually funds our domestic investments. It is this investment that go on to ensure domestic production of goods and services. That, in turn, provides domestic employment and consequently ensures domestic consumption. Domestic consumption ensures taxes for the local government. All these virtually insulates India from any exogeneous shocks and global gyrations of both financial markets and economy. If the four limbs of an economy – production, consumption, savings, and investments – are domestically rooted in any country, it is indeed blessed.

That is not all. The high savings-to-GDP ratio makes any foreign investment less significant than it is made out by the media. It is in this connection that a 2009 Report of the 'High Level Committee on Estimation of Saving and Investment' set up by the Ministry of Statistics and Programme Implementation under the chairmanship of Dr C Rangarajan concludes: "More than 98 percent of investment is funded by domestic savings. As a result, the savings-investment gap has remained relatively in a narrow range reflective of modest reliance on foreign savings." That implies that domestic savings virtually funds the domestic investment, leaving a meagre two percent to be sourced as foreign direct investments. Though this report is of 2009 vintage, the situation at the ground level has not undergone any significant changes. No wonder, it is this paradigm that goes on to provide the necessary confidence to political leaders to tide over any crisis – internal or external. It may be interesting to note that approximately 70 percent of this gargantuan saving comes from Indian households. Needless to add, that the balance thirty percent of our national savings comes from the private corporate sector and public sector put together.

Yet, not many within the establishment recognise the fundamental role and civilisational reasons of savings in the Indian context, especially that of households. Indians, it may be noted, have a civilisational connect to save. This is another unexplored characteristic of the Indian economy. Savings is a habit, culture, and civilisation – all rolled into one. Post-liberalisation,

India has provided increased market access. Despite these developments, Indians have achieved higher savings rate post liberalisation – a theoretical contradiction. This savings is an outcome of certain civilisational restraints and makes Indian economy, by design, to operate within certain restraints. And such an economy is necessarily resilient, especially in a crisis. This contradiction was well-explained by Shri S Gurumurthy, in a lecture titled *Current Economic Crunch and Problems of Industries Particularly MSMEs*, which was organised by National Confederation of Small Industry and Industrial Estate Manufacturers Association in August 2013. Pointing out to that in 1992, (coinciding with the initiation of economic reforms in India) when Manmohan Singh was Union Finance Minister, there were certain differences within the government on the approach to manage the Indian economy. It was at this time that Dr Jagdish Bhagwati, a noted economist, was invited to India to provide some fresh ideas. Dr Bhagwati then, according to Shri Gurumurthy, gave a 72-page report, arguing for reorientation of the Indian economy. One of significant shifts advocated by Bhagwati was to provide a consumerist thrust to the economy, as there was excessive savings in India, which was stymying growth. That was when the savings-GDP ratio was a mere 17%. Despite such suggestions of 'well-meaning economists,' and possibly policy interventions arising out of such recommendations, India grew, and so did her savings.

But how did India manage it by breaking free from the conventional wisdom of eschewing blind consumerism while maintaining a healthy growth rate? How could it record both robust economic growth as well as spectacular rise in savings rate? The answer probably lies in the fact that, in India, there is a symbiotic relationship between the spiritual and practical life. We shall look into this when we discuss the idea of *Ardhanareshwara* in Chapter 10. Some economists now concede that there is a live demonstrable link between the way people live and their philosophical aspirations. As explained in Chapter 6, all these abstract issues are incapable of being reduced to a mathematical equation. Since all these cannot be reduced to a mathematical equation, modern economists refuse to factor this in their analysis.

This requires some explanation. The goals of human life – *Artha, Kaama, Dharma, and Moksha* – collectively called as *Purusharth*, dominates the individual Indian psyche. We have dealt with the first three and their interplay in some measure in chapter 5. Moksha, the fourth goal life, is unique to Hindu philosophy. Simply put, it seeks liberation for the individual from repeated cycles of birth and death so much so that the individual, after his *Moksha*, gets subsumed by the Lord himself. That is the belief of those pursuing this path. The surest and possibly the easiest route to attain *Mokhsha* is to do one's duty, though, there are other approaches to achieve it. Every individual, a householder, teacher or farmer, qualifies without any precondition or qualification to attain *Moksha* simply by doing his duty. Every believer seeks to attain *Moksha* and understands the process to attain it instinctively. What is pertinent to note is that there is no need for any external agency to direct one to *Moksha.* This compelling force of performing one's duty and that individual and his efforts alone matter in attaining *Moksha*. Verse 5 Chapter VI of the *Bhagavad Gita* adds that "One should elevate oneself by one's own efforts and should not degrade oneself; for one's own self is one's friend, and one's own self is one's enemy." The commentary by the Gita Press, Gorakhpur, explains that that the Lord confers on every individual the rare boon of a human body. This affords every individual a golden opportunity whereby he can by spiritual discipline get out of the slough of metempsychosis. Therefore, a man should take particular care that the rare opportunity vouchsafed to him in the shape of a human life is not thrown away and should make the most of it by pursuing a course of discipline. This is what is meant by lifting oneself by one's own efforts. If a man exerts himself, he is sure to get out of the slough of degradation and attain the highest summit. Man should, therefore, constantly strive with the utmost care and diligence to elevate himself; lift himself from where he is. In practical terms, it means, he who strives to redeem himself is his own friend, and he who acts otherwise, is his own enemy. Therefore, man has no friend or enemy other than his own self. He is the cause of his success; he is the cause of his own downfall. This is the spiritual underpinning of the Indian civilisation. The highest goal of life is an extremely privatised affair and requires no external force or agency. And since the duty of self is central to the scheme of things, even god becomes secondary to attain *Moksha*.

Compare this with the goal of salvation in the Christian theology. Salvation implies being rescued from peril. And pray what is that peril? Christian theologists have summarised that the real problem for man is the original sin of Adam and Eve. Resultantly, everyone is a born sinner because of Adam and Eve and their original sin. And there are no exceptions. (In contrast, Swami Vivekananda, a great Hindu Saint believed that every soul is divine). God, according Christian theologists sent Jesus Christ to rescue sinners. Thus, for Christians, Salvation by any other means is a theological as well as a practical impossibility. It cannot therefore be a privatised affair. It does not matter whether a person is consumed by his own passions or exhibits a degree of self-control and discipline. To them, all are sinners without any exception. In effect, the act of sin and sinner do not bear any connection, for anyone born is a sinner. And unless something dramatic happens, like the intervention of an external force like Christ, sinners are on their way to eternal hell. That explains the importance of Salvation in Christianity. In previous chapters, we have discussed the profound impact of this idea of original sin and its impact on Western consciousness and culture. As already pointed out, Boyce in his celebrated work *Born Bad* brings about the theological impact even in the writings of celebrated atheists like Marx and Richard Dawkins. The legacy of original sin takes many forms, including the discontentment of Western people – the feelings of guilt and inadequacy associated not with committing any sin, but simply being labelled as sinners.

Now look at the contrasting Indic situation. On one hand, the idea of *Moksha* places every decision in the hands of the individual. It privatises faith and its attendant consequences. Elevation of the individual by his own efforts is its ultimate objective. In contrast, salvation is impossible without an external agent. It corporatises faith. For the former, individual discipline alone matters. For the latter, only the external force matters, as individual acts have little relevance. Liberation from the cycle of birth and death is linked to one's own efforts. In this, individual's life-long discipline and duty becomes crucial. Salvation on the other hand relies solely on Christ. To attain *Moksha*, birth as a human being is a godsent opportunity while birth as a human being is a sin, requiring salvation through an external agent. Naturally, all these theological understanding has great impact on shaping, de-shaping and reshaping our respective approach to life.

The differentials in various theologies are not the subject matter of this work. But it becomes an imperative to recognise them to understand the functioning of economic theories. Suffice to say that there are different approaches to life and religion. Religion has played a significant role in shaping civilisations. The lessons of the 20th century, especially post-cold war, is all about sustaining and celebrating plurality of life. This multiplicity of approach to life (with or without religion) has for time immemorial recently given rise to the idea of the rise of parallel civilisational states. The unipolar global order was an avoidable distraction of the 20th century. Thankfully, we are witnessing the re-emergence of civilisational states in the 21st century. This has been dealt with in the previous chapter. Naturally, it is a development that will have profound impact on several disciplines, one of them being economics. Global order, unwittingly or otherwise, gave rise to a unitary economic idea. With the rise of civilisational states, the unitary economic idea will necessarily give rise to civilisational economics. This will be the natural fallout of the rise of civilisational states. Why are economists not taking the quantum leap in understanding civilisational economics? Are modern economists, incapable of factoring civilisational aspects in their studies? While political leaders are asserting their civilisational importance in the global order, economists are hesitant to bring about a civilisational perspective to their debates. Why are the pantheon of economists reluctant to break free from their doctrinal positions?

Inexplicable fact of life

Let us at this point return to the spectacular rise in the Indian savings rate post-liberalisation. As pointed out earlier, the Indian savings rate, contrary to expert opinion and popular belief, virtually doubled in this three-decade period. It may be recalled the prescriptions of reducing savings rate made out by certain economists. As pointed out above, not only did India record robust economic growth, but she also recorded a near doubling of her savings rate during this period. Economists have been unable to comprehend this. How did this happen? Why did India turn to higher savings, even as her economy was increasingly getting liberalised? How did these savings become the chief drive of the national economy during this period? Why did India adopt a savings-led model in contrast to the consumer-led model prescribed by well-intended economists? Did this happen by design of the government or by default? Questions that have no answers in economic textbooks.

There is a fascinating dimension to this issue. The 2017 Report of the Household Finance Committee of the Reserve Bank of India (RBI) has summarised the Indian household savings landscape. The key findings of this Committee are that Indian households are unique when compared to their global counterparts and summarised hereunder:

- Several attributes of Indian households that are exceptional in the international context.
- The distinctive features of Indian household balance sheets cannot be explained by any known differentials.
- It appears that these patterns are likely driven by unique aspects of Indian households' financial decision-making.
- A large fraction of the wealth of Indian households is in the form of physical assets (in particular, gold and real estate). This is unusual in the international context.
- Social arrangements in which households' bequest housing wealth to future generations and in turn receive support during retirement are an underlying determinant of these patterns.
- Such traditional approaches to household financial management have likely evolved over time as a rational response to prevailing economic conditions.
- The Indian household finance landscape is distinctive through the near total absence of pension wealth.
- There are low levels of insurance penetration (life and non-life).
- This is further evidence that traditional and cultural factors are strong determinants of observed allocations.

According to the findings of this committee, the average household holds saves 77 percent of its total assets in real estate, seven percent in other durable goods, 11 percent in gold and the residual five percent in financial assets (such as deposits and savings accounts, publicly traded shares, mutual funds, life insurance, and retirement accounts). Further analysis of the smallest share of the pie – the financial assets – and how this five percent is invested in various asset class reveals an interesting pattern. It may be noted that along with the liberalisation of the Indian economy, Indian financial sector has undergone spectacular reforms. Despite such sweeping reforms, regulatory oversight and tightly supervised intermediation, Indian households have refused investments in high-risk instruments. For instance, the share of investment in stock and bond markets has been a mere 3 percent of the total financial savings of households. Despite the spectacular rise in the Indian stock markets, Indian households have not been sufficiently enticed by it to shift their financial savings into the stock markets, not to speak of debt markets. In direct contrast to the meagre savings investment in the stock markets, the savings retained in the form of cash and bank has been at a whopping 13 and 42 percent respectively aggregating to 55 percent of the total financial savings. Substantial amount of financial savings is also retained as investments in insurance (17 percent) and in pensions (19 percent). Thus, amount in excess of 90 percent of household savings is either held as cash or in sectors which are very tightly regulated, low yielding but also having little or no risk. Again, economic textbooks will be unable to provide any clear answer to this phenomenon why domestic investments in high-risk high yielding avenues are marginal and disproportionately higher in low yielding yet relatively safe sectors.

Regretfully, there is yet another piece of statistics that one needs to consider: farmers' suicide. It refers to the national catastrophe of farmers committing suicide, often by drinking pesticides, due to their inability to repay loans mostly taken from private sources. The National Crime Records Bureau (NCRB) is an office in the Ministry of Home Affairs, Government of India. It has been collecting and publishing suicide statistics for India since the 1950s in its reports. It started separately collecting and publishing farmers suicide statistics from 1995. As per records available with this Bureau, approximately three lakh Indian farmers have committed suicide since 1995. There are accusations of states manipulating the data on farmer suicides, hence the actual figures could be much higher. Activists and scholars have proffered conflicting reasons for farmer suicides, such as high interest rate burdens, flood, drought, GM crops, poor government policies, corruption in subsidies, crop failure, public mental health, personal issues and family problems. Several state governments have set up expert committees to suggest the way forward.

The reference to these disconnected data points is not without reason. There is no reliable literature from the economist stable that comes to any definitive conclusion on what caused the spike in savings rate post-liberalisation, or the rationale behind the allocation of financial assets to various asset classes by the Indian household or the reason behind suicides by farmers in India. It is often said that the only the right questions beget right answers. Economists, as already pointed out in the previous chapters, have long been reluctant to study the impact of cultural forces at play as obviously such factors cannot be part of a testable hypothesis using normal statistical tools. Remember, economists like in most other disciplines want to be peer compatible. But they cannot ignore the interplay between culture and economics for too long. The big blind spot in the discipline of economics is now slowly getting identified if not addressed. For too long, we have ignored this symbiotic relationship and have continued to fashion the laws of economics in 'cultural and civilisational vacuum.' Obviously, it has come to a point where the elephant in the room is too big for anyone to deny.

Along with the rise of the civilisational state, economists will be now compelled to pay attention to the correlation between economics and culture. As must politicians, while framing their economic policies. In fact, politicians will need to pilot this idea. Politicians cannot, henceforth, take umbrage under a vague 'emerging global order.' As they are accountable to the very people whom they represent, they will have to necessarily factor the impact of culture and civilisational values in their economic policies. Ignoring this impact for too long has brought an existential crisis to the discipline of economics and disrepute to politics, its frontend. The importance of both culture and civilisational values in influencing the functioning of an economy from now on will be increasingly recognised. This is what one can call as the civilisational economics where modern economic laws will be subjected to civilisational pulls and cultural pressures. Does culture explain the increase in savings rate post liberalisation in India? Yes, it does to a great degree. Are cultural factors of holding oneself guilty of not repaying debts a cause of farmer's suicide? Probably yes. Culture and civilisation may be providing broad pointers, if not precise answers, to a host of such questions. Of course, one must hasten to add that all indeterminable factors cannot be aggregated in the civilisational basket. Given these empirical evidences as listed above in case of savings in India, can anyone deny the impact of culture and civilisational values on economics? The answer to this question will be an emphatic no. The rise of civilisational economics is inevitable and co-terminus with a civilisational state. Admittedly measurement of any link between civilisation and the discipline of economics is a challenge and is a subject of future works of scholars. But the correlation is palpable. And that to us is what matters.

Do economists comprehend this tectonic shift in the field of geo-politics which is directing the rise of civilisational economics? But for that to happen the guild of economists probably must do some serious introspection on their very functioning. For starters, is classical economics still alive? Is modern economics overemphasising on something what the classical economists refused to do? Is big money influencing economic research? Are economists the root cause of flawed policy construct? Or is it something bigger? Is the lure of big money holding them back from genuine researches? Why do economists with great pedigree often fail to see the writing on the wall, especially on boom and doom? Crucially, is the discipline of economics itself imploding under the weight of its own internal contradictions? Since economists themselves will not answer some of these inconvenient questions, let us attempt it for them.

Blurring of lines between Economics and Finance

Incidentally, the answer to these questions came from the most unexpected quarter – an American documentary movie titled *Inside Job*. There is a compelling lesson in this. When one fails to introspect his own repeated failures, others will necessarily do it. And when others do it, it will surely sound harsh. *Inside Job* is no exception to this maxim. Directed by Charles Ferguson, *Inside Job* is a critical analysis about the 2008 financial crisis that erupted in the US and ended up as global economic crisis. According to Ferguson, the movie is about "the systemic corruption of the United States by the financial services industry and the consequences of that systemic corruption." The operating word is corruption. The movie was critically acclaimed, and it won the Academy Award for Best Documentary Feature, popularly called as the Oscar Awards in 2010. The documentary has raised some fundamental questions that continue to haunt us even to this date. As mentioned above, these questions should have been raised and answered by the economists themselves. For starters: what is the link between the world of finance and economics? Or, are they two sides of the same coin? How and why did the American financial crisis metamorphose into a global economic crisis?

To comprehend this, we must appreciate the fundamental difference between a financial crisis and an economic crisis. Technically, a financial crisis is a situation whereby the value of financial assets falls rapidly. On the other hand, when a country itself experiences a sudden downturn in overall economic activities including fall in manufacture, employment or services, it is said to be in an economic crisis. Put simply, financial crisis by itself may only affect the financial and banking sectors whereas any economic crisis affects all economic activities in an economy including the financial sector. Traditionally, finance was a small but important sub-set of the world of economics. There was a thin but clear line of distinction between the world of finance and economics. However, over the years increased financialisation of the economy meant that finance no longer remained as a subset of the economy.

In due course, the world of finance began to dominate the world of economics so much so that over time economics became a sub-set of the world of finance. The thin line of censorious distinction that existed and practiced by both sides for time immemorial was not only erased, finance integrated economics and economics happily submerged into finance. It was a change that happened so rapidly that not many even realised the tectonic changes has already engulfed the discipline of economics with its attendant consequences. One of them being economics as a discipline came to be afflicted with the same vice as the profession of finance – the influence of big money. That ensured command performances, tailored reports and designer researches. With unlimited access to media, the world of finance ensured that even an ordinary research paper written by some could, if need be, become gospel overnight. A few economists fell for the trap and came out of their obscurity to occupy centre stage and limelight. The net result: economists began to peddle heavily in predictive modelling under an exceedingly rewarding and highly incestuous relationship with the world of finance. This was profitably used by the latter in making sentiments and marring markets. In the process the world of finance made money both ways. But this sounded the death knell for the reputation of economists. The world of economists was turned upside down; the hunter became the hunted.

The chaos in the US financial markets exposed the crisis of credibility amongst economists. That in brief is the story of the *Insider Job*. When Ferguson received the Oscar for best documentary, he observed: "Three years after a horrific financial crisis caused by massive fraud, not a single financial executive has gone to jail. And that's wrong." When asked specifically about the absence of prosecutions, senior officials in the Obama Administration gave evasive 'non-answers,' suggesting that nothing illegal occurred, or that investigations were continuing. Subsequently, only one Wall Street executive, Kareem Serageldin, went to jail in the aftermath of the financial holocaust. In 2013, he was sentenced to thirty months in prison. None of the major Republican candidates for the US presidency in 2008 and in 2012 have raised these issues at all. President Trump on assuming office in 2016 too has not seen any virtue in taking any action. Nor will anyone in future. The incestuous relationship extends beyond financial professionals and economists and obviously involves politicians too. The overwhelming evidence that Ferguson presents in his work is that over the last thirty years, the US financial sector has become a rogue industry that has gone berserk. The gravamen of Ferguson's charge is that as it grew exponentially, the US financial sector clinically subverted the political system, government institutions and regulators. 'Efficient Market Hypothesis' (EMH) and with it, 'Deregulation' as a core mantra became the accepted framework for policy framers within the government. Simply put, it is the withdrawal of most and if possible, all regulatory oversight mechanism by the government.

Ferguson argues that till the 1980s, a combination of tradition, reputation, and greater regulation relating to the compensation of bankers in fact prevented major systemic abuses. This is where the incest began. Many steps of the deregulatory process were cut under the suggestion of academic economists who steadfastly maintained that once freed from obsolete regulatory constraints, the financial world would automatically allocate the world's capital flows with unparalleled skill and precision. In fact, deregulation was suggested for all factors of production including labour. Economic models were prepared by the academia and hailed by the media. Simultaneously, beginning the 1980s, thanks to deregulation, the compensation practices underwent enormous changes to favour the financial sector. Excessively high salaries, obnoxious bonuses and benumbing perks ensured that the world of finance had a disproportionate influence on every institution, including the US Congress. Once US accepted an idea, it was a matter of time that it was accepted as a global order. Thereafter, some countries were cajoled by multilateral institutions, some accepted it as a matter of faith. Some were co-opted, by appointing keymen into important posts. Naturally, what was in quintessence financial crisis in the US, ultimately became a global economic crisis. The only saving grace for economists is that they were no exception to this corrosive influence of filthy lucre. This is the crisis within economics. The economic crisis, its causes, size and its debilitating impact across continents is secondary.

In sum, Ferguson's assertion that the profession's faith in markets – read deregulation – comes from the corrupting power of money. Yale Law professor Daniel Moskovitz also speculated that because American universities are funded by 'capital and finance,' they have bent the economics profession in a 'neo-liberal direction' – a charge that will continue to haunt the profession. By assuming that capital markets worked perfectly, did economists ignore on purpose the blatant risks in the financial sector? Did de-regulation lead to funding of academics? Or did such funding of academicians lead to deregulation? By playing ball with the US financial sector are some economists guilty of mis-selling the idea of EMH and deregulation?

Whatever be it, the profession of economists lost their independence and merged with the world of finance as they not only did not see the crisis coming, they positively denied the oncoming crisis. In one of the very few research papers on the issue, economist Luigi Zingales of Chicago University precisely pointed out the dark underbelly of economists by alleging that they have powerful incentives to generate theories and research that suit the powers that be. Or, if one can add, remain silent. Zingales adds, "The natural audience of their work outside of academia is either businesspeople or government officials applying some of that knowledge. The popularity and support among businesspeople or the government gives credibility to a piece of research and the person who did it." And it does not take someone special to point out what sells and how.

The lessons of 2008 economic crisis are compelling. And the coincidences are indeed remarkable. Yet, one cannot expect the economists themselves to come with a research paper establishing the link between 'funding received' and 'researches conducted or concluded.' And even if it is done it will be rightly accused of bias. In the absence of such a report, one cannot exonerate them either. Whatever be it, economists stand discredited before the entire world. Let us examine this in greater detail.

Where the Insider did not do his Job

Half-way around the globe, India may not be a witness to such brazen nexus between financial sector and economist-academia combine. Instead, India offered a unique solution to the entire problem faced by the world of finance. Unlike the finance professionals in the US who laboured for decades to get an insider do their job, in India's case, it was simple – the insider was required not do any job. If the American economy had an issue with the 'Insider Job,' the charge in the case of India is that the 'Insider' did not do his job. And the results were equally disastrous.

To explain what has been stated above let us decode the extant Non-Performing Asset (NPA) crisis that has been dynamiting the Indian banking sector for over a decade. Indian banks, under law are tightly regulated by the Reserve Bank of India. This is where things get intriguing. A 2012 Credit Suisse Report on top ten Indian corporate groups (Adani, Essar, GMR,

GVK, JSW, JPA, Lanco, Reliance ADA, Vedanta and Videocon) revealed the extent of the rot within the Indian banking system, and more particularly the laxity in RBI oversight. According to this Report, the aggregate debt to the above-mentioned ten select corporate groups had jumped five times since 2007. This equated to 13 percent of total commercial bank lending in India in 2012, and approximated to 98 percent of the banking system's net worth at that point in time. Again, this is not merely a case of crony banking alone. There is a question of competency if not integrity. The report also pointed out that four out of these ten group did not earn enough to pay their interest. Yet, they remained the biggest borrowers of the Indian banking system at that point in time. Due diligence? Banking oversight? Regulatory intervention? Well, all these were conspicuous by their absence. A repeat exercise conducted in 2013 by the very same Bank revealed that the financial position of these ten corporate groups had in fact worsened as compared to 2012 – overall debt of these groups increased in 2013; the debt increase was far higher than the concomitant asset increase and finally earnings of a majority of these ten corporate groups was not adequate to even pay interest costs. Even then the watchdogs refused to bark.

Meanwhile, another Credit Suisse Report of November 2012 had brought about the overall state of affairs of Indian corporates. According to a sample survey of about 3,700 companies (with an aggregate debt of approximately Rs 21 lakh crores at that point in time), earnings of 28 percent of the companies surveyed was insufficient to cover even their interest payment. Interestingly, 54 percent of the companies surveyed did not earn enough to cover their interest costs in four quarters of the previous eight. The report further estimates that 12-25 percent of the small and medium enterprises were under enormous financial stress. Alarmingly, the report concluded that the banks have been behind the curve on declaring such delinquent loans as non-performing and providing for the same in their accounts. Remember all this was in 2012. Independent assessment by various banking experts reveals that in 2008-2009, the share of corporate borrowing from the commercial banking sector was approximately 25 percent. In 2014-2015, it rose well over 35 percent. The world of finance was fully aware that most of it was stressed and sticky, except of course, those who mattered.

Now, all these were reported by a global bank operating in India. What did RBI, the regulator of banks, do? What was its official position? Not to be left behind by Credit Suisse, the RBI in September 2014 brought out a comprehensive analysis of the performance of 2,854 listed non-government non-finance companies for the year 2013-2014. Accordingly, aggregate sales growth of these corporates declined in 2013-2014 as did the net profit margins when compared to 2012-2013. What is galling is that the net profit growth of these 2,854 companies was -16.8 percent for 2011-2012, -2 percent for 2012-2013 and -5.1 percent for 2013-2014. As compared to 2007-2008 when the net profit margins of these corporates were 11 percent, the corresponding figure for 2013-2014 was a mere 5.8 percent – a near 50 percent drop in a span of a few years. All these points out to a massive drop in the profitability of the Indian corporates, well known and documented even by the regulator, RBI, in the instant case. And pray what did the RBI do? Why did it not follow up with the banks on identifying and providing for such delinquent loan? Crucially, who was at the helm of affairs at the RBI then? Who was the insider who was not doing his job? A billion-dollar question indeed.

The answer to this question will stun everyone. The person at the helm of affairs during those heady days was Dr Raghuram Rajan, who had an impeccable academic record, especially when it came to banking. Dr Rajan shot to fame when he warned about the increasing risks in the US financial system at the 2005 Federal Reserve annual Jackson Hole conference. And when the financial crisis did explode in 2008, Dr Rajan's warnings, which were contrarian to the mainstream thinking at that point in time, came to be viewed as prophetic. An economist from the Chicago university, he received his PhD in 1991 for his thesis titled *Essays on Banking*. In 2003, Dr Rajan received the inaugural Fischer Black Prize, given every two years by the American Finance Association (another piece of evidence of how the world of finance began to shepherd and hand-hold the thinking of young economists) to an economist younger than 40 who has made the most significant contribution to the theory and practice of finance. Subsequently, his book *Fault Lines: How Hidden Fractures Still Threaten the World Economy*, won the Financial Times Business Book of the Year award in 2010. In 2016, he was named by Time in its list of the '100 Most Influential People in the World.' Interestingly, what should not be lost in the melee is that he was extensively interviewed for the award-winning documentary *Inside Job*.

Therefore, it was perfectly in order that in 2007, the Planning Commission drafted Rajan to write a report proposing the next generation of financial sector reforms in India. A high-level committee on Financial Sector Reforms was constituted consisting of twelve members, with Dr Rajan as its chairman. The committee, in its report titled *A Hundred Small Steps*, recommended broad-based reforms across the financial sector, arguing that instead of focusing on a few large, and politically controversial steps, India must "take a hundred small steps in the same direction." In a remarkable coincidence, it was precisely at the same point in time that the Indian banking industry had begun its lending binge to the favoured ten corporate group. In 2008, the then Indian Prime Minister Dr Manmohan Singh appointed Dr Rajan as an honorary economic adviser and subsequently, in August 2012, Dr Rajan was appointed as chief economic adviser to India's Ministry of Finance, only to be elevated as Governor of RBI in 2013, a post which he occupied till 2016.

Dr Rajan had a brilliant academic background and as pointed out was probably one of the very few who stunned the world with his prediction about the 2008 financial crisis. Since 2007, he was well connected with the Indian establishment and more particularly, the Indian financial system. For nearly a decade, till he demitted the office of the Governor of RBI, Dr Rajan strode the Indian financial scene like a colossus. With such an illustrious academic and post-academic background, Dr Rajan was the archetypal insider who probably knew every development in the world of finance and economics. As an advisor to the then Prime Minister, Dr Rajan could have been the first to know of the emerging skew in the Indian banking system even as ten corporate groups were beneficiaries of a lax banking system. Yet, he did not prevent the seeds of NPA crisis being sown between 2008 and 2012. Surely, he as chief economic advisor could not have been oblivious to what was public knowledge in 2012 through the Credit Suisse report. Yet, he did not react. And finally, he as RBI Governor could not be seen ignorant to the RBI's own assessment of the state of financial affairs of major corporate borrowers in 2013-14. Yet, he chose to remain silent. And when he sought to act, it was a classic case of too little, too late. In hindsight, it would seem that it is precisely at this point in time several 'high-flyer' borrowers were literally toying within the Indian banking sector, even as RBI the regulator failed – a failure that continues to cost Indian economy to this date and probably well into the foreseeable future.

Why did Dr Rajan the man who foresaw the 2008 economic crisis in 2005 failed to see the build-up of Indian NPA crisis even as he was at the wheels for nearly a decade. Yet, he is christened 'Rockstar Economist' by the Indian media even to this date, and his tenure uncritiqued. Is that the power of the financial world and its hold over the media? Is that how formidable reputations are built and built for some oblique purposes? Questions that beg answers. But all this is secondary. What is relevant here is that Dr Rajan was the quintessential finance man who was marketed as a 'Rockstar Economist' who failed in his duty to prevent the NPA crisis. This is a classic case of the insider not doing his job even as economics merged into finance. It is a merger that will haunt Indian and global economy even in the distant future.

The Hydraulic Pressure of Financial Flows

Before anyone concludes that all these were restricted to the rarefied world of economists, let us assure them it is not. In fact, media, academicians, thinkers, writers, editors, NGOs, bureaucrats, accountants, advocates and of course politicians had to necessarily fall in line to the calculated takeover of the discipline of economics by the world of finance. Nothing would illustrate this fact better than the dramatic rise of an economist in a poor third world country into a successful politician in a span of three decades. To plot his successful rise, let us revisit the formation of a little-known private think-tank formed over three decades ago, probably in the late 1980s.

The South Commission, the little-known private think tank in question, was formally established in 1987 following years of informal discussion among intellectual and political leaders from the South – a shorthand for the developing countries or Third World countries as it was popularly called then. It was made up of individuals – a sort of a think-tank – from various developing countries acting in their personal capacity. It has its origins in the recognition that developing countries have many problems and experience the same in common, but that no singular institution within the developing country was responsible for looking at these things in a comprehensive manner, or at the lessons about appropriate development strategies which could be drawn from them. Further, it was feared that none of the developing countries knew what was going on in other developing countries, what were the ideas of its people, what was its potential and the manner in which co-operation amongst developing countries could widen development options for all countries. The idea was obviously to learn from the mistakes of the other and to benefit from the experience of their successes.

The 1990 report of this South Commission notes that "A prominent feature of the last two decades has been the increasing globalization of the world economy, particularly of production and finance. The role of transnational companies has grown. Take-overs and mergers of companies across national boundaries have multiplied, helped by the explosive growth of international private financial flows." These observations need to looked in to the context of the relentless march of the financial world since the 1970s which began to accelerate by early 1990s backed partly by fall of the Soviet Union, some by multilateral institutions like the IMF and the World Bank and the others, of course by academicians. This was three decades ago when probably globalisation was still in its infancy. That was the time when several countries including India had not opened their economy. Even at that early stage the report prophetically warned of the downsides of allowing unregulated financial flows, both inwards and outwards into a country. And since the report, the global economy has been a mute witness to two major economic crisis – the Asian currency crisis, and of course, the 2008 financial crisis in the US, not to mention a host of other financial crisis cause by unbridled financial flows. We had already dealt with the Asian currency crisis in detail in Chapter 6. We are dealing with the second crisis in this chapter. That in more ways than one demonstrates the scholarly approach of the persons who authored this report.

More to the point, the authors of the report were worried about the debilitating impact of unregulated flow of finance that could eventually lead to the flow of capital from the capital starved South to the developed countries. We had dealt with the issue of "capital flowing uphill" in previous chapters in the context of how US trade deficit is being counterbalanced by gargantuan capital flows from developing countries. It is in this connection the report adds "The spread of the deregulation of financial movements and electronic trading in developed countries has opened the way for massive transfers of funds and trading in securities-stocks and shares, bonds and other financial instruments-among the major financial centres as well as facilitated capital flight from the South. Private financial flows have become a substantial multiple of world merchandise trade. These very large cross-border movements of assets tend to cause more frequent shifts in exchange and interest rates, affecting the competitive position of individual countries." In short, the report warns of financial flows, especially outbound investments from developing countries, being a "substantial multiple" of the merchandise trade and the consequential debilitating effect it can have on the economy.

The world is witness to several events since the report sought to forewarn us in 1990, for if there is one economic idea in recent history that has captured the imagination of the people across continents, it has been globalisation. To a common man, it implied cross-border flow of various means of production viz., men, materials, technology, and of course capital. But in practice, cross-border movement of all means of production became irrelevant except capital. Globalisation, shorn of its veneer, was in fact a frantic search for highest returns by the finance world for its capital. The world of economists rationalised it as EMH. Some rationalised it as inevitable. Others welcomed it. This sudden entry and abrupt exit of foreign capital caused substantial changes in ownership status of domestic firms. Further, such movement impacted macroeconomic variables such as money supply, inflation, currency valuation and of course interest rates.

This impact on ownership and macroeconomic variables explains the obsession of the financial world with free movement of capital. This results in making and marring markets. Consequently, economies gyrate further, and a volatile market lends itself for further manipulation. And that feeds on the rapacious appetite of this cabal. Despite all these, the free flow of capital from one country to the other is often explained by economists as a logical and natural consequence of how money would flow to places which maximise rewards and minimise the risks! Economists had eventually distorted the study of economic phenomenon by turning the cause into effect and effect into cause.

Now, who was the author of this prophetic report who warned us against the negative impact of surges in financial flows? Who was the person sagaciously warning the world of the perils of financial flows? It was, believe it or not, Dr Manmohan Singh, the then Secretary General of South Commission. This was Dr Singh the economist and well before his entry into active politics. Paying rich encomiums to the contribution of Dr Singh, the then Chairman of the Commission Julius Kambarage Nyerere stated "We in the Commission have reason to express our own heavy debt to the individuals who have constituted our Secretariat, and the team they became under the exemplary leadership of our fellow-member Dr Manmohan Singh." That was in 1990. Too much water has flown through the Ganga since then.

To comprehend what has been discussed here the contents and emphatic assertions contained in the South Commission Report needs to be contrasted with the address by Dr Singh to the nation immediately after assuming the office of the Prime Minister of India in June 2004. Outlining the approach of his government to globalisation Dr Singh opined "We will pursue policies that enable our economy to be better integrated with the world economy without hurting the interests of our people." Circumspection that was the hallmark of the South Commission Report had indeed given way to some brazenness. Likewise, when asked as to what was the message that he would like to give 'global managers' about India, Dr Singh in an interview in January 2006 said: "If I have any message, it is that it is our ambition to integrate our country into the evolving global economy. We accept the logic of globalisation. We recognise that globalisation offers us enormous opportunities in the race to leapfrog in development processes." Suddenly on assuming the office of the Prime Minister of India, Dr Singh saw virtues in integrating the Indian economy with the global economy – a virtue that he did not see as the Secretary-General of the South Commission. Ironically, the ideas of Dr Singh the Prime Minister were not seemingly in consonance with the ideas of Dr Singh, the Secretary-General of the South

Commission. It is often remarked that where you stand on various issues depends on where you sit. Dr Singh was no exception to this maxim. Here was an insider who knew the job fully well, yet he refused to do it.

Further, since 1991, the Indian economy underwent a series of liberalisation. Outbound Indian FDI too were permitted subject to certain stringent conditions as part of our new economic policies. But under the Manmohan Singh administration the outbound FDI was substantially liberalised in 2005 to four hundred percent of the net-worth of the investing Indian company. Consequently, till 2004-05, India's annual outbound FDI was negligible – a mere $2 billion of outbound debt and equity was reported in that year. However, since 2005-06, the position turns dramatically when $7.8 billion as debt and equity was invested by Indian businesses outside India through this route. Subsequently, $13.30 billion was invested in 2006-07, $18.50 billion in 2007-08, $18.60 billion in 2008-09, $13.60 billion in 2009-10, $16.8 billion in 2010-11, and $8.9 billion in 2011-12. In short, in the seven years between 2005-06 and 2011-12, India's outbound FDI had been approximately a whopping $100 billion! This is indeed scandalous for a country that struggled to get $10-15 billion as inward FDI into India at that point in time. Recall that flight of capital from developing country to the developed is precisely what the South Commission Report had prophetically warned.

Dr Singh's ultimate tryst with the financial sector came in March 2006 when he sought for full capital account convertibility (CAC) of the Indian currency. CAC, it may be noted is the end-game in financial sector deregulation, and as experiences of the East Asian currency crisis demonstrated, fraught with extreme risks. With several vulnerabilities, India could ill-afford to allow free convertibility of her currency. In this connection, he observed: "There is merit in moving towards fuller capital account convertibility within a transparent framework. Our own position, internally and externally, has become far more comfortable. I have requested the Finance Minister and the Reserve Bank to revisit the subject and come out with a roadmap on capital account convertibility based on current realities." One wonders, how could Dr Singh, the author of the South Commission Report, and who had forewarned about the negative impact of such deregulation prescribe the ultimate deregulation for India? The honest assessment of several well-meaning economists is that India, even a decade and half later in 2020, is not prepared for CAC. Then, what was the compulsion for Dr Singh to toy with an outlandish idea that was bound to be a non-starter?

Interestingly, at the peak of the global financial crisis in 2008, the very same Dr Singh who advocated CAC in 2006, instantly sought to insulate the Indian economy "to the maximum possible" extent. No one in India took such observations of the then Prime Minister seriously. This volte-face by Dr Singh – first, from pointing out to the downsides of financial flows in 1990 to next, seeking greater integration of the Indian economy with global economy in 2004 as well as in 2006 and finally, seeking to insulate the Indian economy in 2008 is indeed a fascinating and compelling story in our macro-economic management. Economists largely depend on the willing suspension of disbelief by the gullible to explain their positions. Thus, for much of their legitimacy, economists have relied upon the blind faith of the masses. Dr Singh, the economist, is no exception. Did the economist Dr Singh not know of the consequences? Or was Dr Singh, the Prime Minister, under some compulsion? Was Dr Singh like Dr Rajan, the consummate insider who was feigning ignorance to global developments? It may be noted that both were economists of great repute. It was not a question of competency or the lack of it. It was something more. If so, what and why? We will answer this question shortly.

Where are Economists or Politicians in all this?

As discussed above, since the 1980s, there was a consistent move in US too in favour of successive rounds of deregulation, which ultimately led to the 2008 financial crisis. Big money manifesting through campaign contributions, ruthless lobbying and appointment of 'preferred' regulators in the aggregate explain the relentless drive by the financial sector towards financial deregulation. If the main cause of the 2008 financial crisis was deregulation in US, then responsibility for the crisis should lie squarely with politicians and regulators who decided to play ball by deregulating the financial system without supervising it closely. It was their decision and their responsibility. Or were they under some sort of compulsion? Was it a command performance? The Final report of the National Commission on the Causes of the Financial and Economic Crisis in the US brilliantly encapsulates the entire paradigm. It points out: "The sentries were not at their posts, in no small part due to the widely accepted faith in the self-correcting nature of the markets, and the ability of financial institutions to effectively police themselves. More than 30 years of deregulation and reliance on self-regulation by financial institutions, championed by former Federal Reserve chairman Alan Greenspan and others, supported by successive administrations and Congresses, and actively pushed by the powerful financial industry at every turn, had stripped away key safeguards, which could have helped avoid catastrophe. This approach had opened up gaps in oversight of critical areas with trillions of dollars at risk, such as the shadow banking system and over-the-counter derivatives markets. In addition, the government permitted financial firms to pick their preferred regulators in what became a race to the weakest supervisor." Obviously, it is not a case of policy or ideology that has gone bad but a typical case of a rigged casino.

But that was in 2011. The trillion-dollar question is whether we have learnt appropriate lessons arising out of this crisis? To do so would demand clinical diagnosis of a problem. When a crisis is explained by a mere occurrence of a highly improbable event, breakdown of economic mechanisms or factors beyond human control, our responses will be tailored accordingly. In fact, such events do not lend by itself for providing any humanly possible solutions. On the contrary, when a crisis is explained by human greed, regulatory failures and political decisions, our solutions obviously will be different. And since politics is manned by humans, there are significant lessons for us to handle future as well. For starters, deregulation, by complicit regulators, did not happen all by itself. It was a political decision, backed by academicians, endorsed by the multilateral agencies, hailed by the intellectual class and marketed with missionary zeal by the media. Why did successive US governments decide to deregulate the financial system in the first place? How was the bi-partisan support gathered for such acts? How did the support come from multilateral institutions? How did the system co-opt everyone? How and why did the sentinels go to sleep? Why did the watchdogs refuse to even watch, let alone bark? Finally, is deregulation the result of lobbying by the financial sector, and of revolving doors between Wall Street and Washington?

Economic researcher Marie Daumal, in a paper, brings the cosy relationship between the world of finance and politics, especially since the days of President Clinton. Daumal brings about the frightening fact that the dominance of the world of finance is so complete that even contrarian ideas are not welcome or for that matter discussed. For instance, Daumal points out that The Independent Evaluation Office (IEO) was established in 2001 by the IMF to conduct 'independent and objective' evaluations of IMF activities – a sort of internal peer review. In a 2011 report, the IEO explains why IMF failed to give a clear warning in the 2000s about the financial crisis. The IEO underlines that, during the period 2004-2007, the main message of the IMF was characterised by great confidence in the soundness of large financial institutions and endorsement of financial practices. Crucially, IEO Report finds that the IMF's ability to identify the risks was mainly hindered by 'a culture of groupthink,' implying that economists were afraid to express a view that was contrary to the mainstream or the majority. In general, dissenters were often treated like those boring old aunts at a family wedding. Obviously, contrarian views within this profession are systematically stymied. The dominant view among economists is that the market by itself is enough to stave off any serious problem in financial institutions. If this is a fundamental and a non-negotiable position, where is academic research in this? Where is intellectual rigour in all these? Nevertheless, this elevated economists into prophets. And when prophets failed, there was only doom and gloom.

As per IEO, the assumption was that the crisis, if at all, was unlikely to happen in advanced economies, as sophisticated financial markets can thrive safely with minimal regulations. These are fundamental assumptions governing the discipline of economics even today. And convenient one at that. Not many can question these assumptions, as no one wants to be a contrarian. Studies in the top five economic journals over time show that there has been a sharp fall in the replies, rejoinders, or comments to articles. After peaking in the 1960s, there has been a steady decline, indicating groupthink and homogenisation with the discipline. Even when questioned, there would be not much of answers forthcoming from anyone either. Those who question will be either co-opted or side lined. Of course, the question by itself will never be answered.

In a remarkable coincidence, even as India embraced liberalisation of her economy, the Democratic party in the US had undergone a conversion towards acceptance of free-market ideology. This conspiracy of coincidences never ceases to amaze us. Needless to emphasise, among other things, this included financial deregulation. During the 1992 presidential election, Bill Clinton ran as a New Democrat for more limited government. The Democratic Party in 1992 had stated that "we believe in free enterprise and the power of market forces." Wall Street deregulation was pushed by Clinton and his advisers Robert Rubin and Lawrence Summers – a step that ultimately led to the 2008 financial crisis. Both Rubin and Summers brought the Clinton administration and with it, the Democratic party closer to the financial sector than even the Republicans could ever fathom. Nonetheless, the party has been split on this issue since the 2008 financial crisis. Probably atoning for their lapses and wiser by experience, the Democrats had revised their position and emphatically conceded that "we will also vigorously implement, enforce, and build on President Obama's landmark Dodd-Frank financial reform law." Who said volte-face is the sole preserve of Dr Singh? The newly minted Democrats under President Obama, in 2016, opined: "We must tackle dangerous risks in big banks and elsewhere in the financial system." And in conclusion, they dramatically added: "Democrats will not hesitate to use and expand existing authorities as well as empower regulators to downsize or break apart financial institutions when necessary, to protect the public and safeguard financial stability."

Despite all this public posturing, in March 2018, in a rare demonstration of bipartisanship, 17 Senate Democrats voted with Republicans to once again dilute Dodd-Franck banking regulations. This underlines the divide in the party. In May 2018, 33 House Democrats voted for that bill. Daumal adds that it would be interesting to investigate why each of these legislators, 17 senators, and 33 representatives, voted in favour of a bill that eases regulations. As the Republicans go about deregulating the financial system once again in 2018, it raises the question why they want to do so. Crucially, why are some Democrats supporting? Remember, deregulation was promoted big time by Clinton only to be partially reversed by Obama. Trump is once again moved away from Obama towards Clinton. Is the world of finance ultimately bringing Trump and Clinton together all over once again? Is there an invisible hand that is at work? Democrats or Republicans, does it matter? That invisible hand would explain how obscure personalities are pitchforked into limelight, as advisors, regulators, ministers, or even heads of governments.

Therefore, in the big bad world of finance nothing or no one matters. To it, the ideological difference in the approach to economics between economists, academicians and political parties is a minor irritant. All these can be counter-balanced by lobbying, political contributions, media, and of course by academia itself. For instance, The Centre for Responsive Politics collects data on federal campaign contributions. According to data compiled and published in public domain, the financial sector has been the single largest source of campaign contributions to federal candidates, since 1992. Data that is available demonstrate that the amount of campaign contributions has greatly increased since 1992, from $126 million in 1992 to $1.1 billion in 2016. This massive contribution by itself makes them indispensable to the political parties. Further scrutiny reveals that on most occasions, Republicans received more money than the Democrats. In 2012, there was a huge shift of finance sector money to the GOP which received nearly two-thirds of its contributions. Obviously, Dodd-Franck along with other pro-regulation sentiment within the Democratic Party led to the reduction of contributions from the financial sector to the Democrats. In this murky world, if gratification is instantaneous, so is chastisement. In 2016, once again when Hilary Clinton was the candidate of the Democrats, she was widely expected to have adopted a pro-deregulation position, parity was immediately restored. While Americans are divided along party lines, ideologically and on the basis of personalities, it is apparent that the financial sector had 'purchased options' on the success of either Hilary or Trump. For the world of finance, the political success of Trump or Hillary does not matter. Or for that matter the advice of Dr Bhagwati or Dr Singh as Prime

Minister of India or elevation of Dr Rajan as Governor of RBI. It would seem that each one of them is play acting in this charade.

There is another interesting data that Daumal presents – the challenge arising out of 'Revolving Doors.' The revolving door is the shift in roles of a person back and forth as legislator and regulator to the industries affected by such legislation and regulation. For instance, Daumal points out that Robert Rubin served as Treasury Secretary during the Clinton Administration. He is credited with leading the charge in the Democratic Party to embrace the deregulation of Wall Street. Before his government service (1995-1999), he spent 26 years at Goldman Sachs. Henry Paulson served as Treasury Secretary during the GW Bush administration. Before his government service (2006-2008), he spent 32 years at Goldman Sachs. Steven Mnuchin has been Treasury Secretary since 2017 in the Trump administration. Before his service, he spent 17 years with Goldman Sachs. Many Secretaries of the Treasury (Brady, O'Neill, Snow, Geithner and Lew) joined private equity firms in Wall Street after their service as Secretary. Likewise, the United Nations committee on the crisis led by Nobel laureate Joseph Stiglitz pointed out that regulatory capture occurred through the realm of ideas, rather than mere lobbying for a specific cause. It also reiterated the risks posed by the revolving doors between the world of academia, government, and investment banks. Bush, Clinton, or Trump it would seem that the Treasury Secretary was always from Goldman Sachs. The unsaid portion is that there was no global order; at best there were orders from the world of finance that were carried out globally. Does all these explain why sentinels were at sleep, not only in the US but even in distant India? Is it now clear why no one of great significance has been jailed in the aftermath of the 2008 financial crisis?

There is an important lesson to be drawn from all this. Capital, as we have seen in the previous chapters flows 'uphill,' from the poor developing countries to the rich developed countries. This is yet another imbalance within the global economies that resulted in several imbalances. This imbalance needs to be addressed. This imbalance has not happened spontaneously. This is definitely not EMH at work. This is voodoo economics (however, with due respect to John Perkins, EMH was marketed by various Economic Hit

Men – EHM!) Naturally, it requires a good number of managers, regulators, politicians and of course, economists. All of them need to fall in line in substantial measure by bringing in appropriate policies and administering them or looking at the other way. Of course, global capital neither respects economists nor politicians. But it requires them in abundant measure. If we assume that our elected representatives and economists are contestants in a gladiatorial contest debating with each other for our betterment, we are wrong. If we assume that they are batting for us, again our assumption is flawed. They are at best cheerleaders in a huge stadium, and unabashedly so, in front of a global audience. But pray who are contestants? Well, it is a no contest. The world of finance has ensured that it has none. Needless to reiterate, economists and politicians, Tweedledum or Tweedledee, do not matter in all this.

But What about Economics itself?

Economics, from time immemorial, has always been a dismal science. It was never intended to be colourful. But that is what it had come to be after being subsumed by the world of finance. It tried for a genetic makeover and it failed. With focus from the media, adulation from the public, recognition from those in power and money from the world of finance, the discipline of economics came under unprecedented public glare since the 1990s. When the going was good, it basked in its own glory. In this, most of what the economists spoke and wrote till 2008 was never questioned. On the contrary, some of them celebrated without anyone critiquing them. In those heady days, economics, had been elevated into an exact science. It is this fixation with science (and mathematics) that eventually has resulted in its downfall. As briefly pointed out in Chapter 5, as economic theory increased its mathematical sophistication, economic modelling became extremely complex. As complexity increased, the need for much powerful machines too increased. Economists felt they had arrived at their destination point. In the process, no one could introduce additional variables, especially those that were hard to measure or compute. Economic debates had well and truly become economical about fuzzy logic. For these reasons, not only did economics disregard culture as a factor influencing economic theories, but as economists became more self-confident, expressing themselves through mathematics, economists often dismissed culture as an innocent malleable idea. Mathematics, computing, and modelling made economics a precise science. At least so assumed the economists.

In an excellent 2006 summary of the study of culture in economics, Guiso, Sapienza, and Zingales point out that the increasing use of mathematics meant that qualitative variables such as culture were neglected in economic analysis. This was not accidental. On the contrary, these were the natural outcome of a defined process. "Not only did economics lose interest in its relation with culture, but as economics became more self-confident in its own capabilities, it often sought to explain culture as a mere outcome of economic forces," wrote Guiso, Sapienza, and Zingales. The reason for the same is stunning. Is not Marxism mirroring certain ideas of these economic theories? We have dealt with this idea in Chapter 3. "This movement, which is mostly associated with the Chicago School, is Marxian in spirit, but with no trace of class struggle. On the contrary, the Chicago School pursues a rational Marxian agenda, where people's beliefs, tastes, and values are individual or societal rational choices, and any element of conflict can be resolved through the price system." If man is assumed to be an animal, and if he is expected to behave only in a particular manner, any economic theory made with such a flawed assumption is bound to struggle in real-life situations. Marxism failed because of this fundamentally flawed economic thinking. So has unregulated market economics.

Economist William Pearse puts it succinctly "Economists, so the story goes, had successfully grasped the essence of human behaviour: rational, and therefore, highly predictable. With this discovery, an age-old question whose answer for millennia had eluded humanity was finally laid to rest. Where philosophers, psychologists, and sociologists had failed, economists had struck gold. They had cracked it. As a result, imperfect theories – as economic theories inherently are – started to be treated as laws of nature, like facts, and confidence among economists erred towards hubris." Hubris, it was, that eventually caused the downfall.

What followed was even worse. Following the crash, economists were expected to take centre stage and steer the global economy towards recovery.

On that front too, they failed, as we will see shortly. For nearly a decade after the crisis, economists are in a state of denial, and those who are not, are unable to come out with any meaningful solution to move forward. Crisis or no crisis, in response to many of the challenges faced by mankind, the foremost one being inequality, the discipline of economics has always remained wanting. The net result: reliance on their theories is withering, and general trust in their practice has waned.

One of the biggest theories on which the consensus of the modern economists rested is the 'rational expectations model,' implying that the markets were capable of self-correction. This, in turn, provided the intellectual basis for 'light touch regulation,' that is, left to themselves, markets have the power to auto-correct, and any state or regulatory intervention can be counter-productive. Why did this model fail? The answer is simple. The model relies on simplistic assumptions and has not been able to respond to real-life complexities. The model collapses when one of the fundamental assumptions of the model is disturbed or taken away, or when there is some external instability. It is not that economists did not know the downsides of their theories – what they did was to side-step the problem by simplifying assumptions. Nevertheless, extraordinary care was taken to brilliantly package these theories, present it suavely, and of course explain it through inscrutable aphorisms.

"If you homogenise all individuals and commodities in aggregate models, it is mathematically easy to build stability into the defining equations as a pure assumption," wrote the Harvard Business School scholar Jonathan Schlefer in his 2012 book on the subject *The Assumptions Economists Make*. "But it is a pure assumption. If you want, you can just as easily build instability into the model's defining equations." Schlefer's provides several such examples where economists have chosen to just ignore real-life quandaries or have ruled them out through gross assumptions. The problem with economists is not that they make assumptions. After all, any theory or model will have to rely on simplifying assumptions, as Schlefer too acknowledges. But when critical assumptions are made just to circumvent well-identified complexities in the quest to build elegant theories, such theories will simply end up being elegant fantasies! EMH was one of them.

Dynamic Stochastic General Equilibrium (DSGE) is yet another economic macro-economic model that has come in for greater scrutiny. DSGE attempts to explain economic phenomena, such as economic growth and business cycles, and the effects of economic policy, through econometric models based on applied general equilibrium theory and micro-economic principles. DSGE, over time, became the new workhorses of macro-economics, as they have been defined, and widely adopted by various central banks. But now, we realise that the model suffers from a fatal flaw. Their micro-foundations are hardly compatible with several real-life situations including credit cycles and financial dislocations. Neglect of uncontrollable variables became part of macro-economic modelling. As did risks arising from the world of finance.

Obviously, all this created consternation even within the close network of economists. For instance, *The Economist* in 2009 observed that Robert Lucas, hailed as "one of the greatest macro-economists of his generation," and his followers are "making ancient and basic analytical errors all over the place." It further commented that Harvard's Robert Barro, another towering figure in the discipline, is "making truly bone-headed arguments." And *The Economist* concludes that "The past 30 years of macro-economic training at American and British universities were a costly waste of time." Speaking at a conference at the London School of Economics (LSE), Paul Krugman and William Buiter of the LSE respectively indicated that the world economic crisis is a crisis of economics too. In the last of his Lionel Robbins lectures at the LSE, Krugman caustically observed that most macro-economics of the past 30 years was "spectacularly useless at best, and positively harmful at worst." Why did the discipline of economics come to this pass? One must understand that most such reactions were probably exaggerated in the aftermath of the 2008 crisis. Therefore, to quote all this as gospel or clinical analysis of the discipline of economics, on the whole, may be uncharitable. But one must hasten to concede that the discipline of economics has been having certain structural and fundamental flaws in its approach for the past few decades. It is indeed missing something vital and fundamental. In its anxiety to be seen as an exact science, it is reducing every phenomenon into a mathematical model – and ignoring those influences which cannot be subjected to mathematical modelling – using advanced computing techniques. Obviously, it is guilty of over-simplification of some issues, and unnecessary complications of others. In the process, it has possibly boxed itself to ridicule, if not complete irrelevance.

What about My Money, Our Money

But why are we getting enmeshed in macro-economics, that too at the global level? How are these recent developments in global economics affecting us? Why should we be concerned about the financialisation of economics? Why are we concerned about the ethics, or the lack of it, among economists? The answer to this is simple. What is being discussed here is not merely theoretical economics, but involves my money and of course your money too. The increased financialisation of the global economy has hooked us all in one way or the other into the world of finance. We are all innocent onlookers in this fascinating game – a game being played with only our earnings, our savings, our money. We better be concerned about a game where faceless managers of our own finances have a first right on the upsides that it generates, and we, to every downside. All of us, without any exception, have been sucked into this vortex. Do we realise the world of finance itself has undergone genetic modifications? Do we realise that we must face all its consequences – the bad and the ugly? People, for instance, no longer park their savings in bank deposits alone. Banks, in turn, no longer characterise themselves as commercial bankers, as they did traditionally. Over the years, they have metamorphosised into investment bankers with a wide range of exotic financial services. Some of these are incomprehensible even to finance professionals. Some are highly risky. Of course, it is played with our money. Apart from banks, we have a wide range of mutual funds and stock markets to invest, which carry their own inherent risks, multiplied manifold with lax regulators or soft-touch regulations. Then comes the opportunity of investing in derivatives (Warren Buffet called them weapons of mass financial destruction), which are a class in themselves. In this grand sweep, no one is spared. The traditionally under-banked poor have suddenly been included in this all-encompassing idea. Greater financialisation is argued to be integral to not just growth, but 'inclusive growth' – the new mantra.

The explanation is that it allows the poor to enter into financial transactions efficiently, while simultaneously expanding their investment horizon. Likewise, insurance penetration of both life and property has increased dramatically worldwide. This has ensured insurance companies access to a greater share of our income and savings. Naturally, the solvency of insurance companies and their efficiency in providing reasonable returns is assuming greater attention.

These have profound implications for the way markets operate. Life Insurance Corporation of India (LIC), for instance, has more money in its portfolio than say State Bank of India (SBI), the largest commercial bank in India. Naturally, the financial health of LIC is of more concern then even the SBI. And in all these, we rely on the ethics of the borrower, men who run these institutions, internal systems, rating agencies, analysts, independent directors, auditors, regulators, economists, and of course politicians to make appropriate steps to safeguard our money. And should any of them fail, as often they do, it is our money that is in peril. Worse still, in an interconnected market, a failure at a distant land can cause a downfall of markets across continents. The underlying fact in all these is that at every twist and turn, our money is increasingly handled by strangers, completely unregulated or handled by a soft-touch regulator. This is akin to the faceless unaccountable bureaucrat who handles public affairs (discussed in Chapter 7) – Faceless and unaccountable – a fact that unites governments and markets. There is another dimension to this issue. Much of the assets we buy today are those mortgaged to the world of finance. But in fact, that implies our future earnings are mortgaged. Either way, whether we lend our savings to the financial sector or borrow from it, we are in its collective hold. And should we, the borrower, fail the financial markets, the financial markets will fail us, the investor! We depend on our jobs to earn and subsequently pay back our borrowings – and our jobs are deeply integrated to the world of finance, one way or the other. And if the world of finance fails or its investment collapses, concomitantly, we the borrower fail to repay. This creates a domino effect. It is a spaghetti bowl out there – each leg of a transaction intertwined with the other. Consequently, the risks are not appropriately mapped, quantified, and addressed. The world of finance is sitting on the head of a volcano.

Technology too has played its part. The next quantum leap in the world of finance is the idea of digital money, which is now slowly replacing the physical money, fundamentally altering the way we view money itself. Some are seriously toying with digitalisation of their currency. Economic policies too have played their part. These include reducing cross-border capital controls and lax regulatory systems. Countries around the world, with more than a gentle nudge from multilateral financial institutions have embraced such friendly policies. Resultantly, global economies have repeatedly faced elevated solvency risks, currency risks, inflation risks, extreme volatility, contagion risks and sovereignty risk in the past three decades.

What is most distinctive about the present era of finance, however, is the shift in financial intermediation from banks and other institutions to financial markets – a shift from the 'visible hand' of relationship banking, to the axiomatic 'invisible hand' of supposedly anonymous, self-regulating financial markets. Investments in stocks, for instance, were originally driven by personal choices and preferences. The pension fund as well as insurance money all are being subjected to increasing financialisation, that is constantly in search of high- yielding investments (probably high-risk too), of course with the aid of 'soft touch' regulators. With the advent of the mutual fund industry, stock markets are subject to the inclinations of the fund managers; its gyrations subject to their mood swings. With index-based trading, the age-old industry or company-wise evaluation has given way to a simple analysis – will the index rise or fall! Shareholder wealth maximisation has become a new mantra, which rationalises every act by the world of finance. Even reckless speculation, of course sanctified by economic theories, became perfectly acceptable. The ascendancy of 'shareholder value' as a sole determinant of corporate governance is a façade to cover the growing dominance of capital market financial systems over traditional bank-based financial systems. This displacement of financial institutions by financial markets has an all-pervasive influence on the motivations, choices and decisions made by households, firms, and states as well as fundamental impact on growth, inequality, and poverty – all of which we are only beginning to understand only now. And these are having profound implications on the state of play of the national and international politics.

Most importantly, 'financialisation' in the end has resulted in a marked shift away from manufacturing to financial markets within an economy. It is this shift – read imbalance – that is coming to haunt us.

Economists, as pointed out earlier, were either oblivious to all these developments or were party to the run-up to this crisis. Likewise, they had very little to offer on the road to recovery. The decade following the crisis has been marked by rising inequalities in income and wealth, unprecedented levels of indebtedness, and mounting uncertainty about macro-economic stability. The crisis of economics and the economic crisis have now spilled over and become a major political issue within every nation. Even as there are extraordinary risks that are building within the national economy, the question that needs to be asked: what will happen to our savings and our wealth in the interregnum? Is it safe? Is it secure?

To answer this, a brief reference to the global debt position and the build-up of this debt, is inevitable. The Institute of International Finance (IIF) is a Washington-based institution that has been collating data about global debt. The IIF declares in its official website that it is the global association of the financial industry, with more than 450 members from more than 70 countries. Its mission is to support the financial industry in the prudent management of risks; to develop sound industry practices; and to advocate for regulatory, financial and economic policies that are in the broad interests of its members and foster global financial stability and sustainable economic growth. IIF members include commercial and investment banks, asset managers, insurance companies, sovereign wealth funds, hedge funds, central banks, and development banks. According to IIF, the global debt exceeded $255 trillion by end-2019, which according to it stood at a staggering 322 percent of the global GDP. This debt is $87 trillion more than what it was in 2008. By end-2020, it was $281 trillion and set to rise in 2021. It is now estimated that for every one dollar rise in global GDP results in more than five dollars of global debt. This debt has been sustained by artificially supressing interest rates. A sharp contraction in corporate earnings and mounting job loss is already exacerbating the debt service burden for businesses and households. This coupled with aggressive fiscal responses to the tepid economic growth by various governments has already caused an explosion in global debt which includes private, corporate and public borrowings. Remember, we are both lenders to and borrowers of this debt. As borrowers, we have the luxury of throwing up our hands, as lenders too, we may also have to do that, but with despair.

One of the crucial yet under-debated reasons for the tepid economic growth is the increasing burden of global private debt – the combination of business debt and household debt. The promised green shoots, visible only to the eyes of the economists every spring, refuses to grow. Even though government debt for some strange reason grabs all the headlines, private debt is larger than government debt and has more negative impact on economic outcomes. When private debt is high, households and businesses must divert an increased portion of their income to paying interest on that debt. Consequently, they spend and invest less. Moreover, the repayment of the principal portion stunts the cash flow. Naturally, as private debt reaches such high levels, demand begins to get suppressed. It is for this reason that the interest rates were lowered by the central banks in the first place as a response to the 2008 financial crisis. Lower rates may help but do not solve their financial stress, especially in cases where there is not much increase in incomes. In hindsight, lowering interest rates were akin to providing a simple pain balm where perhaps a treatment like chemotherapy is needed.

Moreover, extraordinary high private debt contributes to lower rates by reducing demand for credit itself, a fact lost on many. Highly leveraged balance sheets do not have the ability to either attract capital or further debt, or both. Lenders and investors are chary of such balance sheets. This in turn stymies growth. What is galling is that the world has now reached a point where combined global government and private debt to GDP is the highest by far in recent history. And the debt of all three sectors – government, household and corporates individually too stand at a historical high. To be honest, we are at an unprecedented, epochal time. Politicians are unlikely to provide solutions. Economists do not have one. In the absence of an alternative, we will almost certainly continue down this path, not knowing when to de-leverage and how.

Importantly, the spectacular rise in the global debt implies that we are a wink away from yet another economic crisis – and this time it will be a full-blown debt crisis. It is evident that the assets backing these debts are not generating enough income to pay even the historically low rates of interest, not to speak of servicing the debt. If the problem is one of insolvency, injection of liquidity only postpones the day of reckoning. But that day of reckoning will arrive sooner than later.

One way out, as suggested by some experts, will be to convert a portion of this massive debt into equity. Debt for equity swaps, as a means of crisis resolution and greater recourse to risk sharing instruments, could probably help prevent future crises. That, experts argue, would also de-leverage the entire financial landscape. But to do so requires huge institutional framework, structural changes including change in ownership of firms. Besides this, there is something more fundamental – conversion of debt into equity is at best converting one form of investment into the other in paper. Will that ensure income generation from the very same asset to pay the interest, repay the debt and service the capital? After all, even after restructuring the quality of the asset remains the same. If it were that easy, people would have precisely done that. Obviously, it is not a workable solution in all cases, though, in some cases it may provide marginal relief. Therefore, the only alternative left out is large-scale debt restructuring or write-off, both of which will have direct consequences for all those whose savings are involved – that is you and me. The ants will continue to pay for the profligacy of the grasshoppers – as taxes as we saw in Chapter 7 and as debt write-offs, as we see in this chapter. There is one inherent danger: there is a distinct possibility that both the ants and the grasshoppers could very well be crushed by this mammoth debt.

Flawed Diagnosis; Wrong Remedy

In retrospect it would seem that the diagnosis of the 2008 financial crisis was fatally flawed as were the solutions proffered post-2008 crisis. The solutions merely postponed the economic apocalypse; it did not resolve the outstanding issues. They were superficial as well as temporary. Worse still, it contained the seeds of a greater financial crisis that is bound to make the 2008 crisis look like a trailer of a badly directed horror movie. At the core of the 2008 financial crisis was a defunct economic and financial ecosystem.

Bereft of the civilisational and cultural values, it resulted in the bankruptcy of the financial sector. Fundamental law of economics demands that the bad performers had to be punished. Instead, they were resurrected and rewarded. That, in short, is the story of the revival plan. Inexplicably, the crisis was diagnosed as a liquidity issue and was sought to be symptomatically treated by injecting extraordinary quantum of liquidity into the system. This artificial injection of liquidity solved the solvency issue temporarily, but neither did it help growth, employment or economic stability. Economic recovery looks fragile even a decade later. Critically, the underlying assumptions in economic theory post the crisis are the same as before the crisis; the players too more or less remain the same.

In the aftermath of the crisis, ultra-easy monetary policy soon became "the only game in town." Crucially, higher quantum of money made available by the central banks ensured that the interest rates declined to a point where there is virtually no interest cost. The impact of this requires some detailed explanation. At the core of the financial crisis, money was used to re-finance assets that were not yielding enough to pay back the interest and loans, especially in US. It may be noted that the decade leading to the crisis was a period of boom where the rest of the world were exporting goods to the US. In return the former unquestioningly accepted the currency of the latter viz., Dollar. This reflected in the spectacular growth of foreign exchange reserves of several countries. These reserves were once again lent to US which was the world's single largest borrower. Thus, the world in effect was financing the great American consumption and simultaneously producing it for their consumption. We had dealt with this aspect in earlier chapters. This is global imbalance – the mother of all economic imbalances spawned by the idea of globalisation. The world is paying a very heavy price for this arrangement.

With surplus money flowing into the US, the challenge was to utilise the money within US. This was done by first promoting the housing industry within the US. Secondly, with such a spectacular flow of easy money, virtually every Tom, Dick, and Harry became willy-nilly a borrower to purchase primarily his house or some other asset for that matter. Technological advancement ensured that at a click of a mouse, a loan virtually was a distinct possibility. That they had no job or that their earnings were insufficient to service the borrowings was of little consequence. Or the assets by itself would not yield enough to repay the borrowings. Thus, to begin with, the doubtful assets of Tom, Dick, and Harry, were mortgaged to the American financial sector. These were then subsequently bundled and even marketed to other financial players across continents as complex synthetic derivatives. In the resulting frenzy, no one realised they were in effect carrying the dubious assets of Tom, Dick, and Harry in their books. And if anyone unwittingly questioned, the rating agencies ensured that these loans were rated much higher than what they really were. As these borrowers were unable to pay back their debt obligations, the world of finance came to a screeching halt, resulting in the 2008 financial crisis.

Subsequently, the US Fed had to necessarily step in and was compelled to buy such dubious debts from the financial institutions. This injected enormous liquidity into the system and kick-started the stalled world of finance. But why did the Fed do this in the first place? Luigi Zingales points out an interesting event to explain the incestuous world of regulators, politicians and economists during this crisis too. According to him, regulators naturally rely on their network of trusted friends to gather information 'from the outside.' If everyone in that network is drawn from the same milieu, the information and ideas that flow to policy-makers will be severely limited. A revealing anecdote comes from a Bush treasury official, who noted that in the heat of the financial crisis, every time there was a phone call from Manhattan's 212 area code, the message was the same: "Buy the toxic assets." Such uniformity of advice makes it difficult for even the most intelligent or well-meaning policymakers not to be influenced. Everyone had to buy the toxic assets. That the US Fed has an unlimited power to issue dollars helped matters. Importantly, what went into the asset side of the US Fed's Balance Sheet (for the dollars issued by it) was the money owned by Tom, Dick, and Harry in the first place to the banks and other financial institutions. What they originally owed to the US financial institutions came to be owed subsequently to the US Fed. In effect, the original lender gave way to a new party viz the US Fed. The borrower and the asset, whose inability to repay was the cause of the mess in the first place, remained the same. Yet this shift was expected to solve the US financial crisis. Can something be more incestuous than this?

Put pithily, the US dollar came to be backed by assets of doubtful quality – of Tom, Dick, and Harry! And several central banks follow this idea – popularly called Quantitative Easing (QE) repeatedly since 2008 to tide over sticky borrowings of banks. This is how easy money began circulating world over resulting in the decline of the interest rates. But there is a crucial difference between the US dollar and other currencies; the dollar is the de-facto global currency. Why is it so? It faces a near perennial demand by other countries to maintain their foreign exchange reserves while other currencies do not enjoy this exalted status. Likewise, oil trade is denominated in dollars, ensuring a continuous demand for dollars. But there is something more. Some experts opine that the dollar is probably the only currency in the recent history to be backed by an army more than anything else. Thus, while QE did not result in runaway inflation in the US, as excess dollars were absorbed for the reasons mentioned above, other central banks could not imitate the policies of the Fed fully. Nevertheless, the bloating of the Balance Sheets of their respective central bank over the past decade is a case in point. It is obvious that their options are relatively narrower. Nevertheless, hooked on to this easy option, world over the central banks through QE have become the "weapons of mass protection" to counter the challenges posed by the "weapons of mass destruction." Central banks know for sure that their economy is on a tailspin. But they have no policy choice either. If they continue with the same set of policies, they are damned; if they do not, they are doomed. Capturing the entire fiasco, the then US President George W Bush said in an interview in 2008 that he abandoned free-market principles "to save the free-market system, to make sure the economy doesn't collapse." A stunning admission indeed. That marked the death of modern economics.

But the carcass remains. Experts now contend that the situation we face is arguably fraught with greater danger than was the case when the crisis first began. First, by encouraging the very same policies of credit and debt expansion, monetary policy has dug the hole still deeper. Repeatedly indulging in QE, the global debt has bloated. By March 2020, thanks to

Covid-19 QE limited of 2008 had become QE infinity. Obviously, the underlying vulnerabilities for the dollar are deep. The dollar might face a serious crisis sooner than later. This is a matter of concern to all watchers of the global economy, and to central banks in India and abroad. Secondly, interest rate often had a risk element, apart from rental equivalent for using money for a period. By successively lowering interest rates, central banks signalled that they were discounting potential future risks. But this was not market driven but was an administered rate. Seen from another perspective, low rates of interest indicate no great foreseeable economic risks even in distant future. And this policy stance by central banks, their macroeconomic risk assessment and pricing of future economic risks have resulted in interest rate rigging which have become a risk in itself. Commenting on this John Plender, a columnist in *Financial Times*, states "The risks have been building in the financial system for decades. From the late 1980s, central banks – and especially the Fed – conducted what came to be known as "asymmetric monetary policy," whereby they supported markets when they plunged but failed to damp them down when they were prone to bubbles. Excessive risk-taking in banking was the natural consequence." As interest rate pricing eliminated risks in the equation, massive debts were accumulated. This rise in global debt post crisis significantly increases the vulnerability of the global economy to any interest rate shocks. Paradoxically, the interest rates are lower in most countries than at any time since the 1970s. If rates continue to stay low because of tepid growth, this can undermine the creditworthiness of those with high debt levels and expose their vulnerability. And should rates rise, it could be economic equivalent of a nuclear holocaust.

As interest rates plummeted as explained above, investors have found it difficult to achieve positive yields in any of the traditional safe-haven investments. In fact, experiences suggest that lowering interest rate has been counter-productive in some cases. As returns from investments plummet, people save more to compensate for the fall in the interest rates. As will be seen below, a similar logic affects the behaviour of insurance and pension fund companies who have committed to providing annuities or those who offer defined benefit pensions. Life insurers, for example, struggle to meet their guaranteed rates of return. So do some pension funds. It is now no more the inter-generational imbalance as we discussed in the previous chapter – an imbalance of a different kind. It is a financial imbalance that is being created within our own life and of our own finances where we are in effect drawing our retirement money from our pension funds to keep ourselves going and the economy afloat for now. In the process, we are not only doing a great disservice to the next generation but also to our own future. When past is present, future is indeed tense.

Such a decline in portfolio returns is significant and has already led to certain reactions on the part of the insurance or pension funds which have been mostly affected. The response has been on predictable lines. Dividend pay-outs of insurance companies have been lowered. This being a capital-intensive industry, such interest rate declines make it difficult to raise successive rounds of capital. Who would knowingly invest in such businesses where income gets squeezed? And in extreme cases, companies have withdrawn from business lines that no longer seem possible thereby lowering choices for consumers. One seeming alternative is that some of these companies might gamble by substantially increasing their exposure to risky investments. Evidently, this is a possible outcome not just confined to insurance companies, but to all financial institutions who suffer income depression in an artificially depressed interest rate regime. As such desperate money chases stocks and other risky investments, as it did between 2015 and 2019, stock markets record spectacular rise. This is when the stock markets get too decoupled with the economic fundamentals and is purely driven by liquidity. Low interest rates have created a stock market boom (and at times, boom in real estate and commodities) without concomitant growth. This is yet another imbalance that needs to be addressed.

There is another issue, probably unexplored. Lower interest rates, as already pointed out, theoretically boxed out all potential economic risks. That implied a risk-free environment in future, a real-life absurdity! Economists had to ignore most future risks to justify low rates of interest – a willing suspension of disbelief. At near zero risk, any business could be theoretically demonstrated to be profitable. But in real life, risks exist and have an uncanny knack of emerging at the most inappropriate moment. Most finance professionals face this challenge while fixing the discount rate in valuations, especially while dealing with cash flows. In the process, substantial future risks are ignored. This is how valuations, based on discounted cash flows, get skewed. Astronomical valuations are arrived for selective businesses by using such extraordinarily low rates of interest. Thus, in effect, a 'virtual pharmacist' could be valued several times a pharma company itself. Evidently, the risks of an online store are much lower than setting up a manufacturing unit. Kiran Mazumdar-Shaw, a leading industrialist in her own right, in an article precisely pointed out this imbalance in our valuation mechanism when she opined "An online pharmacy that operates out of a single room with a few people and smart software may be working smart, but by over-valuing it, aren't we starving a pharma company – which has to invest in research, development and manufacturing – of funds?"

Every finance professional is conscious of the fact that funding a pharma company is fraught with real-life risks, and is riskier than funding a virtual pharmacist. But the templated valuations models are not programmed to capture such risks. Modern 'valuation models' cannot weigh, capture, and evaluate certain real-life risks. And even if they capture, the low interest rates do not support such investments as the 'risk premium' germane to these businesses do not get adequately reflected. Manufacturing, infrastructure, and certain services industry like airline and insurance are capital-intensive and prone to greater risks. The risk premium has not only to compensate for the attendant risks, but also for the artificial depression of the interest rates by the central banks. Obviously, low interest rates which are in effect 'administered' make certain businesses unviable even at the funding stage. Hence financing such businesses, especially manufacturing, is increasingly becoming scarce. The net effect, instead of business determining valuation, valuation models have begun to determine viable businesses and profitable investments. All these have allowed several start-ups and tech driven companies to leverage on the appetite of the market for higher returns. This skew is unacceptable. It distorts the world of finance and economics too. And if important businesses like manufacturing do not get funded, how will employment get generated? How will growth be sustainable? Low interest rate by itself has created a serious imbalance. This too needs to be addressed.

Civilisational Economics – A Primer

At the height of the final war in the great Indian epic *Ramayana*, the antagonist King Ravana loses a day's battle with the protagonist, Lord Rama. Humiliated, tired, and disheartened, Ravana returns to his palace after a hard-fought day. To rub salt in his wounds, Lord Rama compliments Ravana for his efforts and asks him to retire for the day, and comeback fresh the next day. Surely, this must have been extremely humiliating for any warrior to be so applauded and chastised, all in one go in a decisive battle with his sworn enemy. Naturally, it is very difficult to capture the emotions ranging in the mind of Ravana, that too in a poem. That is what an unknown Tamil poet attempted, and successfully so, when he describes the state of the mind of Ravana to be as disturbed as the mind of a failed borrower. Surely, this comparison is unparalleled in any other epics or in other literary works describing similar situations, across continents. More to the point, this has stood the test of time and is appreciated across generations. While granting that it was indeed a colourful description of a poignant situation, the use of the allegory of a failed borrower is indeed civilisationally instructive. It brilliantly captures what the prevailing situation was as the poet saw and sought to convey to his reader. It is not that a borrower was feeling as humiliated as Ravana on failing to repay the loan, but it was exactly the opposite – Ravana was feeling as disturbed as a delinquent borrower. The benchmark in humiliation, if at all there is one, is of a failed borrower. Let us not forget that.

Interestingly, this description of the mental state of King Ravana finds resonance with the ordinary person in India even to this day. Why did the poet use this nuanced reference to explain a delicate position of King Ravana? Obviously, debt is not a mere contractual obligation in the Indian context. And is losing a battle or a war akin to failing a financial obligation or debt repayment? Is it a matter of life and death? To students of law or economics, the very comparison itself may be odious. Modern economics, as we have seen above, has demonstrated that there is always a fall back – the central banks through QE to take care of the inability of every Tom, Dick, and Harry to repay their debts. Moreover, most countries have legislated an insolvency or bankruptcy laws, precisely to facilitate such situations. For students of law and economics, this would suffice. Yet, despite all the instruments available, some people have committed suicide when they are in no position to repay their debts. Therefore, non-repayment of debt cannot be seen from the prism of strict legalities or modern economics, especially in societies that are civilisationally rooted. Needless to emphasise, the repayment of debt has moral dimensions to those civilisationally rooted. It is this characteristic that was obliquely referred to by the poet. Let us not forget that reducing debt to a mere contractual obligation has brought the global economy to the threshold of a debt crisis.

From a civilisational perspective, the 'force majeure' clause does not apply in any debt agreement. Likewise, the legal concept of supervening impossibility too does not apply. If a loan has been taken, it is the duty of the borrower to repay, come what may. And this duty is sacrosanct. It is inviolable. Isn't this idea of placing responsibility on the individual to repay debt central to the idea of our civilisation? Unhesitatingly, the answer to this question is yes. Is that why India's household debt to GDP is one of the lowest globally? Again, the answer to this question too is yes. The central bank of India (RBI) along with several other economists have been enticing the average India to contract more debt. Banks have structured several products. RBI has repeatedly lowered interest rates. Yet, the average Indian has refused to bite the bait. On the contrary they have saved more.

Loan and its repayment are not the only differential. There are several others which have been highlighted by the Report of the Household Finance Committee of the RBI and quoted earlier in this chapter. Why is India an outlier? Why is her household savings an exception to the global norm? Can it be explained by culture? Or by civilisational values? And how does it play out in real terms? The answers to these questions are simple. Indians, for instance, believe that investment in physical gold is kosher. Gold is goddess Lakshmi for Indians. And that is cultural. Gold is also easily convertible into liquid cash at most places in India, any time. That explains the economics behind Indians buying gold. It is also historical as for over five thousand years of recorded history Indians have been storing gold. And, war or peace, it has always stood in good stead. Barring cash, gold and fixed assets, time and again investments in formal financial instruments have failed an average Indian. Promoters have vanished even in case of companies. Audited Balance Sheets of listed companies, audited by the best, have never inspired confidence. Regulators have invariably ended second best to the shenanigans of the corporate delinquent. Savings have vanished and virtually no one barring a few have ever been punished for serious economic offences in India. The failure of Dr Rajan in preventing the NPA crisis, explained in greater detail above, would not surprise a civilisationally rooted Indian. Incidentally, those who have created the NPA crisis in India eventually is the Indian establishment, not the common man. In fact, regulators in India, manned by faceless and unaccountable bureaucrats have consistently breached the trust reposed on it by the households. That explains why most Indians believe the financial sector has a predatory approach. Instinctively, Indians rooted to civilisational values understand this. Hence, they would never fall for the alluring yet highly fallible suggestions of the world of finance or economists or for that matter 'Rockstar economist' or 'Eminent economist.'

Likewise, people believe that they must purchase a property in their lifetime and bequeath it to their children in return for old-age support. It does form part of a loose privatised social security programme. That is purely from an economic standpoint. But there is something deeply civilisational about it too. Parents assume that it is their duty to bequeath something tangible to their children. In return, children believe it is their duty to take care of their parents in their advanced years. That also explains why Indians do not invest much in pension funds. As parents, Indians seek to leave behind a property for the next generation; as children, they assume it is their duty to take care of their elders.

It is these differentials that makes the civilisations unique. This naturally reflects in the investment patterns. There is a self-discipline in regulating one's own affairs. Eschewing debt, frugal lifestyle and acceptance of individual responsibility that makes such economies structurally different. This was the strong civilisational foundation that the Mahatma referred to when he highlighted the case for India. This is what made Pranab Mukherjee confident at the height of the rating crisis. Narendra Modi too drew comfort on the state of the economy from this civilisational approach. But remember, these are mere refences at the times of the crisis. All these explain the resilience of the Indian economy – not its ability to soar high. For it to soar it must leverage on these very strengths. For that it needs to adopt a distinct set of economic policies that is suited to its own distinct needs. It cannot blindly adopt imported economic theories and hope to succeed. On the contrary, the time for an indigenous economic model engrained to civilisational issues is just now. And to do that we need to revisit our root assumptions about economic policies. We need to clearly spell out the end game in reforms. Crucially, we need to redefine economics and reforms of economics as a discipline before we spell out what we seek from economic reforms. Simply put, it is not that India or for that matter the world that is in search of economic reforms, it is economics that is in search of reforms.

References

1. Fundamentals of Indian economy strong, policies are clear – Economic Times – March 6, 2020.
2. PM Modi says fundamentals of Indian economy strong, has capacity to bounce back – Economic Times – January 9, 2020.
3. Contribution made by MSMEs at heart of Indian economy – New Indian Express - 24th August 2013.
4. Savings and capital formation in India – NIPFP Working Paper Series No. 271 By Ila Patnaik and Radhika Pandey – June 10, 2019.
5. https://en.wikipedia.org
6. Inside Job -The Financiers Who Pulled Off the Heist of the Century – By Charles Ferguson – 2012.
7. The Economic and Political Causes of the 2008 US Financial Crisis – By Marie Daumal- University of Paris – September 15, 2018.
8. Budget 2015 – will it provide pragmatic solutions? By M R Venkatesh -Niti Central – February 2015.
9. Crony capitalism happened right under Rajan's nose – Interview with M R Venkatesh by Shoba Warrier-www.rediff.com- June 22, 2016.
10. Will PM explain his volte-face on globalisation? www.rediff.com- November 9, 2008.
11. The Final report of the National Commission on the Causes of the Financial and Economic Crisis in the United States – January 2011.
12. The Challenge to the South – The Report of the South Commission – 1990.
13. The Economist's Decline – By William Pearse – 08 November 2019.
14. The seven sins of economists – By Pramit Bhattacharya – 18 Sep 2017.
15. Financialization and Economic Development: A Debate on the Social Efficiency of Modern Finance By Servaas Storm – Institute of Social Studies, The Hague.

16. Financialization and the World Economy By Gerald A. Epstein.
17. The seeds of the next debt crisis – John Plender- Financial Times – March 4, 2020.
18. The Private Debt Crisis – By Richard Vague – Democracy A Journal of Ideas – 2016.
19. Globalization and Monetary Policy Institute – Working Paper No. 126 – William R. White – 2012 – Federal Reserve Bank of Dallas.

9. The Power of Restraint

Economists discount any factors that would not influence the thinking of a rational person – Richard Thaler

Supply creates its own demand – J.B. Say

The ancient temple town of Kancheepuram is located approximately 75km south-west of Chennai. In the distant past, this town was at the centre of a flourishing and prosperous Tamil civilisation. As the capital city of the great Pallava dynasty, Kancheepuram had attracted in good measure both secular and spiritual activities. That was some 1,500 years ago. It was, and remains, to this day the meeting point between arts, science and religion. To the Hindus, this non-decrepit town is one of the seven holy places to visit during one's lifetime. Several temples in this town probably predate known history. To this extent, the antiquity of this place remains indeterminate and was celebrated as *"Nagareshu Kanchi"* (best among cities) by the great poet Kalidasa. It is no wonder that this great seat of learning wielded extraordinary influence on international affairs too, during the Pallava regime. The legendary monk Bodhidharma who travelled to China and initiated martial arts to the Chinese in the 5th century AD, is believed to have hailed from this small sleepy town.

Incidentally, it is also home to one of the five Shankara mutts established by the great Hindu seer – Adi Shankara who is regarded as one of the greatest philosophers and spiritualists the world has ever seen. Sages and scholars, who have shone through the centuries after his time, have regarded him as an incarnation of the divine. Many a thinker and scholar of different climes and times has been attracted by the philosophic discipline of *Advaita* (Monism), effectively propagated by Adi Shankara, almost two-thousand five hundred years ago. It is understood that the mutt in Kanchipuram established by

Adi Shankara, has the distinction of an unbroken line till date of seventy acharyas, beginning from Adi Shankara himself. This long line of successor acharyas, each one distinguished for their extraordinary learning, discipline and penance, have since then adorned the Mutt and have guided the faithful.

Pertinently, the sixty-eighth acharya, the world-renowned Sri Chandrasekhara Sarasvati Swami, became pontiff in 1907 when he was barely 13 years of age. He shone as the Acharya of the Mutt for the next eighty-seven years. Like his illustrious predecessors, Sri Chandrasekhara Sarasvati Swami imparted great knowledge and wisdom to his followers and disciples. He is regarded as one of the greatest sages of the 20th century and aptly celebrated as *Paramacharya* by his countless devotees across the globe. One of his poems – *Maitrim Bhajata* – of the several authored by this great pontiff is relevant, and probably central, to the understanding the idea of 'Retaining Balance: The Eternal Way.' Though it is not possible to literally translate the poem into English and still preserve its pristine meaning, sources available from the internet suggest the following translation of the venerable pontiff's profound idea expressed through in mellifluous Sanskrit:

> *Maitrīṃ bhajata akhilahṛjjetrīm* – Cultivate Friendship which will conquer all hearts
>
> *Atmavadeva parānapi paśyata* – Look upon others as similar to yourself
>
> *Yuddhaṃ tyajata* – Renounce war
>
> *Spardhāṃ tyajata* – Forsake (unhealthy) competition
>
> *Tyajata pareṣu akramam ākramaṇam* – Give up aggression; acquiring by force
>
> *Jananī pṛthivī kāmadughā(ā)ste* – Mother Earth yields all that we require
>
> *Janako devaḥ sakaladayāluḥ* – The Lord, our father, is most compassionate
>
> *Dāmyata* – practice 'Restraint'
>
> *Datta* – be kind and give unto others
>
> *Dayadhvaṃ* – Be Kind to others
>
> *Janatāḥ* – Oh People of the World
>
> *Sreyo bhūyāt sakalajanānām* – May all people be happy and prosperous

Fittingly, this song was rendered at the United Nations on October 23, 1966, on its founding day by Bharat Ratna (the highest civilian award in India) and the great Carnatic musician M S Subbalakshmi. And this was no ordinary event as some may believe and tend to dismiss. It is widely known that Subbalakshmi was a devotee of the Pontiff. He is believed to have specifically referred to this song as an anthem for the challenges faced by the comity of the nations. It is thus, no wonder, that the UN issued a stamp in 2016 to commemorate the fiftieth anniversary of her memorable performance at the UN General Assembly. Why did the pontiff choose this song and ask her to render it on such a momentous occasion? What was the underlying message conveyed to the world by rendering this song? Crucially, does this song – and the ideas embedded in it – have any relevance to the issues on hand?

Before we proceed to answer these questions, let us refer to the preamble to the charter of the United Nations which is reproduced hereunder:

We The Peoples Of The United Nations Determined:

- to save succeeding generations from the scourge of war, which twice in our lifetime has brought untold sorrow to mankind, and
- to reaffirm faith in fundamental human rights, in the dignity and worth of the human person, in the equal rights of men and women and of nations large and small, and
- to establish conditions under which justice and respect for the obligations arising from treaties and other sources of international law can be maintained, and
- to promote social progress and better standards of life in larger freedom,

And For These Ends

- to practice tolerance and live together in peace with one another as good neighbours, and
- to unite our strength to maintain international peace and security, and
- to ensure, by the acceptance of principles and the institution of methods, that armed force shall not be used, save in the common interest, and
- to employ international machinery for the promotion of the economic and social advancement of all peoples,

Have Resolved To Combine Our Efforts To Accomplish These Aims

Accordingly, our respective governments, through representatives assembled in the city of San Francisco, who have exhibited their full powers found to be in good and due form, have agreed to the present Charter of the United Nations and do hereby establish an international organisation to be known as the United Nations.

From a plain reading of the preamble to the UN charter it is obvious that the pontiff of Kancheepuram had written this song with an extraordinary clairvoyance. Peace is a prerequisite for prosperity and progress. And this, in turn, is possible only when we as individuals, families, societies, communities and as countries voluntarily restrain ourselves from committing any excesses. Apparently, the Pontiff had a powerful yet subtle messages to mankind – one, to eschew unwanted competition and the other, to be voluntarily restrained. The operating word, let us reiterate, is voluntary restraint. It may be recalled that The United Nations was formed after several excesses in the field of economics, politics and militarily were committed by mankind in the first half of the 20th century. The lessons of those excesses cannot be ignored; neither should they be. That, in quintessence, is the message of the wonderful song that is *Maitrim Bhajata*.

The Paradox of Prosperity

Yet, this invaluable message of the pontiff is lost on modern economics (and economists too). The discipline of economics as we have seen in previous chapters is rooted to extremes, especially consumption, which in turn encourages unbridled competition. Modern economic policies seek to free, for one reason or the other, an individual from any self-imposed (or by the family or the society or for that matter even by the state at times) fetters and consistently goads him to commit excesses at every twist and turn. Recall the idea of 'animal spirits' that we discussed in Chapter 4? Recall what Harari commented about the evolution of the state in chapter 6? Well, modern economics has the calculated effect of converting a man into an animal – a ferociously competing, unrestrained and unforgiving one at that. This is simply because contemporary economists assume that absolute unfettered competition brings about substantial increase in output. This, they argue, goes on to increase production in the aggregate, while resulting in concomitant surge in profits. This stimulus, according them is the formulae for sustained growth, possibly to eternity. The underlying assumption is that such increase in production, productivity and profit alone will pave way for an all-round sustainable prosperity for the individual, society, and the economy. And should there unwittingly be any excess, the markets or governments have the necessary in-built mechanism for self-correction. Economists do not realise that this relentless pursuit of profits as an end in itself, comes with attendant catastrophic consequences. Little do we realise that profits when treated as the sole elixir of businesses contains the toxic seeds of impending doom. Recent events, as have seen in Chapter 4, have demonstrated that these 'modern economic' ideas are unsustainable even in the short run. Needless to emphasise, we need to revisit several root assumptions that guide our understanding of the discipline of economics. But how? We will look into this issue later in this chapter.

In contrast, civilisations are, as we have seen right through, essentially rooted in self-imposed restraints. They eschew competition, especially excessive ones. By definition, they seek to co-opt all and sundry. They believe that there is undoubtedly a room for everyone. Certainly, the civilised do not believe in the crass idea of 'survival of the fittest.' In essence, post-modern economics is in quintessence a battle of ideas – battle between those who are inclusive and those who assume that only the fittest will and should survive. The idea that fittest only will, can, and should survive takes away the moral persuasion in any theory. On first blush, they are indeed alluring and hence, persuasive. But surely such ideas as we have repeatedly seen are not durable. Nevertheless, such a ruthless approach creates distinct dichotomies in real life situations – a fact that cannot be lost sight of either. Civilisations by their very construct can never successfully participate, much less compete, with the uncivilised and the unrestrained, especially in the short run. This is akin to an athlete who is compelled to compete with another who has taken recourse to a certain performance enhancing prohibited substance. Likewise, of late, the democratic world is realising, albeit belatedly, that they cannot compete fairly and squarely with non-democracies in the global trade regime where uniform rules apparently prevail, much to the former's distinct disadvantage. Such an arrangement skews competition in favour of those who do not care for the very rules of the game. That explains substantially, if not wholly, why civilisations historically rise only to be run over by those who do not share the idea of sharing, caring, and being restrained. Naturally, it is not just in the interest but the responsibility, of the civilised that the unrestrained must be restrained. What modern economics seeks to achieve is exactly the opposite – un-restrain the restrained as we saw in Chapter 3 by collapsing the idea as well as the institution of family.

What applies to the real-life situations applies in equal measure to the field of economics. More to the point, modern economics is a software that works on and only on the hardware of the unrestrained or those who are at best subjected to minimalist restraints. In fact, economics as we see today are designed by the unrestrained, for the unrestrained and, of the unrestrained. Restraint, if any, is minimal and superfluous. Therefore, it is natural that the rules of engagement as considered by modern economics are skewed heavily against the cultured and decisively in favour of those who have made such rules in the first place. Consequently, in every contest between the restrained and the unrestrained, it is the latter who would more often than not emerge victorious as it is the unrestrained who have a systemic upper hand.

Nevertheless, it is the restrained who have ensured, nurtured, and sustained civilisations for time immemorial. The unrestrained, by definition, cannot. Civilisations, developed by the restrained, right through the history of mankind have been the cradle for arts, science, philosophy, religion, politics, economics, or for that matter anything and everything. Humans as a race have advanced only when the civilised have delivered, not otherwise. This is a responsibility that the civilised have carried on their shoulders since the dawn of history. It is these telling attributes of restraints practiced by a silent and an overwhelming majority that ultimately results in durable peace within societies. Peace, let us not forget, is an important prerequisite for prosperity. Recall that economic prosperity (*Artha*) was the first definitive step in the path to the final goal for Hindus (*Moksha*). And it is this economic prosperity that always contains the seeds of human development including fulfilment of all his material and non-material goals.

But this prosperity regrettably results in the Catch-22 situation. Though prosperity may have some unintended perils, ironically, it is this prosperity that instantly attracts predation from the unrestrained, in one way or the other. For the unrestrained, it is the easiest and surest way to prosperity. This, in short, is the history of mankind. But when the civilised fall, as often they have in the history, unable to stand up to the barbarism of the unrestrained, it is human race that has collectively suffered. Thus, it is obvious that prosperity brings along with it, extraordinary risks. This is what is loosely termed as the paradox of prosperity. Ensuring continued prosperity and balancing it with security is a challenge that has been confronting mankind since the dawn of civilisation. Our forefathers quickly realised that prosperity was often a self-defeating idea as it exposed them to increased risks from their predatory counterparts. Typically, this predation should have discouraged them from continuing in their relentless march to prosperity. Yet, this risk by itself did not deter them as the history of mankind would tell us.

Modern nation-states too face similar if not identical challenges. We saw one in chapter 6 – between freedom and equality and how it remains unresolved to this day. The framers of the Constitutions of modern nations assume that to quell potential violence (recall the Christian idea that man is always born bad) as well as to deal with every challenge faced by the society, they needed an omnipotent, omnipresent state. The state by design wielded extraordinary authority and power. Such a skew in the Constitution construct invariably undermined their ability to respect individual freedom and their private rights. That in turn, gave rise to the idea of certain inviolable 'Fundamental Rights.' Modern nation-states have temporarily solved this issue of the lack of balance caused by the need for an omnipotent state on one hand and the pressing need to allow individual rights on the other. This has been possible by ideating newer political institutions that midwife solutions in most situations. Yet, experiences demonstrate that such solutions worked out are fleeting at best. Consequently, such arrangements seemingly lend credence to the entire system, but do so only in the short term. What is not realised in the melee is that the deeper fault lines in balancing between an omnipotent state and individual rights within the constitutional construct remain unaddressed. And that comes to haunt us all in the long-term.

Therefore, the enduring clash is thus a primordial conflict that continues to fashion the present and probably the foreseeable future too. And this is not a mere historical fact as we too face myriad risks of predation as faced by our forefathers. Although the rise of civilisations and their repeated resurrection after every fall is arguably the most fascinating story in the history of mankind, modern political economy has paid much less attention to it. To begin with, civilisation entails the joint achievement of both prosperity and security. Societies that held production close to subsistence levels possibly mitigated predation, but simultaneously ran the risk of slowing future progress. Societies that did not pay much attention to security invariably were overrun. Our forefathers quickly realised that they needed a robust balancing mechanism between surplus production and protection for the surplus. Civilisations that succeeded in achieving this delicate balance succeeded for a longer period.

On the other hand, civilisations that over-balanced in favour of security became a threat to others and collapsed under the resultant imbalance. A nation that over-spends on its security than on the welfare of its people and their prosperity is sooner than later bound to acquire imperialist tendencies. And no nation that has an expansionist design has ever succeeded in the long run. Soviet Russia is a classic case in point in recent history. Therefore, societies for time immemorial have been in constant search for arriving at an ideal balance between progress and security; between peace and prosperity, and between the supremacy of the state and of individual freedom. Those who have been able to achieve balance on all these fronts have been in a position to sustain their societies for long. Societies that have been unable to arrive at this delicate balance have invariably floundered. In short, a pacifist state is as much at risk of being overrun as is an expansionist state of imploding from within. The challenge for every state is to get the right balance between the two.

The Collapse of the Exceptional

As briefly mentioned above, nothing illustrates this better than the stunning collapse of the Soviet Russia in the last decade of the 20th century. This collapse has often been heralded in the West as the ultimate triumph of capitalism and democracy, though this event was probably accelerated by certain calculated policies of the Reagan and Thatcher governments in the eighties. This self-congratulatory analysis has little relation to measurable facts, circumstances, internal political and economic dynamics that were the real historical causes of the stunning collapse of the Soviet state. The key to understanding the reasons for the demise of the Soviet Union is to be found not in the celebratory speeches or acclaimed policies of politicians in the West, but in the simple analysis of internal Soviet history, especially the unique brand of its iron-fisted political system and skewed economics in the years leading to its implosion.

It may be recalled that the economy of Soviet Russia was plagued by several factors. At the outset, it would seem that the Soviet empire was in a perverse ideological competition with market economies and democracies. In retrospective analysis, it is clearly seen that it was ultimately this impulse to dominate the world that was the cause of their undoing. Russians, in the quest for their own security, forsake progress, and instead became a threat for the rest of the world. In view of the ideological war with others, notably the West, the skew in its own domestic policy formulation turned decisively in favour of security and against domestic prosperity. This is precisely what the venerable Pontiff of Kancheepuram obliquely warns in his poem *Maithrim Bhajatha.* That explains why it seeks to avoid unwanted competition, ideological or otherwise. There is yet another important lesson for us here. A state that places any ideology above the interests of its own people is bound to suffer significantly on account of the ensuing imbalance. As the horrors of Soviet Russia emerge, it is now seen that significant quantities of industrial output were routed to military production, leaving very less for civil-domestic consumption. Societal prosperity is a natural incentive for an individual to work. When governments lose sight of this fundamental fact, people refuse to work or in the least, be productive. That is what happened in Soviet Russia too. An anonymous Soviet citizen, widely quoted in the media, captured the then prevailing situation. He is reported to have said: "They pretend to pay us and we pretend to work." The Russian economist, Grigory Yavlinsky, who ultimately became an important advisor to Mikhail Gorbachev, was convinced on the need for reform when he investigated the low productivity in the Soviet mines. Yavlinsky hit at the root of the problem when he added "The Soviet system is not working because the workers are not working."

The Soviet command economy coordinated economic activity through the issuance of directives, by setting social and economic targets, and by instituting regulations. Soviet leaders decided on the state's overarching social and economic goals. To achieve these goals, Communist Party officials assumed control over all of the country's social and economic activities. The Communist Party legitimised its control by claiming repeatedly that it had the ideology to direct a society that would rival and overtake any competing market economy. Officials managed to obtain significant amounts of information necessary for centralising the planning of both production and distribution. Hierarchical structures were instituted at all levels of economic activity, with superiors having absolute control over the norms and parameters of planning assignments, as well as setting regular performance evaluations and rewards. All these curtailed individual freedom and enterprise.

Expectedly, this created severe problems and the Soviet leadership was acutely aware of the same. As a result, they attempted some half-hearted reforms which failed to revive the increasingly stagnant Soviet economy, with productivity growth falling below zero by the early 1980s. This ongoing poor economic performance led to a more radical set of both economic and social reforms under the leadership of Mikhail Gorbachev. While attempting to maintain socialist ideals and control over primary societal goals, Gorbachev aimed to decentralise economic activity and open up the economy to foreign trade. This restructuring, referred to as Perestroika, encouraged individual private incentive, creating greater openness. Perestroika was in direct opposition to the previously hierarchical nature of the command economy. But having been habituated to the command structure for several decades, the system refused to respond to any stimulus or reforms in any significant manner. It was a classic case of too little, too late.

When the Soviet leadership relaxed control to save the faltering economic system, they ultimately helped create conditions that would lead to the country's ultimate collapse. While perestroika initially appeared to be a success, as Soviet firms took advantage of new freedoms and new investment opportunities, optimism soon faded. A severe economic contraction characterised the late 1980s and early 1990s, which would be the last years of the Soviet Union. Soviet leaders no longer had power to intervene amidst the growing economic chaos. Newly-empowered local leaders demanded greater autonomy from central authority, shaking the foundations of the command economy, while more localised cultural identities and priorities took precedence over national concerns. With its economy and political unity in tatters, the Soviet Union collapsed in the early nineties, fragmenting into fifteen separate countries.

But the West, notably the US did not see this implosion of Soviet Russia due to the latter's own internal weakness – read excesses. The West assumed that the collapse of Russia automatically signalled the triumph of democracy and market economics, values and ideas that the Western world loves to cherish. Fascinatingly, it inspired the thesis in Francis Fukuyama's *The End of History and the Last Man* in 1992. We have dealt with this issue of the post-Soviet collapse and the resultant euphoria in the West in greater detail in Chapter 3. A mere two decades later, that euphoria dramatically transmogrified into a deep despair following the implosion of the Western financial system in 2008. Fukuyama's *mea culpa* took the following form: "The American political system has decayed over time because its traditional system of checks and balances has deepened and become increasingly rigid. With sharp political polarisation, this decentralised system is less and less able to represent majority interests, but gives excessive representation to the views of interest groups and activist organisations that collectively do not add up to a sovereign American people."

Why did Fukuyama err in his assessment of post-Soviet collapse of the emerging global order? Why did the promise of durable peace elude him? Why did he fail to identify the fault lines in the American political landscape? Was the evidence concealed from him? Or like in the case of Russians, did his theoretical prism disconnect him from the realities that existed on the ground? It is most likely the latter. Whatever be it, the fetish to dominate and triumph others, ideologically, militarily, or otherwise has been the undoing of several empires in the history of mankind, including the contemporary West.

It may be appropriate at this point to once again recall the sagacious advice of the Pontiff of Kancheepuram contained in his song *Maithrim Bajata*! Market economy, as it is practiced now suffers virtually from the same vices of 'excesses' as was the case of communism in Soviet Russia. May be, the excesses are different. May be not. But they are excesses nevertheless. In the case of latter, it was an idea to dominate others that went awry, while in case of former it is once again the non-negotiable idea that markets are supreme, a self-correcting and self-balancing system that has increasingly come under scrutiny. Either way, it is the idea of domination that needs to be eschewed. Many analysts now acknowledge that there are serious problems with market economy, but they are not able to visualise the terms of a viable and functional alternative. German sociologist Wolfgang Streeck is one of those puzzled analysts. He notes: "The problem is, while we see capitalism disintegrating before our eyes, we see no successor approaching." The world's best thinkers have reflected on the global crises, which they associate with the capitalist economy; but they are unable to isolate the root causes to explain the consequent damage inflicted on communities and the environment. More importantly, they have been unable to precisely identify the reason why markets failed.

As Complexity Creeps into Economies

It has been over a decade since, on a visit to the London School of Economics, Queen Elizabeth II asked her hosts: "Why did no one see it coming?" She was referring to the global financial crisis of 2008. On June 17, 2009, the British Academy convened a group of leading academics, economics journalists, politicians, past and present civil servants, and other practitioners for a roundtable discussion to precisely address this question. The chairman, Professor Peter Hennessy, explained that a purpose of the British Academy Forum was to provide the basis of an 'unofficial command paper' that attempted to answer the Queen's question. They pointed that 'some of the best mathematical minds' were involved in risk management but "they frequently lost sight of the bigger picture." In summary, they concluded, "the failure to foresee the timing, extent, and severity of the crisis and to head it off, while it had many causes, was principally a failure of the collective imagination of many bright people, both in this country and internationally, to understand the risks to the system as a whole." Interestingly, they pointed out that "economics has turned virtually into a branch of applied mathematics, and has been become detached from real-world institutions and events." Yet, the forum probably did not consider how the preference for mathematical technique over real-world substance diverted many economists from looking at the issue holistically. It failed to reflect upon the drive of modern economists to specialise in narrow areas of enquiry, to the detriment of wholesome vision. For example, it did not consider the typical omission of psychology, philosophy, or economic history from the current education of economists in prestigious institutions. It mentions neither the highly questionable belief in universal rationality nor the 'Efficient Markets Hypothesis' – both widely promoted by mainstream economists and academia. It also failed to consider how the pantheon of economists have also been "charmed by the market" and how simplistic and reckless market solutions have been widely and vigorously promoted by them. As a case in point, the letter points out that the American Economic Association set up a commission as early as 1988 on the state of graduate education in economics in the US. In a crushing indictment published in the *Journal of Economic Literature* in 1991, the commission expressed its fear that "graduate programs may be turning out a generation with too many idiot savants skilled in technique, but innocent of real economic issues." Well, the subsequent happenings over the past three decades seem to suggest that this was indeed one forecast that the economists had indeed got correct.

To understand the complexity associated with modern economics we need to retrace the evolution of economics over the two-hundred years. Classical market economics, it may be recalled, functioned on the assumption that individuals are led by their supreme self-interest in the pursuit of their respective economic activities. In the aggregate, their individual decisions and actions collectively so taken promote the good and welfare of the society as a whole. Thus, according to Adam Smith, though an individual is motivated by self-interest and personal gain, he is led, as it were by an invisible hand to promote the social welfare as well. It is the impersonal forces of market mechanism which represent the invisible hand. Adam Smith writes: "Every individual necessarily labours to render the annual revenue of the society as great as he can. He generally, indeed, neither intends to promote the public interest, nor knows how much he is promoting it....... he intends only his own security; and by directing that industry in such a manner as its produce may be of the greatest value, he intends only his own, and he is in this, as in many other cases, led by an invisible hand to promote an end which was no part of his intention. By pursuing his own interest, he frequently promotes that of the society more effectively than when he really intends to promote it."

When life was simple, economics as natural consequence too was simple. Large number of firms ensured higher degree of competition and sovereignty of the consumer. This was the classical position that is referred by Adam Smith. Subsequently, rapid technological progress began to dramatically alter the position. This is where the discipline of economics as was traditionally understood gets turned on its head. Introduction of newer technology required greater amount of machinery as machines replaced men in the manufacturing process. Up to a point this yielded greater overall benefits. But this required large amount of capital in the first place. Obviously, the economies of scale to serve this greater amount of capital were significantly different. To achieve the optimal result, players required ever-expanding markets and complex and huge managerial set-up and. Simultaneously they required large, efficient and reliable supply chains. This in turn required firms to operate on a very large scale not only in the absolute sense but also in relation to the size of the market. Economists cheered these rapid developments. Theories were written substantiating such ideas. This, in turn, spawned the academia-industry nexus where the former was reduced to play the role of a cheerleader for the latter. In the process little did economists realise that maximum productive efficiency achieved through employment of modem technology necessitated the existence of a few large firms rather than a large number of small firms. This is where things go awry.

Before we proceed further, it is pertinent to note that economists have often failed to answer a fundamental question – are all technological advancement good? Are we suffering from an imbalance, at-least in the field of economics, caused by rapid technological developments? On the face of it, it is obvious that it probably does. The next obvious question is how do we measure the resultant imbalance? Just as a technically challenged society is at a disadvantage, the technologically advanced too probably have a downside. It is only a matter of time when we would figure it out the optimum technology required for the most efficient functioning of the economy. For starters, Robert Solow, a Nobel Laureate in economics demonstrated through a model that the source of long-term economic growth is technological growth. Before Solow's 1956 and 1957 papers outlining the model, some economists (Harrod-Domar model for instance) believed that a country could boost its rate of economic growth by increasing its savings rate or adding more workers to its labour force. But Solow's model shows something else. Increasing the savings rate could get an economy to a higher level of output after the increase, but the long-run rate of economic growth would not increase. Doubling the savings rate would increase a country's GDP per capita, but it will not change the fact that the economy would still grow at the same rate as before. But a "technological" advancement boosts the long-run growth rate of the economy. By technology Solow's Model does not mean just advances in computers or robots, but rather anything that allows for a more efficient use of capital and labour. In that way, technology is essentially the same thing as total factor productivity. What determines the growth over time is still very much an open question in economics. Just as Solow's model was an advancement over the Harrod-Domar Model, probably it is time to refine the Solow model itself to find its optimality and its consequential impact. And once the optimality is breached, common sense tells us that it will have a telling effect, mostly a debilitating one, on the economy. Determining optimality will restore the balance between technology and consequent growth arising from it.

Reverting to the issue of the consequences of technology on economy, experiences demonstrate that emergence of newer technologies resulted in the concentration of production in the hands of fewer firms. This resulted in the decline of competition and the emergence of oligopolies and monopolies. This substantially distorted the very foundation of market mechanisms. Consequently, there was a concomitant downside to these disturbing developments. The decline of competition and the simultaneous emergence of oligopolies and monopolies have resulted in a dysfunctional market. What is indeed worrying is that the classical function of markets in allocating resources in accordance with the wishes of consumers has virtually ceased to exist. Prof J K Galbraith, captures the entire issue when he points out that the emergence of multinational corporations or big businesses have significantly reduced consumer sovereignty. These big corporations do not merely seek to satisfy or fill the wants of the people. On the contrary, they themselves create these wants by massive expenditure on advertisements which influence the public to buy their products. To them, as we saw in Chapter 3, even a toddler is at best a potential who must be compelled to become a compulsive consumer of their product. The final denouncement came when finance, as we saw in Chapter 7, took over economics. What remains of the debris is merely exotic mathematical modelling.

Empires and Hubris

What gravity is to physics; competition is to economics said a good friend of mine. Remember *Artha* is vital. For *Artha* to succeed, competition is inevitable. Even the Pontiff of Kancheepuram was conscious of the fact and wanted us to eschew only unwanted competition. That by implication meant restraint. It goes without saying that every individual, economy, society and country needs to be competitive. Therefore, the notion of competition is fundamental to a market-oriented economy; the market and competition cannot exist without each other. But there is a thin line that differentiates between competition for common good and unwarranted competition. Let us not forget that without competitive spirit most of us will simply wither away. Therefore, every government needs to foster competition so that every player is spurred to greater heights. It is this competitive spirit that often has brought the best out of men. And this has fuelled human progress from time immemorial. But every society needs to draw a line, as invariably governments cannot do so. Competition cannot be absolute and unbridled. It needs to be tempered and measured. It cannot have the calculated effect of converting men into animals, as what modern economics seeks and substantially succeeds. To do so, it needs institutions to temper competition. And this is where nations and societies are floundering. We will deal with the issue of institutions that can temper competition within societies shortly.

But first, the downsides of unbridled competition. Francesco Duina an American associate professor at Bates College, in Maine, USA, and author of the celebrated book *Winning* deals with the rather nebulous subject of competition and competitive spirit. This book chronicles the dominant traits of American society and the American love for unrestrained competition. Duina describes the 'American obsession' with competition and winning, very vividly. This book is important because it poses the critical question - how much competition is really needed in rich nations, especially those with high levels of economic and cultural productivity. The answer to this question is relevant in discussions about the role of governments and about the optimal levels of liberalisation or regulation of markets. It is obvious that any nation cannot get its direction of economic reforms and macroeconomic policy right unless it answers this question in the first place.

Americans, for several reasons, are motivated by the desire to distinguish themselves. This obsession or mindset is a cultural reality. Such cultural realities are usually embedded in the social structure of a society and hence, not so easy to change. Americans believe that winners are supposed to have a better grasp, not only on the competitive event itself, but also on the world in general. Loss, by contrast, raises questions about the way losers approach the world. According to the General Social Survey, more than 75 percent of Americans believe that God plays a role in shaping their success or failure. With victory comes the belief that God was instrumental in shaping their performance. Americans assume consciously or sub-consciously that if they win, God rewards them for something they are doing right, not just in the particular realm in question, but life in general. They believe they win because they are worthy of God's grace, and are living a virtuous life in line with God's desires. In contrast, Hindus not only believe that they have won because of God's grace, but also have lost because that is the way the Lord has willed. Probably this is an outcome of the Protestant work ethic that Weber described and discussed in Chapter 5. But this approach has a tremendous downside. Much as the Protestant work ethic is welcome, it is apparent that the Protestants do not have the benefit of the sagacious advice of the Pontiff of Kancheepuram. Unbridled competition and the American way of life is not only a problem for the Americans, but now it is an issue for all those who blindly imitate the Americans.

Duina precisely identifies problems associated with such unbridled competitive spirit. Competitiveness has become one of the great unquestioned virtues of contemporary culture, especially in the US. This obsession with winning is very notorious and brings with it a debilitating effect for several reasons. It generates enormous tensions in a society, most of all because of its adversarial nature. A competitive mindset assumes a position of aggressiveness toward the world. This would be harmless if people were thoughtful and selective about competition, but unfortunately in real-life situations, it is deployed without much thought in countless areas. Remember, it is now part of the American culture to be competitive, combative, and aggressive. Sadly, the world, post the collapse of Soviet Russia, had modelled itself based on what the Americans did and did not do. After all, everyone loves a winner. And it was not limited to the American economic model but also American approach to life too.

In more ways than it would seem, the world had turned Protestant, without probably adopting the Protestant work ethic. This unrestrained competition creates its own share of problem. As long as people view all their activities merely as tests of their worth, they will be doubtful about themselves. The idea that winning alone matters is also problematic as this approach demotivates people to think about the process and fixates them to the end result. Where winning alone matters, contriving ways to exterminate competitors becomes legal and even morally acceptable. The end result is that we end up creating a population that is possessed by self-doubt and a society that is constantly in war with itself. And such a society which places a premium on the end result than on the process, is sooner than later, bound to degenerate.

Contrast this with the Indic approach of doing one's duty and leaving the fruits of his labour to the lord as discussed in Chapter 5. Clearly, such a society has a greater chance to be at peace with itself than the one which sees competition as an end in itself and not as a means to an end. This is the subtle but significant difference in the approach to life, competition, and winning between Hindus and Protestants, a fact lost on Weber. Constantly stretching the idea of a work ethic may surely benefit in the short run. But the moot question is whether it is sustainable in the long run? Regardless of the outcome, the fact remains that ideally a balance needs to be stuck between outcomes and processes. Without competition and the alluring promise of betterment that goes along with it, no society will have the incentive to invent and innovate. But carrying it to the extreme to declare that outcomes alone matter has its own unintended consequences, mostly on the downside. Surely, every individual, society, and nation must decide for itself the right quantum of competition that is necessary for its material and other successes. Of course, balancing this idea through a neat mathematical model would be virtually impossible. Yet, this needs to be done. We will look into how of it shortly.

There is yet another important lesson in all these. Like the Russians, the Americans too are currently engaged in a mindless game to dominate others. Americans, term this as 'exceptionalism,' – a rather polite term for bring exclusivist and by extension, supremacist. The idea that the US is unique among nations has been around for a long time. It dates back at least to 1835, when French historian and author Alexis de Tocqueville published the first volume of *Democracy in America*. In the book, he marvelled at the young country's fortunate circumstances: vast territory, abundant natural resources, and a spirit born from having freed itself from the colonial masters. He wrote that the country had a strong enough connection to Europe to reap the benefits of 'European civilisation' without being crippled by its attendant consequences. We have dealt with Tocqueville and his views on American society in some detail in previous Chapters. Somewhere along the line, though, the idea of 'American Exceptionalism' evolved into a conviction that the US, as a country, had little to learn from the rest of the world. More importantly, Americans, as exemplified by Fukuyama's writings, believe they have virtually left others behind in every sphere. To them, as a nation, they achieved a sort of perfection in all spheres. Consequently, there is nothing for Americans to learn from or compete with others. At the height of the Soviet empire and probably even a year before its implosion, most Russians too would have felt the same way. The Communist leadership too felt that they had conquered history and eliminated all competition. But the fact of the matter is that they did not. Past experiences of mankind demonstrate that a period of intense hubris is the penultimate chapter in the history of most civilisations. Russia was no exception. Neither is US to the rule that excesses dynamite the best of empires. *Maitrim Bhajata* seems to be ever relevant to entire world even to this day.

Is that why monarchs from India, barring rare exceptions, historically never ventured to send their army to conquer alien lands? And even when they sent their army, there is no historical record demonstrating that their army was violent or brutal. Did our kings and their army genuinely believe that coveting alien lands would be abhorred civilisationally by their own people? Or was it that the sustained internal prosperity of India by itself acted as a deterrent to such expansionist ideas? On a similar footing, is that why Indic religions never believed in religious conversions, by force or allurement? Whatever be it, it is apparent that the civilised and the restrained do not believe in the idea of expansionism, domination, war, supremacy, conquests, unwanted competition, ideology, aggression, bigotry, or intolerance. Great civilisations have consistently desisted from adopting such ideas as they were aware of its debilitating consequences in the long run. And those who did, possibly encountered fleeting successes at best, nothing more. Yet, the history of the world is the story of clashes arising for that momentary success. The great Pontiff of Kancheepuram precisely warns us on these points.

The Tolerance Conundrum

But there is another dimension to this issue best exemplified by modern India and her approach to tolerance. If the rest of the world is notorious for being intolerant, and hence violent, India, especially for the past few decades has mistaken tolerance for acceptance, to the point of being a pacifist. Resultantly, she has been a victim of her own diffused thinking. As Goethe wrote in 1829: "Tolerance should be a temporary attitude only. To tolerate means to insult." In the Indian context, tolerance of late means in effect acquiescence or passivity – a supinely indifferent attitude that denudes the word of its meaning. In the process, tolerance in post-independent India has been conflated for love, universal brotherhood, and of course approval for even the most ridiculous ideas put forth in public domain. Let us not forget that the very idea of intolerance has a convoluted chapter in the long and complicated history of mankind. Yet we do not realise that tolerance of the intolerant often results in proliferation of the latter in a society, especially those filled with certain underlying tensions. Tolerance only weakens a society from within over a period of time. Tolerance, passivity, or sheer indifference to the violence in thoughts or in deed unleashed by the unrestrained, makes a society vulnerable to repeated predatory attacks. And unless a society learns to resist such attacks and repulses them effectively, it cannot progress. Peace at any cost is not a sure way to progress either.

This is the conundrum of tolerance that has been gathering attention of many sociologists and of late many economists too. How much should an individual, society or a nation tolerate the intolerant? To begin with, modern nation-states must stop revelling in the non-existent virtue of endless tolerance, which on even a superfluous examination would demonstrate, is a far greater malice that afflicts the vitals of the society. This is popularly called as the Tolerance Conundrum. One of the most well-known works on this subject was explained in greater detail by Austrian philosopher Karl Popper in his 1945 book *The Open Society and Its Enemies*. Popper was a non-religious Jew who witnessed the rise of Nazism in the 1920s in his hometown of Vienna and fled to England, then in 1937, to Christchurch, New Zealand, where he was appointed lecturer at the University of Canterbury. There, he wrote *The Open Society*, where the famous passage in connection with the paradox of tolerance appears in a footnote: "Unlimited tolerance must lead to the disappearance of tolerance. If we extend unlimited tolerance even to those who are intolerant, if we are not prepared to defend a tolerant society against the onslaught of the intolerant, then the tolerant will be destroyed, and tolerance with them. In this formulation, I do not imply, for instance, that we should always suppress the utterance of intolerant philosophies; as long as we can counter them by rational argument and keep them in check by public opinion, suppression would certainly be unwise. But we should claim the right to suppress them, if necessary, even by force; for it may easily turn out that they are not prepared to meet us on the level of rational argument, but begin by denouncing all argument; they may forbid their followers to listen to rational argument, because it is deceptive, and teach them to answer arguments by the use of their fists or pistols. We should therefore claim, in the name of tolerance, the right not to tolerate the intolerant."

Obviously, the idea is to balance between tolerance of extreme ideas on one hand and acceptance of diverse and plural thoughts on the other. Popper recognised the inevitability and healthy necessity of conflict of all ideas, but he also affirmed the values of cooperation and mutual recognition, without which a liberal democracy cannot survive – a fact lost on many liberals themselves. Popper welcomed criticism, but he refused to tolerate views that reject reason, facts, and arguments in order to incite and perpetrate violence and persecution. It is difficult to imagine any democratic society surviving for long if it decides that, while a particular idea may indeed be objectionable, nevertheless needs to be tolerated for the sake of being tolerant.

The Mythical Rational Man

Modern economics in more ways than one reflects this conundrum – the tolerance of excesses. If experience of the past few decades is anything to go by, and as pointed out in the earlier chapters, modern economics has been a victim of this excess. Yet it refuses to cognise the root of its consternation. And one of the fatal flaws in the approach to modern economics is that it oversimplifies the rationality (or the lack of it) of men in their approach to life and their affairs. In fact, much of our contemporary policy discussion remains infused with principles grounded firmly in the concept of homo economicus – the perfectly rational human being. Strangely, this *homo economicus* is a mythical character – never heard or seen in real life. Yet, it is this rational behaviour of the mythical man – the man who as a constant in and vital to every economic modelling – and is presumed to pursue all his activities in his own supreme self-interest.

It may be stunning to note that the entire edifice of modern economics is built on this mythical rational man. Like modern India and its liberals who have shut their eyes to the all-pervading chapter of intolerance in the history of mankind and hence have come to the sweeping conclusion that intolerance does not exist in real life, modern economists too have turned a blind eye to the persistent irrational behaviour of men and its consequent debilitating impact on macro-economics. Benumbing as it may, the fact of the matter is that complex economic theories are built on such oversimplified assumptions. The roots of such politically correct and acceptable behaviour stem from the prevalent culture within the pantheon of economists. In their zeal to protect certain non-negotiable tenets – market efficiency, the invisible hand, comparative advantage – economists do not realise that they have been reduced to a cheer leader by a 'visible behaviour' of the irrational man.

Expectedly, economists continue their romance with this mythical man only to conjure a vision of a perfect economy expressed through fanciful economic theories embellished with complex mathematical equations or models. Obviously, only a rational man with a predictable behavioural pattern meets their imperial professional requirements. With the advent of the computers, 'mathematics and quants' dominate the discipline of economics. In the process, the rational man is reduced to a binary expression to suit computing. Worryingly, the irrational man is long dead and forgotten up to the time his irrational acts surface in the form of an economic crisis. Till the Titanic hits the iceberg, what matters to the world of economics is only the mythical rational man who lends himself, as we have seen, to mathematical modelling, divorced from the real-life situations. This creation of the ideal man and perfect market by economists are, as we saw in the previous chapters, partly intended to suit political and ideological narratives. And in substantial measure, economic theories are a command performance catering to the insatiable greed of an external agent, mostly the world of finance. In this paradigm, contrarian views will never be part of mainstream as the deeply entrenched eco-system would never allow alternative thoughts even to blossom, much less to flourish. The overwhelming desire of the economists to be politically correct and intellectually elegant in their approach means that they ignore men, his fallibility, his irrationality and penchant to act against his own self-interest.

In this sanitised view of real life, economists deliberately choose to ignore all things that could probably go wrong. They repeatedly turn a Nelson's eye to the limitations of human frailty and irrationality – of greed, dominance, war, expansionism and of course, supremacy. They have chosen to ignore the irrational behaviour of men that often lead to excesses. They have overlooked the quixotic behaviour of men which ensured regulations which, instead of regulating an economy, ended up smothering it. They have forgotten the fact that it is the unreasonable men who have caused institutions to run amok and create chaos. It is the irrational man who has by his seemingly rational acts caused sudden unpredictable booms as well as crashes in an economy. In short, they have deliberately disregarded the irrational man and his actions bordering on excesses – the root cause of imperfections of all real-life situations. And when the irrational man hits back with a vengeance, economists usually end up being clueless. As Paul Krugman points out "economists will have to acknowledge the importance of irrational and often unpredictable behaviour, face up to the often-idiosyncratic imperfections of markets and accept that an elegant economic "theory of everything" is a long way off. In practical terms, this will translate into more cautious policy advice – and a reduced willingness to dismantle economic safeguards in the faith that markets will solve all problems."

For economists, the crisis in modern day economics offers both a blazon example of the shortfalls as well as an opportunity to revisit the nature of the root assumptions in their approach. The idea that there exists a species, homo economicus, who operates according to predictable axioms and abstract theories, is partially responsible for every boom and successive busts that follow it. In a world of this idealised mythical economic man, economic theories fashioned on such idiosyncrasies need to stop. Great strides were made over the course of the 19th century to align economics to physics and then subsequently to mathematics. This may have marked the retreat of values from economics and with it, the absence of the human aspect of this social science. How far we have fallen from Adam Smith's economic man! One could look at the bursting of the tech bubble in the late-1990s as the first in a continuous series of manias and crashes that have led us to the present precipice. With each bubble burst money fled into new areas: tech money to commodities; commodities to consumer credit and real estate; real estate to bailouts; and now bailout to bailout? We have come full circle where nothing looks worth inflating. Even today, the major hope is that by keeping interest rates low, one could somehow revive the economy.

In effect, the world is in search of a brand-new development model that could deliver inclusive and sustainable high growth while simultaneously enhancing economic prosperity for all on a sustained basis. Responding to this challenge, economists have repeatedly come up with ideas that is nothing but repackaging of the hackneyed commonplaces to make it appear novel. We have seen this happening a number of times in the past few decades, especially as the world of economics alternated between the grand ideas of Keynes and Hayek. We have dealt this subject in greater detail in earlier chapters. One of the recent shifts in the never-ending debate between markets versus state is now evolving more as an optimal combination of the two. Traditionally, markets are believed to ensure efficient allocation of resources that is necessary for higher economic prosperity while the state was to enforce regulations enabling markets to function effectively. This was to provide a level playing field to market participants, and undertake redistribution to address inequality. But as we saw in the previous chapters, this too is a dysfunctional idea. For reasons, obvious and not so obvious, this hybrid model, passed off as a novel idea by some economists, too has not been working.

Beginning of a Grand Idea

In effect, the world of economics is not suffering from lack of fresh ideas, but it is also subject to excessive recycling of old ideas and decrepit prescriptions as something original, fresh and innovative. Economists and policy analysts are in constant search of a magic bullet that would make economic policy meaningful, state intervention effective and, markets functional. Increasingly, realisation seems to dawn on economists that markets and state alone cannot shoulder the responsibility of a complex economy. This is what is termed as the missing middle and has been dealt in good measure in chapter 5. In his interesting book titled *The Third Pillar: How Markets and the State Leave the Community Behind*, Raghuram G Rajan, the former Governor of the RBI, has shed some new light on the missing middle – besides market and the state. In his book, Rajan has attempted to portray the economy as an interplay between the three pillars of state, markets and community. The signal service of the book lies in moving beyond the realm of traditional economics markets and the state by highlighting the important role of the community. While one may or may not agree with the views of Rajan, it must be conceded that it is probably for the first-time a mainstream economist has explicitly conceded the need for a third pillar besides the outworn prescriptions of markets and state or its combinations thereof. Importantly, community by itself is a complex thought lends itself to multiple interpretations and suggestions. Nonetheless, Rajan's novel idea of encompassing community is indeed welcome and laudable for it breaks the monopoly of both the markets and the state in economic policy formulations. However, the moot questions remain: whether a community by itself is sufficient to make economies stable and sustainable? Is it the missing middle that the world is in constant search? Does it provide the necessary fillip to the economy? Or do we require something more?

While the idea of community is indeed nebulous, Rajan argues that the community performs a number of roles. It gives individuals a sense of identity and belonging; it supports members in times of social and economic distress; it allows members to participate in local governance structures thereby improving the provisioning of public services while giving members a sense of control over their lives. In fact, according to Rajan, vibrant communities can serve as a watchdog to prevent corruption and crony capitalism by mobilising protests. It is obvious that Rajan's idea of community corresponds to the idea of civil society of Western democracies. Notwithstanding its usefulness, intriguingly Rajan points out that community can also be regressive if community members put too many restrictions and over-emphasise traditions to protect the power structure within the community. Thus, Rajan with some trepidation, concludes that what is needed is the 'right balance' between the three pillars: state, markets and community in order for society to prosper.

Further, Rajan argues that the source of much of the problems of our times lies in the 'imbalance' between markets and the state. Of course, politically such imbalance expresses itself as extreme nationalist or ultra-left movements in different parts of the world. As Harari points out and detailed in chapter 6, Rajan too concedes that communities have become too weak relative to markets and the state. Fascinatingly, Rajan views the said imbalance again from the prism of the developed world, and not from the standpoint of a sustainable idea. Implicit in the argument of Rajan, is the fact that excessive reliance on the markets in the Western and developed world has led to the idea of globalisation. Even as corporates in the west conjured of a global markets and sole pursuit of profits, little did they realise the collapse of middle-income jobs for the moderately educated workers in these very countries that became the champion of such ideas. This loss in employment opportunity within their own country has taken a huge toll on the families and communities. This, according to Rajan, is manifesting in poor school performance, drug addiction and increased crimes. The long-term consequences of all these are frightening even as the west grapples with the Frankenstein that it has unleashed on itself. As communities and neighbourhood came under increasing pressure, functional families moved to better neighbourhoods to escape the unhealthy environment. To paraphrase Gresham's law – when bad circulates with good, bad will drive out good. Somehow the ants have contrived to distance from the grasshoppers in the West.

This resulted in a downward spiral effect even as dysfunctional communities deteriorated further and faster. Thus, Rajan points out how economic decline – even in the relatively affluent countries – eventually leads to decline of the very idea of family as an institution. It is indeed instructive to note that economic prosperity of family and its long-term sustainability combine to reinforce each other to form a virtuous cycle. That explains the ancient Indian wisdom of placing *Artha*, that is economic prosperity, at the centre of any policy formulation. Absent economic prosperity – individual, family and society will invariably collapse. This results in the alienation of individuals. Once alienated, individuals of dysfunctional families then fall prey to various rabid ideologies and isms propounded by the radical groups that blame the everyone for the problems at hand. It is this breakdown of families that is at the root of our economic problem even as global economic downturns have a debilitating impact on the families. Once family breaks up, invariably markets or the state, the only known instrumentalities, have to necessarily step in to fill in the void. When they do so, it comes with the attendant consequences, usually at extraordinary costs. The cost and consequences of the collapse of the families are compelling if not chilling. Let us not forget that the net result of global economic prosperity has to ultimately result in the prosperity of the families as well. As it is not happening, then something somewhere is seriously wrong.

The West has quickly realised the shortcomings of globalisation including its inability to transfer economic prosperity to the family and there on to the individuals. Hence it has recently distanced itself from the very idea of globalisation, more so after the economic crisis of 2008. In the final analysis, this is the definitive cause for the failure of globalisation even as it collapses right in front of our eyes. Obviously, this comes with a bout of fresh challenges. It is in this, Rajan proposes 'inclusive localism' as a tool to ensure balance of the three pillars. The author describes localism as "the process of decentralising power to the local level so that people feel more empowered in their communities." According to him, empowerment of local communities will give them a sense of responsibility, freer markets will create greater competition to ensure that it remains efficient. Apparently, this arrangement according to the author will by itself ensure that the state will not become corrosive, and the markets oppressive. But the moot question is whether this alone will suffice? The emphatic answer is that it will not. While conceding that communities do have a limited role, the fact is that they do not have the necessary formal authority of law or for that matter, moral suasion. To this extent, communities suffer from certain inherent limitations. What Rajan has suggested may be merely the beginning of a grand idea but not the conclusion. Obviously, it must be taken to the logical conclusion. While the idea of community is indeed welcome to a limited point, the fact of the matter is that we need to go far beyond, and must include families at the core of our economic policies. Rajan was willing to strike, but afraid to wound.

The Counterfactual Question

Obviously, Rajan stopped short of suggesting something spectacular and pointed. Rajan understood the need for a balancing factor between the state and the markets but in the extreme orthodoxy of our times chose to ignore instrumentalities any further than local communities. Of course, local communities have a role, but as mentioned earlier, it is extremely limited. And mostly, local communities are conceptually limited to Western countries. Being inorganic, unorganised, and without the compelling force of law or societal approval, it is often observed even in the Western world that communities are at best, loose association of people lacking the ability to bring the necessary traction to the table. And whenever they do, it is at best local, for a limited period and importantly for a limited cause. No wonder, Rajan like several of his ilk is spot on with the diagnosis but is unable to proceed further with the prescriptions.

That brings us back to the central issue of identifying the balancing factor that ensures we as individuals eschew excesses. Is family the necessary balancing factor that Rajan implicitly advocates but desists from identifying? Is family the crucial factor that has been missed by economists in their understanding of the discipline itself? Let us not forget that the family is perhaps the oldest institution known to man that has survived over the millennia. It has shown a great deal of flexibility and resilience over the centuries. It is the first institution that takes care of us. The essential functions historically of a family has been to contribute to the basic economic survival of its immediate members through a range of what is now called as mundane yet crucial chores for our very survival. These would include something as simple as teaching, cooking, nursing and cleaning.

In economic terms, the concept of a household is an economic unit that lives together and shares resources for the common benefit. The family consumes together, gaining the benefits of economies of scale in consumption. The family raises children and cares for the old and sick. It allocates its capital resources between its members, generating investment in both enterprise and in education. It allows risk sharing between its members, ensuring that temporary downturn does not permanently damage an individual member's prospects. In some cases, the family is also a production unit and organises the division of labour, sometimes based on gender. The extended family, because of its long-term relationships based on trust, allows risk sharing and the efficient allocation of capital between its members. It also serves as an important source of information flows. Finally, the family acts as a mechanism for social inclusion, ensuring that individual members are not permanently alienated from society. It satisfies a psychological need for belonging and represents commitment and security in an uncertain world.

The reason for such behaviour is not far to seek. Individuals have evolved and have survived as a species by placing his own interests and those of his immediate family above the interests of all others. Human beings are indeed self-centred to a great extent. Evolution built us this way. We can sneer at it or ridicule it. But we cannot help it. Thus, given a man the choice between devoting his efforts to himself and his family versus the welfare of strangers, and he will choose the former. And it is not bad or evil for individuals to act in self-interested ways. In fact, it is a natural order. The human species exists probably because genes that impelled the individual toward personal survival were replicated more frequently and survived in the following generations. Therefore, our genetic programming compels us to be self-centred. Yet, most of the economic ideas devised, and particularly those promoting the idea of a welfare state, suggest that it is possible to find a vast number of politicians, bureaucrats and public servants who will selflessly serve the interests of strangers rather than act in their own self-interest. Given the nature of humans, it cannot be done. So are the markets with all its oversight bodies. When we attempt to build a system that violates this fundamental law of nature, we are guaranteed to fail as deliverables from the state or the market is a fraction of what is needed to be done in the first place.

But that is not all. When people make decisions, they seldom think in terms of national or global consequences. However, they also seldom act entirely as individuals. Most often the family or household acts in light of likely consequences and perceptions of how they will affect the family unit. Economic decisions on where to work, how much to save and invest, and what education to acquire are most often made at the family level. Households are the primary decision-making units in most societies. While economists tend to focus on gross national product, the family, not the nation, makes decisions about spending, number of children, migration, education, and the roles assigned to parents and children within the household. Thus, an understanding of household decision-making is critical to an understanding of the relationship between economic development of the nation and that of the family. As family economics and impact of family in economics are still in an embryonic stage of understanding, only a small literature is available on the impact of family on other branch of humanities, especially economics. The family, let us not forget, is such an important institution that progress in understating how it functions is vital for any discipline. In addition to what has been stated above, families play a role of insurer of last resort, providing aid and solace when all else fails and preventing temporary setbacks from becoming permanent. Crucially, it is also the vehicle of transmission of civilisational values from one generation to the other. However, in the academic agenda of modern economists, family has played only a limited-minimalist role. Economists have studied the market, government, the firm, the polity, the business system, civil society, and many related topics such as guilds, democracy, and even religion and their individual and collective impact on the economy. But very little study has been carried out about the family as an institution and its impact on the economy or for that matter, polity. Fascinatingly, none of these activities of the families are captured while computing the national GDP.

The repeated glamourisation of the state and markets means that the role of the family and its impact on economics has been substantially ignored. Crucially, it means family remains a black hole when it comes to the discipline of economics even as most economic decisions including savings, investments, and of course current consumption are taken by families. Further, families contribute to the production too in substantial measure in several economies. This family businesses have their own grammar of functioning. One plausible explanation for this massive oversight by economists is that the study of family invariably involves the study of gender relations, more particularly the role of women, which as we know came to be monopolised by feminists. Recall how the feminists have fallen into the 'rights trap' as discussed in greater detail in Chapter 2. Feminists, by their very definition interdict the very idea of families. And having done so, there is no other alternative but to play by their idea of women and family. In this volatile and surcharged scenario, economists probably believe that they should not enter where, forget angels, even demons fear to tread. Thus, economists and policy framers have built theories on what is practically plausible and not on what is economically correct. More particularly, as discussed in Chapter 8, economists considered the family, the underlying norms, and values as part of a nebulous idea called 'culture' which obviously does not lend to elegant mathematical quantification.

In modern societies, theoretically the dominant economic institutions are the market and the state. However, while these institutions seek to provide alternatives to the family, as pointed out by Harari in *Sapiens* as discussed in Chapter 6, they have their own problems. Market mechanisms can produce efficient outcomes, but pervasive market failure exists in many areas. Corporate entities, in theory, maximise shareholder value but are often conflicted with other goals of the society. This conflict means that they are incapable of playing the larger role required – to be a substitute for the state or the markets. The idea that the state should intervene in such cases is commonplace, but the state itself is not omnipotent as it is made out to be, and state failure, in the sense that it fails to deliver as much as is expected of it, is also common. Other institutions, such as religious organisations, clubs, and community associations, play important roles in limited social arena, but usually lack resources to do the needful. Moreover, these informal associations of men lack the moral, legal or societal approval to step into the role of the markets or the state. Thus, the alternative to the failure of both the state and the market or for that matter any institution, it is the family and family alone.

Yet, family remains largely outside the remit of economists. And whatever be the explanation, the fact of the matter is that the family has been largely absent from the agenda of economists – a classic case of undeserved neglect. One easy way to understand the importance of families is to imagine a world without families. Theoretically, every adult could live alone and gain all the things a family provides from the state or markets or from derived institutions. People could work, consume, save, and invest individually without any of the filial commitments. Risk sharing, old age care, health care and childcare could all be carried out by the state or through the private sector. Children could, in principle, be born not knowing who their parents are. They could be raised by private firms to start their working lives with a debt, or by the state, in which case they would face excessive tax liability. The underlying argument is of course that in almost every illustration mentioned above artificial constructs, institutions, and synthetic mechanisms can supplant the role of the family. For some, the dreadful idea of a world without family is not only deep-seated but also instinctive. Probably, such a world is possible in theory, and indeed, both Plato and Marx postulated such ideas. So do absolute free marketers, liberals, and even feminists with their weird variations. In their understanding, the market merely replaces the state or vice-versa. And implicit in their hypothesis is that whenever markets fail, it is incumbent on the state to step in and do the needful. The fact that some individuals manage to live full lives without ever being associated with a formal family are cited as conclusive evidence that family is not essential for an individual to survive. But is it so simple? Do exceptions make a general rule? All these discussions bring us to a singularly vital counterfactual question: Are families important? Do we require families in the first place? Can we have a world without families? Critically, what will be the impact of the world without families on the discipline of economics?

All these imply a unique social (though we cannot term this social, for want of a better word, we do) experiment where children, parents and siblings are complete strangers to each other. They could all be neighbours or live elsewhere several hundred miles away. In this convoluted scheme of things, DNA and genetic studies cease to matter any longer. Importantly, there is nothing called a spouse -a husband or a wife – in this arrangement. As the idea of family completely melts away, family supervision, so very crucial in the conduct of men and their affairs would become non-existent. Without the brooding omnipresence of filial oversight, there would be no restraints for individuals. This is what modern sociologists, economists and constitutionalists seek to achieve in the long run – complete atomisation of the individual without any filial, social or any other oversight whatsoever with the only exception being that the state and state alone should be the sole arbitrator of men and their affairs. In effect, men and women stripped of their cultural moorings would be converted into animals – acting purely on this instinct and not on their supreme collective self-interests. In this scenario, cultural and civilisational values expressed through layers of restraints, assiduously built over the millennia, will also evaporate. As a result, men and women would be prone to commit excesses without any let or fear. And when individuals become more unrestrained in their behaviour it is the state that would have to necessarily become coercive. Obviously, one feeds into the other and definitely both are undesirable. In the alternative paradigm, in the absence of any incentive that arises from a functional family system, men and women may become recluses and hence cease to participate meaningfully or purposefully in any economic function. Either way, excesses in any form is bound to have a debilitating impact on the economy. It is often remarked that the importance of anything gets expressed only in its absence. Nothing would be closer to truth in the case of family and its impact on economics.

Nevertheless, in the absence of any precise study on the economic behaviour of men (and women too) in the absence of families, it is impossible to fathom an economic model that would precisely address the quadrat of production, consumption, saving and investment and *inter se* arriving at a delicate balance between them. However, one can safely surmise that the entire economic model of such an experiment of a society without family will be significantly different from the society that nurtures family, culture and civilisational values. The communist regimes of yesteryears are the closest examples that one can think of. Stunningly, modern economic models and constitutional constructs are precisely conjured on such fantasies that tend to ignore the importance of families. In short, they ignore real life situations, more particularly of families on the national economies. In the pursuit of being intellectually sophisticated and politically acceptable, experts have preferred to place an individual and individual alone at the centre of their ideas. And that is the real shortcoming of modern economics.

Put differently, even though families and its omnipresent role in real life economic decision making is well acknowledged, understood, and summarily debated, it is virtually ignored in most economic models and constitutional constructs. That is simply because the modern mind refuses to think beyond individuals as the sole basic unit as a reference point. Thus, this creates the ultimate paradox – what is stated in modern theories is divorced from real life situations and what is practiced in real life is never captured in good measure by most modern theories or models. To this extent modern theories remain incomplete as they assume facile positions and tend to ignore real life complexities.

To illustrate, we have dealt with the distinction in the spending pattern of an individual and that of a family in previous chapters. Individuals, without the restraint imposed by the family, revel in current spending. Family, in contrast, will seek to postpone current spending and save. Just as excessive current spending needs to be frowned, excessive savings too brings with it, certain disadvantages. And the self-balancing mechanism – probably a gift of mother nature – is often provided by the families themselves as the urge to spend in the form of celebrations or festivities (or for that matter rituals) is also driven by families but tempered once again by certain restraints. This is best exemplified by the contrasting positions of the Chinese and the Indian economy – both of which are family-based societies and consequently significant saving economies. Nevertheless, the differential between the two is that while civilisational India even to this day scores high on domestic consumption, communist China is compelled to depend on to a great deal on external consumption for dealing with its domestic production. The destruction, by Communist China, of its civilisational past has been dealt in Chapter 3. In fact, little did the communists realise that celebrations of festivals, rooted to civilisational values, results in a million micro-triggers within the economy as it arrives at a delicate balance between both demand and supply. More importantly, such festivals act as a seamless mechanism in redistributing wealth within the society. Absent such mechanisms it probably lends to some corrosive expansionist economic programs including but not limited to currency manipulation and dumping of their goods into other markets. Naturally this internal imbalance in the Chinese economy between their production and consumption is exported by the Chinese to the outside world and manifests itself as a global imbalance. This is akin to the societal imbalance described in greater detail in chapter 1 within polygamous societies and the resultant violence spilling over to the rest of the world. Is this transformation of civilisational China into a communist state in the 20th century the cause of this consumption-production imbalance? Are the Chinese guilty of disconnecting their present to their past? Is this preventing China celebrating its festivals and traditions? Is this in turn causing this imbalance within their economy which in substantial measure makes China dependent on global consumption for its production? Is the destruction of traditional Chinese values the root cause of the present global imbalance?

In real-life situations we as a family are likewise confronted with several alternative and equally compelling alternatives. And like policy makers at the national level, our resources too are finite. But unlike policy makers, families find it natural and hence easy to answer in real time when such convoluted paradigm presents itself. Economists are unable to comprehend this innate ability of an individual to seamlessly provide effective solutions to seemingly irreconcilable real-life situations for himself or for his family. Thus, it is easier for a family, to decide whether to indulge in current consumption or save and therefore, provide for future consumption by deferring the present consumption. This is just as easy for the family, as it is for a migratory bird to find its way back to her home despite flying thousands of miles to avoid adverse weather conditions. Surely, this is done by migratory birds without any modern electronic or magnetic gadgets. Similarly, there is a natural mechanism at play within the family that is able to guide an individual within the family to take these decisions effortlessly. Let us call it the 'invisible mind' which is ceaselessly at work and programmed to take the best of decisions in the overarching interests of the family as well as each and every individual member of the family. Interestingly, the 'invisible mind' lets us know when to save, when to invest, or for that matter take any decision with regards to the collective interests of the family. Most of us do feel it but yet the 'invisible mind' does not lend itself to any precise mathematical modelling. Exactly for this reason and this reason alone economists ignore family in their theoretical abstractions and policy formulations. Despite all this family exists. This is economics at work at the micro level. And when millions of families take decisions in their supreme self-interest, it is pure play macroeconomics. More to the point it exposes an interesting contradiction in our collective thinking – at an individual level we are rooted to our traditions, family and civilisational values and take decisions that are in the supreme interests of our families. But together, at a national level we seek policies that are aimed at the individuals (or at times for the nation) and not collectively for the family. More importantly, when governments take decisions aimed at the individuals and not at the family, and the individuals take decisions favouring the family, the fault lines between the individual, family and government get dramatically exposed.

Family – A Robust and Efficient Institution

In the spring of 2020, as the threat of Covid-19 virus loomed large on the nation, the Indian Prime Minister Narendra Modi announced an unprecedented lockdown of the entire country from March 25. With factories and workplaces shut down, millions of migrant workers had to deal with their loss of employment and consequential debilitating impact on their incomes. The World Economic Forum estimates that there are 139 million migrants in the country. That implies that one out of every ten Indian is a migrant within India – a statistically significant number. It is estimated that most migrant labour in the country originate from the states of Uttar Pradesh and Bihar, followed by Rajasthan, Madhya Pradesh, West Bengal, and probably Odisha. This is where things get intriguing. With their future uncertain in the wake of the lockdown, tens of thousands of India's migrant workers began walking back home, hundreds of kilometres away. With no means of transport due to the lockdown these poor migrant workers had no other choice but to walk back to their homes – to their very homes from which they had migrated to India's great cities like Mumbai, Bengaluru, Chennai, and Delhi in search of greener pastures in the first place. This action of the migrants is all the more inexplicable because these cities had apparently better medical facilities than the hinterland from where these workers had migrated. Sadly, as per various press reports, more than 300 migrant workers died in the process while going back to their homes, with reasons ranging from starvation, suicides, exhaustion, rail accidents, police brutality and denial of timely medical care.

In response, both the Union Government and the respective state Governments did announce a slew of measures to tackle the extant migrant crisis. In the wake of mounting media pressure and possible interventions by the Courts, the Union and state governments took various measures to help them by arranging transport facilities for these workers to reach their respective homes. Further, there were several reassuring measures by the

Union Government including free food grains, ordering waiver of rent and other related measures. Yet, why did the migrants in the time of a grave crisis choose to ignore these promises by the state and migrate during the harsh Indian summer, walking hundreds of kilometres to reach their homes? Why should these workers get back to their homes in a distant place at the time of an extreme national health crisis risking their life? Was the reward of merely reaching their home under such trying circumstances overweighing the risk of walking hundreds of kilometres in the most trying circumstances? If so, what was it?

In fact, the conservative academia in India have not yet asked these pertinent questions. To them, this mass migration of labourers represents the failure of state or markets, depending on their ideological persuasion – nothing more. For some, the migration represented the failure of the state while for others it represented the failure of the markets to take care of the "poor migrant labourers." What was and is lost in the din in the wake of such unprecedented mass migration of human beings and the resultant human sufferings is that these migrant workers were and are in turn supported by an invisible economy – the traditional Indian household – back home from where they had migrated in the first place. Migrants can afford to migrate back, at least in the Indian context, simply because there is an extended family back home. This is despite the fact that the extended family could be only with meagre resources, span across generations, children, siblings and elderly parents (and at times their siblings too). What is crucial is that it is this institution that promises care and succour even in the most desperate of times without any chance of any failure. Economists unfortunately are unable to fathom this invisible structure and its impact on the behaviour of every individual. Indians know, so do many outside India, that the state or for that matter despite its best of intentions cannot be a pale substitute for the efficacy of family. The migrant knows that should he somehow make it back to his home in the distant land, his family will take care of him.

That explains in a nutshell the role of family qua the state or the markets. But to understand this inexplicable human behaviour we need to analyse the economics that drives such behaviour in greater detail. Balance sheet of the world is the aggregate of the balance sheets of the family, businesses including those of corporates, banks and of course finally of the governments. It may be fascinating to note that the family invests in the business as well lends to the corporates, banks and governments. Resultantly, the balance sheets of latter are steeped in debt with such debts in effect represent the savings and investments by the household. For instance, what is held as deposits by banks is in effect lending by the household; investments into the government bonds are in effect assets of the family as it will be in case of corporates. Thus, in case the balance of the world is indeed drawn up, the assets side will be represented predominantly by the savings of the household and invested into as shares and bonds of the business, banks and government. Needless to emphasise, the aggregate of all these makes up the liability side. It is this strength derived from this balance sheet that makes the family not only a socially robust institution but also economically an efficient one.

This is what experts call the natural law at work and hence tend to be dismissive about it. Sadly, they believe that it would work under any circumstances and can be milked to the bone. While the state or market cannot fashion the natural law to work especially in trying circumstances, they surely can by their corrosive functioning and destructive interference make families dysfunctional. A discussion on the proposition that a family requires a solid economic basis in order to carry out the natural functions assigned to, it would amount to belabouring the obvious. Recall the ancient Indic idea of *Artha* and how it is a vital cog in the scheme of things? Yet, it is oblivious to our policy framers. It is also evident that whenever the drift of social and economic forces leads even to a partial breakup of the certain preconditions for the effective and efficient functioning of the family, the institution of the family is put to great peril. That it survives in extreme excruciating trying circumstances is a tribute to its survival ability. It is also a telling commentary on the policy makers who frame such corrosive policies without foreseeing the impact on the families. The policies brought about by Daniel Patrick Moynihan in the early 60's and discussed in chapter 2 in connection with the black families in the US and its subsequent debilitating impact on black families in US is a case in point. Consequently, any economic system which fails to produce conditions permitting families to continue living together as a unit would fail to measure up to the requirements of the natural law itself. And this, in more ways than one, sums up the modern economics.

It is necessary at this point to clarify first the somewhat ambiguous term "family as an economic unit." People living together in a household and consuming all or part of a joint income are referred to as a spending unit. If the income is being produced and earned entirely outside the home, these families constitute economic units only in terms of consumption. But in the long experience of mankind, the vast majority of families were also producer units, working together on the land, small businesses and in small shops to earn the family income with their own productive assets. This was the case to such an extent that there has been an almost de facto identification between families and ownership of income producing assets such as land or business capital. Prior to the industrial revolution of the last two hundred years, most economic units in business and farming were centred around the family. Families were coextensive with productive economic units to such a degree that one did not seem to be viable without the other. While post industrial revolution much has changed probably in the Western world, the fact remains that in several developing countries notably India, families continue to own some income producing asset, which enables the family to generate income and based on such income, maintains its consumption patterns. Protecting these income generating assets should be the priority of any government as it ensures that families manage to be self-sufficient, albeit with meagre resources and minimal income. Crucially, they do not turn into a burden on the state, a fact lost on most economists. Therefore, the question arises – how can the family as a functional economic unit be preserved and strengthened in a current socio-political setting?

Why Families should be Preserved

Before we proceed to answer this question, first let us answer the question why should family as a functional unit be preserved? To answer this, let us draw reference to the hypothesis of financial instability first developed by the noted economist, Hyman Minsky. He argued that financial crisis is endemic in pure play capitalistic economies because extended periods of economic prosperity encouraged borrowers and lenders to be progressively reckless. It is entropy, as we discussed in Chapter 4, at play, pure and simple. Therefore, Minsky rightly pointed out that extended period of prosperity by itself contains the seed of self-destruction. If economic history of post war period is any guide, this excessive optimism (which is another form of excess) ends up definitely creating financial bubbles. As we all know, bubbles are prone to collapses and economic implosion. And fascinatingly, no amount of government regulation or intervention has been able to solve this issue of mass irrational exuberance. Financial instability thus could be summed up as excesses caused by rapid bouts of economic successes which leads to an economic crisis caused by the building up of asset bubbles in the first place.

The Minsky moment refers to the point where the financial system moves from stability to instability. It is that point where over-indebted borrowers start to sell off their overvalued assets to meet other repayment demands. This causes a fall in asset prices and a loss of confidence. It can cause businesses to become illiquid – they can't meet the demand for cash to repay their debts. It may cause a run on the banks as people seek to withdraw their money. Usually, the Minsky moment comes when lending and debt levels have built up to unsustainable levels. The work of Hyman Minsky was largely ignored by mainstream economics in the 1970s and 1980s. Instead, there was widespread support for financial deregulation. But the credit crisis of 2007 onwards understandably created renewed interest in his work when mainstream economists once again favoured governmental regulations.

Understandably, Minsky's hypothesis revolves around irrational exuberance exacerbated by extreme levels of debt. According to Minsky, market capitalism is inherently unstable because the forces that cause periodic finance, output and debt crises are systemic. According to Minsky, the surest way to ensure that irrational exuberance does not go out of hand is conceivable only when we give importance to institutions that can manage such excesses. But experiences of the past seven or eight decades since the war demonstrate that most of the regulatory mechanisms and institutions set up by the governments or markets have failed in identifying or dealing with any irrational behaviour, exuberance or otherwise. We have seen the unsuccessful tryst with macroeconomic stability by the former British Prime Minister Gordon Brown in Chapter 5.

This is where the importance of family as an institution comes up in counter-balancing irrational exuberances. For starters, for most family, debt is a four-letter word that's synonymous with risk, vulnerability and outside control. High-profile cases of family that have buckled under enormous debt become cautionary tales for most families. It is therefore no surprise that most families manage to operate with little or virtually no leverage. And when families are compelled by force of circumstances to contract debt, they are relieved when they repay the same. We have dealt with the issue of the psychological scare on the delinquent borrower in Chapter 8.

The case of Ford in the first decade of this century is a classic case in point as to how families deal with debt and mortgage of family silver. Ford Motors borrowed $23.5 billion in loans as means of implementing a daring plan to transform the business and remain independent. As luck would have it, Ford borrowed the money in 2006, on the eve of the financial crisis and a severe downturn in the auto market. And to qualify for the loans, Ford put up nearly all its assets as collateral, including its blue oval trademark, a move the descendants of Henry Ford did not take lightly. "When we pledged the blue oval it was enormously emotional for me personally and for my family, because we weren't just pledging an asset, we were pledging our heritage," William Clay Ford Jr., fourth-generation executive chairman, said in a conference call when Ford got the logo back in 2012.

A professionally managed firm would have that logo as a mere asset and not a heritage as did seem for Ford Jr. And therein lies the subtle but crucial difference between firms that are professionally managed and those which are managed by the family. A professionally managed firm could have probably leveraged the asset, in this case the Ford Logo, by borrowing more and spending more, at times even recklessly. In case things go well the professional managers would seek to be rewarded first up. But if things go bad, there was always a route through the insolvency proceedings. For the Ford family it was a matter of prestige as the Logo was a priceless piece of heritage. That emotional bonding with the logo ensured that the Ford despite the fact they had borrowed significant sums during the great economic recession were able to repay the same and got back the logo released from pledge. Why did the Ford family attach so much significance to the Logo?

Did that impact its performance and spur it to greater heights? Crucially, is there is a difference in a firm managed by a family and those which are professionally managed?

It is in this connection that the Centre for Management and Economic Research at École Polytechnique, compiled a list of 149 publicly traded, family-controlled businesses with revenues of more than $1 billion. They were based in the US, Canada, France, Spain, Portugal, Italy, and Mexico. Likewise, a comparison group of companies from the same countries and sectors, which were similar in size but not family controlled was created. Then a rigorous analysis of the manner in which those two sets of companies were managed differently and how that affected their respective performance was carried out. Results demonstrated that during good economic times, family-run companies do not earn as much money as companies with a more dispersed ownership structure. But when the economy slumps, family firms far outshine their peers. When the study looked across business cycles, it found that the average long-term financial performance was higher for family businesses than for nonfamily businesses, in every country it examined. It is evident that those cycles are speeding up. If that trend continues, the resilience-focused strategy of family-owned companies may become more attractive to all companies. In a global economy that seems to shift from crisis to crisis with alarming frequency, accepting a lower return in good times to ensure survival in bad times may be a practical trade-off that conservative owners will be thrilled to make.

The conclusion of the study was on expected lines yet profound. It found that that family businesses focused more on enhancing its resilience prowess than on performance. They forego the excess returns available during good times in order to increase their odds of survival during bad times. A CEO of a family-controlled firm may have financial incentives similar to those of chief executives of nonfamily firms, but the familial obligation will invariably lead to very different strategic choices. Executives of such family businesses often invest with a 10 or 20-year horizon, concentrating on what they can do now to benefit the next generation – something that professional managers do worry about, but rarely. Needless to emphasise, caring for the next generation is a classical trait of a business scion. Fascinatingly, they also tend to manage their downside far better more than their upside, in contrast with most CEOs, who try to make their mark through out performance. At a time when executives of every company are encouraged to manage for the long term, the research demonstrated that well-run family businesses can serve as role models. In fact, the research was able to identify several companies with dispersed ownership whose strategies mimicked those of family firms. Those companies also exhibited a similar performance pattern: below their peers during upturns but leading the pack in times of crisis. So how do family-run firms manage for such resilience? What is the secret formula which repeatedly ensures that family managed firms sustain in the long term? Significantly, the study identified seven differences in their approach:

1. They're frugal in good times and bad.
2. They keep the bar high for capital expenditures.
3. They carry little debt.
4. They acquire fewer (and smaller) companies.
5. Many show a surprising level of diversification.
6. They are more international.
7. They retain talent better than their competitors do.

Put pithily, family firms triumph the professionally managed firms by simply putting into practice the idea of restraint contained in *Maitrim Bhajata.* They are frugal in good and also at bad times, carry little debt, are not ostentatious, continuously invest, diversify while continuously investing in their employees and retain them rather than firing them. It is the restraint at every twist and turn that ensures that these firms are fully equipped and hence survive the Minsky moment as and when it arrives. And as bubbles burst, it is these firms by putting in place an internal countercyclical policy are able to quickly beat the downtrend and more often than not outpace their competitors as when upswing happens.

What holds true for family managed business firms holds true for family-based economies as well as societies. Such economies and societies will be well and truly be restrained. It will have the place for the weak, women, the aged, the environment and of course the flora and the fauna. It will place women and her welfare central to every decision. It will care for the children as it will for the aged and the disabled. It will constantly seek to look at the long term as it will provide for the next generation. It will seek to co-opt rather than ruthlessly compete. And when it does compete it will do so only up to a point of establishing systemic efficiencies. It will be inclusive as it will be efficient. It will be frugal and not flashy. Consequently, it may not make spectacular headlines for the media but will be efficient during upswings as well as downswings. Importantly, it will not cause any downturns. It will absorb technology at its own pace without being flashy about it, as it will be, in case of employment. It will eschew debts and drive its future growth on its own earnings and savings. Such societies in effect sustain themselves for a long run. In short, it will be restrained and hence an anti-thesis of everything that modern economics stands for and professes. No wonder modern economics has no place for it either.

Minsky, let us not forget, posed questions that surpassed the mechanisms of capitalism and inquired into the very core of modern economics. He may have very well posited – "Are crises inherent to modern-day economics?" Such questions would require a deeper view of the functioning of modern-day economies. This deeper view is the object of this work too. From the origin of economics, its grand purpose, to the very nature of economics, to the disappearing human values, we ask scholars and economists alike, how we ended up where we are today. Crucially, what are the solutions? Part of what emerges from the discussions above is whether values have left economics or, more aptly, whether economics has divorced itself from values. And when values take leave, what remains is only abstract theory. And how do we bring values back? If it is the institution of families that can bring stability to the inherently instable system, how do we strengthen the families?

The regulatory and policy responses thus far have been more symptomatic than attacking the root of the issue; more or less on predictable lines. While not completely devoid of merit, none of these responses address the core issue of reinfusing filial values in the functioning of the economy. Let us not forget that it is some sort of short-termism that landed us in our current mess. The blind focus on GDP, the stock market indices, incremental quarterly earnings, and the latest consumer confidence level put enormous pressure on individuals, corporates and even governments to short-circuit existing rules and lobbyists to erode such regulation in the name of competition. This narrow focus diminishes the humanistic elements of the economy. It is precisely for all these reasons that the institution of family must be well and truly preserved. The ubiquitous focus on bringing analysis down to the individual as the agent of every analysis (we will deal with this issue in Chapter 10) forgets that economics stems from oikos, meaning the family. Keynes famously stated that, "the biggest problem is not let people accept new ideas, but to let them forget the old ones." We may be wise to remember what we have forgotten for too long and to our own peril – economics is after all a social science.

References

1. NBER Working Paper Series – The Paradox Of Civilization: Pre-Institutional Sources Of Security And Prosperity – Working Paper No – 21829 – By Ernesto Dal Bó, Pablo Hernández and Sebastián Mazzuca.
2. Why Did the Soviet Union Collapse? By Michael Ray – www.Britannica.com
3. How the Economics of Civilisation can Save the Global Economy – By Fred Harrison – DOC Research Institute – 27th September 2017.
4. Civilization and Economic Growth By Bryan Caplan – 1995.
5. https://equitablegrowth.org/appreciation-robert-solow/
6. How much Competition do we need in a Civilized Society? By Jan Ott – March 3, 2011.
7. Why we missed the storm – By David Orrell- World Finance – November 23, 2018.
8. Letter to the Queen – By Geoffrey M Hodgson – https://www.geoffreymhodgson.uk/letter-to-the-queen
9. How a belief in American exceptionalism is making America less exceptional – By Eric J. Lyman – Pacific Standard, Feb 22, 2018.
10. Does Democracy Demand the Tolerance of the Intolerant? Karl Popper's Paradox – By Josh Jones – Open Culture – 29th March, 2019.
11. How Did Economists Get It So Wrong? By Paul Krugman – The New York Times Magazine – September 2, 2009.
12. Reserve Bank of India Occasional Papers Vol. 40, No. 1, 2019 By Ipsita Padhi, Manager Department of Economic Policy and Research (DEPR), RBI.
13. Family Systems and Economic Development By Sarah G. Carmichael, Selin Dilli & Jan Luiten van Zanden- January 2016.
14. The Family and Economic Development By David Canning, Marc Mitchell, David Bloom, and Erin L. Kleindorfer- Harvard Institute for International Development.

15. https://en.wikipedia.org/wiki/Indian_migrant_workers_during_the_COVID-19_pandemic
16. The Family as an Economic Unit By Friedrich Baerwald- Fordham Law Review – 1955.
17. Financial Instability Hypothesis By Tejvan Pettinger – Economics. Help- 12th February 2018.
18. What You Can Learn from Family Business By Nicolas Kachaner, George Stalk, Jr. and Alain Bloc – Harvard Business Review – November 20.

10. Ram Rajya is Less of Lord Rama, More of Rajya

Life is like riding a bicycle. To keep your balance, you must keep moving

– Albert Einstein

Minimum Government, Maximum Governance

– Narendra Modi

So, who are we? Merely animals? Or are we a species of animals; at best its subset – mammals? If merely animals, are we to be scientifically explained as direct descendants of primates; also termed as *homo sapiens*? Or are we something much more and different – cultured, civilised, and hence an evolved species of animals? If that were so, what then is the ultimate test of this culture, civilisation and their associated derivatives? What are their ingredients? Crucially, do culture and civilisation matter in our modern constitutional and macroeconomic arrangements? And pray how and to what extent they impact and hence become relevant, especially in arranging our public affairs? If, on the other hand, culture and civilisation do not matter in our existence at all, how do we then claim with certainty that we are an evolved species of animals in the first place? As a sequel, who is to determine what is culture and its larger set, civilisation? More specifically, what are the crucial differentials between those who claim to be cultured and civil and those who are alleged to be not? Who is to arbitrate this divide? Are culture and civilisation at best an idea based on certain religious or habitual preferences of a particular group? Is it homogeneous? Or heterogeneous? Are plural thoughts and ideas possible within the broad prism of culture and civilisation?

Fascinatingly, if human behaviour has to be uniformly collectivised, corporatised and monochromatised, then what about individual initiatives and individuality? If the latter triumphs all collective good, as some believe and practice, then why do we then seek to surrender individuality at the altar of some nebulous, yet overarching, idea called overall or collective good? Put differently, do we as individuals possess distinct characteristics which is non-violable and that which cannot not be subjected to some higher idea and greater ideals? Is the clash then being played out concurrently between extreme individualism and common collective good, with little or no balancing factor in-between the two? And is this belief in the two extreme positions – in Marxism and in the alternative Markets – the cause of several cycles of economic boom and doom as much as they are the cause of repeated social, political and economic instability as we witnessed in the 20th century? And is the antidote to such repeated cycles of boom and doom available with us in the form of cultural and civilisational values rooted to individual restraints? Is it therefore inevitable that the constitutional mechanism and macroeconomic arrangement globally that are at play in these troubled times should now focus more on these individual restraints even as we move forward in redesigning our public affairs?

There is yet another dimension to this issue. In the extant process of arranging our collective affairs we should not forget the fact that we are heavily tethered to others, notably to our fellow human beings? Is this arrangement with our fellow human beings contractual, and hence artificial? Or is this entirely natural and hence does not require any interference whatsoever? Is there a need for balancing the two contrasting positions? Further, if we naturally do come together why do we have to necessarily come together yet again, as the preamble of the Indian Constitution declares? Crucially, is this coming together only for the limited purpose of guaranteeing our specific individual rights while managing our collective affairs? Or is it much more? Much as it may sound quixotic and paradoxical, are we to come together under an artificial written charter to collectively cognise our natural individual rights? And pray what about our collective rights – as members of the family, kinship and society arising out of coming together naturally? Is atomisation of the individual the sole viable option in arranging our public affairs? Is the coming together as prescribed by the preamble the only way with no alternative in sight? Or do we once again need to balance between the two? If so, how?

And in all these, what would be the role of women, men and families? Is not the family the very microcosm of society? Should we then not first seek to arrange the private affairs of men and women primarily and also decisively through the institution of family and marriage before we proceed any further to set right any public affairs? Or, is it entirely desirable to build the entire constitutional and macroeconomic edifice bypassing this natural yet crucial institution that is at once intensely private, yet has a profound influence on all affairs that is public? Does the extant constitutional arrangement indicate that all it matters is the individual good and his material well-being, achieved, either by the active assistance of the state, or the markets? Implicitly, is gross individualism the destination point in arranging our public affairs and macroeconomic structure? Thus, are we reduced to mere individuals that the state has to step at every twist and turn to fulfil all our wants and probably desires – the perfect backdrop that necessitates an omnipotent and an omnipresent state? As we saw in chapter 3, the destruction of family leading to absolute individualism suits both the Marxists and the champions of free markets.

In short, do we inadvertently but, heavily borrow from the central idea of Christendom in having an external corrective agent in the form of the state (or markets, as the case may be) at every twist and turn of human affairs? In the alternative, are we to reduce the state to a residuary idea, thereby placing individual duties and responsibilities at the centre of all our public policy formulation? How are we to arrange the affairs of the state? For starters, how much do we tax? How do we balance the conflicting ideas of welfare and taxation on one hand and liberty and private initiative on the other? By repeatedly expanding the idea of welfare, are we not making everyone dependent on welfare rather than on private initiative? Is this idea durable? Is this arrangement sustainable in the long run? Does this lack of balance between the state and the individual dynamite the very idea of state, especially its finances? Is this overdependence on the state, triggered by excessive welfarism, the root cause of the crisis within the discipline of economics that we are currently witnessing? Does not a pauperised state become dysfunctional one sooner than later? Finally, what is the impact of a dysfunctional state on the macroeconomic outcome of a nation, its society and the assiduously built arrangement between the individual and the state? Some of these questions are indeed difficult to comprehend. Answers to some of these questions can be done only by indulging in an extensive counterfactual analysis, the impact of which the human mind may find extremely difficult to conjure, much less compute.

Nevertheless, and fully mindful of these limitations, we have sought answers to some of these convoluted questions in the preceding chapters of this book. It may be recalled that one of the haunting questions which remains as the primary trigger for this book and was dealt with extensively in Chapter 1 is the role of the institution of family. Research clearly shows that the institution of family is the first form of community and government and, as pointed out repeatedly by various philosophers the first, best and original department of health, education and welfare, and probably much more. The antiquity of this institution and its impact on the economic and scientific progress of mankind is indeed stunning. The reason for the same is not far to seek. The family, even to this date, remains as the basic social unit of society. Centuries ago, Aristotle opined that the family is nature's answer for the supply of mankind's everyday wants. Since then, neither the state nor the markets have been able to replace it in substantial measure, despite concerted attempts to do so by both. And this has profound impact on the way our economy remains structured and functions. Let me amplify.

Core of the Conundrum

Without attracting the charge of exaggeration or crass generalisation one can safely surmise that a nation, society and the state solely stands on the edifice of family. And family necessarily involves the issue of marriage or two persons of opposite genders. It is natural that we are interested in the relationship between the sanctity of marriage in every society and the consequent importance given to the institution of family by it. This is simply because family is the most basic social unit on which the entire edifice of society is built. Also, marriage and family are linked to other social institutions such as the economy, government and religion. Charles Murray in his book, *Coming Apart*, examines to find that the great secrets of the successful upper class (in the US) lay in dedicated practices of traditional family values. Simply stated, it means that successful families are those which have practiced self-restraints leading to sustained hard work, frugality and living within one's means. Some would know of it as Calvinist spirit in action and others, as *Karma Yoga*. This belief in sustained hard work explicitly ushers in self-reliance and implicitly eschews dependency on others, notably the state. Put differently, families have become great by their dint of sincere hard work, not otherwise. More to the point, families have definitely not become great through doles given by the state. Of course, welfare programs of the state might have sustained some families in their bad times and for short periods, but have never made anyone among them, great.

If we examine dispassionately the economic history of the 20th century, it is apparent that welfare and doles are not elixir that fights the scourge of poverty. And, definitely not over a sustained period of time that too for extended sections of population. It is pertinent to note that no family and by extension country has found its way to economic nirvana merely through welfare and doles dished out by an indulgent state. Nor has the individual. This is the core and recurring theme of this book. On the contrary, it is the natural urge of both woman and man, as members of the family, to provide for their family that compels them to indulge in sustained hard work and to be self-dependent. This natural urge cannot be created by a fiat. But the state, through repeated intervention in the affairs of the family, can weaken it substantially, probably even destroy it, as it has done successfully in the case of black American families. It must be remembered that it is this sustained hard work of family members that makes a family successful. Therefore, men and women who get married, stay married and have children within marriage are more likely to be economically successful. It must be noted that economically successful families collectively transform into economically successful nations. Family, as we have seen, is a bedrock on which the edifice of macroeconomics is built. Thus, sanctity for the institution of marriage, the importance of family in the harmonious functioning of the society and their symbiotic link with the national economy cannot be understated in these tumultuous times.

Yet, modern economic policies precisely ignore the importance of family, marriage and impact of culture on economics. If there is one institution whose importance has been downplayed in modern socio-economic-political discourse, it is the institution of family. The reason for the same is not far to seek and has been explained in previous chapters of the book. Most of the modern policies are rooted in an individualistic view of society, one that emphasises maximising one's human and financial capital over building any social capital, that is, the ability to develop and maintain strong family and community institutions. Yuval Levin, for instance, argues in *The Fractured Republic* that the prevailing "view of society as consisting only of individuals and a state" must be tempered by "putting power, authority, and significance as close to the level of the interpersonal community as reasonably possible." This view corresponds to the view of Yuval Noah Harari in *Sapiens*. It is the birth of individualism, the consequent break-down of families and the concomitant rise of both markets and state that has been at the core of the conundrum. The net consequence of this rise in individualism and purging him of his connections to the family is of recent origin. We have discussed the chilling consequence of these developments in Chapter 6.

Ideally, policy formulation should reflect in a less than modest role for government coupled with a more than robust role for social institution including markets. The government, once seen as a crucial provider of law and order, and social institutions, have unfortunately been over a period of time redefined to serve solely the needs of the individual. As political scientist Daniel Elazar observed, whereas in the colonial period it was understood that "the fabric of society had to be kept intact, even at the expense of individual liberties and rights." Accordingly, from 1789 to the 1940s "the maintenance of the social fabric was given equal billing with individual rights." Subsequently, in the late 1940s or so, "maintaining the social fabric became distinctly secondary if not incidental in the face of individual rights challenges." While modern constitutionalists sought to secure individual rights by strengthening institutions and balancing forces within society, postmodern constitutional thought looks to the guaranteeing of individual rights through judicial fiat, almost without regard to the other institutional arrangements and relationships. The net result was absolute atomisation of the individual with near complete destruction of family as an institution. As families were destroyed the nanny state was inadvertently born. Remember the fundamental laws of physics – nature abhors vacuum. The sociological vacuum created by the collapse of families was at-once occupied by the emergence of the nanny state. As state became the surrogate family, it slowly yet steadily expanded its sweep and scope of interfering into every single affair of a traditional family. This was possible only by the extensive bureaucratisation of the state, of course with disastrous cost and consequences. We have dealt with all these issues in Chapter 2.

This combination of increased bureaucratisation of the state and concomitant weakening of family eroded the emotional bonds between individuals and their communities. More importantly, the bureaucratisation of the state meant that the state had considerable difficulty in internalising the moral code of the society – of differentiating between good, bad and the ugly. To expand further, the state is simply incapable to impart or enforce the needed ethic for the efficient conduct of business, economy or for society, a function so seamlessly, efficiently and naturally done by families. Absent such mores and mechanism to enforce them, there is nothing to lubricate every bend and joint for an efficient functioning to the society. Bureaucracy, as is its wont, tends to see everything in a binary mode, i.e., things that are completely right and that are clearly in the wrong – leading to unintended consequences for the smooth functioning of the economy. In the process we run the risk of becoming a rule-based society rather than a law-based one. The end result of all this is perceived equality, not functional equity. The difference, though subtle, is crucial. It is no wonder that we are unable to wipe the scourge of poverty with such a pedantic approach. Let us not forget that real life, as we all understand, is a kaleidoscope of emotions where a rule-based approach is a surest way to make every system dysfunctional.

And that is crucial to the issue on hand – is there an institution that allows individual initiative to flourish while simultaneously ensuring that animal spirits do not takeover an individual completely, that too on real time basis? As discussed in Chapter 1, unrestrained individuals run the risk of dynamiting every system and man-made construct. They are at once a risk to peace and prosperity. At the core of the conundrum is the absence of a cost-effective oversight body that addresses these individual excesses while allowing individual initiatives to flourish. This in short is the challenge to modern economics as it is unable to balance between igniting individual initiatives and curbing individual excess. This individual gyration, sometimes with gay abandon, invariably results in the cycles of economic boom and doom. Individual excesses arise invariably when such persons are not integrated into the moral universe of the society. The solution to this conundrum is obviously when the institution of family integrates an individual into the moral universe of the society, and probably even to that of the nation. That is easily done as it is the family that determines the moral universe of the society and by extension of the nation, in the first place. Conversely, it is entirely possible that a nation purged of family and civilisational values would be without a moral universe. National morals are indeed built on family morals. This is the first and the foremost contribution of the family which most observers tend to ignore. More to the point, as the state cannot legislate morality, there are very few institutionalised checks and balances as would be possible in case of a traditional family to hold back the self-aggrandizing, predatory, animalistic behaviour of an individual. When individuals go berserk, nations too follow suit. On the contrary it is the family that tempers the individual to conform to a socially accepted behavioural pattern. We have dealt with this aspect of the family induced restraints in great detail in chapter 9. Since the days of Plato, communists have been attempting at a designer society where family and family values are given a go by. Much to their chagrin and probably to the relief of the entire world, they have been by and large unsuccessful in their attempts to create a designer society. Despite its failure, the idea of Plato has often made remarkable comeback only to fail and be rejected by the subsequent flow of events. The platonic society has been unable to take off for the simple reason that it is at odds with the behaviour of men and thereby in conflict with the laws of nature. That, in more ways than one, makes marriage and family important as a naturally cost-effective balancing factor while dealing with every individual and his excesses.

Explaining the Inexplicable

Indians have, for time immemorial, realised the importance of family and marriage in restraining individuals from wanton excesses exemplified by the great Indian epic *Ramayana*. In more ways than one this epic offers certain solutions to the challenges faced by the modern world. Anybody, intending to know the solutions to the present cannot ignore our past – in the least as a diagnostic tool, if not as a prescriptive one. The popularity of the *Ramayana* over the millennia is a monument to the recognition of idealism in India; its high esteem of moral values and resolute belief in the ultimate triumph of good over evil. Although, the *Ramayana* earns the distinction of great antiquity in world literature, it is still accepted as a splendiferous literary specimen for all times due to its universal appeal in affording perpetual solution of most the problems that confront us in every stage of life. At a personal level, *Ramayana* beautifully presents the ideal filial relationship between individuals of a family, viz. between the brothers, between the husband and wife, between the mother/father and their sons. Naturally, its appeal remains eternal to all the citizens of our country and those abroad. At a broader level it blends religion with morality and statesmanship with common sense in such a manner that it presents an eternal referral point for all future generations. Consequently, and without any hesitation one can safely declare that no other work in the literary world has exercised such a significant influence on the collective mind, life and thoughts of the masses over the millennia and in several countries. Jawaharlal Nehru, the first prime minister of independent India, not known for exhibiting any sentiments for traditional India had given to his emotion while commenting on the *Ramayana* (and also the *Mahabharat* the other great Indian epic) – "I do not know of any books anywhere which have exercised such a continuous and pervasive influence on the mass mind as these two. Dating back to a remote antiquity, they are still a living force in the life of the Indian people."

The reason why the *Ramayana* occupies a unique place in the realm of literary development and religious thoughts is not far to seek. Various scholars at every point in time have pointed out that it exerts great influence on the activities and thoughts of successive generations of Indians. It shows us that all good attributes like faithfulness, sincerity, obedience, truthfulness etc. are central to a civilised social order. No wonder, the high ideals of life as portrayed in the epic, influence the people even to this day. Thus, it is not only a very popular epic but also an undeclared universal ethical code for humanity. The teachings of the *Ramayana* are easily comprehended because of its ethical contents. The *Ramayana* teaches us how an ideal king, an ideal father, an ideal mother, an ideal son, an ideal brother, an ideal servant, an ideal husband and an ideal wife should behave in life – each one of them exemplified by their retrained behaviour in the most trying circumstances. It also tells us what is not ideal behaviour. It is for us to choose between the two. And only the consequences of our choices are explained in these epics. In direct contrast to what Boyce puts forth in *Born Bad* about how Christendom seeks an external agent for salvation and discussed in greater detail in chapter 3, the ideas contained in *Ramayana* are invariably to seek redemption to all problems, personal or otherwise, from within. It is this message that reflects in an established social order that has been extended through the ages. Not even the modern India despite its proclaimed idea of being irrelevantly neutral to all religiosity is free from the eternal message contained in this epic. Thus, the *Ramayana* exercises a tremendous influence on the individual, social or religious life of the common people of India in every respect even to this date. It will not be an exaggeration to say that the *Ramayana* serves as the foundation stone of Indian culture and social life through the ages, on which, the entire edifice of the present society is even to this day firmly rooted.

Of the several ideas discussed, ethics prescribed and morals preached, the life of the central character of *Ramayana*, the Prince of Ayodhya has an eternal message for all of us – that of monogamy. Arising out of monogamy is a tranquil social order that guaranteed durable peace which in turn enabled sustained progress. Monogamous marriage was probably the greatest discovery of mankind, exemplified by the life of Lord Rama. Over the millennia, Indians have come to understand that it is this individual restraint that brings about a benign social order that was established and sanctified by Lord Rama himself. This has been internalised by the society over generations so much so that is now seen as an inviolable law of the land which goes on to establish an eternal, functional and fair mechanism. Thus, as the life of Prophet with numerous marriages to various women has become the benchmark for emulation for devout Muslims, the life of

Lord Rama with his lifelong message of monogamy had become the gold standard of personal behaviour for devout Hindus (Interestingly, for both, the standard prescription both by our Constitution and modern economists has been remarkably anchored to the Hobbesian view of the world arising from what the devout Christian believes – 'Broken Self'). Of course, this may be breached by a few individuals occasionally through an act of adultery or polygamy. Yet, to the ordinary Hindu mind it cannot be an acceptable social order – an order that was created by Lord Rama himself. No wonder, amongst the pantheon of gods in the Indic fold, Lord Rama for the sheer idea of monogamy is considered as a civilisational god – a fact lost on many. In contrast to the deep understanding on this subject by our society, the Supreme Court decided to go ahead of the curve in Joseph Shine case as discussed in Chapter 1. Accordingly, adultery was reduced to a mere civil wrong by the modern constitutional mind and therefore, it did not involve any criminality on part of the errant spouse involved in such act. But to the traditional, adultery is sacrilege. Traditional Indian society or for that matter any society will never accept adultery as a minor indiscretion on part of an individual. It is breach of trust at an individual level and at a national level, it is much more. Constitutional morality cannot be built by those who care less for personal morals – a point missed by many. In fact, constitutional morality has to be dovetailed into the social values, not otherwise. More to the point, to a student of *Ramayana*, any lack of personal morality would be perfidy. Adultery, or for that matter polygamy, does disturb the assiduously built social construct and dynamite the economic order. The life-message of Lord Rama explained through *Ramayana* only re-emphasises the prerequisite for building the national economy through individual restraint. Once this natural order is disturbed, society is left to be constantly on the boil. Such a society has no chance of being at peace with itself. And a society which is not in peace with itself cannot bring in prosperity or for that matter usher in progress. This explains why Lord Rama is considered as a civilisational God by many across the world.

Thus, there is a twin-layered magnus opus in operation – one, that deals with monogamous marriages at the first level and the second – being a derivative of the former – is how monogamy transmutes itself into overarching peace and prosperity for the society. Of course, the link between monogamy and economic prosperity, though demonstrable, is incapable of being put to some precise mathematical formula. As we have seen in chapter 5 modern economists eschew anything and everything that is incapable of being subjected to a precise mathematical formula. Monogamy is one grand cultural idea that has profound impact on several aspects of mankind. We have seen this argument being put forth right through the book, more particularly in Chapter 1. But since it is incapable of being mathematically being calculated or demonstrated, economists for good measure have rejected the very idea of culture, more so monogamous marriages, in their understanding of economics. In direct contrast to the economists, the ordinary people understand the symbiotic link between macroeconomic functioning and culture propelled by monogamy. Probably, it is the lack of some obscure mathematical formula presented in the most convoluted manner by economists that facilitates the understanding of this phenomenon by the commoner in the first place! Inexplicable as it may sound, the fact remains that the ordinary men are eminently capable of understanding the causal relationship between practicing monogamy at an individual level and peace, progress and economic prosperity at a macro level. Of course, unlike economists, it may be impossible for them to articulate their overarching concerns in precise terms about how individual indiscretion adversely impacts national economic functioning. Unable to explain, their consternation is expressed in other forms, often through uncivil means and at times through violence. That explains why Tamils were incensed and dismayed with the statements of Khushboo as discussed in chapter 4. Importantly, in such surcharged atmosphere it is these uncivil protests that come to occupy the centre stage in any socio-economic-political discourse, and not the main issue viz., monogamy as well as cultural restraints and their link to macro-economics. To make matters worse, courts then take over and seek to discuss what is purely a fundamental economic idea, explained through lawyers and understood through the constitutional rights and morality, especially of individual. In the resultant cacophony, matter of greater import gets buried fathoms deep. Denuded of any opportunity to understand the thinking of economists and denied of the prospect to articulate their position to these very economists, the ordinary person finds solace in the life and message of Lord Rama. Economists miss this vital point. In a way, the life of Lord Rama, comprised in the *Ramayana* is also a message for economists.

Abhijit Naskar, author of the celebrated book *Wise Mating: A Treatise on Monogamy* sums up the issue brilliantly when he opines: "Monogamy is not a choice, it is a responsibility of a genuine human" and adds "Polygamy is a luxury of the cave-people, and monogamy is an existential responsibility of the civilized society." Tellingly, he concludes "Religious fundamentalism advocates homophobia, misogyny, xenophobia, polygamy, and many other primitive evils. Can you imagine, somebody telling you, your love for your dearly beloved is a sin! Can you imagine, somebody telling you, women are inferior to men, and are meant only serve the men! Can you imagine, somebody telling you, a man can have multiple wives, and yet be deemed civilised! Here that somebody is a fundamentalist – a theoretical pest from the stone-age, who somehow managed to survive even amidst all the rise of reasoning and intellect. Such a creature with no modern mental faculty whatsoever, knows nothing beyond the words of a book, written hundreds or thousands of years ago, when ignorance was the default mode of thinking in the society. It does not only believe every single word of a book to be literally true, but puts all its efforts to convince others to believe the same. This way, it would be an understatement to say, such is a worthless creature. In reality, such a creature can cause a catastrophic contagion in a society, especially if that society is already going through socio-political turmoil."

More to the point, there is a lesson for policy-framers in all these. Modern theories as propounded currently by economists, bereft of cultural moorings, are probably in embryonic stages of their formulations. Policy framers needs to jettison such ideas and simultaneously adopt policies that find acceptance with the ordinary people of India. Family and monogamy are one such grand yet simple idea that surely finds resonance with all people across continents. Paradoxically, despite overwhelming evidence to the contrary, both the constitutionalists and economists direct themselves and their policies towards the individuals, not to their families and definitely not towards encouraging monogamy. Isn't it time that we need to redirect our policy focus away from individualism and towards family, monogamy and self-restraints? Should we not rethink of re-structuring of our otherwise sublime Constitution to include families as a vehicle of socio-economic importance? Is it not time to address the missing middle in macroeconomics? Is it not time to answer some of the questions raised by Arjuna in Chapter I of the *Bhagavad Gita* and discussed in Chapter 4? For too long, our constitutional arrangements and by extension our understanding of economics have been imbalanced and favoured the individual over other social structures. For too long, we have tolerated, why, even celebrated individual excesses. Little did we realise that every individual excess contained the seeds for a macro-economic boom and an impending doom. And for every boom and doom we have alternated between the policies of Keynes and Hayek which in turn fuelled further imbalance in the national economy. It is time that we rebalance all these. It is time we punish individuals committing excesses and address the lack of individual restraints. It is time that our economic policy formulations favour of the family and reward individual restraints. It is time that the Constitution realises the importance of families and is amended to bring families as an integral part of its basic structure of its Constitution.

Reengineering the State

Needless to emphasise, the role of family in providing macroeconomic stability probably has been outside of the radar of economists for too long. To understand the importance of family and culture in the functioning of an economy, we need to have comprehensive re-look into the discipline of economics all over again including its root assumptions to understand why the exclusion of family is now proving fatal to macroeconomics. With the successive failures of state in managing the economy and repeated cycles of boom and doom of markets it is obvious that the very discipline of economics that needs some serious re-engineering. This assessment of the efficacy of the discipline of economics should not be solely based on the global financial crisis of 2008. In fact, modern economics, especially the discipline of macroeconomics, as we know it was in deep crisis even before the 2008 imbroglio. It was structurally flawed even before the economic crisis hit us. At best, the 2008 crisis was the proverbial last straw on the camel's back. It may be recalled that the accumulated excesses caused by irrational behaviour of most market players exaggerated the crisis. And an incompetent apparatus simply buckled under the onslaught. In fact, even in the aftermath of the crisis, little did we realise that the 2008 crisis was not merely an economic crisis but exposed the discomforting truth that the discipline of economics was in effect, in deep crisis. Worse was to follow. We have attempted to provide solutions to the issues on hand by using outworn theories that were the cause of the problems in the first place thereby exacerbating the crisis further. Post 2008 crisis, economics continues to be structurally flawed as before. It is a matter of time that it explodes. We have dealt with these issues in Chapter 8 of this book.

Most of the post crisis criticisms concern the broad assumptions governing modern economic theories, the inadequacies of these theories for dealing with the make-believe world of big finance and the consequent spill over effects for the entire economy. Some of the most articulate and well-informed criticisms of these theories have come from several of its best-known practitioners of the discipline, like Nobel laureate Paul Krugman for instance. He asserts, as we have noted in the previous chapters of this book, that we are living through the dark age of macro-economics in which the hard-won wisdom of the ancients has been lost. Well, it is this wisdom that is embedded in the *Ramayana* and is so well understood by the common man in India. Crucially, Krugman singles out Chicago School of Economics that invariably bats for deregulation of markets for special criticism. He believes that "the economics profession has gone astray because economists, as a group, mistook beauty clad in impressive-looking mathematics, for truth" and adding, "Not only did few economists see the current crisis coming, but most important, was the profession's blindness to the very possibility of catastrophic failures." Other economists of repute too have expressed similar views like that of Krugman. Writing in the *Financial Times*, Paul de Grauwe (2009) has claimed that macroeconomics is in deep trouble and went on to blame some of its baseless assumptions for the mess. Further, Robert Skidelski (2009) had pointed out that "economics has displayed the Ricardian vice of excessive abstraction," and economics opted for maths instead of aligning itself with other social sciences in their study of human behaviour and "bankers displayed blind faith in their mathematical forecasting models."

This unquestioned adherence to mathematics and quantitative techniques had the calculated effect of concerting economics into a subset of finance when theoretically it should have been the other way around.

But is the dalliance of economics with mathematics the core issue? Or is there a lack of civilisational values that is dynamiting national and global economics? One would indeed guess that it is probably both. Thus, in more ways than one, these critics of modern macroeconomics are spot on in pointing out to the lack of realism in its fundamental assumptions in macroeconomic models and the non-functionality of the complex mathematical models in predicting a crisis. Simultaneously, we do not realise that repeated waves of financial crisis hitting markets across the globe are due to the spectacular failure of modern economists, more particularly of having reduced economics itself into a subset of finance. Having successfully done and being jubilant about it, modern economics now suffers from the same vice as that of the world of finance! For starters, a better understanding of macroeconomics and elevating it to be a superset of finance would surely help. Traditionally, it may be noted that macroeconomic theories largely ignore finance and give only a cursory role to financial markets. Modern macroeconomics has been heavily criticised for presuming the efficacy of financial markets. We have already dealt with EMH and its inherent limitations in chapter 8. Further, there is a near consensus emerging within the pantheon of economists that a macroeconomic theory is more likely to be useful if it is simple and purpose-built than if it is designed to be fit for all purposes, when it is likely to be far too complex and cumbersome. But there is a catch in all these. These critiques of modern economics, being fundamentally Keynesians, are those who are highly sceptical of markets in the first place. These economists were the ones who have been extremely critical of macroeconomics in the backdrop of the 2008 crisis. The peculiarity of their timing post 2008 economic crisis has made their otherwise just criticisms, spectacular. Inadvertently, such criticism gets conflated as a criticism of macroeconomics, and not to the overall discipline of economics as a whole. Therefore, while the prognosis of the problem is indeed spot on by such Keynesians, one must realise that their sole prescription to the challenges faced by the economies arising out of a dysfunctional market post the 2008 crisis was to embrace once again the age-old Keynesian ideas. We have seen this swing in ideas from markets to state and back in chapter 4 of this book.

But why do some economists of repute, like Krugman for instance, have deep suspicion in the functioning of the markets? At the core of their belief is that markets have serious limitations in their very functionality, especially of dealing with the issue of equity. Recall the need for balance between equity and liberty and discussed in chapter 6. It is the fundamental belief of these economists that equity is more important than liberty and can be decidedly done only through affirmative action of the state. Needless to reiterate that their suspicions about the markets is reasonably well-founded but to some extent their opposition to the markets is deeply ideological and consequently suffers from such a bias. Despite repeated market failures one must hasten to add that their blind opposition to markets is without evidence of great persuasive value. Put differently, it is ideologically impermissible for some economists to accept the functionality of markets. Therefore, one has to evaluate their criticism of economics or macroeconomics as the case may be, only after negating their ideological bias.

Further, their argument is that Keynesian idea rests also on the premise that certain services cannot adequately be provided through free competition among players in the marketplace and must in contrast necessarily be provided by the state. Originally, the primary services falling into this category were defence from external aggression, police protection from domestic criminals, and a justice system for arbitration of disputes – in effect all sovereign functions. But the system, as we saw, creepingly acquired other non-sovereign services into its fold. And once a particular service was drawn into the state's fold, there was no reversing it. Likewise, where private enterprises did not have a risk appetite for many ventures, as roads, canals, postal services, schools, and management of the airways and airwaves, the state readily stepped in to bridge the entrepreneurial diffidence to invest in such high-risk ventures. The net result in emerging democracies was that the list was constantly and rapidly expanded in the name of providing welfare to people and began to include a myriad of activities by the ever-growing list of services to be provided by the state, such as the retirement benefits and disability security, basic health care, insurance, adequate housing, food, safe food, drugs, air, water, wildlife preservation, and even culture. The list as we have seen in chapter 6 is endless which dynamites the finances of the state. It is not out of place to mention that this ever-expanding list corresponds to the constantly expanding basic structure doctrine of the Indian Constitution as expounded by our courts.

Underlying this approach is the view that all individuals in a society are entitled to share, to some extent, in the prosperity enjoyed by those who are hardworking and hence prosperous. This belief, in turn, rests on the premise that many of those at the lower end of the economic spectrum are victims of those who have succeeded in the first place through the dint of their hard work and sincerity. Let us not forget that such an assumption has the calculated effect of delegitimising hard work and individual initiatives within the economy. It may equally be a fact that many of them probably owe their prosperity to a more fortunate toss of life's dice. But is reckless welfare the solution? Does it guarantee equity and equality? If so at what price? The assumption, that welfare funded through taxation has run its full course in our socio-political-economic arrangement. Needless to emphasise, much of it is without scientific analysis and credible evidence. Thus, the extant debate on the functioning of the state and the scope of welfare to be offered by it does not rest on whether it is economically optimal and practically possible for the government to provide for the needy, but rather on what is appealing to be seen as a benevolent government. In the process we miss something far too fundamental. Do we realise that in every idea of welfare and taxation there is an inbuilt trade-off with growth? As welfare deepens, it is elementary that it hits at overall economic prosperity. Taxes, let us not forget, transfers money from the hands of the most productive viz., households into the government. But taxes are indeed needed to carry out the sovereign functions of the state, is it necessary to fund welfare through taxes? Is this the right way? In catering to equity are we not sacrificing growth? Excessive taxation is clear admission that modern economics is yet to find the delicate balance between growth and equity. We need to do it pronto.

Nevertheless, welfare as an idea has become a bottomless pit; absolutely insatiable in its scope and sweep. This endless supply-based welfare is limited only by one's imagination – and definitely not by the finances of the state, its revenues or even its gargantuan debt. Distasteful as it may be to the student of economics or moral science, in a democracy this is nonetheless electorally a profitable approach as results at the hustings, especially in India, have repeatedly demonstrated. As political parties face success from subscribing to the idea of welfare, there is a near unanimity of thoughts amongst otherwise warring politicians that the state by definition has to be a welfare state. Once there is a near consensus within the political parties in a democracy, then there is an absolute race to the bottom to define its sweep and scope. It is elementary human nature. But worse is to follow. Invariably, as any government increases its role as provider and guarantor, the size of that government too grows and the inequities that its programmes were supposed to have redressed, have in effect increased. For instance, as more public money is spent on support for single mothers, more families break up and more children are born out of wedlock. It seems that whenever the state steps in to alleviate a social problem, the effect is to make the problem worse.

In 1875, Karl Marx stated the principle underlying the welfare state quite succinctly: "From each according to his abilities, to each according to his needs." The welfare state is founded on the proposition that it is necessary to take the property of those who have it to meet the needs of those who do not. As Marx and Engels said in *The Communist Manifesto*, "...the theory of Communists may be summed up in the single sentence: Abolition of private property." But we do not realise that the state does not create property. It is not traditionally designed to create wealth. Only hard-working people do create wealth and the concomitant prosperity. And while there may be no 'God-given' right to keep what is produced, elementary economics also guarantees that any system which uses force to take property away from those who produce it and give it to others in the form of welfare will result in lowering overall economic efficiency and progress. This is a fundamental law of economics that we cannot ignore either.

Strangely, for every market failure there are Keynesians waiting in the wings to suggest that the state must once again occupy the commanding heights of the economy. We have seen in Chapter 6 as to how such Keynesian ideas quickly turns a state into a welfare state sooner than later, subsequently degenerates into a populist state which quickly spirals downwards chillingly into a reckless state. This inevitable cycle that results in endless oscillation of macro-economic ideas between state and markets, alternating between one extreme to the other. Frighteningly, every law, regulation, and programme in every democratic government rests squarely on a single premise: One person's need is a just claim on the property of another. Taxation merely legitimises, even sanctifies, and codifies it. John Pugsley, a writer of great repute, puts it succinctly when he states "Sadly, this premise, which is truly the ultimate foundation for the welfare state, is never debated, and never questioned. It is rarely even articulated. Yet it is the issue that should be debated first. If it is wrong, then all of the great debates raging in society over the questions of which needs are genuine needs, and whose property will be forfeited to supply those needs, are totally moot." The debate on taxation was summarily settled when we, in our formative years were taught that the taxation by the British colonial masters on pre-independent India was both exploitative and extortionist. Strangely, the constituent assembly debates, that we have seen in Chapter 7, seems to suggest that our independence was fought over the principle that taxation without representation is unjust, but that somehow taxation with representation is appropriate. Either way, there was not much debate by the founding fathers of the modern Indian Republic on the need and extent to tax India's free citizens. Equally, they did not debate on the responsibility to be undertaken by the state and match it with an appropriation taxation regime. Probably they left the matter to be settled by each generation according to its needs. The debate, if at all, was how much share of the taxes could be taken by the Union or the state governments. While taxation for the limited and original role of government as envisioned by Keynes is by and large welcome, taxation for recklessness of the state is surely unacceptable; and that for funding electoral ambitions of political parties, absolutely unpardonable. More importantly, the cost of administering welfare through a highly inefficient, unaccountable and expensive idea that is bureaucracy is another deterrent in this apparently benign yet toxic idea of welfare. We need to balance between taxation and welfare too. For that we need to deal with the issue of individual duties. We will revert to this issue shortly.

Markets Failure is because of Regulatory Failures

But what is the viable alternative to a welfare state? If a welfare state through a mechanism of elaborate taxation and equitable distribution is still unable to deal with the scourge of poverty, inequality and social disorders what else will? Is there any natural way out of the quagmire? Why are people agitated over failure of economics and direct their anger at economists? Crucially, how do we make economics deliver? Economics, let us not forget, has a great deal of influence on the lives of every citizen compared with other disciplines. It helps form policies that have a significant impact on peoples' lives than any other profession barring teachers. And so, economists rightly attract exacting scrutiny as is not only important but also a highly impactful discipline. No wonder, as more people understand lately that the mess in their life is caused by some botched up economist sitting in a distant land. This, coupled with the scepticism of experts and lack of consensus from within the discipline, appears to be having a stunting effect when it comes to economic policy making. It would seem policymakers are lost in the wilderness – not knowing exactly what is to be done and more particularly, how. That explains why someone as decisive as Narendra Modi, the prime minister of India who instinctively realises the pitfall in Nehruvian economics, has been unable to break free from economic ideas that are distinctively Nehruvian. So could not Reagan, who also talked of small and effective government but failed to deliver one. On top of this, there are charges that the academia has bent theories to favour certain policies on the basis of funding received from vested interests. It is these theories that are peer reviewed, awarded and celebrated. As both theories and theorists become 'rock stars,' collectively the accompanying cacophony compelled by shrillness associated thereunder, suspend our sense of disbelief. The denouement is complete when sections of the media instead of critiquing such fanciful theories instantly turn to become cheerleaders. That simply compounds the cacophony. In the melee, regulatory captures happen brazenly – an issue that we have elaborately dealt in Chapter 8 – and where insiders have been used to devastating effect. When that happens, nothing survives as markets.

All that is stated above, let me hasten to add, is recent economic history. In reality, it is worse, when measured in terms of outcomes in addressing the challenges of modern economics. In more ways than one market failures have been caused by irrational exuberance of players. As markets failed, this in turn necessitated repeated and sustained intervention by the government. The high degree of state intervention in these economies was not only due to the fact that many governments ideologically had a tryst with socialism during the 20th century, but also due to the fact that for some time even such multilateral agencies such as the World Bank assumed that government intervention was necessary as markets by itself could not function optimally. On a deeper scrutiny, it is obvious that this it is the Hobbesian view, discussed in the previous chapters, at play. Interestingly, government intervention to address repeated market failures is no longer the norm, but a structural necessity. In fact, post 2008 economic crisis, countries across the globe now are keen to participate virtually on a concurrent basis with the others to soften the macabre consequence of any future market failures. To this extent government intervention in the market functioning is the modern-day rule, not an exception, anymore.

This is not the market economics as we traditionally understood. Some scholars have termed this as a rigged casino. But where does the slide begin? Is intervention of governments in markets fallacious? If not, are governments to be supinely indifferent to market failures? And for how long? Also, who is to be blamed for academic incest with market players leading to regulatory capture and resultant distortions of the market functioning? For starters, it would be counterproductive to assume that any economic policy can engineer the best of all worlds. Markets and people are unpredictable, and economic models are always incomplete as they have to comprehend a billion minds in action. Attempting to strike a right balance is indeed messy and is exactly what policy formulation should aim to achieve, naturally and without much external intervention. We also need to proceed with a clear understanding that there are no markets failures but only regulatory failures. Regulation is at the heart of the functioning of markets and its failure it often seen to be fatal for the smooth functioning of the markets. And when the state takes over the regulation of the market, it is no longer a regulatory failure; it is the failure of the state. Given that we are confronted with such a scenario fairly on a recurrent basis, the moot question is 'What remains?'

It may be noted that several scholars have proffered, that markets remain the most efficient way to coordinate transactions in societies, and rightly so, simply because of its decentralised nature. This is the market of 3Bs – the brewer, butcher and the baker as originally envisioned by Adam Smith. It is the 3Bs that, economists belatedly realise, is the "wealth" of nations. The underlying idea in the success of a classical market is that probably unknown to others, the excess of one of them was identified, questioned and instantly corrected by the rest. This is possible as markets originally contrived by Adam Smith was a personal one – a market where everyone had stakes in its stability and durability. To this extent the players were also performing the secondary yet crucial role of an oversight-regulatory body. This implicit arrangement ensured a harmonious functioning by various players that gave rise to the "wealth" of the nations. The quintessential point here is that such markets functioned only if they were decentralised, not otherwise. It is this decentralisation that allows players to play a dual role – one, as that of players and the other, of oversight bodies. A dispassionate analysis of the functioning of the markets will demonstrate that absent one of the two aforementioned characteristics, markets will tend to fail. Pointedly, the self-interest of the actors involved ensures a natural oversight as well as a balanced order – a fact is missed by many. The excess of the brewer for instance became the excess of the local markets directly impacting the supreme self-interest of the butcher and the baker. This, at once prompted their instantaneous intervention to remedy the excesses of the brewer. But this is no longer possible in the modern markets which are faceless and impersonal. Consequently, there is no self-interest in overseeing their functioning or for that matter, correcting their excesses. Once self-interest is divorced from its functioning, markets no longer retain the essential features of a classical market. This point is vital for the orderly functioning of the markets. What economists do not fancy, is that by destroying the family, the connect with local communities is irretrievably lost. Once the link is lost, markets become dysfunctional.

That said, market economics by itself is a nebulous concept with the level of state or personal intervention, indeterminate. Large markets, it may be noted are necessary in these times as it brings in economies of scale. Some are by-products of technological developments and are inevitable.

Such markets are impossible to function at a personal level and therefore necessitate a functional regulator. That implies we are compelled by the force of circumstances to let markets, with some sort of regulation, grow and succeed. Regulation is a sine qua non in the efficient functioning of any markets. Of course, there is no clear formula for this. We need to feel the stone and cross the river. It is pertinent to note that none can deny that the world has experienced a decisive shift toward markets since the adoption of the economic ideas propounded by Hayek in mid-seventies. The net result is that there is near universal political consensus on convoluted issues such as deregulation, privatisation, financial liberalisation and individual enterprise. But it is not yet clear whether they constitute market economics in the first place and how is it to be regulated. Thus, there is a need for precise definition of large markets and clearly identify the manner in which larger markets will be regulated and by whom.

Yet, our craving for free markets – one without any regulation – remains. The repeated emphasis on free markets is because certain players, especially the large ones, want a market divorced from regulations, oversight or intervention. That explains why free market champions seek to dilute the influence of family on an individual, as family is definitely the biggest stumbling block in preventing reckless decisions of the individuals. Champions of free markets do not even remotely realise that markets with soft touch regulation are our best bet out of the current economic morass. Therefore, markets in its pristine form needs to be preserved and made functional. That is the surest bet for humanity to succeed in its war against poverty. For that to happen it is important that we build appropriate checks and balances that function on a real time basis. But before we prescribe anything constructive it is better that we answer the fundamental question: what precisely is market economics? In broad terms, it denotes a preference for private initiative over government, economic activities to be preferred over cultural norms, and private entrepreneurship over collective action. Put pithily, the term over the past decade or two has come to be seen as a catchall phrase for anything that does not emphasise a role for the government or its agencies.

Whatever be it or its role, the fact of the matter is that today, market economics is routinely reviled for the ideas and practices that have produced growing economic insecurity and inequality, led to the loss of our political values and ideals leading to populist backlash. The Oxfam Report discussed in Chapter 6 is a case in point. Why is it that despite overwhelming academic literature pointing to the success of markets at a theoretical level, it continues to fail in practice, especially when it comes to the crucial question of addressing inequity? Why does market suffer from a disconnect between theory and practice? The answer for the same stems from the fact that – what we see as markets is at best rigged casinos. More importantly, despite overwhelming evidence that market economics was not delivering even at a national level, globalisation – which was seen as the destination point in the evolution of market economics – was a stunning failure. Strangely, this found instantaneous acceptance by the economic establishment, especially by developing countries. To those who refused to accept, several state and non-state actors ensured the same with more than gentle persuasion. The others were pummelled into acceptance. Governments were put under tremendous pressure to adopt market-friendly policies by even multilateral agencies. Globalisation accelerated further, thanks to free flows of finance, trade in intellectual properties and ambitious trade agreements, both multilateral and plurilateral. Thus, market economics which, in the absence of an effective oversight body could not meet expectations even at a national level became a grand global experiment and thrust on unsuspecting people as a successful economic model for all times to come in future. This led to people like Fukuyama coining the phrase "triumphant capitalism," implying we had hit a sweet spot in economic policy formulations. Crucially, the world of economists began deluding itself into a belief that nothing more needs to be done in this field as we had reached economic nirvana.

Little did we imagine as to how could markets be expected to deliver at a global level when even at the national level, oversight bodies, so vital for the efficient functioning of the markets, were conspicuous by their absence? Crucially, globalisation converted markets, which required participants to function diligently at a personal level, into faceless players operating behind the veil of incorporation. The net result was that markets became largely impersonal, highly transactional and definitely unaccountable. More particularly, with remuneration for managers getting firmly linked to the profits of the firms, this faceless-impersonal-unaccountable paradigm ensured a free run for multinational corporates by facilitating stripping of local assets and resources in more ways than one that resembled the marauding armies of the medieval era. Of course, obscene salaries to managers led to window dressing of books and the resultant accounting scandals too. But who cared? Large accounting firms were created only to operate out of tax havens with a clear mandate to be a party to this arrangement. In the process no one got punished as every firm indulging in such operation is either termed systemically important or is deemed as too big to fail. Either way, in both cases the state is compelled by the market players, as we saw in the case of President George Bush, to suspend markets to bail them out. Crucially, as we saw in the context of the 2008 economic crash in the US, none barring one small market participant, got punished. Lack of exemplary punishment is a conclusive evidence that market economics has since long become dysfunctional.

The next step was a logical culmination of these factors at play – globalisation of finance and the inevitable consequence thereof – trade and currency wars. All these are unfolding before us with unprecedented monstrosity. The worst, one fears, is yet to come. As this model worked with all ferocity, local cultures and home-grown business practices were neatly destroyed. We have dealt with the resultant issues in chapter 6. Having realised the havoc wrecked on themselves, now political leaders across the globe and policy framers are loath to see any upsides in globalisation. The cabal including academia, corporates, market participants, policy framers and the ubiquitous media that championed the idea of globalisation with missionary zeal at the beginning of this century has strangely become silent. The attempts to homogenise the world through globalisation was indeed unworkable to begin with. That it failed within a decade or two is indeed reassuring for, had it prolonged any longer, the costs associated with its failure might have been several times more.

Naturally, post the ideological denunciation of globalisation, the world of economics is in a state of suspended animation with an uneasy truce prevailing between markets and the state. Already, several countries are unabashed proponents of de-coupling indicating reversal of their globalisation process. To many, globalisation especially that of finance was an experiment to nowhere with very little or no upsides and guaranteed downsides. QE, as we have seen has flushed in gargantuan liquidity into the system to salvage it from complete devastation. This has helped us in tiding over the economic crisis by literally postponing the fallout. As we have argued in greater detail in Chapter 8, currencies are now no longer being backed by gold or for that matter anything precious. But as supply of currency increases, fundamentals of economic theory demand that the currencies could face significant downward pressure in their values. Monetary policies too have run their full course where many currencies are now backed not by anything precious but by the toxic assets of every Tom, Dick, and Harry who have borrowed far beyond their means to repay. In the alternative they are backed by currencies of other countries, whose value are equally questionable. Policy framers are in a bind. If they do not allow such borrowings, growth will definitely be hampered. And if they do, the economy chokes. Caught between Scylla and Charybdis, policy framers have completely frozen. Central banks are equally in a bind. If they reverse QE, it could well strangulate the fragile recovery process. If they continue with QE any further, asphyxiation of the economy through explosion of their currency is inevitable. If the past decade or so since the 2008 crisis is any indication, one is certain that it is lull before the storm. Given the state of affairs, as things play out, one can be near certain that the next economic crisis would indeed be a currency crisis. Nevertheless, we need to make the best out of the intervening period.

Women, Women's property and Women as Property

The role of women in modern societies has evolved over time, the fate of women, at least in the Western world, was decided long back in history when the first sin was committed by Eve. This decision of Eve continues to haunt not only women but collectively impacts human civilisation to this date. As noted in Chapter 3 these have roots in Christian theology. Subsequently, Christendom faced several rights movements and underwent reforms, especially in the past few centuries. As a consequence of all these developments, women have begun to enjoy several rights in the Western world today though much of these are of recent vintage. Women's suffrage to wage equality, were results of extraordinary efforts put forth by activists and champions of women's liberties throughout this period in the Western hemisphere. Likewise, property rights linked to women too underwent some serious correction. It may be recalled that during the colonial period, most of the newly-formed American states followed British common law, which stipulated that husbands had complete control of any property their wives brought into the marriage. This went by the legal doctrine of coverture, whereby, upon marriage under common law, a woman's legal rights and obligations were subsumed by those of her husband. Implicitly, coverture held that no female had a legal identity, especially after marriage. At birth, a baby girl was covered by her father's identity and then, when she married, by her husband's. That legal idea in more ways than one dramatically reduced the status of women to being virtually a property of a man. By taking over the property of women, for all practical purposes, women could be "owned" by men. Worse was to follow. Married women had no rights to their bodies. That meant that not only would a husband have a claim to any wages generated by his wife's labour but he also had an absolute right to sexual access. Within marriage, a wife's consent was implied, so under the law, all sex-related activity, including rape, was legitimate. Of course, a man wasn't legally allowed to beat his wife to death, but he could beat her nevertheless. This was the explicitly stated legal position in the Western world till say the 17th century.

It may be noted that this ban on property ownership by women in 18th century England and the related issues that flow from it became a major plot in quite a few novels authored by Jane Austin. Further, women were prevented not so long ago in Europe and in US, from conducting business without a male representative. Married women could not exercise control over their children without the permission of their husbands. They had no access of higher education and were invariably banned from taking most professions. Equally, suffrage was another contentious issue which was extensively debated within the Western world for centuries before agreeing to it, again in the 20th century. While one is not sure whether Eve committed a sin or not and if at all it was the original sin or not, the fact of the matter is that even after several centuries women continue to pay for the same. And in a society where one half of the population viz women, is under some stress, the prosperity of that society is doubtful or unsustainable.

Of course, centuries of oppression of women in the Western world had to come to a logical end. And it is coming to an end sooner than later. The imbalance in the manner in which women were treated spawned several bouts of rights movements. These culminated in what is now termed as feminist and women's liberation movement, beginning the middle of 20th century. The first success was the grant of suffrage to women. The next logical step in the women's liberation movement was when it pushed for political representation of women in government, fuelled the sexual revolution, brought about the legalisation of abortion, and sparked debates in every denomination about women's ordination and the relationship of husband and wife. But more was to come. Having more or less settled the issue of patriarchal society, feminists have now turned their final attention to the root of the problem – patriarchal theology. Remember within Christendom the triumvirate of the Father, Son and the Holy Spirit are all males. As a natural fallout, in the 1980s and 1990s women have turned in increasing numbers to search a feminine form for worship. Meanwhile, in some churches the feminist movement has successfully pushed for the publication of new Bible translations that remove references to God as Father or Jesus as Son. The process to create feminine divine and divine that is feminine has well and truly commenced within the Christendom. That it may take probably another century or two to fructify to establish gender balance even within an avowedly patriarchal theology like Christianity is well understood but welcomes nevertheless.

But there is a downside to all these healthy developments – the birth of an Alpha female. Feminism, it may be noted, has over the past few decades swung to the other extreme where instead of addressing the primary issue – gender equity – has unintentionally uncorked a new genie. The evolution of mankind, it may be recalled and discussed in chapter 1, was all about taming the Alpha male through family and monogamous marriage. But like many isms before it, feminism also seeks to dismantle the traditional family unit for its own gain. The reason for the same is not far to seek. To any ism, old loyalties interfere with an individual's ability to pledge unwavering allegiance to new ones. That is always an imperial demand posed by any ism which therefore seeks absolute control on the individual. Feminists realise that families tend to put family members and their needs before the demands of the ism, reducing its power and influence. The abhorrence of Communists and the champions of free market towards the institution of family, is a case in point. In the process, feminists also seek to destroy the family without realising the unintended consequence – the re-emergence of the Alpha male! This will have a debilitating impact on other males, females, and even children. And should that happen the feminists have no one to blame but themselves for the mess wrecked on women in the aggregate by their own excesses. In a way, if polygamy with its theological backing of Islam has resulted in a set of problems, Christianity with perceived lack of gender equity have fashioned a different set of issues.

In contrast, the traditional Indic way was to concede to gender equity as exemplified by the powerful imagery of *Ardhanareshwara* – one of the sixty-four manifestations of lord Shiva. Roughly translated it symbolises the Lord as half woman (and implying the other half to be a man). However, the image of *Ardhanareshwara* transcends beyond the mundane idea of gender equity, as we understand, as Lord Shiva fuses into oneness with his consort, Goddess Shakthi. This fusion, at a physical level, conveys the importance of balance – not by negating one force or the other, but by finding a harmony in the functioning of conflicting forces. Some scholars opine that beyond physical fusion *Ardhanareshwara* mystically symbolises the spiritual life, represented by Shiva himself coalescing with and the materialistic life of the householder, denoted by Shakthi. In the Indic traditions, the ascetic is as important as the householder. If the ascetic sustains the householder through spirituality, the latter provides for the former and sustains him. At the individual level, the ascetic side of an individual is as significant as the hedonist. Absent the ascetic, the hedonist runs the risk of going berserk the consequences of which were discussed in the previous chapters. On the other hand, if it were only the ascetic, procreation and consumption, so very vital for the sustenance of the secular world, will come to a rapid end. Obviously, one cannot exist without the other and both are necessary in the right measure for the orderly functioning of the society. Both of them as also the balance between the two, will ensure the sustainability of the society. This is economics based on spirituality – or what one may call spiritual economics - one that is sustainable simply because amongst other things it is devoid of any excess. If Lord Shiva connotes the inevitable destruction – we have dealt with the idea of entropy in chapter 4 – Shakthi symbolises the power that lies within us to rebuild. Destruction is as important as creation as without the former the latter cannot proceed. It is this repeated cycle of destruction and creation that goes on by the simple appellation called life. *Ardhanareshwara* merely alludes to this simple yet powerful truth.

While *Ardhanareshwara* answers gender equity from a higher philosophical plane, the *Mahabharat*, the great epic of India settles the matter decisively and, in a manner, that can be understood by the commoners. Of the several underlying themes in this great Indian epic was the dignity of women personified by Draupadi, one of the central characters of the epic, and the extent one should go to protect it. As briefly stated in chapter 4, the story is of warring cousins for inheriting the kingdom – Kauravas on one side and Pandavas on the other. Duryodhan, the eldest of the Kauravas, gets a vile idea from his uncle Shakuni of inviting the Pandavas for a feast that is to be followed by a game of dice. This was sought to be played between him, represented by his cunning uncle Shakuni and Yudhishthira, the eldest of the Pandavas. Shakuni, who was the master of deceit kept winning game after game and Yudhishthira kept losing the bets that ranged from his domestic aids, jewellery, cattle, army, chariots, elephants, horses to finally even his kingdom. Reaching almost a point of no return and with the faint hopes of reclaiming all that was lost, Yudhishthira went on loser's frenzy. But the die was literally cast against him. Expectedly, he began losing his own brothers one by one and finally even himself. So obsessed he was, Yudhishthira fell an easy prey to the diabolical suggestion of Shakuni that he could pawn his wife Draupadi as one last attempt at gambling and win all that he had lost.

It is here that one is compelled to draw a reference to one of the most celebrated works *Panchali Sabadam* (the fiery vow of Panchali aka Draupadi) penned by the great Tamil poet of pre-independence times, Mahakavi Subramania Bharathi. The work is a near dramatised version of the most important of incidents comprised in the grand epic – the game of dice played between the cousins. Beginning with the envious rant of Duryodhan, who gleefully approved a suggestion of his uncle Shakuni and invited Pandavas for a dice game, knowing fully well that Shakuni could and would somehow manipulate a win, right up to the earth-shattering vow of Draupadi at the very end – the mini-epic of Bharathi within the great epic spans to 412 verses comprised in 5 chapters. It would be impossible for anyone to bring the emotional fervour or the rage of Bharathi in any translated version. Nevertheless, what has been attempted here is to briefly capture the work of the great poet on the indignation heaped on Draupadi by the Kauravas. After losing all his brothers and himself in the game, Yudhishthira loses all his sense of proportion and pawns his wife Draupadi as his final bet. As one recoils in horror at the very thought, Bharathi brings about a series of metaphors to describe the melancholic situation in a manner that only he could. Read in pristine mellifluous Tamil, the agony of the poet contained in his immortal works would run a chill down our spines. As fate would have it, deceit once again won and Draupadi too was lost in the game of dice.

Duryodhan sent his charioteer to fetch Draupadi – his purported slave by now – to the courtyard. Rightly, Draupadi refused to accept the fiat and pertinently posed a question of great importance to the issue of gender equity: "Did Yudhishthira lose himself before he lost me in the game of dice or did he pawn me first, before he bet himself?" This was a neat question of law pregnant with a spiritual riddle: "Does a man own his wife like other property?" For if the husband had lost himself first, he had no business in pawning her later. But if he had pawned her first, that too without her consent the entire process was obviously vitiated as a husband does not own a wife in the first place. Of course, such legal niceties when conveyed by the charioteer did not cut ice with Duryodhan who directed his younger brother Dushahshan to physically bring her to the hall. Dushahshan literally drags by her hair to the courtyard. Draupadi, inconsolable at her pitiful plight, poses the very same questions of law to Yudhishthira and elders present in the courtyard. Yudhishthira the authority on dharma, responded to his wife's question in the gambling hall with catatonic silence. He said nothing, good or bad. Bheeshmacharya, the senior most of the Kuru clan and supposedly the most sagacious and experienced person in the court, while agreeing on the validity of her questions did not clarify the matters. His nebulous analysis was that one without property cannot stake the property of others; but women were always the property of their husbands. Bheeshma's opinion, if at all there was one, was neither here nor there. It was decidedly ambiguous – like a note on a contentious issue written by an under-secretary to the Government of India. The assembled nobility too did not have answers to her questions.

Even as Draupadi was arguing with the elders, the most horrendous thought came to the mind of Karna who suggested disrobing of Draupadi in the courtyard in front of everyone present. Dushahshan faithfully began the despicable job. Realising that she had a hopeless situation on hand unless there was a divine intervention, Draupadi surrendered to the Lord, extolled His virtues and prayed fervently to save her honour. Miracle unexpectedly happened. Or was it expected? As Dushahshan kept pulling her robes, she kept getting seamless extensions of the same – miles and miles of them in resplendent colours, obviously through the intervention of the Lord. Exhausted Dushahshan finally gave up. The Kauravas were stupefied by the turn of events. Draupadi, who was already incensed by the silence of the elders to her questions was now livid at personal humiliation attempted on her. At this point she took the gut-wrenching vow – that she would leave her hair with which Dushahshan pulled and dragged her, untied till she would be able to drench them with the blood of Dushahshan and Duryodhan. Years later, when the war happened between the warring cousins, the vows of Draupadi got fulfilled exactly the way she intended it to be.

The lessons from the *Mahabharat* are indeed compelling – gender equity and honour of women needs to be upheld at any cost. That a woman, that too a princess, was sought to be disrobed in the courtyard is one of the lowest points in the Indian civilisation. And for restoring the honour of a women, if annihilation of a clan is necessary, so be it. Importantly, a wife is certainly not the property of her husband. Gandhaari, the mother of Kauravas realised and conceded to this point more than any scholar present in the courtyard. On her decisive intervention, Draupadi and her husbands were set free and their kingdom with all that was lost, immediately restored. Both Gandhaari and Draupadi understood that a wife had an identity independent of that of her husband. But how far and how much were left to the collective conscience of successive generations. And this open-ended stance has stood in good stead in the collective conscious of the Indians since the days of *Mahabharat*. At a superficial level, Draupadi's tryst with gender equity settled the debate decisively in favour of women.

There is yet another fascinating perspective to this. At pivotal points in the *Mahabharat*, two important players viz., Lord Krishna and sage Vyasa, appear to direct the plot, most often by resolving tricky issues involving moral dilemma of the characters involved. In fact, sage Vyasa moves in and out of the epic narrative both as an author and character. Scholars are of the view that sage Vyasa appears forty-one times in the epic, mostly to counsel and direct characters. It is important to note that sage Vyasa was absent during this crucial event involving Draupadi and the unsavoury events that followed. One opines that probably he could have appeared like he had done on several other occasions and easily settled the questions posed by Draupadi. Likewise, Lord Krishna comes very late to protect the honour of Draupadi but he too does not opine on the questions posed by her. Some scholars are of the view that a resolution by either Vyasa or Lord Krishna would have definitely established the law, possibly for all time to come. Probably, both Lord Krishna and sage Vyasa have left it to the collective conscience of future generations to answer the seemingly vexatious questions posed by Draupadi. The other inference, that one can draw, from their absence at a crucial turn in the epic stems from the fact that the questions posed by Draupadi merited the obvious answers. Gender equity is, definitely, an inviolable natural law that warrants any amount of reiteration by anyone at any point in time. The obvious answers to the questions posed by Draupadi did not lend itself for their decisive intervention by them in the first place. That, substantially, if not fully, explains their absence. The Lord, it may be noted, not only signals through his presence but also through his absence. Stunning, isn't it?

Woman, property rights of woman and woman herself as property, are not contentious issues as they are made out to be. Such thoughts are by-products of infertile minds. But if ignored, it could ignite mayhem as it has done in the case of Draupadi or modern feminism. The process adopted by Draupadi is an extreme one and cannot be a model for everyone to follow. Hence, while Draupadi is revered in India she is never considered as a role model. This is probably because her subsequent actions resulted in the annihilation of the Kaurava clan and sadly even included her own children. Likewise, gender equity cannot be established by destruction of the family as modern feminists sought to achieve. At best, it seeks parity with men, that too on a superficial level. We need to settle gender equity, not through the idea of modern feminism along its corrosive instrumentalities, but by religious, social and legal reforms. But since we refuse to indulge in these difficult processes, we seek the easy way out. Hence, the ocularly alluring, yet superficial idea of feminism. Will Christendom give up its stated position on women and patriarchy? Will Islam give up on polygamy? Will the Abrahamic faiths address these issues pronto? Gender equity, established through religious reforms alone will ensure the emergence of a new global order and overseen through family, culture and civilisation is probably the road forward and not in line with what was contemplated by Samuel Huntington and discussed in chapter 3. It is a long road ahead but one worthy of travel.

Genetic Re-Engineering of Economics

The Selfish Gene, a highly acclaimed book by evolutionary biologist Richard Dawkins explains the process of evolution in biology using genes as its basic unit. That was in 1976. It was a path breaking work of its times demonstrating how genes manifest in the form of organisms, what they do to ensure their own survival, how they program our brains, which strategies have worked best throughout history and what makes humans so special in this context. The basic idea captured in the book was that evolution happened to genes, not to individual species. The radical argument that the *Selfish Gene* makes is that the natural selection process in the evolution of living beings is not about making the species, community or group secure. It is about making the individual secure. More specifically, it is about making the individual a mere vehicle for carrying it. Altruistic behaviour, according to Dawkins, happens only when individuals gang up for purely genetically selfish purposes so that the species and their societies carry on. In fact, Dawkins's proposition is that pure altruistic behaviour has never helped anyone in the history of any species. The Selfish Gene theory is still debated hotly among evolutionary biologists, because it brings about an uncomfortable but a completely new view of our existence. As most of the book is devoted to the radical theory that all living creatures are essentially vehicles for their genes, the moot question remains – whether we exist to transmit and propagate our genes. Do we then count for nothing more than being mere carriers of some double-helix structures? Is it that these double-helix structures, also called genes, owns us as it transits us for its own betterment? Probably that would answer the first question raised at the beginning of this chapter, of course, from an evolutionary biologist's point of view.

It is pertinent to note that similar ideas challenging the notion that people are born selfish, have surfaced in several diverse fields, such as psychology, sociology, political science and economics. Put together, these compelling ideas are bringing forth a paradigm shift in the fundamental changes to approaches in diverse disciplines and researches involving human actions. Until the late 1980s, our understanding of what motivated the human mind was marked by the remarkable rise in precisely defining the idea of self-interested rationality, which provided the sole basis for predicting human behaviour. Studies suggested that people will necessarily be selfish and such people, if need be, will ruin things for everyone else. Based on this assumption of a self-interested rational human, various behavioural patterns were mapped. In more ways than one, the rational but selfish man was the theoretical foundation on which several systems in diverse disciplines were created. But this rational man cared for none except himself. Therefore, to save ourselves from freeloaders, systems after systems were built in diverse disciplines by assuming the worst in every single individual, more so in the discipline of economics. In the case of macroeconomics, policies began to be made merely to deal with the excesses of the rational man. And the more irrational he became; policies were tailored to further exacerbate his excesses. It is apparent that we built systems only for the "sinners" and amply reward them for their sins.

But just as one thought the selfish-rational-economic man had attained immortality, things changed dramatically. Yochai Benkler writing in 2011, points out that this widespread conviction about the power of self-interest is based on two long-standing, partly erroneous, and opposing assumptions about getting people to cooperate. One of them inspired the philosopher Thomas Hobbes's *Leviathan* in 1651: Humans are fundamentally and universally selfish, and governments must control them so that they don't destroy one another in the short-sighted pursuit of self-interest. The second is Adam Smith's alternative solution: *The Invisible Hand.* Smith's 1776 book, *The Wealth of Nations*, argued that because humans are self-interested and their decision making is driven by the rational weighing of costs and benefits, their actions in a free market tend to serve the common good. Though their prescriptions are very different, both the *Leviathan* and *The Invisible Hand* have the same starting point: a belief in humankind's selfishness. And both as we saw in previous Chapters have their origins in Christian theology, more particularly the original sin.

While the work of Dawkins had become a pioneering work in evolutionary biology, and continues to be so even to this date, some realised that there were inherent limitations to this idea. But by 2006, the tide had begun to turn even within the discipline of evolutionary biology. Harvard University's mathematical biologist Martin Nowak pointed out the evolution of cooperation in *Science* magazine: "Perhaps the most remarkable aspect of evolution is its ability to generate cooperation in a competitive world. Thus, we might add natural cooperation as a third fundamental principle of evolution beside mutation and natural selection." As evidence in several fields began to demonstrate the innate ability of the humans to cooperate, the challenge is to redesign systems that are based on such deeply flawed fundamental assumptions. Simultaneously, it may be noted that in contrast to the idea of Dawkins, another pioneering work on this subject interestingly titled was *The Cooperative Gene* by Mark Ridley. In this celebrated work, Ridley presented a new and contrarian explanation of how complex large life forms came to exist, demonstrating that the answer to the greatest mystery of evolution for modern science is not the 'selfish gene,' it is the 'cooperative gene.' In his thought-provoking book, Ridley explains how two major biological hurdles had to be overcome in order to allow living complexity to evolve; the proliferation of genes and gene-selfishness. And this, according to Ridley, was achieved through *The Cooperative Gene.* To his eternal credit, Dawkins did acknowledge in sebsequent editions of his book that "without departing from fundamental laws of the selfish gene theory … cooperation and mutual assistance can flourish" and that he could have called his book *The Cooperative Gene*. Looks like pioneers like Dawkins and Ridley were right, but up to a point. Theories and studies suggest that nature has probably evolved us primarily as a selfish creature but also there is a cooperative gene lurking besides every selfish one. More importantly, it is my hypothesis that there is a third one – the 'Balancing Gene' – one that determines when to alternatively make the idea of Dawkins or Ridley functional! And it is this balancing gene that is dormant and hence unmapped, yet so powerful that it makes decisions to suit it at every possible turn of events.

These developments in the rarefied field of evolutionary biology have direct interest to the discussions on hand. It is interesting to note that like biology, the discipline of economics too has begun to undergo tectonic shifts over the years in overcoming its root assumptions about individual self-interest. Economic theory, in more ways than one, mimics biology. Both share similar approaches in so far as both fields of inquiry deal with complex, hierarchical, and evolving systems. As many economists and biologists have noted, the controversies in biology and economics are remarkably similar. Since the former has gone further in explaining the dynamic behaviour of living systems, economists have much to gain from an understanding of current controversies in evolutionary theory. One controversy of particular importance to the concept of group selection and the related issue of altruistic behaviour. The existence of natural pro-social behaviour, that is neutral or detrimental to the individual but positive for the survival of the group, has far-reaching implications not only for biology but also for modern economics. But there is a serious challenge in the road ahead for both. Just as evolutionary biologists are yet to come to a consensus whether the gene is selfish or a cooperative one, economists are yet to come to any definitive conclusion on the economic man is a rationale person, altruist or something more!

Modern economic policy, as we have seen in the previous chapters is dominated by welfare, occasionally peppered by extending irrational faith in free markets. Over the past few decades, the scientific validity of the assumptions of human behaviour underlying these policies has come for sharp attack, mostly from within the economic mainstream. The cornerstone of these policies is the radical individualism embodied in the notion of the rational economic actor. As the assumption is deeply flawed, most of the economic models built on such assumption are reduced to being theoretical fantasies. The economic man is a case in point. Yet, the economic-man continues to be the basis for the policy recommendations of modern economics despite the fact that behavioural literature demonstrates that humans do not act according to these simplistic assumptions.

The net result? The state is inherently inefficient and markets volatile. The post-war Keynesian welfare state is in crisis – it has become too large to be manageable, it is collapsing under the burden of excessive taxation, and it is generating ever-higher rates of cyclical inflation. Consequently, it cannot be sustained any longer, especially in a world that is now characterised by highly mobile capital and by vigorous economic competition between nations. Hence, economists have begun attempting to roll back the state. Some suggest, in particular, that the state should concentrate on making policy decisions rather than on delivering services. As a consequence, they want the state to withdraw from direct delivery of services. They want to replace state provision of public services with an entrepreneurial system based on competition and markets. But there was a serious catch in all these. Governments functioned in economies of scale and worked in near monopolistic conditions. Market players demanded equivalence. So large corporates were created as surrogates for governments. That made these corporates unaccountable. And now we seek to regulate markets through government, a task that is not within its genetic makeup. In the process we have collapsed the governments, made markets dysfunctional and corporates unaccountable.

At the root of this conundrum is the flawed assumption of the selfish gene and of course its relevance to modern economists – the economic man. Events of the past few decades have demonstrated that the idea of *Homo Economicus* has run its full course. The time for displacing individuals as central to policy formulations has come. It is time to genetically mutate the economic man to a far superior idea. For that to succeed, it is crucial we jettison policies that gave rise to him in the first place. Dawkins is passe, at least in economics. It is time to recognise the co-operative genes within us. It is time to welcome Mark Ridley wholeheartedly while framing our policies. We must realise that altruism does exist and is eminently workable at the immediate family levels. That would imply that it is the individual who is responsible, not the state, for the welfare of the family. That implies we need to relook at the idea of welfare itself. Equally, it is also appropriate that we need to provide incentives to the disciplined and crucially punish those who are not. For all these to happen we need to genetically reengineer the discipline of economics. But such efforts cannot be limited merely to the discipline of economics. Such an exercise, truncated in its sweep, would be futile. It has to be far more encompassing – socially, politically and also constitutionally. We have dealt with all these in the length and breadth of this work. Wherever appropriate, we have suggested possible reforms too. Of course, the areas of reforms are exceedingly large to merit repetition once again. Nevertheless, some of them are a new global order, a workable and sustainable economic model, marriage, polygamy, welfare, bureaucracy, market regulators, taxes, role of state, gender equity; we can go on as the list is indeed endless. The challenge is indeed humungous but well within our ability to deliver, but should we fail, the future generations will never forgive us.

Flawed Assumptions – Imbalanced Construct

But there is a crucial reform that is necessary to make all others reforms work and systems functional – the constitutional reform. It is in this connection that the inclusion of individual duty to the state, society and family as a basic structure of the constitutional arrangement has been one of the recurring themes of this book. Resultantly, many questions posed in the previous chapters are essential to this political philosophy and are focused on the desired political institutions, their rights and responsibilities, to make this new idea work. Associated questions arise: What rights and liberties should the state grant its people? Let me turn the question upside down – how much should, we the people, empower the state to meddle with our affairs? What makes a state, a legitimate, economically viable and functional entity? Should the state be at the centre of our political landscape? In the alternative, should it be the family? What kinds of equality should the state concern itself with, and how much inequality, is too much? Critically, how should it deal with inequality?

Answers for all these questions, for too long, have been riveted on the Christian idea of 'broken self.' Consequently, we have made an individual central to our constitutional construct – and that mending the 'broken self' forms the sole basis for resolving complex socio-political-economic conundrums for all times to come. This assumption of a broken self, as we saw, gave rise to social contract theory. This theory in turn culminated in the rise of the modern state. We have discussed this in some detail in Chapter 6. To amplify further, for yielding to this arrangement, the state in turn provided a significant concession to the individual in the form of guaranteed fundamental rights including the right to life and liberty. That in turn further legitimised the state with enormous powers to intrude into the affairs of men. The consequential evolution of the basic structure doctrine was inevitable to protect the citizens from an all-powerful institution called the government. The underlying idea is that a citizen needs to be protected from an omnipotent, omnipresent and omniscient state. As a consequence, basic structure became a natural by-product of this structurally flawed design. Nonetheless, the state and its coercive agencies became the sole arbiter in deciding the affairs of men.

Paradoxical as it may be, the fact of the matter is that the state despite being a creature of the collective will of the citizens had to be repeatedly restrained from attacking the very citizens who came together to create it in the first place. This was despite all the checks and balances created by the Constitution. Given this paradigm, courts and civil society had to repeatedly step in to broker a workable truce between the state and its citizen. Definitely, such interventions were not intended to be a design fix. This was achieved by repeatedly expanding the idea of the basic structure to include several rights of the citizen precisely to guard him from a marauding state. But is this truce durable? Is it sustainable? Is the contract desirable in the first place?

This post-independence byzantine arrangement, between the citizens and the state, has never been our civilisational aspiration. Neither was it sought for by our forefathers who fought for our freedom. But inadvertently we have created this blackhole. Needless to emphasise, this constitutional reform is the ultimate reform that awaits our decisive intervention – where imbalance between the state and citizens are promptly addressed. Equally it is important that the duty of the citizen is incorporated into the basic structure of our Constitution. We need to fix the bug in our Constitution at two levels – one, by incorporating duties of the individual into the basic structure of our Constitution and two, by addressing the skew in the arrangement between the state and the citizen. That in turn requires a serious re-assessment of the omnipotent state. Is that what we seek? What is the precise role of the state? Does it correspond with our civilisational aspirations and moorings? Consequently, should the state be an all-powerful one or a residuary one? The founding fathers of the Indian Constitution probably did not have time to delve much into these matters. The events leading to the independence of India from our colonial master, the British, and immediately thereafter did not probably lend itself into such detailed civilisational analysis of the role of the state. That explains why some scholars are of the view that the Indian Constitution is at best a mere rehash of the Government of India Act, an enactment of the British vintage. Consequently, several features of the Indian Constitution are those which already figured prominently in the said enactment. A Rights based constitutional arrangement may suit the British, or for that matter the Americans even today, but cannot be thrust on a nation which has deep-rooted civilisational values, especially on individual duties. Obviously, we need to look at the constitutional arrangement, afresh.

A duty-based Constitution – both for the state and its citizens – will be a remarkable shift from the present structure. Gandhiji was one of the earliest political leaders to visualise its importance. He realised very early the need to link our post-independent constitutional arrangement to our civilisational values and individual duties. Naturally, this found resonance with Indians in the run up to our independence. When he was asked about the ideal state, without any hesitancy, he referred to Ram Rajya. The reason for the same is obvious. According to many authors who have researched on the subject have concluded that Ram Rajya is not a myth or imagination, it is an historic truth of its times. It represented a model kingdom, with a perfect king and notably, ideal citizenry. It is pertinent to note Ram Rajya

– the ideal kingdom – is dependent on the ideal King Lord Rama as well as its ideal citizens. By using Ram Rajya as a slogan, Gandhiji implied an ideal post-independent government where values of justice, equality, idealism, renunciation and sacrifice are practised, both by the state and its citizens. "By Ram Rajya, I do not mean Hindu Raj. I mean by Ram Rajya Divine Raj, the Kingdom of God." That is how he describes the contours of the eternal idea of Ram Rajya. Gandhiji further explains the concept further in 1929 in *Young India*: "Whether Rama of my imagination ever lived or not on this earth, the ancient ideal of Ram Rajya is undoubtedly one of true democracy in which the meanest citizen could be sure of swift justice without an elaborate and costly procedure. Even the dog is described by the poet to have received justice under Ram Rajya." Gandhiji revisits this subject once again in 1937 when he states "By political independence, I do not mean an imitation to the British House of commons, or the soviet rule of Russia or the Fascist rule of Italy or the Nazi rule of Germany. They have systems suited to their genius. We must have ours suited to ours. What that can be is more than I can tell. I have described it as Ram Rajya i.e., sovereignty of the people based on pure moral authority." Again, on the eve of India's independence Gandhiji opined in 1947 on this civilisational idea: "There can be no Ram Rajya in the present state of iniquitous inequalities in which a few roll in riches and the masses do not get even enough to eat." Given its powerful reach and civilisational moorings, the slogan was sufficient; the idea powerful enough to reach to the masses. It is indeed strange that despite its tremendous impact during the independence movement, political leaders, post-independence are reluctant to use the phrase, much less live up to its ideals. Sadly, like Gandhiji, Ram Rajya has ceased to be politically correct post-independence. It is time we revive it, draw appropriate conclusions and make it contextually relevant.

It is to be noted Gandhiji was not alone and this exhilarating idea of the state, its role and the role of citizens have always held the attention of Indians. Various statesmen and seers of this land have pondered different aspects of the science of polity and presented their views on the subject in various treatises at different points in time. *Rajasastra, Rajadharma, Dandaniti, Arthasastra*, and *Nitisastra* are the synonyms for the *Rajanitisastra* or the science of polity as expressed in Sanskrit language. Fascinatingly, the philosophy of these seers lays greater emphasis on the premise that inner spirituality and character that must govern both the conduct of the rulers as well as citizens. It was never the traditional Indic view that the citizens must be divorced from the state. This is what we have done post-independence probably with unforeseen downsides.

Like the *Ramayana*, the *Mahabharat* too has dealt with this subject of governance and has been brilliantly explained in the chapter appropriately titled *Shanti Parva* (chapter of peace) of *Mahabharat*. This chapter is collection of political philosophy of Bheeshma, Vyasa, and various other sages of that time. More particularly, it incorporates several ideas of Bheeshma on various dimensions of politics, the origin of state and duties of the King. In brief, all these conversations revolve around the conduct of those involved in governance to adhere to the highest standards of morality and ethical behaviour. In a nutshell, these conversations lay emphasis, like other texts on the premise that inner spirituality and character must alone govern the conduct and behaviour of the leaders. Apart from Shanti Parva, *Vidura Neeti*, is another reference point within the *Mahabharat* that has substantial referral points for good governance. It may be noted that while *Vidura Neeti* is a pre-war advice by the minister Vidura to the King Dhritharashtra, Shanthi Parva is a post war advice by Bheeshma to the victorious Pandavas. The unsaid part in all these was that the citizens were indeed equally spiritual and did not correspond to the 'Broken Self' of Christendom. If that is a fact, why does our Constitution mirror the Western idea of the state?

World over, political philosophers and scholars too, have also turned their attention to this vexatious issue. From a legal perspective, a citizen is a person who is an official member of a political community and who therefore has certain *de-jure* rights and privileges and legitimate expectations of his/ her government. One important question is how do these impose corresponding obligations on citizens. In other words, what do people as citizens owe something to their governments and societies apart from the secular issues of taxes and adherence to laws? The cardinal virtues of classical thought would obviously serve citizens and their society well – justice, wisdom, courage, and temperance. We can add several more that are explicitly civic; a political society will function better when the citizens are also tolerant, self-disciplined, take care of their family, dedicate to the common good and remain supportive of their government. The uniform thought in all these discourses is the eternal goodness in man that needs to be leveraged. It is time we as a nation revert to these discussions enshrined with eternal wisdom.

But modern Constitutions precisely ignore these positive virtues in any men. It sees only flaws in them. Neither does it encourage higher thinking in its citizens nor allows them to flourish. Once the state distrusts its own citizens, the citizens contrive to belie the expectations of the state from them. That in turn brings about a downward spiral from where it becomes virtually impossible to recover. Christendom, is rooted even to this day to the 'Original Sin' and the resultant 'Broken Self,' dominates our public discourse. It has got so far under the skin of Western culture that even in the modern age, the idea of 'Broken Self' remains the dominant paradigm for any discussion on any discipline involving humanities. Let us not forget that at the core of every idea that has been put forth by any Western thinker is that a man is a wayward, selfish being in need of an external remedy. In a way we are all born sinners, and consequently we need an external powerful state for our own salvation. It is this Hobbesian thought, rooted to Christian theology, that created the contract theory and an omnipotent state in the first place.

Let us flip the arguments. Absent the 'Broken Self' the need for an omnipotent state vanishes almost instantly. Thus, the theory of 'Broken Self' is the cause; the brutal state the effect. If this presumption is set aside, we can conjure a state which is far less vicious, yet be more efficient. To reiterate, it is this fundamental assumption of the brutal nature of citizenry that necessitates a meaningful response in the form of a powerful state. More pertinently, it is this flawed assumption about men that has led to a constitutional construct that is highly imbalanced. It is time that we re-balance the equation between the citizens and the state. That would imply reworking the fundamental assumption about men and their conduct. That would instantly bring down temperatures, reduce the scope of the state and its functionalities. For that we need to believe in the goodness of men and cast away the Hobbesian idea of 'Broken Self.' Once we do so, we can immediately envision a minimalist state.

That is what in essence Ram Rajya is all about, where the state is a minimalist state, yet remains an efficient one – where it is caring, based on equity, goodliness of people, yet, one that is purposeful. The fundamental assumption within Ram Rajya is that the citizens are honest and diligent; not otherwise. Only such a citizenry can deserve Lord Rama. Consequently, laws need to be framed to provide incentives to the citizens to be honest, sincere and dutiful. A dutiful citizenry reduces the dependency on the state and its welfare mechanism. A self-dependent individual is the ideal citizen in Ram Rajya. In such a scheme of things the state has a minimalist role with the consequent taxation and welfare mechanisms. Welfare if at all is limited to the needy and is never fanciful – mostly concentrated in enablers like health and education. The state bereft of sundry distractions concentrates on its sovereign function of defence and dispensing justice. Promptness in punishing the deviant, and that too punitively, will ensure that there are virtually not many who prefer to take the risk of breaking the law.

In all fairness the Part III of the Constitution relating to Fundamental Rights of the individual has to necessarily undergo serious changes in the sense that it has to necessarily include the idea of Fundamental Duties. Without mandating duties for our citizens, we are completely disconnecting them from their civilisational roots. We must not place the 'Broken Self' central to the constitutional construct, but we must include the divinity in our self in our remaking of the constitutional order. That would imply reimagining Ram Rajya – one where there is less of emphasis on Lord Rama i.e., the government but a more renewed focus on Rajya – the nation. And that would imply reorienting all our policies to focus on 'self' rather than the 'broken self.'

References

1. Stronger Families, Stronger Societies By William Bennett – The New York Times – April 24, 2012.
2. A Systems Approach to Social Disintegration By Seth D. Kaplan – National Affairs - 2017.

3. Influence of Ramayana on the Life, Culture and Literature in India and Abroad Ramayana By Dr. Y. Ramesh Associate Professor, Department of History & P.G. Centre, Government Arts College, Bangalore, Karnataka, India – IJESC Vol 6, Issue No 8.
4. What's Wrong with Modern Macroeconomics? Why its Critics have Missed the Point By M.R. Wickens- Department of Economics, University of York; Cardiff Business School, Cardiff University -CESifo Economic Studies, Vol. 56, 4/2010.
5. The Welfare State as a Failed Experiment By John Pugsley.
6. In Defense of Economics By Allison Schrager – September 24, 2019 – Quartz.
7. History of Women's Property Rights and Ownership By Rebecca Winke- March 12, 2021 – Family Handyman.
8. All About Eve: Feminism and the Meaning of Equality – www.bible.org
9. Why Feminism Wants to Dismantle the Family By Nikita Coulombe -www.nikitacoulombe.medium.com
10. The dilemma of Draupadi's disrobing By Rohini Bakshi- November 22, 2016 -www.livemint.com
11. The Selfish Gene: an alternative theory of evolution By Sandipan Deb – September 10, 2016 -www.livemint.com
12. The Unselfish Gene By Yochai Benkler- August-September 2011 – Harvard Business Review.
13. The Cooperative Gene: How Mendel's Demon Explains the Evolution of Complex Beings By Mark Ridley – www.goodreads.com
14. Civic Duties, Civic Virtues, and the Barriers to Effective Citizenship By Christopher A. Callaway – American Bar Association.

Index